"'Community punishments' are characteristic of criminal justice systems everywhere, but as this new volume vividly illustrates, the nature of these measures varies markedly from place to place and from time to time. Drawing on specially-commissioned expert accounts of community penalties in eleven European nations, Robinson and McNeill provide a fascinating, indispensable guide to the problems, trends and controversies that affect community-based punishment in Europe today. The result is a deepened theoretical understanding of the important issues at stake."

David Garland, Professor, School of Law and the Department of
Sociology, New York University, USA

"Notwithstanding new interest in comparative criminology, and descriptions of what is available in Europe, we know relatively little about how community punishments and interventions are conceived, so this is a hugely welcome book. The editors and contributors have put together a scholarly collection of European case studies which not only locate different forms of community punishments in different contexts, but reveal adaptations over time, and in particular the interplay of managerial, punitive, rehabilitative, reparative and technological pushes and pulls. This is an insightful and rich text which addresses how community punishments have evolved and survived in late modern social and penal conditions; it is a wholly? interesting and original book of real importance."

Loraine Gelsthorpe, Professor of Criminology and Criminal Justice,
University of Cambridge and President of the
British Society of Criminology, UK

COMMUNITY PUNISHMENT

In *Community Punishment: European perspectives*, the authors place punishment in the community under the spotlight by exploring the origins, evolution and adaptations of supervision in 11 European jurisdictions. For most people, punishment in the criminal justice system is synonymous with imprisonment. Yet, both in Europe and in the USA, the numbers of people under some form of penal supervision in the community far exceeds the numbers in prison, and many prisoners are released under supervision. Written and edited by leading scholars in the field, this collection advances the sociology of punishment by illuminating the neglected but crucial phenomenon of 'mass supervision'.

As well as putting criminological and penological theories to the test in an examination of their ability to explain the evolution of punishment *beyond the prison*, and across diverse states, the contributors to this volume also assess the appropriateness of the term 'community punishment' in different parts of Europe. Engaging in a serious exploration of common themes and differences in the jurisdictions included in the collection, the authors go on to examine how 'community punishment' came into being in their jurisdiction and how its institutional forms and practices have been legitimated and re-legitimated in response to shifting social, cultural and political contexts.

This book is essential reading for academics and students involved in the study of both community punishment and comparative penology, but will also be of great interest to criminal justice policymakers, managers and practitioners.

Gwen Robinson is Reader in Criminal Justice at the University of Sheffield, UK. She is co-leader of the COST Action on Offender Supervision in Europe's Working Group on Practising Supervision.

Fergus McNeill is Professor of Criminology and Social Work at the University of Glasgow, where he works in the Scottish Centre for Crime and Justice Research and is Head of Sociology. He is the Chair of the COST Action on Offender Supervision in Europe.

COMMUNITY PUNISHMENT

European perspectives

Edited by Gwen Robinson and Fergus McNeill

Routledge
Taylor & Francis Group

LONDON AND NEW YORK

cost

**EUROPEAN COOPERATION
IN SCIENCE AND TECHNOLOGY**

First published 2016
by Routledge
2 Park Square, Milton Park, Abingdon, Oxon OX14 4RN

Simultaneously published in the USA and Canada
by Routledge
711 Third Avenue, New York, NY 10017

Routledge is an imprint of the Taylor & Francis Group, an informa business

This publication is supported by COST.

British Library Cataloguing in Publication Data
A catalogue record for this book is available from the British Library

Library of Congress Cataloging-in-Publication Data
    Community punishment : European perspectives /
    edited by Gwen Robinson and Fergus McNeill.
        pages cm
    Includes index.
    1. Community-based corrections–Europe. 2. Punishment–Europe.
    I. Robinson, Gwen, 1969- II. McNeill, Fergus.
    HV9344.A5C66 2015
    364.6'8094–dc23   2015005251

ISBN13: 978-1-138-78378-2 (hbk)
ISBN13: 978-1-138-81864-4 (pbk)
ISBN13: 978-1-315-76848-9 (ebk)

Typeset in Bembo
by Sunrise Setting Ltd, Paignton, UK

Printed in Great Britain by Ashford Colour Press Ltd

CONTENTS

FIGURES

TABLES

PREFACE AND ACKNOWLEDGEMENTS

This book is the second edited collection to be published as an output of the COST Action *Offender Supervision in Europe*, which was established in March 2012 and is funded until March 2016 (Action IS1106). However, it is fair to say that it also builds on the foundations laid in a number of previous projects. Of particular importance, as we explain in Chapter 1, is a chapter we wrote, together with Shadd Maruna, for the *Sage Handbook of Punishment & Society* (Robinson *et al.* 2013). In this chapter we considered the development of community sanctions in 'late modern' Western societies. We focused in particular on the ways in which such sanctions had evolved since the decline of 'penal modernism' (Garland 1990) and, with it, the dominant narratives of rehabilitation and welfare which had given birth to probation and parole. In the chapter, our focus fell on those jurisdictions with which we were most familiar (namely, England and Wales, Scotland and the USA), and – in the vein of Garland's *Culture of Control* (2001) – on the commonalities between those jurisdictions. Our analysis centred upon the emergence of four overlapping narratives for community sanctions, which we characterised as *managerial*, *punitive*, *rehabilitative* and *reparative*. These narratives, we argued, had served (at different times and in different combinations) to legitimate or re-legitimate community sanctions in the last 40 years, and could help to make sense of their survival and proliferation in often hostile climates.

Subsequently, we thought about developing the ideas in that chapter into a book. However, we soon ran into problems in respect of the potential scope of such a book. We were forced, both by our own academic experiences and by recent scholarship, to acknowledge the problem of over-generalisation stemming from the reference to 'late-modern societies', which have been noted by several commentators. For example, Nicola Lacey (2007: 26–9) has raised questions about the utility of an overall category of late-modern society as a unit of analysis and has argued for more comparative analyses, capable of discerning and explaining some important differences between the criminal justice systems of democratic societies with relatively similar profiles in terms of economic development. Meanwhile our involvement in networks of European scholars (initially the European Society of Criminology Working Group on Community Sanctions; later the European Union (EU)-funded COST project on Offender Supervision in Europe) was exposing us to some significant variations – as well as some convergences – in policy and practice in respect of community sanctions in Europe, increasing our scepticism about the feasibility and desirability of doing further analytical work with late-modern societies as the unit of analysis. Instead, we committed ourselves to a project that would seek deliberately to expose and make sense of the different trajectories of community sanctions in a variety of European jurisdictions. We wanted, however, to retain a focus on legitimacy or, more precisely, strategies of *legitimation*, which we had also explored in other research – separately (Robinson 2008) and together (McNeill and Robinson 2013). In other words, we wanted to examine the rationalities or narratives underpinning community sanctions in a range of jurisdictions: not just those with long traditions of such sanctions and/or recent histories of 'penal turbulence'.

When we pitched this idea to colleagues in the COST Action, we were delighted by the response, which was overwhelmingly positive. We found among our colleagues a strong appetite for exploring the contexts (social, political, economic etc.) in which community-based sanctions and measures have arisen and evolved across jurisdictions: indeed, '*contextualising offender supervision*' had been an important theme in our original network proposal to COST, but it had been somewhat lost in the evolution of working groups with other, more substantive themes. Proposing this collection thus enabled us to recover and examine the challenge of contextualising the evolution of supervision under the umbrella of our COST network. We proceeded to secure the commitment of its contributors by inviting them, in early 2014, to a 2-day workshop at Ross Priory in Scotland (on the shores of Loch Lomond), to discuss the analytical framework we had by that time set out in a draft version of the book's introduction (Chapter 1).

It has been a great pleasure to work so closely with the contributors to this volume, all of whom have worked extremely hard and responded with great patience and good humour to our comments on their draft chapters. It is to them that we dedicate this book. We do, however, also wish to acknowledge the contributions – albeit indirect – of other scholars from whom we have had the great pleasure to learn along the way. In particular, Louise Brangan's presentation to the COST network in 2013 offered an engaging insight into comparative research that has been very valuable to us. Similarly, David Garland's address to the European Society of Criminology's annual conference in Budapest, also in 2013, offered some extremely useful new tools for thinking comparatively (see Chapter 13). We would also like to take this opportunity to thank Shadd Maruna for inviting us, back in 2010, to work with him on the chapter that ultimately inspired us to embark upon the process of producing this book. Thanks also to Wiley for their permission to reproduce previously published material in Chapter 7 of this book. Finally, we would like to acknowledge the support of the EU COST office, and our publisher, Routledge. Particular thanks are due to Tom Sutton and Heidi Lee, who have helped make the production of this book such a pleasure.

Gwen Robinson and Fergus McNeill
January 2015

References

Garland, D. (1990) *Punishment and Modern Society*. Oxford: Clarendon Press.

Garland, D. (2001) *The Culture of Control*. Oxford: Oxford University Press.

Lacey, N. (2007) *The Prisoners' Dilemma: Political Economy and Punishment in Contemporary Democracies*. Cambridge: Cambridge University Press.

McNeill, F. and Robinson, G. (2013) 'Liquid legitimacy and community sanctions', in A. Crawford and A. Hucklesby (eds) *Legitimacy and Compliance in Criminal Justice*. London: Routledge.

Robinson, G. (2008) 'Late-modern rehabilitation: The evolution of a penal strategy', *Punishment and Society*, 10(4): 429–45.

Robinson, G., McNeill, F. and Maruna, S. (2013) 'Punishment in society: The improbable persistence of probation and other community sanctions and measures', in J. Simon and R. Sparks (eds) *Sage Handbook of Punishment and Society*. London: Sage.

ABOUT COST

COST – the acronym for European Cooperation in Science and Technology – is the oldest and widest European intergovernmental network for cooperation in research. Established by the Ministerial Conference in November 1971, COST is presently used by the scientific communities of 36 European countries to cooperate in common research projects supported by national funds.

The funds provided by COST – less than 1% of the total value of the projects – support the COST cooperation networks (COST Actions) through which, with EUR 30 million per year, more than 30 000 European scientists are involved in research having a total value which exceeds EUR 2 billion per year. This is the financial worth of the European added value which COST achieves.

A "bottom up approach" (the initiative of launching a COST Action comes from the European scientists themselves), "à la carte participation" (only countries interested in the Action participate), "equality of access" (participation is open also to the scientific communities of countries not belonging to the European Union) and "flexible structure" (easy implementation and light management of the research initiatives) are the main characteristics of COST.

As precursor of advanced multidisciplinary research COST has a very important role for the realisation of the European Research Area (ERA) anticipating and complementing the activities of the Framework Programmes, constituting a "bridge" towards the scientific communities of emerging countries, increasing the mobility of researchers across Europe and fostering the establishment of "Networks of Excellence" in many key scientific domains such as: biomedicine and molecular biosciences; food and agriculture; forests, their products and services; materials, physical and nanosciences; chemistry and molecular sciences and technologies; Earth system science and environmental management; information and communication technologies; transport and urban development; individuals, societies, cultures and health. It covers basic and more applied research and also addresses issues of pre-normative nature or of societal importance.

Web: http://www.cost.eu

CONTRIBUTORS

Kristel Beyens is Professor of Penology and Criminology at the Vrije Universiteit Brussel, Belgium, where she works at the Department of Criminology. She is a member of the research group Crime and Society (CRiS), where she is leading the research line Penality and Society. Her research focuses on penal decision-making and cultural, organisational and social aspects of the implementation of prison sentences and community penalties. Together with Mike Nellis and Dan Kaminski she published a book on electronic monitoring (2013, Routledge). She is a founding member of the ESC Working Group on Community Sanctions (chair 2009–2012) and the vice-chair of the COST Action on Offender Supervision in Europe.

Ester Blay is lecturer in Criminal Law and Criminology at Universitat Pompeu Fabra, Barcelona, Spain. Her research focuses on judicial decision-making and sentencing, community service, individual supervision practices and, outside the field of penology, on policing. She has recently co-edited with Elena Larrauri *Penas Comunitarias en Europa*. She regularly publishes, in Spanish, peer-reviewed publications, and has also published research in English regarding community service orders. She is a member of the COST Action on Offender Supervision in Europe's Working Groups on Decision-Making and Practising Supervision.

Miranda Boone is Professor of Penology and Penitentiary Law at the University of Groningen and Senior Lecturer in Criminology and Criminal Law at the University of Utrecht, the Netherlands. Her PhD thesis was on the subject of community sentences and measures, and she has continued to publish on that topic. Other recent research projects include criminal records and reintegration; prison experiences; and the sentencing and detention of irregular migrants. She is co-leader of the COST Action on Offender Supervision in Europe's Working Group on Decision-Making and is currently involved in a comparative study of electronic monitoring led by the University of Leeds, UK.

Nicola Carr is Lecturer in the School of Sociology, Social Policy and Social Work at Queen's University Belfast. She previously worked as a Probation Officer in a youth offending team. Her main research interests are youth justice, probation and community sanctions. With colleagues, she is currently working on a number of research projects, including a study funded by the British Academy on young people's experiences of paramilitary violence in Northern Ireland's 'post-conflict' society. She is co-author of *Understanding Criminal Justice – A Critical Introduction* (Routledge, 2012). She is a member of the COST Action on Offender Supervision in Europe's Working Group on Practising Supervision.

Ioan Durnescu is Senior Lecturer at the University of Bucharest, Romania, teaching subjects such as comparative probation and prison resettlement. He used to work for the Probation Department in Romania for a number of years. He is currently involved in numerous international projects dealing with education for, development of and research on probation. He is also co-editor (with Anton van Kalmthout) of the book *Probation in Europe* and the co-editor of the *European Journal of Probation*. He is co-leader of the COST Action on Offender Supervision in Europe's Working Group on Experiencing Supervision.

Deirdre Healy is Lecturer in Criminology at the Sutherland School of Law, University College Dublin. She is also a member of the UCD Institute of Criminology. Her research interests include desistance from crime, community sanctions, victimisation and criminological theory. Deirdre has recently published two books: *The Dynamics of Desistance: Charting Pathways Through Change* (Willan, 2010) and *Rape and Justice in Ireland* (with Conor Hanly and Stacey Scriver, 2009, Liffey Press) and is currently editing the *Routledge Handbook of Irish Criminology* with Claire Hamilton, Yvonne Daly and Michelle Butler (2015, in press).

Martine Herzog-Evans is Professor in Law and Criminology at Reims University, France. She has published extensively (see http://herzog-evans.com). Her latest books are: *Droit de l'Exécution des Peines* (Sentences' Implementation Law), Dalloz, Paris, 2012–2013; *French Reentry Courts and Rehabilitation: Mister Jourdain of Desistance*, Paris, l'Harmattan (2014); and *Offender Release and Supervision: The Role of Courts and the Use of Discretion* (ed), Nijmegen: Wolf Legal Publishers (2015). She is co-leader of the COST Action on Offender Supervision in Europe's Working Group on Decision-making and Supervision.

Elena Larrauri is Professor in Criminal Law and Criminology at Universitat Pompeu Fabra, Barcelona, Spain. Her research focuses on criminal records, sentences, and gender and criminal law. She obtained the Fulbright-La Caixa and Alexander von Humboldt Scholarship, was given the prize Rafael Salillas of the Spanish Society of Criminology (2007) and has been awarded an All Souls Visiting Fellowship for 2013–2014. She was president of the European Society of Criminology (2007–2010). She is co-leader of the COST Action on Offender Supervision in Europe's Working Group on European Norms, Policy and Practice.

Fergus McNeill is Professor of Criminology and Social Work at the University of Glasgow, where he works in the Scottish Centre for Crime and Justice Research and is Head of Sociology in the School of Social and Political Sciences. He previously worked in drug rehabilitation and as a criminal justice social worker, and has researched and published extensively on 'offender supervision', community sanctions, prisoner resettlement, sentencing, youth justice, and on rehabilitation and desistance from crime. He is chair of the COST Action on Offender Supervision in Europe.

Christine Morgenstern is Lecturer in Criminology and Criminal Law at the University of Greifswald, Germany. She studied law in Freiburg, Hamburg and San Sebastian. Her PhD on international standards for community sanctions and measures was published in 2002. In 2012 she was awarded a 3-year grant from the German Research Council to conduct a study on pre-trial detention in Europe. She is predominantly interested in comparative and human rights aspects of the criminal justice system. She is co-leader of the COST Action on Offender Supervision in Europe's Working Group on European Norms, Policy and Practice.

Gwen Robinson is Reader in Criminal Justice at the University of Sheffield, UK. After qualifying as a probation practitioner in 1996, she has pursued a career in academic research and has published widely in the areas of community sanctions, offender rehabilitation and restorative justice. Her recent publications include *Restorative Justice in Practice: Evaluating What Works for Victims and Offenders* (co-authored with Joanna Shapland and Angela Sorsby) published in 2011 by Routledge. She is co-leader of the COST Action on Offender Supervision in Europe's Working Group on Practising Supervision.

Kerstin Svensson is Professor in Social Work at Lund University, Sweden. Her research concerns professionals and their practices in human service organisations in general, with a special focus on organisations and professions within the criminal justice system. She has written several books in Swedish on social work, drug abuse and prevention, professions and organisations. Her publications in English are mainly articles about probation and victim support. She is co-leader of the COST Action on Offender Supervision in Europe's Working Group on Practising Supervision.

1

INTRODUCTION

Studying the evolution of 'community punishment' in comparative context

Gwen Robinson and Fergus McNeill

Introduction

Looking at criminological topics comparatively has become a popular endeavour. Indeed, in a review of comparative research in criminology published in 2007, Heidensohn noted that the field had already grown to the extent that it would not be possible to provide a comprehensive overview. Limiting our focus to punishment, and to the Anglophone literature, the field is a little less crowded, but nonetheless expanding. Given that most reviews of the comparative penology literature start with Downes' (1988) now classic *Contrasts in Tolerance*, it is fair to say both that comparative work in this area is still relatively new and that it is developing quickly. In the last 15–20 years a number of influential scholarly works have pointed to some important convergences and global trends in penal policies and configurations of criminal justice (Garland 2001; Pratt *et al.* 2005). However, more recent scholarship has begun to draw attention to the role of *local* – as well as global – influences on the penal sphere. These influences (economic, political, cultural, social), it is argued, help to explain why we are not witnessing penal convergence on a global scale[1] (Cavadino and Dignan 2006; McAra 2005; Lacey 2007).

Comparative penology then, is 'on the up'. But although scholars are gravitating towards comparative research, their spotlight has not been focused evenly across the punishment field. To a large extent, the focus of comparative projects (as in penology more generally) has been the prison: in particular, imprisonment rates and prison conditions, with youth justice systems also having attracted some attention (Cavadino and Dignan 2006; Ruggiero and Ryan 2013; Tonry and Doob 2004; Muncie and Goldson 2006). Meanwhile, forms of punishment in the community for adult offenders have attracted little scholarly attention, despite the fact that in many parts of the Western world there are far more people subject to some form of punishment in the community than are serving their punishment behind bars (see Robinson *et al.* 2013; McNeill and Beyens 2013).

Part of the rationale for this book therefore stems from our desire to address a real lacuna in comparative penology; but more importantly we want to examine what analyses of the developing field of 'community punishment' might bring to the table. What, in other words, might a better understanding of the evolution of punishment in the community contribute to our understanding(s) of penal systems, policies and actors, *both* nationally *and* in comparative perspective?

Our comparative methodology

In this book we adopt a case study approach to analyse the development of community punishment in a selection of European jurisdictions. Our case studies comprise a part-purposive, part-convenience sample, drawn from different parts of Europe and from scholars whose work we know and respect. Our approach has been developed *not* with a view to presenting any kind of definitive (or complete) picture, but rather to expose examples of sameness and difference in the field of community punishment and thus, ultimately, to contribute to theory building. In providing not just *accounts* of sameness and difference, but *analyses* of how and why things are as they are and how they came to be so, our contributors and our collection of case studies aim to push at the boundaries of existing explanations of penality and of penal change.

In choosing this methodology, we have sought to avoid the duplication of existing knowledge in the field, particularly that which is already available via survey-based research on probation in Europe (van Kalmthout and Durnescu 2008) and on offender or case management systems (www.domice.org/). As valuable as these kinds of contributions are in terms of accruing knowledge about arrangements for Offender Supervision in a wide range of countries, they offer limited insight into the sorts of analytical issues that interest us in this book.

In choosing Europe as our sampling frame, we have consciously conceived this as a project under the umbrella of the ongoing European Cooperation in Science and Technology (COST) Action on Offender Supervision in Europe, which has brought together a network of scholars with an interest in the field of community punishment.[2] Our sample has been selected with a view to exploiting the knowledge, interests and talents of members of that network who represent eleven jurisdictions. No doubt some readers of this volume will note with disappointment the lack of a chapter on particular countries that are missing in this collection; others may criticise the inclusion of all three UK jurisdictions. We, however, are happy with the selection of case studies and would defend our decision to develop a high-quality collection from which we might be able to build theory, rather than a 'representative' one.

In methodological terms, we have not emulated the approach taken by Cavadino and Dignan in their celebrated book *Penal Systems* (2006). This 'multistudy' (Heidensohn 2007) involved Cavadino and Dignan distributing structured questionnaires to 'experts' in twelve nations, the results of which were used as the basis for the manuscript which Cavadino and Dignan co-authored, and on which the same 'experts' (credited as associate authors in the book) were invited to provide comments. Nor have we emulated the approach taken by Tonry and Farrington (2005) in their volume on crime and punishment in Western countries in the 1980s and 1990s. Tonry and Farrington developed an extremely detailed template (described by Heidensohn (2007: 210) as 'complex, demanding and somewhat unwieldy') to capture information about crime and criminal justice matters and to structure the contributions (chapters) of authors from eight countries.

Our approach is perhaps best described as a 'hybrid'. On the one hand, we take the view that the contributions in our book ought to be written by our scholar-colleagues themselves: they are best placed to explain and make sense of the field in their own jurisdiction and, in particular, to notice the particular cultural, legal, institutional, political and social features and dynamics which have played or are playing a role in shaping community punishment there. However, in order to facilitate comparison across jurisdictions, and to minimise the risk of too much heterogeneity of approach between the different contributions, we have had to give serious thought to the benefits of a common analytical framework to structure the chapters. This framework, which has both conceptual and theoretical elements, is outlined below. In addition, we have put together a set of questions which authors have been asked to address. We hope we have been successful in avoiding 'ethnocentrism' implicit in producing an 'Anglo-Saxon template' (see Beyens and McNeill 2013) that fails to allow for expressions of difference or the generation of topics and questions we could not anticipate.

There will thus be two types of comparison at work in the collection. First, *vertical comparison* will occur whereby each contribution will consider the relevance of the key conceptual and theoretical tools presented in this introductory chapter. Second, *horizontal comparison* will occur in our final chapter, in which we will examine similarities and differences among the jurisdictions included, consider explanations for observed patterns and try to draw some conclusions. Each chapter should, however, also stand alone as an important contribution to the penological literature.

In a sense therefore, we have tried to create or curate a collection that allows the reader to be, in Heidensohn's terms, an 'armchair traveller' or, in Nelken's terms, 'virtually there'. Of course, this approach carries certain risks. No one author can represent a nation objectively or dispassionately. The armchair traveller is at the mercy of the positions, dispositions and interpretations of their guide. However effectively the guide brings alive the people, places and practices they describe, we are not there observing these things for ourselves. But equally, merely being there (as every thoughtful tourist knows) is no guarantee of really understanding what we are seeing; and, without a knowledgeable and trustworthy guide, we risk missing much of the social worlds we see. Nelken (2000) might be right in arguing that only a committed and lasting engagement in and with the places in which we find ourselves can enable deep comparison. But, of course, such an approach imposes significant limits on comparative research itself; and it creates the risks that the incomer simply becomes as compromised and partial an observer as the indigenous 'expert'.

In essence therefore, we have picked guides we trust, asked them to engage reflectively with their own positions and partialities and told them (below) what it is that we want them to show and explain to us. At the same time, recognising that the questions that we begin with, the concepts we use and the theories we want to test are bound to be the products of particular places and partialities, we have also asked our guides to point out where and when we might need to shed aspects of our agenda and our preconceptions if we are really to make sense of their worlds in their terms. In the conclusion of the collection, we return to these methodological questions and conundrums, and try to make sense of what we have learned from our grand European tour, and what we have failed to learn.

A framework for comparison

Conceptual issues

The penal field (Page 2013) is, at least in some parts of the world, an increasingly complex and differentiated one. The part of the penal field which concerns us in this book is no exception. In recent years many jurisdictions have seen the expansion and diversification of forms of punishment in the community, as well as growing numbers of offenders being made subject to them. As researchers keen to expose and encourage comparison of developments in this part of the penal field across European jurisdictions, our first problem was finding a label to describe our subject.

Some possible labels were easy to dismiss because of their 'foreignness' in a European context (e.g. the American term 'community corrections'). Another option we rejected quickly was 'probation'. Although 'probation' is a term which is recognised internationally and in a European context (Hamai *et al.* 1995; van Kalmthout and Durnescu 2008), we were uncomfortable with the idea of continuing the tradition of using it as a shorthand to describe the field. This was for two main reasons. 'Probation' is a term with interwoven meanings that connote both *institutions* (typically public services/an arm of the state) and a *type of sanction* (or alternative to a sanction – see further below). We wanted to ensure that our focus, and the scope of the book, would extend beyond the confines of both definitions. In other words, we wanted to ensure, firstly, that forms of punishment other than standard probation disposals be included. For example, we wanted to include those forms of mandatory supervision which often follow or directly substitute a period of incarceration; we also wanted to include electronically monitored punishment. To put this another way, we wanted to encourage attention to all of the *technologies of government* (Miller and Rose 1990) or *penal technologies* – not just probation – that have developed, and often compete with one another for their share of the penal 'market' (Raynor 1997). Secondly, we were also aware that, whilst in some parts of Europe probation services have only been established relatively recently, in others they are already obsolete, in the process of being dismantled or else entering mixed markets of penal providers. So we also wanted to escape the institutional straitjacket of probation, enabling our purview to include the entire field of supervisory sanctions and providers.

We were also keen to avoid labels that define the field in terms of what it is not: popular examples being *non-custodial penalties* and *alternatives to prison*. There were two main reasons for wishing to avoid such terms. The first, and most important, is that they tend to reinforce the popular idea that prison/imprisonment is the 'norm' against which 'alternatives' should be considered, and that imprisonment is the dominant form of punishment in quantitative terms. The other, more pragmatic reason, was that we intended to include within our conceptual frame some sanctions that are properly conceived as custodial or quasi-custodial penalties, such as suspended sentences of imprisonment and periods on licence or parole which involve offenders 'doing time' outside the prison walls.

Given our European focus, we began with the distinctly European term 'community sanctions and measures' (CSM), defined by the Council of Europe (1992) as those 'which maintain the offender in the community and involve some restriction of his liberty through the imposition of conditions and/or obligations'. Initially, this seemed to be an unproblematic choice. However, further investigations[3] revealed that CSM was too broad for our purposes, incorporating 'any sanction imposed by a court or a judge, and any measure taken before or instead of a decision on a sanction as well as ways of enforcing a sentence of imprisonment outside a prison establishment'. In other words, whilst all possible 'sanctions' (being sentences imposed by a court or a judge) would fall within our purview, only a sub-set of 'measures' would: ways of enforcing a sentence of imprisonment outside prison (e.g. electronically monitored curfews; parole) would certainly fit; but those imposed as diversionary or other pre-trial measures would not. This left us with the possible option of 'post-conviction community sanctions and measures' as one accurate label, but we could hardly see this as a title for our book.

We were thus grateful when our colleague Kristel Beyens[4] said the following:

> As a sociologist I prefer the word 'punishment', because sanctions and measures refer to rather judicial categories (in Belgium) and both deny the punishing element of these sanctions. As I battle to get accepted that also 'alternatives' and community penalties have each their own punitive bite, I prefer the word punishment in this context.

This intervention was particularly helpful. We had already considered (and rejected) the term 'punishment in the community', because of its particular association with the Anglo-Welsh context (Worrall and Hoy 2005). We have ultimately opted to delineate the field of interest with reference to the term 'community punishment'. On the one hand, we could justify it as the least problematic of the available choices. But we prefer to justify its choice with reference to Kristel Beyens' observations: that is, as a term which conveys the *penal* character – intended or unintended – of a range of community sanctions and measures which share in common a restriction on the offender's liberty through the imposition of conditions and/or obligations.

Imposed post-conviction (i.e. at the point of sentencing), these are properly conceived as punishments rather than diversionary measures. Whilst it is acknowledged that all such sanctions and measures may not be strictly defined as punishments *legally* (the pre-1991 Probation Order in England and Wales is one such example) and that they may not claim retributive punishment as an objective, they nonetheless entail a degree of coercion, or at least the threat of coercion, in their implementation or enforcement. Ultimately, even if remotely, they are always and everywhere underwritten by the potentialities of coercive power legally exercised by the penal authorities of the State.

The choice of 'community punishment' to delineate the field of interest is also intended to be provocative: we want to engage contributors (and readers) in discussions about the particular labelling and branding of the relevant sanctions and measures, as well as broader discourse in the penal field, in comparative perspective. We therefore remain open to debate in this important area of language and labels, and have explicitly encouraged contributors to this volume to reflect on our choice of label and its applicability in their own jurisdictions.

Theoretical issues

The theoretical framework for the collection builds upon the approach used by the editors in our recent joint work (Robinson *et al.* 2013; McNeill and Robinson 2013). We adopt a broadly *social constructionist* perspective, proceeding from the basic idea that community punishment is neither an inevitable nor a necessarily static part of the penal field. Rather, it is one which emerges in particular forms in specific contexts and which is subsequently vulnerable to a whole host of influences which may impact upon its legitimacy in the eyes of powerful stakeholders. Once established, then, the future survival of punishment in the community is not guaranteed; nor does its survival necessarily indicate stasis or continuity in its forms and functions. In order to retain legitimacy within (and beyond) the penal field, community punishments may be required to adapt or evolve.

In our previous work, and in this collection, we understand legitimacy as a *social process* (Johnson *et al.* 2006). In other words, legitimacy is not an objective category, but rather a quality which is bestowed (or not) upon a social object, institution or set of practices by various stakeholders. For example, a much-cited definition of legitimacy is Suchman's (1995: 574), which refers to 'a generalized perception or assumption that the actions of an entity are desirable, proper or appropriate within some socially constructed system of norms, values, beliefs and definitions'. The idea of legitimacy as a social process implies that social objects strive to obtain – and subsequently retain – legitimacy by claiming consistency with the larger social and cultural framework(s) in which they are situated (Berger *et al.* 1998). Based on a review of research in the fields of social psychology and organisational studies, Johnson *et al.* (2006) discern a number of general principles which appear to apply to the legitimation of social objects of various types, which we think provide a useful framework for thinking about community punishments as objects of legitimation.

How do new social objects achieve legitimacy? Johnson *et al.* (2006) identify four stages in this process: innovation, local validation, diffusion and general
validation. Initially, they argue, social innovations emerge at the level of local actors
in response to particular structural conditions that create strategic interest for those
actors. In order to acquire legitimacy, they must then be locally validated; that is,
they must be understood – more or less explicitly – as consonant with the prevailing cultural framework. Having acquired the status of a 'valid social fact', they
may be diffused or imported into new local situations, where they are likely to
need less explicit justifications. Ultimately, this process of diffusion and the appear-
ance of consensus which it communicates results in a 'general validation of the
social object', such that it becomes a 'normal social fact' or part of the 'status quo'
(Johnson *et al.* 2006: 72).

Having attained the status of general validity, or 'a normal part of the social
fabric', social objects tend to remain relatively stable, but implicit or explicit
endorsement and authorisation from powerful stakeholders will help to sustain their
validity over time. However, as Johnson *et al.* go on to observe, 'not all legitimated
objects remain so' (2006: 73), and it is important to understand the social processes involved in the *de-legitimation* of a social object (see also Beetham 1991).
This, they argue, is something we know less about; though they suggest that it is a
process which is likely to begin as a result of a change in the structural conditions
that provide the foundations for the social object – even if these are different from
those which underpinned it when it was first conceived. Johnson *et al.* conclude
their review with a number of questions which might be relevant to studies of
de-legitimation. Among these is the question of what happens when a social object
loses widespread acceptance by an audience, but there is nothing there to replace
it. When this happens, we argue, social objects may strive to adapt to their changed
context and, ultimately, re-establish or reinforce their legitimacy.

Resources for thinking about penal 'objects' (institutions, cultures, practices
etc.) as essentially malleable or elastic can be found in the Foucauldian literature
(Foucault 1977; Miller and Rose 1990; O'Malley 1996). In *Discipline and Punish:
The Birth of the Prison* Foucault understood the prison as a 'technological apparatus' which could be made to work in the context of a variety of governmental
programmes or rationalities. We can apply the same logic to the sanctions and measures which comprise punishment in the community: that is, they can be conceived
(generally) as *technologies of government*, or (more specifically) as *penal technologies*,
the precise purposes, scope and targets of which are not set in stone. In short,
community-based punishments are capable of evolution, in response to a variety
of potential forces within and beyond the local and/or national penal field which
they occupy. At any point in time, their contemporary forms and characteristics
may bear little resemblance to their original design or else tell a story of relative
stability. Both kinds of story – of stability and change – tell us something useful
about the penal field in a particular place. Yet rarely do accounts of change in the
penal field attend seriously to community punishment, let alone consider its role as
a barometer of the penal climate more broadly.

Some analytical resources

We have gone some way towards exploring ideas about 'penal evolution' in our previous work, both separately (McNeill *et al.* 2009; Robinson 2008) and jointly (Robinson *et al.* 2013). In the most recent of these pieces, a book chapter entitled 'Punishment in society: The improbable persistence of probation and other community sanctions and measures', we analysed the fate of community sanctions in the UK and the USA since the decline, in the 1960s and 1970s, of the dominant narratives of rehabilitation and welfare which had underpinned their inception (Garland 1985, 1990). We argued that, in those jurisdictions, the survival (and indeed expansion) of community sanctions could be explained with reference to a process of evolution and a series of adaptations, involving the appeal of community sanctions to four particular narratives, each with some cultural purchase or resonance. We characterised these adaptations (and their associated narratives) as *managerial, punitive, rehabilitative* and *reparative*. At different times and in different combinations, each of these adaptations, we argued, represented an attempt to re-legitimate community sanctions since the 1980s and might help to make sense of their survival and proliferation in fundamentally altered social and/or penal contexts. We also proposed these as 'key dimensions against which community sanctions might be analysed, compared and contrasted across time and space' (Robinson *et al.* 2013: 322).

The *managerial* adaptation of community sanctions reflects wider processes of managerialisation and systemisation within criminal justice (and in many other aspects of state provision). For Bottoms (1995), this process of 'systemisation' has, in most jurisdictions, tended to embrace characteristics such as: an emphasis on inter-agency cooperation in order to fulfil the overall goals of the system; mission statements for individual criminal justice agencies which serve those general system goals; and the creation of 'key performance indicators' for individual agencies which tend to emphasise the efficiency of internal processes rather than 'effectiveness' in relation to any overarching objective. As Garland (1996) has observed, systemisation has enabled the cooperative adoption of a variety of devices to deal with the problem of crime in a reconfigured field characterised by an acceptance of crime as a normal social fact: a risk to be managed rather than a social problem to be eliminated. The key imperatives of a 'managerial' penology are thus focused on the limited goals of 'managing a permanently dangerous population while maintaining the system at a minimum cost' (Feeley and Simon 1992: 463). With respect to probation institutions, we identified three main ways in which their roles and functions shifted in line with or as a response to these developments. Firstly, their role in affecting the system came to the fore, most specifically in terms of their putative capacity to offer 'alternatives to custody', thereby reducing prison populations or at least containing their growth. This connected to a second development; a shift in emphasis from the pursuit of outcomes (such as crime reduction or social inclusion) to outputs (such as meeting minimum quality standards). Thirdly, they became partners with others in the system in pursuit of wider strategies of 'risk management' or 'offender management' and public protection in pursuit of more narrowly defined system goals. This is not to say, however, that these reframed goals were easily achieved, nor that they succeeded in advancing the legitimacy of community sanctions as a set of mechanisms that played a useful part in the wider pursuit of systemic goals.

If the first adaptation was unashamedly pragmatic and instrumental, the second adaptation – based on a more *punitive* narrative – also had a more expressive or symbolic quality. In sharp contradistinction to their previous identity as an expression of welfarism, late-modern community sanctions (at least in some jurisdictions) emerged as forms of punishment. Three developments shaped this 'punitive turn'. The first was linked to the need to deliver alternatives to custody, referred to above. Achieving that objective seemed to require that community sanctions better establish their credibility with sentencers and with the wider public – and for some policymakers and practitioners this required that they sharpen up their punitive 'bite'. But punitive bite was also required by a second (and more principled) development; the rise of deserts-based sentencing frameworks implied a need to better articulate the punitive 'weight' of community sanctions, so as to more clearly locate them in a range of proportionate penalties. Though this second developments was driven philosophically by liberal academics and policymakers committed to 'limiting retributivism' (Morris 1974), a third development served to skew its effects. This was the emergence of 'penal populism' or 'populist punitiveness'; a less principled, low political response to and/or manipulation of the perceived hardening of attitudes in 'the law-abiding majority'. In practice, the cultural, political and social pressures of the punitive turn, as well as the more liberal demands of penal reductionism and of 'just deserts' placed probation institutions under pressure to substantiate the punitive character and content of community sanctions – and to evidence the rigour of their enforcement. Community sanctions had to be 'toughened up'.

If the second adaptation represents a departure from probation's traditions, the third adaption – the reframing of its *rehabilitative* narrative – had a more familiar ring. Rehabilitation, buoyed by some encouraging new research findings and by reappraisals of existing evidence, re-emerged from the doldrums of the 1970s 'Nothing Works' crisis, but in a new form. In the new political context, rehabilitation's advocates laid less stress on aspirations to restore the offender to full citizenship and more on rehabilitation's capacity to manage and reduce risks and thus to protect the disquieted and insecure 'law-abiding' public of late modernity. Members of this public – and in particular potential future victims – were now the beneficiaries of rehabilitation; offenders were the objects or raw materials on which it would operate *pro bono publico*. While this recasting of rehabilitation's purpose aspired to appeal to a more punitive public, its new instruments and mechanisms reflected the systemisation of justice referred to above. Risk-assessment tools and manualised offending behaviour programmes recast rehabilitation in managerialised form. That said, it is possible to overstate the instrumental aspects of the new rehabilitation; some commentators have highlighted its more expressive and communicative aspects. Offending behaviour programmes can be seen as part of a wider project of 'responsibilisation'; and their common pursuit of 'victim empathy' or 'values enhancement' reveals their more moralising aspects. The rehabilitated offender is expected to manage his or her own riskiness; rehabilitation is a personal project, not a social one.

The final adaptation discussed by Robinson *et al.* (2013) related to a developing *reparative* narrative for community sanctions. Indeed, as early as the 1970s, a number of prominent criminologists and sociologists, some inspired by Durkheim, had suggested that rehabilitation's then crisis might open the way for the development of restitutive or reparative sanctions (Bottoms 1980; Christie 1977; Hulsman 1976). Such sanctions seemed to allow the parsimony of proportionality (and related due process and human rights protections) without defaulting to a 'merely punitive' retributive model of doing justice by imposing harms on offenders. While community service and unpaid work might lay claim to being perhaps the most common and most successful innovation in community sanctions since the 1970s (indeed since the establishment of probation), in fact its goals, purposes and practices have rarely been defined solely in reparative or restitutive terms. Indeed, community service perhaps has been 'all things to all people' – sometimes advocated for its punitive bite, sometimes for its rehabilitative effects, sometimes for its reintegrative potential. Equally, the relationships between community sanctions and the global movements associated with 'restorative justice' and with 'community justice' have been less well articulated than might have been expected; not least because, unlike rehabilitation, reparation seems better placed to provide victim redress, to garner public support and therefore to substantiate the credibility and legitimacy of community sanctions as just sentences.

Robinson *et al.* (2013) also mentioned, but do not elaborate upon, other potential adaptations, perhaps the most important of which is the development of 'techno-corrections' (Nellis 2010; Nellis *et al.* 2013) and in particular electronic monitoring (EM). However, EM might be analysed at least partly in relation to the four adaptations discussed above: What sorts of particular claims for legitimacy do its technologies permit community sanctions to make? Are these claims linked principally to managerial goals, punitive weight, rehabilitative potential or reparation; and are there other claims that are specific to EM?

In preparing this book, we offered these narratives and their associated adaptations as analytical resources for our authors to consider in the context of their own analyses of community punishment in a variety of European jurisdictions. However, conscious that our analysis is rooted in the UK and US jurisdictions that we know best, we did not wish to impose an Anglocentric viewpoint on our contributors or to imply an analytical straitjacket from which they may not escape. In essence, the questions we asked them to address[5] are the same questions we set ourselves: How has community punishment evolved and survived in late modern social and penal conditions? What sorts of legitimation strategies have emerged and to what effect? If our earlier answers provide a helpful starting point, so be it. If not, we should learn something interesting by considering why not and what other explanations make more sense in different contexts.

Notes

1 It is further becoming clear that there can be considerable variation within some countries (Barker 2009; Phelps 2013).
2 For more information, see www.offendersupervision.eu.
3 We are grateful to our colleagues Kristel Beyens, Christine Morgenstern and Sonja Snacken for helping us get to grips with the legal distinctions here.
4 Personal communication by e-mail, 11 August 2013.
5 A more detailed list of questions we asked authors to address can be found in Appendix 1.

References

Barker, V. (2009) *The Politics of Imprisonment: How the democratic process shapes the way America punishes offenders*. Oxford: Oxford University Press.

Beetham, D. (1991) *The Legitimation of Power*. London: Macmillan.

Berger, J., Fisek, M. and Norman, R. (1998) 'The legitimation and delegitimation of power and prestige orders', *American Sociological Review*, 63: 379–405.

Beyens, K. and McNeill, F. (2013) 'Conclusion: studying mass supervision comparatively', in F. McNeill and K. Beyens (eds) *Offender Supervision in Europe*. Basingstoke: Palgrave Macmillan, pp. 155–69.

Bottoms, A. E. (1980) 'An introduction to "the coming crisis"', in A. E. Bottoms and R. H. Preston (eds) *The Coming Penal Crisis*, Edinburgh: Scottish Academic Press, pp. 1–24.

Bottoms, A. E. (1995) 'The philosophy and politics of punishment and sentencing', in C. Clarkson and R. Morgan (eds) *The Politics of Sentencing Reform*, Oxford: Clarendon Press, pp. 7–49.

Cavadino, M. and Dignan, J. (2006) *Penal Systems: A Comparative Approach*. London: Sage.

Christie, N. (1977) 'Conflicts as property', *British Journal of Criminology*, 17: 1–15.

Council of Europe (1992) *Recommendation No. R (92) 16 of the Committee of Ministers to Member States on the European Rules on Community Sanctions and Measures*.

Downes, D. (1988) *Contrasts in Tolerance*. Oxford: Clarendon Press.

Feeley, M. and Simon, J. (1992) 'The new penology: notes on the emerging strategy of corrections and its implications', *Criminology*, 30: 449–74.

Foucault, M. (1977) *Discipline and Punish: The Birth of the Prison*. London: Allen Lane.

Garland, D. (1985) *Punishment and Welfare*. Aldershot: Gower.

Garland, D. (1990) *Punishment and Modern Society*. Oxford: Clarendon Press.

Garland, D. (1996) 'The limits of the sovereign state: strategies of crime control in contemporary society, *British Journal of Criminology*, 36(4): 445–71.

Garland, D. (2001) *The Culture of Control*. Oxford: Oxford University Press.

Hamai, K., Villé, R., Harris, R., Hough, M. and Zvekic, U. (eds) (1995) *Probation Round the World*. London: Routledge.

Heidensohn, F. (2007) 'International comparative research in criminology', in R. King and E. Wincup (eds) *Doing Research on Crime and Justice* (2nd edition). Oxford: Oxford University Press, pp. 199–228.

Hulsman, L. (1976) '*Strategies to Reduce Violence in Society: Civilising the Criminal Justice System*', an address to the annual meeting of the Howard League for Penal Reform (unpublished).

Johnson, C., Dowd, T. and Ridgeway, C. (2006) 'Legitimacy as a social process', *Annual Review of Sociology*, 32: 53–78.

Lacey, N. (2007) *The Prisoners' Dilemma: Political Economy and Punishment in Contemporary Democracies*. Cambridge: Cambridge University Press.

McAra, L. (2005) 'Modelling penal transformation', *Punishment and Society*, 7: 277–302.

McNeill, F. and Beyens, K. (eds) (2013) *Offender Supervision in Europe*. Basingstoke: Palgrave Macmillan.

McNeill, F. and Robinson, G. (2013) 'Liquid legitimacy and community sanctions', in A. Crawford and A. Hucklesby (eds) *Legitimacy and Compliance in Criminal Justice*. London: Routledge, pp. 116–37.

McNeill, F., Burns, N., Halliday, S., Hutton, N. and Tata, C. (2009) 'Risk, responsibility and reconfiguration: penal adaptation and misadaptation', *Punishment and Society*, 14: 419–42.

Miller, P. and Rose, N. (1990) 'Governing economic life', *Economy and Society*, 19: 1–31.

Morris, N. (1974) *The Future of Imprisonment*. London: University of Chicago Press.

Muncie, J. and Goldson, B. (eds) (2006) *Comparative Youth Justice*. London: SAGE.

Nelken, D. (ed.) (2000) *Contrasting Criminal Justice*. Aldershot: Ashgate.

Nellis, M. (2010) 'Electronic monitoring: Towards integration into offender management' in F. McNeill, P. Raynor and C. Trotter (eds) *Offender Supervision: New Directions in Theory, Research and Practice*. Cullompton, Devon: Willan, pp. 509–33.

Nellis, M., Beyens, K. and Kaminski, D. (2013) *Electronically Monitored Punishment: International and Critical Perspectives*. London: Routledge.

O'Malley, P. (1996) 'Risk and responsibility', in A. Barry, T. Osborne and N. Rose (eds) *Foucault and Political Reason: Liberalism, Neo-Liberalism and Rationalities of Government*. London: University College London Press, pp. 189–207.

Page, J. (2013) 'Punishment and the penal field', in J. Simon and R. Sparks (eds) *The SAGE Handbook of Punishment and Society*. London: Sage, pp. 152–66.

Phelps, M. (2013) 'The paradox of probation: Community supervision in the age of mass incarceration', *Law & Policy*, 35(1, 2): 51–80.

Pratt, J., Brown, D., Brown, W., Hallsworth, S. and Morrison, W. (2005) *The New Punitiveness: Trends, Theories, Perspectives*. Cullompton, Devon: Willan.

Raynor, P. (1997) 'Evaluating probation: a moving target', in G. Mair (ed.) *Evaluating the Effectiveness of Community Penalties*. Aldershot: Avebury, pp. 19–33.

Robinson, G. (2008) 'Late-modern rehabilitation: the evolution of a penal strategy', *Punishment and Society*, 10(4): 429–45.

Robinson, G., McNeill, F. and Maruna, S. (2013) 'Punishment in society: The improbable persistence of probation and other community sanctions and measures', in J. Simon and R. Sparks (eds) *SAGE Handbook of Punishment and Society*. London: Sage, pp. 321–40.

Ruggiero, V. and Ryan, M. (2013) *Punishment in Europe: A Critical Anatomy of Penal Systems*. Basingstoke: Palgrave Macmillan.

Suchman, M. (1995) 'Managing legitimacy: strategic and institutional approaches', *Academy of Management Review*, 20: 571–610.

Tonry, M. and Doob, A. (eds) (2004) *Youth Crime and Youth Justice: Comparative and Cross-National Perspectives*. Chicago: University of Chicago Press.

Tonry, M. and Farrington, D. (eds) (2005) 'Crime and punishment in western countries 1980–1999', *Crime and Justice: A Review of Research*, 33: 541–54.

van Kalmthout, A. and Durnescu, I. (eds) (2008) *Probation in Europe*. Nijmegen: Wolf Legal Publishers/CEP.

Worrall, A. and Hoy, C. (2005) *Punishment in the Community*. Cullompton, Devon: Willan.

2

THE NEW GENERATION OF COMMUNITY PENALTIES IN BELGIUM

More is less...

Kristel Beyens

Focus

This chapter analyses the narratives and practices of community punishment in Belgium at different levels, that is, policy and legislation, application and operation. Having conducted sentencing research on the custody threshold (Beyens 2000a) and having been involved in research into the implementation of both the work penalty (Luypaert *et al.* 2007) and electronic monitoring (EM) (Devresse *et al.* 2006; Beyens and Roosen 2013, 2015), I will focus on these two penalties to tell the Belgian story of community punishment. They can be regarded as illustrations of what Bottoms *et al.* (2004) have identified as the 'new generation of community penalties', characterized by a focus on a punishing rhetoric, a growing reliance on technology to enforce the requirements, the introduction of new public management techniques, the contracting out of responsibilities to other bodies and inter-agency cooperation and partnership (Bottoms *et al.* 2004). I will reflect on how these features connect with the adaptation strategies that have been identified by Robinson *et al.* (2013) and discussed in the introduction to this volume. The emergence of the work penalty and EM will be situated in a broader political context and their acceptance will be compared with earlier community-oriented penal interventions, such as probation and suspended sentences. I will argue that the development of the new generation of community penalties is deeply rooted in the problem of the ever-increasing prison overcrowding and the search for a solution to the prison crisis. I will show how initial rehabilitative narratives and practices of the work penalty and EM have been reframed under the pressures of increasing numbers, managerial objectives and budgetary considerations.

Legal and sentencing developments

Until the 1990s interest in community sentences in Belgium was very limited. However, since the introduction of the so-called Act Lejeune in 1888, Belgium had been one of the first countries to introduce (non-supervisory) conditional sentences (fines and imprisonment) and conditional release. Individualization was the main objective of conditional sentences, which were embedded in a classic sentencing framework, guided by deterrence and retribution. Non-supervisory conditional sentences were widely used and still are today. Judges see them as a warrant or a 'second chance' for the offender, who is regarded as a rational actor who can be deterred by the mere threat of imprisonment (Snacken 1986; Beyens 2000a). However, as there are legal limits with regard to the criminal records of those whose sentences can be suspended, only a selection of first offenders are eligible for these conditional sanctions, hampering the discretionary power of the sentencing judge.

In 1964, almost a century later, probation was introduced as the Belgian expression of the 'era of resocialisation'. This 'probation measure', as judges call it, fitted with a general tendency towards the humanization of punishment and an inclusionary view of the offender. However, Snacken (2007) points out that Belgium never experienced a rise and fall of rehabilitation as was described by Garland (2001) for the UK and the USA. Despite the development of a strong welfare state, Belgian penal theory, legislation and practice remained fairly neoclassical, with an emphasis on individual responsibility, retribution and deterrence. According to the Act of 1964,[1] probation conditions have to be combined with a suspended sentence (previously conditional sentence) or a suspended conviction;[2] with a possible follow-up period of up to 5 years. Initially probation officers were, and since 1999 justice assistants (*infra*) have been, responsible for the supervision of the offender. The philosophy of rehabilitation did not catch on very well with the retributive, just-desert and proportionality oriented sentencing culture, which explains its lack of success with the judiciary (Beyens 2000a). Therefore probation had a very hesitant start and, despite a small recent increase, is still imposed only at a moderate rate (6,964 new cases in 2013, compared with 9,902 new mandates for the work penalty) (Directorate-General Houses of Justice 2014: 106). Although criminologists have denounced its limited use (Snacken 1986), research into the imposition of probation has been very scarce.

After the 1964 Act, it was some 30 years before significant new developments took place in the Belgian field of community punishment. The introduction of community service and training orders as new modalities of probation in 1994, and the broadening of the range of possibilities in which suspended sentences (*uitstel*) and suspension (*opschorting*) might be imposed, have been linked to crises of legitimacy of the political and judicial establishment since the 1980s. Insecurity became an important political topic and was linked with the success of the extremist right-wing party Vlaams Blok (later 'Vlaams Belang') in the national elections of November 1991 (so-called Black Sunday). Policy analyses pointed at the 'gap with the citizen', and citizens were described as feeling more vulnerable because of radical social changes and inevitable contact with other cultures, due to migration, particularly of non-EU citizens. A new political 'Contract with the citizen' (1992) by the government emphasized the importance of tackling major social problems by providing more security, more fairness through better and swifter administration of justice and more attention to the needs of victims (Snacken 2007).

The introduction of community service at the prosecution and sentencing stages was one element of policy initiatives aimed at tackling this legitimacy crisis (Snacken and Beyens 2002; Snacken 2007). As political pressures to demonstrate immediate action were high, community service was hastily introduced in 1994 as a condition of probation at the sentencing stage and as a condition of penal mediation at the prosecution stage. Penal mediation was the first legal initiative that explicitly brought the victim to the fore. Contrary to what the name of mediation would suggest, however, it was an ambivalent penal option, combining offender-oriented measures, such as therapy, training orders and community service of between 20 and 120 hours, and victim–offender mediation. It was therefore merely a symbolic, victim-oriented umbrella concept, rather than a genuine restorative innovation (Beyens 2000b).

The year 1996 was very important for Belgian society and for penal policies. In June 1996, the then Minister of Justice, Stefaan De Clerck, presented his white paper on penal policy and imprisonment in Parliament (Minister of Justice 1996). It was the first time that a Minister of Justice had presented an integrated and balanced approach to the penal crisis and where the priority for alternative sanctions was explicitly promulgated. However, the timing of the publication of the white paper could hardly have been worse: from August 1996 onwards, the notorious and strongly mediatized Dutroux case (which involved the abduction and murder of four young girls), and the following public outcry, dominated the discussion of penal reform, resulting in a focus on the construction of more prison capacity and, as Marc Dutroux was a recidivist sexual offender who had committed his crimes when he was on parole, on the reform of conditional release with particular attention to sexual crimes (Daems *et al.* 2013). The 'White March' of 300,000 citizens with white balloons in the streets of Brussels ushered in an era of constant and greater awareness of the needs and pains of victims. The collective denunciation by citizens of the lack of empathy of the judicial system towards victims was an expression of social solidarity with victims and their families and became part of the Belgian collective memory. Therefore this White March can be interpreted as an answer to the fragmentation of postmodern society and the search for reference points to unite citizens in a morally fragmented world (Boutellier 1993).

This new attention to victims of crime has led to several legislative changes that enhance the rights of victims in the criminal and parole procedures. The Act of 22 June 2005 introduced 'restorative mediation', which is applicable to nearly all offences and at every stage of the criminal procedure, from police investigation to prosecution, judicial inquiry, sentencing and sentence implementation. This was part of a restorative adaptation strategy to enhance the legitimacy of the penal system towards victims. The practice of restorative mediation got a foot on the ground in Belgium mainly due to strong academic support of restorative practices from colleagues of the Catholic University Leuven, with Tony Peters as forerunner and currently Ivo Aertsen as engaged and informed advocates of the restorative philosophy on a national and international level.[3] Other interesting illustrations of the restorative adaptation strategy in Belgium include the systematic addition of a separate article in all post-Dutroux legislation that introduced new community penalties, stating that the judge can take the interests of the victims into account when imposing a sentence. On the initiative of the Parliament, the right of the victim is even explicitly mentioned in the name of the Act on conditional release of 2006.[4]

Since the year 2000 the Belgian era of the 'new generation of community penalties' (Bottoms *et al.* 2004) has been ushered in, with the introduction of intermediate penalties that can be situated between those commonly perceived as 'too soft' (probation, training orders and community service) on the one hand and imprisonment on the other (Morris and Tonry 1990). Community penalties obtained an autonomous legal status and the rehabilitative aspect became reframed in a more punitive, desert-oriented framework.

In 2002 community service as a probation measure was replaced by an autonomous or stand-alone sentencing option, which was named the 'work penalty' (*werkstraf* in Dutch or *peine de travail* in French) (Act of 17 April 2002). The terminology that is used to refer to penal interventions and practice conveys a meaning about how they are conceived and used, and has also an effect on the perceptions of both those who impose and implement them and of the wider public (Herzog-Evans 2012). Using 'penalty' as the official label explicitly conveyed the punitive dimension of this sentence, which was recognized in the restriction of freedom, the requirement to comply with work schedules and being subject to external control. Together with imprisonment and the fine, the work penalty became the third main penalty in the Belgian penal code, which boosted its legal status.[5] To avoid net widening, it was explicitly mentioned in the preparatory work of the legislation that the work penalty should serve as a substitute for imprisonment. It was further officially promoted as a constructive sanction with a reintegrative character (Beyens 2010). Work penalties can substitute a prison sentence of up to 5 years, and to maximize their scope they can legally be imposed for all offences, excluding only a few very serious offences, such as kidnapping, rape, sexual offences with minors, murder and manslaughter. Unlike for suspended sentences, suspension and probation, the criminal record of the offender does not impede the imposition of a work penalty, which has been an important step forward to increase its use. Work penalties can range between 20 and 300 hours (600 hours for recidivists), and the defendant (or his/her lawyer) has to give his/her consent during the court hearing. Very importantly, to avoid social stigmatization, the work penalty does not appear on the certificate of good conduct, which offenders need in order to obtain a job.[6] This possibility to safeguard social and judicial rehabilitation[7] was and still is a strong impetus for defendants and lawyers to plead for the work penalty and a key success factor in its swift acceptance.

Upgrading the legal status of the work penalty from a condition of probation to an autonomous main penalty also initiated a noteworthy change in judges' sentencing behaviour. In 10 years of application, the number of offenders sentenced to a work penalty increased to 9,902 new mandates in 2013 (Directorate-General Houses of Justice 2014: 106). Compared with the very moderate use of community service as a condition of probation and of probation in general (*supra*), this quick increase is an unprecedented success. Small-scale research by Lefevre (2009) and Verbist (2013), repeating Beyens' (2000a) research by using the same four vignettes with a small sample of judges, showed the openness of the judiciary to this sentence. While Beyens found that the experiences of the judges with community service were rather limited and that they did not regard community service as a 'real sentence', reserving it for a small group of well-integrated offenders, 10 years later the judges accepted the work penalty as a punishing sentencing option that could meet different aims, such as retribution and deterrence, but also reintegration and even redress to society. They related the enhanced credibility of the work penalty to its autonomous status as a main penalty and the policy that the substitute prison sentence has effectively to be served in the event of breach.[8] Here the link with the non-execution policy of the short prison sentences comes to the fore (see the section on prison overcrowding, below; also *infra*). Work penalties are regarded by judges as more credible sentencing options than short prison sentences that are not implemented due to prison overcrowding. It shows how the application of the autonomous work penalty in Belgium is linked with the wider penal policy to counter (the public's perceptions of) impunity, due to the non-execution of short prison sentences.

From this success, policymakers obviously understood that creating autonomous sentences could increase the use of non-custodial sentences. So in 2014 two additional autonomous community penalties were introduced in the Belgian penal code, namely EM as an autonomous penalty (Act of 7 February 2014) and probation as an autonomous penalty (Act of 10 April 2014). Many provisions in the Act of the autonomous work penalty of 2002 have been replicated in these acts of 2014. While the Probation Act of 1964 mentions 'judicial accompaniment' or 'guidance' and 'treatment', the Act of 2014 on autonomous probation only speaks about 'judicial accompaniment' or 'guidance'[9] (*justitiële begeleiding*), which illustrates that probation as an autonomous penalty is no longer regarded as a purely rehabilitative intervention (Decaigny 2014). Also the use of probation 'penalty' and no longer 'condition of probation' also shows a punitive shift, which is confirmed by the policy that pre-sentence reports have become optional for the autonomous probation penalty. In fact this is a continuation of an existing situation, whereby work penalties are increasingly imposed without a social enquiry report (Directorate-General Houses of Justice 2014). An explanation given by the judges for this underuse of social reports is lack of staff at the houses of justice to prepare the reports, which would lead to a delay of the judicial procedure. Research by Beyens and Scheirs (2010) with judges indicates that the relatively marginal use of social reports at the sentencing stage is an illustration of the judges' pursuit of professional ownership of 'their' decision: they prefer to rely on judicial documents or police reports, or on their own evaluation of the situation of the offender, which is based on short interactions during the court hearing, rather than relying on the social narratives of justice assistants. Lastly but not less importantly, as for the autonomous work penalty, also for probation and EM as autonomous penalties, there are no restrictions any more with regard to criminal record, which reflects the desire of the legislator to maximally encourage extensive use of these penalties.

Electronic monitoring as the panacea to solve the legitimacy crisis of an encumbered prison system

While autonomous EM has been introduced legally only recently, EM has a long history in the execution phase of imprisonment, since 1998 on a local basis and since 2000 on a national level. Initially, EM was introduced as a back-door measure for prisoners with a prison sentence of up to 18 months. It was promoted as a humane and rehabilitative alternative to imprisonment, a form of virtual detention that aimed to prevent the prisoner from suffering the negative consequences of imprisonment, by letting him remain within his normal social environment and providing the possibility to engage in useful activities, such as performing a job or participating in education. A balance was sought between social support and technical control, and technology served as a means to support rehabilitative goals; an approach referred to as the 'Belgian Model' (Beyens and Kaminski 2013). EM only acquired a legal basis with the Act of 17 May 2006 on the External Legal Position, 6 years after its national rollout. The Act defines EM as

> a modality of the execution of the custodial sentence where the convicted person undergoes his entire custodial sentence or a part of it outside of prison according to a plan of execution, whereby compliance is controlled, among others, by technological means.
>
> *(Art. 22)*

It is interesting to note that the legal definition of EM mentions technological means, among others, as a way of controlling compliance. Human supervision has become, however, less and less prominent nowadays, in particular for EM replacing prison sentences of up to 3 years.[10]

Since 2005, a two-track policy with regard to the application of EM has been adopted, resulting in diverging practices for prisoners with a sentence of up to 3 years, imprisonment on the one hand or more than 3 years on the other. For the group of offenders sentenced to 3 years of imprisonment or more, EM serves as a back-door intermediate phase between imprisonment and conditional release. Here the supervisory-oriented Belgian model is still applicable and justice assistants are still involved in the follow-up of individual conditions. However, for prison sentences of up to 3 years, in recent years EM has increasingly been applied as a purely controlling and retributive way of executing the prison sentence, without any social guidance of the justice assistants or application of individual conditions. Prison sentences are almost automatically converted to an EM during the implementation phase, by the prison governor, or by the Detention Management Service (Directie Detentiebeheer) for 'difficult' cases, such as sexual offences.[11] Individual time regimes are replaced by standard schedules, and contact with the penal system no longer takes place via the justice assistants, but mostly via the technical monitoring and mobile staff of the Centre of Electronic Monitoring (CEM). Here EM serves currently as a front-door strategy, aiming to tackle prison overcrowding. Although, up to 2006, EM numbers rose only slowly, the policy aiming to convert more prison sentences has initiated an almost exponential growth of the numbers of people under EM, particularly since 2012. As of 2014, about 2,000 offenders are subjected to EM on a daily basis, the majority being convicted prisoners sentenced to imprisonment of up to 3 years (69 per cent of the total EM population on 30 May 2014, $N = 1,364$) and 27 per cent being persons serving a prison sentence of 3 years or more ($N = 530$ on 30 May 2014).[12] Also 3.7 per cent ($N = 73$) of the total EM population was serving remand custody under GPS, which is another recent novelty, introduced in 2014.

Prison overcrowding

The emergence and growth of EM has a particular link with the problem of prison overcrowding. Since the 1980s the Belgian prison population has been steadily increasing, leading to overcrowding of up to 124 per cent in 2013 (Prison Service 2014: 67). From the start, back-door policies (Rutherford 1984) have been used to relieve the over-burdened prison system at short notice. 'Provisional release in view of pardon', which was originally introduced in 1972 as an individual decision, has been more systematically and generally applied by the Prison Administration since 1983, releasing all prisoners sentenced to up to 1 year after having served a part of their sentence in prison. In 1994 the application of 'provisional release for reason of overcrowding' was broadened to sentences of up to 3 years and sentences of up to 6 months were not executed any more, due to a lack of prison capacity (Snacken et al. 2010).[13] This policy has led to an instrumentalization of provisional release and raised a lot of discontent and misunderstanding among the public, politicians and sentencing judges. Due to the complexities of the different forms of early release, confusion between the systems of *conditional* release (for prison sentences of more than 3 years) and *provisional* release (for prison sentences of up to 3 years) has arisen, despite their differences in nature and application. The increased use of provisional release for reasons of overcrowding, coupled with the expanding use of EM as a modality of the implementation of prison sentences for those sentenced to imprisonment of up to 3 years, nourished the idea of impunity in society. Research by Beyens et al. (2010) showed that judges anticipate possible release decisions in their sentencing decisions and are inclined to impose sentences of 3 years and longer, sometimes even the symbolic length of 36 months and 1 day, to be sure that the offender will be released through the individual and much stricter system of conditional release.[14] This has led to a vicious circle of longer sentences being imposed by the sentencing judges, which increases prison overcrowding, which in turn increases the resort to provisional release and the use of EM. Provisional releases have made up more than 80 per cent of all releases in Belgium in recent years (Snacken *et al.* 2010); and the more this form of early release has been used as a form of routinized, quasi-automatic early release, the more vehemently it has been attacked.

There is an undeniable and important emotional dimension in this debate, which has been picked up by the media, who have spread the idea of impunity to the general public and the judiciary. It is therefore not surprising that policymakers too are worried about the widespread perception of impunity. Since 2008, white papers on penal policy have explicitly referred to the importance of a credible sentence implementation system (Vandeurzen 2009; De Clerck 2010; Turtelboom 2012). The 'impunity narrative' has thus become an official, authoritative account of the functioning of the Belgian criminal justice system and has insidiously gained legitimacy (Beyens *et al.* 2013). 'Regaining credibility' became the mantra of Minister of Justice Annemie Turtelboom and this was also explicitly formulated in the Ministerial Circular Letter of 7 July 2013 on EM, which insists on a 'resolute and swift execution of all sentences and in particular of short prison sentences, which is necessary for the credibility of the penal system'. The importance of 'the optimisation of the sentence implementation for prisoners convicted to a prison sentence of up to three years' was also emphasized. Furthermore, the Ministerial Circular Letter of 2012, which introduced the so-called system of home detention, being applied to persons serving a prison sentence of up to 8 months and who have to serve 2 months of their sentence under the regime of voice recognition, referred to the 'credible execution' policy. In addition to the introduction of the new technology of voice verification, even more important is that people who are subjected to the regime of home detention no longer have any recourse to support or accompaniment of a justice assistant, nor is a social enquiry report required to investigate the circumstances wherein the home detention will be executed.

In order to cut the costs of staff, accompaniment and supervision of individual conditions by a justice assistant during the execution of the EM measure has thus become less and less frequent. This allows simplifying and speeding up of the procedure, to facilitate the management of more offenders at a lower cost and to eliminate waiting lists of offenders to serve their sentence. Justice assistants are no longer involved in the implementation of EM for a growing group of convicted offenders, nor for the group of remand prisoners who are serving their pre-trial detention at home under GPS. In 2014, the scope of EM was extended once more when it was introduced at the pre-trial phase using the technology of GPS tracking. Reducing the population under pre-trial detention was the main driver, despite the dismissive stance of investigation judges having to apply this alternative to detention. Investigation judges consider GPS tracking to be unsuitable for tackling important risks that lie behind the rationale of imposing remand custody. Also research investigating the possible reductive effect on the prison population has come to very

cautious conclusions (Maes *et al.* 2012). Since 2014, defendants have been confined 24 hours a day, seven days a week (24-7) and are only allowed to leave their
home with the explicit permission of the investigating judge, under exceptional
circumstances that are described in the Ministerial Circular Letter.[15] Paradoxically,
tracking technology is thus mainly used to control the defendant's presence inside
the house on a 24-7 basis, without any access to support or accompaniment of a
justice assistant. The speed and lack of thoughtfulness with which GPS has been
implemented in the pre-trial phase illustrates again the eagerness of the government
to prioritize technological innovations and its belief in their effectiveness (Beyens
and Roosen 2015).

Reinventing the operation of community punishment

The expansion of the different forms of community punishments and their increasing use required a reorganization of the execution of these sentences. In the
first phase, before the 1990s, this para-penal field was not only rather invisible,
but also very fragmented, diffused and uncoordinated, and lacked internal coher-
ence, transparency and management in its operation (De Valck 1999; Storme and
Gyselinck 2012). Probation officers enjoyed considerable freedom in how they
supervised their 'clients' and worked quite independently. Speaking about 'clients'
also reflected their strong social approach, based upon individual guidance. Since
the end of the 1990s, efforts have been directed towards internal centralization and
identity building of the field of community punishment.

Today two key organizations are responsible for the operation of community
punishment in Belgium, the Directorate-General of the Houses of Justice and the
National Centre for Electronic Monitoring (NCEM). They both have a turbulent
organizational history and both agencies had up to 2014 operated under the federal
government. Recently, a new phase was ushered in as a result of the sixth Belgian
State Reform, leading to a transfer of competences of the federal level to the regions
(Flanders, Wallonia and Brussels) and the (language) communities.[16] These changes
raise a lot of questions about the future operation of community penalties and
generate a lot of unrest and uncertainties among staff. It also implies that energy
that has to be invested in organizational matters will continue to be diverted from
more substantive issues.

The establishment of the NCEM in 2000 was an answer to the deadlock that
arose in the debate on who should be responsible for the social supervision and
the electronic control of people subjected to EM. The then probation officers,
who initially were in charge of the supervision and follow-up of those subject
to EM during the pilot in 1998, refused to be involved in prompt enforcement
when, for instance, the offender's time schedule was violated. As a consequence, a
separate agency was created as part of the Prison Service and, from 2000 onwards,
specially created officers, 'EM-social assistants', were made responsible for the social
supervision of people under EM (Beyens and Kaminski 2013). As of 2007, the
NCEM became part of the DGHJ and the supervisory work was taken over by

the justice assistants and it became an important and ever growing player in the field of executing community punishment in Belgium. The increasing and sole reliance on electronic devices for the execution of a sentence, and the removal of the involvement of justice assistants in the execution of EM for a growing group of persons subjected to EM implied that more and more tasks are taken over by personnel and management of the NCEM. Monitoring staff and technicians who install the equipment in homes, and who have no social work background, became the only contacts and thus representatives of the penal system for those under EM.

Since 1999, the Directorate-General of the Houses of Justice and the 27 local houses of justice (one in every judicial district) are, as 'para-penal' actors, responsible for *inter alia* the execution of probation, training orders, the work penalty and EM (for those who are also supervised by a justice assistant). Their establishment was directly linked to the Dutroux case, and was intended to literally and symbolically bring the penal system closer to the public, and thus enhance the credibility of the criminal justice system (Snacken and Beyens 2002). The name 'Houses of Justice' indicates the shift to making justice more accessible and transparent (Bauwens 2009). 'Probation officers' became 'justice assistants', explicitly referring to their role of assisting in judicial tasks, emphasizing the importance of compliance with rules and contracts. A management plan 2006–2012 and a mission statement with six objectives was set out.[17] Reducing re-offending and (re)integrating the offender are bound together as primary policy objectives. It took, however, until 2010 before an official vision statement on 'offender guidance' was available, mentioning that 'social work under judicial mandate' must give shape to the 'primary intended outcome of offender guidance', that is, *non-recidivism* (Bauwens 2011; Bauwens and Devos 2015). This guidance implies fostering a learning process for the offender to encourage him/her to adopt a certain type of behaviour. Building a relationship of mutual trust between the justice assistant and the offender or *justitiabele* (those who are subjected to a judicial intervention) is seen as being of pivotal importance.

A lot of energy, however, has been spent on internal reorganizations and streamlining the social work activities of the justice assistants, aiming to increase the efficiency of the operation of community penalties. The roll-out of the so-called Business Process Re-engineering programme took place between 2006 and 2007 and raised many reactions from the field workers. Jonckheere (2013), who investigated the introduction of the information platform SIPAR (Système Informatique PARajudiciaire), describes the uneasiness, unrest and resistance of justice assistants towards this tool, which directs their work and facilitates closer control of their own activities. Bauwens (2009, 2011), who studied the impact of the organizational changes on justice assistants, describes the ambivalence with which the imposed bureaucratization and managerialization of the organization was met in the field. She, however, observes that newly recruited or junior justice assistants seem to accept the new offender management approach more readily, and that they are more inclined to follow the manuals and prescribed work methods than senior assistants who previously enjoyed great discretion in performing their tasks.

In general few justice assistants disputed the need to standardize some very variable and inconsistent practices across the country, and meanwhile it has also become clear that the field is adapting slowly (but surely) to this change in the execution of guidance tasks. However, the fear of the hollowing out of the social and human dimension of social guidance and of the shift of time investment in individualized supervision towards more administrative burdens, which was expressed by Claus and Schoofs (2010) at the first big conference that was organized to celebrate 10 years of Houses of Justice, was not without reason.

Indeed, with regard to the work penalty for example, we see that the follow-up has become stripped of social guidance and that the amount of contact with persons under supervision has been strictly limited. Consequently the caseload of justice assistants is adjusted to this minimalistic interpretation of their task. The evolution of the social work approach towards a rather 'naked' follow-up is related to the pressure of the increasing numbers of offenders made subject to a work penalty. This does not, however, mean that the social approach has become completely abandoned. The research of Dantinne *et al.* (2009) into offenders' perceptions of their contact with the justice assistants, the dispatchers and the supervisors at the work placement (*infra*) shows that the majority (80 per cent) of the sample of offenders described the contact with the justice assistants as 'helping'. However, 55 per cent describe it as controlling and one-third (34 per cent) as 'punishing'. Helping and controlling thus do not seem to be contradictory. Interviews with justice assistants reveal that, in spite of the official policy, and especially in cases of social fragility of the offender (personal problems of all kinds), social support and guidance are offered as far as possible by the justice assistants. This illustrates the tension between the stated goals of the organization and the real goals of the justice assistants (Denkers 1976), or what McNeill *et al.* (2009) have described as a 'governmentality gap', referring to the contingent relationship between official discourse and practices, the role of penal workers and their capacity to, consciously or subconsciously, resist policy.

The increasing involvement of the 'community'

An important feature of current community penalties is that other, non-penal actors get a role in the execution of the sentence (for example, third-sector involvement for the work penalty). New actors and agencies became involved in the follow-up of the work penalty. The result is a penal field with blurred institutional and non-institutional boundaries, which requires an increased focus on inter-agency cooperation.

In Belgium the work penalty must be carried out in public services within 12 months of the conviction. Luypaert *et al.* (2007) describe the complex configuration of agents involved in the execution of the work penalty: (1) the houses of justice and the justice assistants, (2) the subsidized 'dispatching' and 'work floor projects' (*werkvloeren*) and (3) the voluntary 'work places' (*prestatieplaatsen*). Interestingly, the structure for subsidising the third-sector agencies was established in 1994 from an employment-driven rationale, rather than from a criminal justice approach, responding to the needs and diversity of the offenders who have to serve their work penalty. This brought about a disorganized and fragmented supply of services, entailing considerable differences between the judicial districts and also between the French- and Dutch-speaking parts of the country. Dispatching projects took over two important functions of the justice assistants: finding a work placement for the persons who have to serve their work penalty, and supervising the execution of the work penalty. As these projects are subsidized on a yearly basis, based on quantitative criteria, this led to a fragile existence, characterized by increased job uncertainty, dissatisfaction and pressure to receive enough cases on a yearly basis to survive.

Non-profit-making organizations and foundations with a social, scientific or cultural objective can provide unpaid work for offenders. These organizations all cooperate on a voluntary basis, without being paid for their services to the government (Luypaert *et al.* 2007; Beyens 2010), which is a cheap way for the government to contract out its punishing responsibilities to the civil society. By involving civil actors, who operate outside the strict limits of the criminal justice system, there is a blurring of the 'modern' penality into an undefined, fragmented, seemingly limitless system of penal control. Persons who are made subject to a work penalty become controlled by their fellow citizens, who receive discretionary power, without having been trained to execute this job of control or supervision (Beyens 2010).

Cohabitants become strongly involved in the daily execution of EM. Research by Vanhaelemeesch and Vander Beken (2014) reveals how EM impacts on the lives of cohabitants in order to make EM work. They fulfil a number of roles, ranging from social assistant to controller. Also this group of citizens provides free services to the government that is more and more reliant on self-management of the punished offender.

Conclusion: More is less

In this chapter I have focused on developments with regard to the work penalty and EM, because, from a quantitative point of view, they have dominated the landscape of community punishment for the last decade. Both penalties have evolved from a rehabilitation-oriented 'measure' to an empty, almost meaningless controlling punishment option, being stripped of its social work potential. This adaptation from a rehabilitative approach towards a more retributive, purely controlling approach is intimately linked to the enduring prison overcrowding and the encompassing search of the government for quick and cheap solutions. The growing population serving community sentences has not, however, curbed the rising prison population, which indicates the expressive and even symbolic dimension of this policy. However, the questioning of the credibility of the criminal justice system through the non- or part-execution of prison sentences initiated and stimulated the recourse to work penalties and EM, at the different levels of the criminal justice system.

To restore its political credibility, the field of community punishment has become transformed into a people-processing system focussing on quantity, rather than quality, initiated by a strong managerial dominance in the operation of community punishment.

The increasing group of offenders that has to be processed through the system has brought new organizational challenges. The houses of justice and the NCEM have been confronted with waiting lists, lack of staff and increasing caseloads, problems that are very similar to the penitentiary problems caused by overcrowding. Legitimacy has been sought through a professionalization of the organization by introducing new public management techniques (Bauwens 2011): supervisory tasks have become streamlined and standardized, which has led to more equal treatment, but also reduced or even abolished an individualized approach for certain groups of offenders. The amount of contact between supervisor and supervisee has been formally reduced and house visits replaced by telephone contact. The work of the justice assistants is evolving towards that of mere administrators of sentences, who tick boxes instead of being supervisors or social workers for offenders. This development is reinforced by the outsourcing of social work activities to less skilled staff and workers in the community, hereby creating new kinds of staff, mainly working in temporary and uncertain positions without social work training.

With regard to EM we see an even more extreme evolution, moving away from a rehabilitative approach. Guidance by a justice assistant has been completely removed for the biggest group of offenders under EM, and most of the people who are subjected to EM or GPS are only monitored from a distance through electronic control and contact by phone with anonymous workers at the monitoring centre, who have no social work training.

All this has initiated fundamental changes in the nature of community punishment in Belgium. The rehabilitative dimension has been reduced to working in the community or being locked up in the offender's own house, without giving further substance to the sentence. The mission of 'fostering a learning process for the offender to encourage him/her to adopt a certain type of behaviour' hereby gets a new interpretation of pure control of compliance with time schedules and contracts. Together with the strong technology-driven approach, this has led to erosion, not to say transformation, of the rehabilitative nature of community punishments. From a quantitative point of view, this has initiated more punishment in Belgium, but punishment without (social) content. Thus, more is less. . .

However, managerial adaptations to increase the opportunities to execute penalties are not unambiguously linked to more punitiveness from a qualitative point of view. Less supervision also means less (human) control and thus perhaps less punitiveness. But more or purely electronic control gives less leeway to the controlled, which can increase the risk of failure, and thus the risk of being subjected to the substitute (prison) sentence, thereby increasing punitiveness. The question about the punitive adaptation is, however, a complex one, which has also to be investigated through the experiences of those who are subjected to the punishments.

Notes

1 Act of 29 June 1964 with regard to suspension, suspended sentence and probation, *BS* 17 June 1964.
2 In the case of *suspension*, the judicial response is a declaration of guilt, and the sentencing judge does not impose a sentence. If the offender does not commit a crime over a certain period (between 1 and 5 years), there will be no sentence. In the case of a *suspended sentence*, the sentencing judge imposes a sentence of up to 5 years, which can be suspended for between 1 and 5 years. In the case of a new crime during this period, this sentence will be activated and added to the sentence that will be imposed for the new offence. Probation supervision can be combined with a suspended sentence or with a suspension.
3 For an overview of current national and international activities, see the website of the European Forum of Restorative Justice (www.euforumrj.org/home, consulted on 26 November 2014).
4 In full, the Act of 17 May 2006 on the External Legal Position of sentenced prisoners and *the right of the victims* in the legal framework of modalities of implementation of sentences (my emphasis).
5 Community service as a condition of probation was previously inscribed in a separate law and not in the Penal Code, which weakened its legal position.
6 Nevertheless, the work penalty appears on the central sentence register, where all criminal records are maintained.
7 For an interesting international comparative view, see the special issue on judicial rehabilitation of the *European Journal of Probation* of 2011, vol. 3, no. 1.
8 Ministerial Circular Letter no. 1771 of 17 January 2005 with regard to the early release and the non-execution of certain sentences.
9 The terms 'guidance' and 'accompaniment' are used interchangeably as a translation of the Dutch word '*begeleiding*'.
10 Today the Act of 2006 is still only applicable for those who are serving a sentence of 3 years imprisonment or more, where EM is used as a back-end measure, who have become a minority of the total EM population today.
11 Ministerial Circular letter of 28 August 2012 on home detention with voice verification for persons convicted to one or more prison sentences of which the executable part is *no longer than 3 years and who are 2 months or less from their early release date*. Ministerial Circular Letter ET/SE-2 of 17 July 2013 concerning the regulation of electronic monitoring as a modality for prison punishment where the executable part *does not exceed 3 years.*
12 Data provided by the NCEM.
13 Prison sentences of less than 6 months are actually executed when they are a substitute for a work penalty that has not or has only partly been executed. This was explicitly stated in the Ministerial Circular letter of 2005, to enhance the credibility of the work penalty.
14 For more details about the different systems of early release in Belgium, see Snacken *et al.* (2010).
15 Ministerial Circular Letter ET/SE-3 concerning arrest warrant executed under EM.
16 This means that the federal government is no longer to be in charge of the DGHJ, nor of the NCEM, and that as of 1 January 2015 the Dutch-speaking Houses of Justice and the Dutch speaking part of the NCEM are embedded in the Department of Welfare, Public Health and Family of the Flemish Government and that the French-speaking Houses of

Justice and NCEM become 'une Administration Générale' (somewhat comparable with the structure of the current Directorate General of the Houses of Justice). The House of Justice of Eupen forms a separate division or 'ein Fachbereich' at the Ministry of the German-speaking Community (Bauwens and Devos 2015). From 1 January 2015 on, the National Centre for Electronic Monitoring is replaced by a 'Flemish Centre for EM' (*Vlaams Centrum voor Elektronisch Toezicht*) for the Dutch-speaking part of Belgium and a 'Centre for EM' (*Centre de Surveillance Electronique*) for the French-speaking part of Belgium. In this chapter we will use the acronym 'NCEM', as we discuss policies and practices up to 2014.

17   For more details, see Bauwens (2011) and Bauwens and Devos (2015).

References

Bauwens, A. (2009) 'Probation officers' perspectives on recent Belgian changes in the probation service', *Probation Journal*, 56(3), pp. 257–68.

Bauwens, A. (2011) 'Organisational change, increasing managerialism and social work values in the Belgian Houses of Justice, Department of Offender Guidance', *European Journal of Probation*, 3(2), pp. 15–30.

Bauwens, A., and Devos, A. (2015) 'Belgium', in I. Durnescu and A. M. van Kalmthout (eds) *Probation in Europe*. CEP. Available at: www.cep-probation.org/default. asp?page_id=157&map_id=152.

Beyens, K. (2000a) *Straffen als Sociale Praktijk. Een Penologisch Onderzoek naar Straftoemeting*. Brussels: VUBPress.

Beyens, K. (2000b) 'Vier jaar bemiddeling in strafzaken: 1995–1998', *Panopticon*, 21(3), pp. 260–71.

Beyens, K. (2010) 'From "community service" to "autonomous work penalty" in Belgium. What's in a name?' *European Journal of Probation*, 2(1), pp. 4–21.

Beyens, K., and Kaminski, D. (2013) 'Is the sky the limit? Eagerness for electronic monitoring in Belgium', in M. Nellis, K. Beyens and D. Kaminski (eds) *Electronically Monitored Punishment: International and Critical Perspectives*. Oxon: Routledge, pp. 174–99.

Beyens, K., and Roosen, M. (2013) 'Electronic monitoring in Belgium: a penological analysis of current and future orientations', *European Journal of Probation*, 5(3), pp. 56–70.

Beyens, K., and Roosen, M. (2015) 'Suspects being watched in real-time: Introducing GPS tracking in Belgium', *Journal of Technology in Human Services*, 33(1), in press.

Beyens, K., and Scheirs, V. (2010) 'Encounters of a different kind. Social enquiry and sentencing in Belgium', *Punishment and Society*, 12(3), pp. 309–28.

Beyens, K., Françoise, C., and Scheirs, V. (2010) 'Les juges Belges face à l'(in)exécution des peines, Edition: Déviance et Société', *Déviance et Société*, 34(3), pp. 401–24.

Beyens, K., Snacken, S., and Van Zyl Smit, D. (2013) 'Truth in (the implementation of) Sentencing: Belgium and elsewhere', in T. Daems, D. Van Zyl Smit and S. Snacken (eds) *European Penology?* Oxford: Hart Publishing, pp. 271–92.

Bottoms, A., Rex, S., and Robinson, G. (eds). (2004) *Alternatives to Prison. Options for an Insecure Society*. Cullompton, Devon: Willan.

Boutellier, H. (1993) *Solidariteit en Slachtofferschap. De Morele Betekeniscan Criminaliteit in een Postmoderne Cultuur*. Nijmegen: SUN.

Claus, V., and Schoofs, A. (2010) 'Justitieassistent in het verleden tot nu. Ervaringen binnen een organisatie in evolutie', in FOD Justitie (ed.) *10 Jaar Justitiehuizen. Balans & Perspectieven*. Brussels: FOD Justitie, pp. 51–7.

Daems, T., Maes, E., and Rober, L. (2013) 'Crime, criminal justice and criminology in Belgium', *European Journal of Criminology*, 10(2) pp. 237–54.

Dantinne, M., Duchêne, J., Lauwaert, K., Aertsen, I., Bogaerts, S., Goethals, J., and Vlaemynck, M. (2009) *Peine de Travail et Vécu du Condamné. Beleving Van de Veroordeelde tot een Werkstraf*. Liège, Leuven: Université de Liège; Katholieke Universiteit Leuven.

Decaigny, T. (2014) 'Nieuwe correctionele hoofdstraffen: de straf onder elektronisch toezicht en de autonome probatiestraf', *Tijdschrift voor Strafrecht*(4), pp. 211–25.

De Clerck, S. (2010) *Straf en Strafuitvoeringsbeleid. Overzicht en Ontwikkeling*. Brussels: Kabinet Justitie.

De Valck, S. (1999) 'Naar een meer humane, toegankelijke en efficiënte justitie... De uitdaging Van de justitiehuizen', *Panopticon*, 20(6), pp. 583–91.

Denkers, F. (1976) *Criminologie en beleid*. Nijmegen: Dekker & van de Vegt.

Devresse, M.-S., Luypaert, H., Kaminski, D., and Beyens, K. (2006) *Onderzoek Betreffende de Evaluatie Van de Reglementering, Van de Besluitvorming en Van het Verloop Van het Elektronisch Toezicht*. Brussels: UCL, VUB, FOD Justitie.

Directorate-General Houses of Justice (2014) *Activity Report 2013*. Brussels: FOD Justitie.

Garland, D. (2001) *The Culture of Control. Crime and Social Order in Contemporary Society*. Oxford: Oxford University Press.

Herzog-Evans, M. (2012) 'What's in a name: Penological and institutional connotations of probation officers' labelling in Europe', *EuroVista*, 2(3), pp. 121–33.

Jonckheere, A. (2013) *(Dés)équilibres. L'informatisation du Travail Social en Justice*. Louvain-la-Neuve: Larcier.

Lefevre, J. (2009) 'Rechters en werkstraf: Een kwalitatief onderzoek', Master's Thesis, Vrije Universiteit Brussel, Belgium.

Luypaert, H., Beyens, K., Françoise, C., Kaminski, D., and m.m.v. Janssens, C. (2007) *Werken en Leren als Straf. Le Travail et al Formation Comme Peines*. Brussels: VUBPress.

Maes, E., Mine, B., De Man, C., and Van Brakel, R. (2012) 'Thinking about electronic monitoring in the context of pre-trial detention in Belgium: a solution to prison overcrowding?', *European Journal of Probation*, 4(2), pp. 3–22.

McNeill, F., Burns, N., Halliday, S., Hutton, N., and Tata, C. (2009) 'Risk, responsibility and reconfiguration: Penal adaptation and misadaptation', *Punishment Society*, 11(4), pp. 419–42.

Minister of Justice (1996) 'Oriëntatienota Strafbeleid en Gevangenisbeleid', in T. Peters and J. Vanacker (eds) *Van Oriëntatienota naar penaal beleid?* Leuven: Katholieke Universiteit Leuven, pp. 1–86.

Morris, N., and Tonry, M. (1990) *Between prison and probation: Intermediate punishments in a rational sentencing system*. New York: Oxford University Press.

Prison Service (2014) *Jaarverslag 2013*. Brussels: FOD Justitie.

Robinson, G., McNeill, F., and Maruna, S. (2013) 'Punishment in society: The improbable persistence of probation and other community sanctions and measures', in J. Simon and R. Sparks (eds), *The Sage Handbook of Punishment and Society*. London: Sage, pp. 321–40.

Rutherford, A. (1984) *Prisons and the process of justice: the reductionist challenge*. London: Heinemann.

Snacken, S. (1986) *De korte gevangenisstraf. Een onderzoek naar toepassing en effectiviteit* (vol. 13). Antwerpen: Kluwer Rechtswetenschappen.

Snacken, S. (2007) 'Penal policy and practice in Belgium', in M. Tonry (ed.) *Crime, punishment and politics in comparative perspective, crime and justice: A review of research*. Chicago: Chicago University Press, pp. 127–214.

Snacken, S., and Beyens, K. (2002) 'Alternatieven voor de vrijheidsberoving: hoop voor de toekomst?' in S. Snacken (ed.) *Strafrechtelijk beleid in beweging*. Brussels: VUBPress, pp. 271–316.

Snacken, S., Beyens, K., and Beernaert, M.-A. (2010) 'Belgium', in N. Padfield, D. Van Zyl Smit and F. Dünkel (eds) *Release from prison. European policies and practice*. Cullompton, Devon: Willan, pp. 70–103.

Storme, I., and Gyselinck, L. (2012) 'Van overheidsreclassering naar Psychosociale Dienst en Dienst Justitiehuizen', in R. Roose, F. Vander Laenen, I. Aertsen and L. Van Garsse (eds) *Handboek forensisch welzijnswerk. Ontwikkeling, beleid, organisatie and praktijk*. Gent: Academia Press, pp. 47–69.

Turtelboom, A. (2012–2013) *Algemene Beleidsnota Justitie*, 27 December 2012, Belgische Kamer Van Volksvertegenwoordigers. DOC 53 2586/2027.

Vandeurzen, J. (2009) *Beleidsverklaring Van de Minster Van Justitie*. Brussels: Kabinet Justitie.

Vanhaelemeesch, D., and Vander Beken, T. (2014) 'Between convict and the ward: the experiences of people living with offenders subject to electronic monitoring', *Criminal, Law and Social Change*, 62(4), pp. 389–415.

Verbist, D. (2013) *De visies Van rechters op de autonome werkstraf; Een emprisich onderzoek*, Master's thesis, Vrije Universiteit Brussel, Brussels.

3

THREE NARRATIVES AND A FUNERAL

Community punishment in England and Wales

Gwen Robinson

Introduction

Among the jurisdictions represented in this book, it is probably fair to say that England and Wales is an extreme case in respect of the amount of recent and ongoing turbulence, both in the domain of 'community punishment' and in the surrounding penal field. It is also perhaps atypical by virtue of being a jurisdiction in which the notion of *punishment in the community* has precise – and relatively recent – origins. Today, the concept itself is hardly contested as a way of describing the field, albeit that the origins of 'probation' lie in ideas about the provision of constructive *alternatives* to punishment, and at least some practitioners in the field would seek to minimise their role in the delivery of 'punishment' (understood as something negative or painful).

This chapter begins by considering the foundations of community punishment in England and Wales, before moving on to analyse its evolution in the twentieth century. This account focuses mainly on developments since the 1980s, in the wake of a collapse in confidence in the 'rehabilitative ideal' which formerly dominated the field. It is argued that community sanctions and measures have managed to claw back legitimacy by means of their appeal to three dominant narratives, which are characterised as 'managerial', 'punitive' and 'rehabilitative'. Despite some potential for conflict between them, these narratives are largely intertwined or 'braided' (Hutchinson 2006) in policy and practice, such that both 'old' and 'new' ways of representing community punishment tend to collude in the legitimation of community punishment in the present. The chapter proceeds to consider the present state and future legitimacy of community punishment, with reference to the contemporary programme of reform which is in the process of breaking up a probation service which, for the past 100 years, has enjoyed primary responsibility for delivering punishment in the community, as well as respect across Europe.

Foundations

In England and Wales, the origins of contemporary forms of community punishment are, somewhat paradoxically, to be found in a system of probation established in the early part of the twentieth century explicitly as an *alternative* to punishment and sanctioning. In other words, probation started out as a 'measure' rather than a 'sanction', and its use was restricted to those deemed worthy or deserving of an opportunity to reform in the absence of formal punishment. In his influential study of *Punishment & Welfare* at the turn of the twentieth century, Garland (1985) argued that the establishment of probation at this time was evidence of a penal system newly alive to ideas about the possibility of offender reform, and about bringing the character and history of the individual offender into the calculus of penal thought. Garland (1985, 2001) has described the establishment of probation as one of the key elements in the development of a distinctly modern 'penal-welfare' complex, one which survived until the 1970s.

The roots of this formal system of probation, conceived of as a mode of 'reformative diversion', have been traced back to the 1820s and began in relation to juveniles, later being extended to some adult offenders (Vanstone 2004). Edward Cox, a sentencer in Portsmouth, began the practice of releasing 'suitable' offenders on recognisance, a strategy which became the basis of the Summary Jurisdiction Act of 1879. This Act permitted a conditional discharge on the giving of sureties for good behaviour or reappearance for sentence. Cox believed that this was suitable for unpractised offenders in that it offered them 'a chance of redemption under the most favourable circumstances' (Cox 1877, quoted in Radzinowicz and Hood 1990: 634). A parallel development sprang from the 'rescue' work of the Church of England Temperance Society (CETS), established in 1862 with a view to tackling the problem of drunkenness and the reformation of the intemperate (Vanstone 2004). The extension of the CETS' work with offenders led to the practice of attaching missionaries to the criminal courts – initially in London, but later elsewhere – with a view to 'saving the souls' of those habitual drunkards released to their care and oversight (McWilliams 1983). Between 1880 and 1894 the number of full-time missionaries working in the courts increased from eight to seventy (Radzinowicz and Hood 1990). The police court missionaries were pioneers in the sense that 'they developed the concept of social workers working in and for the courts; they [also] provided the rudiments of the techniques of individual concern for and a personal relationship with, offenders in the open' (Jarvis 1972: 9). By the late 1870s the CETS had extended its focus to include discharged prisoners, who were offered help with accommodation, employment and the like, as well as being invited to sign a pledge of abstinence on release (Ayscough 1923, cited in Vanstone 2004: 8).

Another influential late-nineteenth-century figure in probation's 'pre-history' was Howard Vincent, a lawyer and former Director of Criminal Investigation at Scotland Yard. In the 1880s, Vincent became the most persistent promoter of the cause to offer first offenders, both juvenile and adult, a chance of reform without recourse to the contaminating prison environment. In 1886, having visited Boston, Massachusetts where an early system of probation was in operation, Vincent introduced the Probation of First Offenders Bill. This Bill proposed that any person without previous convictions be released on probation, subject to a form of police supervision modelled on the 'ticket of leave' system (an early version of parole). In a letter to *The Times*, Vincent explained that his proposed scheme was designed 'to save hundreds from a habitual life of crime, to give back to the State many an honest citizen, and to save the pockets of the taxpayer' (26 July 1886, quoted in Vanstone 2004: 17). Although the resulting Act was a drastically amended version of Vincent's Bill, devoid of any formal supervision component, it did constitute evidence of a growing willingness to substitute consignment to a harsh prison regime with an opportunity to reform – albeit that this option was restricted to only those offenders deemed to deserve a 'second chance'.

We might summarise the 'founding narrative' of probation work in England and Wales as a reformative one – albeit fairly strictly limited to the 'deserving' and potentially 'corrigible' among the offending population, deemed worthy of a chance to avoid, or (in the case of ex-prisoners) receive help to mitigate, the moral and social damage caused by imprisonment.

Development: The twentieth century

There is a good number of published accounts of the development of what we describe in this book as 'community punishment' in England and Wales, and all tend towards periodisation, whereby separate eras or phases are identified, albeit differently labelled (McWilliams 1985, 1986, 1987; Bottoms *et al.* 2004). Thus, for example, they all describe the evolution of probation practice in the early decades of the twentieth century under the influence of the emerging discipline of psychology and the development of social casework. In this context, early ideas about the moral reformation of offenders gradually gave way to a discourse centred on diagnosis, treatment and rehabilitation, and University-based training for probation officers was introduced (Raynor and Robinson 2009). McWilliams (1986) has characterised this transition (between the late 1930s and the 1960s) in terms of a shift from the *phase of special pleading* to the *phase of diagnosis*.

Existing accounts also identify a growing crisis of confidence in rehabilitation in the 1960s and 1970s – a crisis which affected penal systems both in England and Wales and the United States – as a key turning-point in the development of probation. The so-called collapse of the rehabilitative ideal (Allen 1981) in these countries was the outcome of a three-pronged attack on rehabilitation which exposed serious weaknesses in terms of its theoretical basis, its ethical credentials and its effectiveness in terms of achieving demonstrable reductions in reoffending on the part of 'treated' individuals. In *The Culture of Control*, Garland (2001) describes the profound effects of what he terms a 'crisis of penal modernism' on those parts of the penal systems in England and Wales and the USA which had traditionally or latterly derived their legitimacy from ideas about 'normalisation', reform and rehabilitation. In England

and Wales, although it has been acknowledged that faith in rehabilitation did not collapse overnight – and, as Vanstone (2004) has argued, certainly did not evaporate among employees of the probation service – there nonetheless followed a period of uncertainty during which the probation service was extremely vulnerable to the charge that it could no longer command legitimacy (Raynor and Robinson 2009). This, then, was a period in which new justifications for existing penal structures and practices were urgently needed.

This was, however, also a period during which a growing prison population was causing concern among policymakers (Home Office 1977), and these twin problems were to provide fertile ground for the development of certain new community-based sanctions and measures in the next decade or so. The Criminal Justice Act 1967 had introduced parole for certain categories of ex-prisoner, and a further Criminal Justice Act in 1972 ushered in the community service order (requiring offenders to perform unpaid work in the community), which was intended to offer sentencers a direct alternative to custody.[1] By the end of the 1970s, academic commentators had begun to recognise the potential for probation to relegitimise itself with reference to 'systemic' concerns: specifically, by asserting the potential of probation to divert offenders from the more expensive and harmful sanction of imprisonment (Bottoms and McWilliams 1979). Thus began what, in historical accounts of probation, has generally been characterised as an era of 'pragmatism' (McWilliams 1987) or, more commonly, 'alternatives to custody'. Probation thus adopted a new, much more modest principal rationale, as 'a non-custodial penalty aiming to increase its market share and reduce imprisonment, rather than a "treatment" aiming to change people' (Raynor 1997: 27).

Contemporary narratives

Looking back at the development of community sanctions and measures over the last 25 years or so, we can see a growing consciousness of the 'systemic' role of probation and newer community sanctions and measures as a key part of an evolutionary process by which they have sought to rebuild their legitimacy. In other words, and following Robinson et al. (2013), a 'managerial' narrative for community sanctions and measures is an important part of the story of their adaptation and survival into the present. It is not, however, the whole story. I shall argue that we cannot fully comprehend the recent history of community sanctions and measures in the Anglo-Welsh context without also attending to two other major narrative strands which emphasise, respectively, the purported punitive and rehabilitative qualities of such interventions. Each of these three narrative strands represents one of the principal ways in which community sanctions and measures have evolved and sought legitimacy in a changing penal field.[2] I argue that the coexistence of these narratives is evidence that we have not (yet) seen the emergence of a single replacement discourse or 'meta-narrative' for community sanctions and measures in England and Wales.

A 'managerial' narrative

At the heart of most accounts of managerialism in the penal field has been the notion of *systemisation*; that is, the transformation of what was formerly a series of relatively independent services or agencies (courts, police, prisons, probation services etc.) into an interlinking 'system'. For Bottoms (1995), this process of systemisation has, in most jurisdictions, tended to embrace characteristics such as an emphasis on inter-agency cooperation in order to fulfil the overall goals of the system; mission statements for individual criminal justice agencies which serve those general system goals; and the creation of 'key performance indicators' for individual agencies which tend to emphasise the efficiency of internal processes rather than 'effectiveness' in relation to any overarching objective. As Garland (1996) has observed, systemisation has enabled the common adoption of a variety of devices to deal with the problem of crime in a reconfigured field characterised by an acceptance of crime as a 'normal social fact': that is, as a risk to be managed rather than a social problem to be eliminated. The key imperatives of a 'managerial' penology are thus focused on the limited goals of 'managing a permanently dangerous population while maintaining the system at a minimum cost' (Feeley and Simon 1992: 463).

In England and Wales, there have been many examples of the recasting of community sanctions and measures in ways that have emphasised their systemic legitimacy: that is, their value in serving the needs of a penal system which has been increasingly under strain. This was perhaps first evident in the adoption in the 1980s (described above) of a pragmatic rationale which emphasised the provision of credible 'alternatives to custody'. Here, the primary motivation for increasing the market share of probation and community service orders was to relieve pressure on (and the expense of) prison places (Raynor 1988). Another important example concerns the extension of post-custodial supervision of ex-prisoners subject to conditional release from custody – a population which in many jurisdictions has been escalating (Padfield *et al.* 2010). Increases in rates of imprisonment and sentence lengths have encouraged the increased use of the 'safety valve' of early release mechanisms which, in turn, have brought greater numbers of individuals under the remit of post-custodial supervision (on licence or parole) (Cavadino and Dignan 2007). For example, the Criminal Justice Act 2003 extended automatic conditional release at the half-way point of sentences of imprisonment to all prisoners serving standard determinate sentences[3] of 12 months or more and increased the length of the non-custodial element of most custodial sentences. The effect of this was an increase in the population of ex-prisoners subject to supervision (on licence) by the probation service. Between 2003 and 2013, the number of prisoners (pre- and post-release) subject to supervision by the probation service rose by 37 per cent (from just over 80,000 to over 110,000) (Ministry of Justice 2014a, Table A4.13).

These developments have been underpinned by a shifting understanding of the probation service and its employees as 'partners' working cooperatively with other parts of the system, such as police and prison services, where previously ideological conflict would have made such partnerships problematic, if not unthinkable.

In England and Wales, formal partnerships have emerged since the late 1990s between police and probation services to manage various categories of 'high risk' individuals in the community, resulting in formal Multi-Agency Public Protection Arrangements (Kemshall and Maguire 2001). More recently, police and probation services have also teamed up in new local structures called Integrated Offender Management teams, which have focused their efforts on the oversight of high-risk offenders released from custody but not necessarily subject to mandatory supervision (Wong 2013). We have also seen attempts to create a US-style 'correctional services' structure, in the guise of a National Offender Management Service (NOMS), combining prisons and probation in the pursuit of the common goal of 'public protection' (Raynor and Vanstone 2007).

Meanwhile, some of the features of the so-called new penology described by Feeley and Simon (1992) in the US context have become evident in England and Wales, most notably in the emergence and spread of new, actuarial technologies oriented to the assessment of risk and (importantly) the rationing of resources in line with those assessments (Robinson 2002). We have also seen the emergence and spread of new types of surveillant sanction oriented to what Feeley and Simon refer to as 'management in place'. The growing popularity of electronically monitored curfews and drug testing (which may be conditions of community sentences or post-custodial supervision on licence) are among the best examples of this trend towards an emphasis on the *management of risks* which offenders may pose and the deployment of new technologies to detect non-compliance with specified standards of behaviour (see Nellis 2010).

The emergence in the last decade of a discourse of 'offender management' in England and Wales is, however, perhaps the most prominent example of the sorts of trends I am describing. In 2005 the probation service implemented an 'offender management model' (OMM), developed by senior managers seconded to NOMS, which consolidated an approach towards offender supervision which had already become preoccupied with risk assessment (Robinson 2005). The OMM identified four levels or 'tiers' to which offenders were to be allocated, each implying a different focus and intensity of supervision. The tiers, labelled 'punish', 'help', 'change' and 'control', were designed to be cumulative, such that every offender would receive 'punishment', most would additionally receive 'help', fewer still would also be expected to 'change', and – reflecting their high-risk status – the final group would be primarily subject to 'control'. This illustrates very well how a fundamentally managerial approach towards offenders subject to statutory supervision in the community – that is, an approach centred on classification and differential resource allocation – has become a firmly embedded and taken-for-granted approach. It also illustrates, however, the continuing currency of other narratives for such supervision; among these, rehabilitation (implied by 'change') and, arguably at the heart of the model, in the common denominator of 'punishment', a narrative centred on making offenders feel the 'punitive weight' of the sanctions and measures to which they were subject. It is to the growing resonance of a punitive narrative for community punishment that I shall turn next.

A punitive narrative

For many advocates of community sanctions and measures, perhaps especially in European jurisdictions, the idea that these might have a deliberately punitive dimension is anathema. Traditionally, such sanctions have been associated not just with the provision of welfare, but also the avoidance of state punishment. As already noted in this chapter, the probation order established in England and Wales by the 1907 Probation of Offenders Act enjoyed the legal status of an alternative to punishment. That said, such 'alternatives' have always involved the exercise of power and control over individuals, albeit a 'softer' form of power than the prison. Drawing on Foucault's (1977) argument concerning the 'power of normalisation', Garland (1985) noted that the new regime of probation established in England and Wales in the early twentieth century represented not just a more humane response to crime, but also a more extensive and subtle network of control. Community sanctions and measures have also tended to be backed up by the possibility of other punitive sanctions in the face of non-compliance (see Raynor and Vanstone 2007; Robinson 2013).

In England and Wales in the last 25 years or so, we have seen a growing tendency to expose and enhance the 'punitive credentials' of community sanctions and measures. As I have argued elsewhere (Robinson *et al.* 2013), this has to be understood in the context of at least two developments in the Anglo-Welsh context. The first concerns the adoption of a desert-based sentencing framework in the early 1990s, a policy development which once again followed the lead of the USA and which embraced the so-called justice model (American Friends Service Committee 1971; von Hirsch 1976). Although largely driven by liberal intentions to reduce the use of custody, the introduction of desert-based sentencing necessitated thinking more consciously about penalties of all kinds in relation to their retributive content, or 'punitive weight'. Probation and community service orders thus came to be reconceptualised and calibrated along a new 'continuum of punishment', within which they were viewed as 'middle range' punishments between custody and financial penalties; that is, relatively inexpensive but nonetheless tough penalties for those guilty of less serious offences (Home Office 1990; Mair 1997). In this context, the constructive potential of such sanctions arguably became less important than their retributive qualities, which could be measured in length, intensity and intrusiveness. The 1991 Criminal Justice Act, which implemented a sentencing framework based on desert, thus inaugurated the concept of 'punishment in the community' which has had currency in England and Wales ever since (Worrall 1997).

The other key driver of the punitive narrative in England and Wales has been the politicisation of crime and criminal justice, and the increasing resort on the part of politicians and policymakers to 'populist punitiveness' or 'penal populism' (Bottoms 1995; Pratt *et al.* 2005). Much has been written in England and Wales about the increasing politicisation of 'law and order' issues (particularly since 1993[4]) and the impact of this on crime-control policy. For example, writing a decade ago, Michael Tonry described the recent history of crime control policy in this jurisdiction as 'tumultuous and schizophrenic' (2004: 1). Tonry evidenced the 'tumult' in the sheer quantity of change witnessed in the preceding decade, and the 'schizophrenia' in the 'sometimes startling contrast between the [then Labour] government's claim to engage in "evidence-based" policy-making, and its determination always and on all issues, no matter what the evidence may show, to be seen as "tough on crime"' (2004: 1). Commentators have also noted the tendency of politicians in the UK parliament to look to the USA, rather than to other parts of Europe, for policy inspiration. For example, Newburn (2007) argues that the Labour Party's rebranding as the party of law and order in the early 1990s followed the example of the US Democratic Party in the wake of the Republicans' electoral victory in 1988. At this time, the shift in Democratic penal policy was in a more punitive direction and this was premised on three core messages taken from that election: that crime had the potential to be a key issue in elections; that candidates should at all costs avoid being seen as 'soft on crime'; and that, irrespective of the substance of any policies they may endorse, candidates must appear 'tough'. It was these lessons, Newburn (2007) argues, which the Labour party took to heart in the mid-1990s and which have arguably shaped penal politics in England and Wales ever since.

Not surprisingly, much of the commentary and critique related to the politicisation of crime control in England and Wales has centred on imprisonment. Between 1993 and 2012 the prison population increased by more than 100 per cent, from 41,800 prisoners to over 86,000 (Ministry of Justice 2013a). Less attention has been paid to the impact of a 'punitive turn' in penal policy on non-custodial sanctions and measures. However, the impact has been significant. First of all, community sanctions such as probation have met with relentless criticism for being too 'soft' or too closely aligned with the needs and/or interests of those convicted of crimes, rather than those of the 'law-abiding majority' or victims of crime (Home Office 2006). One result of this, also in the mid-1990s, was that the Conservative Home Secretary Michael Howard took the decision to sever the longstanding connection between probation and the social work profession, repealing the need for probation officers to hold a social work qualification.[5] At this time, probation officers in England and Wales not only ceased to be social workers, but also saw the context for their work change, from a social work agency, to a 'law enforcement agency' (National Probation Service 2001). In this process the service lost any claim to an identity or pursuit of purposes defined outside government policy (Robinson and McNeill 2004).

Since then, we have witnessed numerous attempts to 'toughen up' both the discourse around community sanctions and measures and the experience of being subject to them. For example, we have seen the rebranding of existing sanctions in ways which have emphasised their retributive or punitive orientation. A good example here is community service, originally made available in the 1970s. In 2008 the UK Cabinet Office published a report which proposed building public confidence in what by then was being called 'unpaid work' by rebranding it as 'community payback'. The author of the report, Louise Casey, suggested that the work involved should not be something the general public would choose to do themselves (i.e. it should be unfulfilling and unpleasant) and that individuals performing it should wear high-visibility vests identifying them to members of the public (Casey 2008; Maruna and King 2008). In 2013, one of the pioneers of community service in England (and until 2001 a chief probation officer) published an article in a leading British newspaper to mark the fortieth anniversary of the introduction of community service (Harding 2013). His article posed the question: 'How did a measure that required offenders to carry out socially beneficial work turn into a form of punishment?'

We have also seen the creation of a variety of new, more 'intensive' sanctions. Examples from the late 1990s include the Combination Order, which combined in one sentence probation supervision and community service. The 1990s also witnessed the introduction of technological innovations to increase the 'punitive bite' of community sanctions or to increase the restrictions placed on offenders under supervision in the community. Thus in the 1990s we saw the introduction of the curfew with electronic monitoring, the Drug Treatment and Testing Order and the Home Detention Curfew scheme for prisoners subject to early release. The Criminal Justice Act 2003 subsequently did away with the existing suite of community sentences and in their place introduced a single community sentence, the Community Order, to be made up of any combination of twelve requirements, including: supervision, unpaid work, a treatment programme, a curfew, and so on.[6] The 2003 Act also introduced a new hybrid custodial–community sentence called the Suspended Sentence Order (SSO), which enabled sentencers to suspend a period of imprisonment whilst also imposing on offenders any combination of the same twelve requirements that could be attached to a Community Order (Mair *et al.* 2007). More recently (2008–2011) we have seen trials of Intensive Alternatives to Custody (IAC) – combining intensive supervision with additional 'demanding requirements and interventions delivered by partner agencies' – intended to divert offenders from short-term custodial sentences (Mews and Coxon 2014: 2).

A further development connected to the 'penalisation' of community sanctions and measures has been a lowering of tolerance in respect of failures to comply (Robinson and Ugwudike 2012; Robinson 2013). According to the Ministry of Justice, harsher 'enforcement outcomes' have made a significant contribution to the rising prison population in the last decade or so. Indeed, Ministry of Justice data indicate a staggering 470 per cent increase in the numbers of offenders imprisoned for breaches of community-based sentences between 1995 and 2009, whilst in the same period the rise in the population of offenders recalled to prison while on licence was 37-fold (Ministry of Justice 2009). It is also worth noting that the traditional requirement of an offender's consent to a community order has become irrelevant in most cases[7] (Raynor 2014).

In 2013, legislation[8] was introduced requiring courts to include a 'punitive requirement' in all community sentences for adults, having already extended the maximum length of curfews and the number of hours offenders can be required to perform unpaid work. A press release announcing this development said:

> In a move to improve public confidence in community sentences, adult sentences will now have to include some form of punishment. [From

11 December] Most sentences will contain an element of formal punishment such as a fine, unpaid work, curfew or exclusion from certain areas. This could affect around 40,000 offenders per year.

(Ministry of Justice 2013b)

There is ample evidence, then, that the evolution of community sanctions and measures in England and Wales has been characterised by increasing attention to and emphasis on their punitive weight, such that the idea of punishment in the community has, since 1994, increased its purchase.

A 'rehabilitative' narrative

In the 1980s and early 1990s, following the so-called collapse of the rehabilitative ideal, several commentators argued that rehabilitation was dead and buried. Heavily influenced by the 'new penology' thesis emanating from the USA at that time, some saw the emergence of risk-based thinking in the probation service as evidence of a decisive paradigm shift, signalling the demise of 'transformative optimism' among those responsible for supervising offenders in the community. For example, Kemshall *et al.* (1997) argued that the new centrality of risk and risk assessment in the probation service indicated that the service was:

> engaged in a transition from the traditional concerns of the rehabilitative and welfare arm of criminal justice [...] and the language of 'need' to an agency of crime control concerned with the accurate prediction and effective management of offender risk.

(1997: 217)

Rumours of the death of rehabilitation, however, turned out to be greatly exaggerated, as a resurgent rehabilitative ideal did in fact emerge. Starting in the late 1980s in North America, what came to be known as a 'What Works?' movement was enthusiastically taken up by a small group of British academic researchers who spread news of the revitalisation of rehabilitation via a series of conferences and workshops with both academic and practitioner participants (McGuire 1995). Ever since then, rehabilitation has crept back into penal policy: for example, being declared one of five legitimate rationales for sentencing in the Criminal Justice Act 2003 (s.42);[9] explicitly underpinning several of the conditions which may be attached to a community order or suspended sentence order; and featuring prominently in the current government's headline penal policy of a 'Rehabilitation Revolution' (Ministry of Justice 2010).

This is not, however, to say that in England and Wales we have somehow turned back time, revisiting modes of rehabilitation prominent in early mid-twentieth-century probation practice. We should not overlook the ways in which rehabilitation has been transformed and remarketed in recent years, such that, far from going against the grain of broader penal developments, it has been rendered compatible with them. As I have argued elsewhere, it is more accurate to talk of the *evolution* of rehabilitation than of its survival or revival, the latter being terms which imply a somewhat static (and inaccurate) picture (Robinson 2008). This evolutionary process has produced visions and modes of rehabilitation in the community sanctions context that have diverged from earlier incarnations in important ways, as I shall outline below.

Firstly, the 'new' rehabilitation has had to adapt to social and political contexts which have become increasingly intolerant of approaches and interventions that appear to put the needs and interests of offenders above those of (actual and potential) victims. This has meant that proponents of rehabilitation have had to de-emphasise its welfarist, humanitarian and essentially offender-centred justifications, in favour of rationales which emphasise the instrumental and more broadly 'utilitarian' value of rehabilitative sanctions. David Garland (1997: 6) was among the first to observe this realignment of rehabilitation in England and Wales when he observed that probation workers had come to 'emphasise that "rehabilitation" is necessary for the protection of the public. It is future victims who are now "rescued" by rehabilitative work, rather than the offenders themselves'. This idea that the legitimacy of contemporary rehabilitation rests on a utilitarian justification (Robinson 2008) helps to explain the spread of 'offending behaviour programmes' under the auspices of the 'What Works?' movement, the resurgence of interest and investment in the re-entry or resettlement of ex-prisoners (Farrall and Sparks 2006) and, most recently, official interest in the findings of research on desistance from offending (McNeill 2006). Thus, for example, what at first sight appears to indicate a heightened concern among policymakers with the welfare and reintegration of ex-offenders or a desire to undo the harmful consequences of imprisonment is, today, arguably more an expression of concern for the communities to which most prisoners ultimately return and resume their lives.

A related point is that rehabilitation has come to be understood less as an end in itself than as a means to other ends (Garland 1997, 2001). Specifically, rehabilitation has come to be understood as part of a toolkit of measures oriented towards the protection of the public and the management of risk. Thus, we have tended to see the repositioning of rehabilitative measures within managerial systems which have come to be dominated by the discourse of risk. In this regard, rehabilitation has not only come to be reconceived of as a means of achieving risk reduction or management, but it is also increasingly rationed in line with assessments of risk which determine the eligibility of offenders for rehabilitative interventions. Such an approach secures a space for rehabilitation among the range of legitimate responses to offending, but limits its reach and influence in new ways. I have already referred (above) to the risk-driven, differentiated approach which characterises the offender management model of probation practice which was introduced in England and Wales in 2005 (see Robinson 2005). As previously noted, this model uses the logic of risk to determine the level of resource appropriate to individual offenders. Only the third tier, 'change', contains an explicitly disciplinary or rehabilitative element, and it is targeted at those posing a medium to high risk of reoffending. This explicitly actuarial model illustrates quite clearly that contemporary rehabilitative interventions are far from inimical to managerial systems.

That said, the reframing of rehabilitation in risk-management terms and regimes has not simply entailed putting a new spin on the same old product. Importantly, the product itself has adapted as part of the evolutionary process I have described. Whilst it is probably unwise to characterise contemporary rehabilitative sanctions and measures as if they were a unified product, it is probably fair to say that, among these, the most explicitly rehabilitative are those offending behaviour programmes which emerged under the banner of the 'What Works?' movement alluded to above. Based on cognitive-behavioural principles and methods, the new offending behaviour programmes proliferated and spread throughout England and Wales in the 1990s, backed by some evidence of their effectiveness in reducing reoffending. At the same time the government convened an expert (accreditation) panel to ensure that programmes that were to receive public resources were in line with contemporary evidence about 'what works' (Raynor and Robinson 2009).

The crime reduction potential of rehabilitative programmes and interventions has then been a major selling point for their inclusion as part of community sanctions in the late twentieth century context and beyond. However, some have argued that we should not attribute the 'new' legitimacy of such interventions solely to their (putative) instrumental effectiveness. For some commentators, the dominance of cognitive-behavioural programmes in England and Wales (and elsewhere) is at least in part attributable to their expressive and communicative qualities and their resonance with advanced liberal forms of governance which emphasise personal responsibility for wrongdoing, and rely upon strategies of 'responsibilization' as the dominant response to anti-social behaviour (Garland 1996; Kendall 2004; Rose 2000). The same has been said of the contemporary resurgence of interest in restorative justice approaches in England and Wales (Dignan 2005). Both modes of intervention, it has been argued, seek to engage offenders in a 'moral discourse' which both communicates censure and seeks to instil in offenders both a measure of victim empathy and a new 'moral compass' which, it is hoped, will dissuade them from future offending (see also Duff 2001). The 'rehabilitated' offender, then, tends to be presented as an individual capable of managing his or her own risks without recourse to externally imposed sanctions or controls, and without making any claims on the state in terms of its duties to create opportunities for reform and reintegration.

Thriving – or just surviving? Analysing trends in community punishment

In this chapter I have focused on what I see as the three main narratives that have underpinned the development of community sanctions and measures in England and Wales in the last 25 years. Until now, it would appear, these narratives have more or less sustained community punishment as a legitimate endeavour – albeit one lacking the kind of 'transcendent justification' which McWilliams and Pease (1990) saw as essential to the longevity of the probation service. However, important questions remain about just how successful the adaptations I have described have been in terms of securing a bigger 'market share' for community punishment and, in particular, its impact on the use of imprisonment.

When we consider the proportion of convictions which resulted in a community sentence between 1978 and 2008, we see a gradual increase in their popularity with the courts. The market share of community sentences rose from 3.5 per cent in 1978 to 6.1 per cent in 1988 and then to 10.2 per cent in 1998, reaching a high of 14 per cent in 2008 (Ministry of Justice 2014b, Table A1.1). At first sight these statistics appear to signal good news for advocates of community sentences. However, there are two additional factors to consider. The first is that the growing popularity of community sentences has not coincided with a reducing market share for imprisonment; indeed, rates of imprisonment have increased in parallel. The second is that whilst community sentences have been used more, the use of fines has dropped considerably.[10] The overall trend, then, has been one of 'up-tariffing', such that sentencing, generally, has become harsher (Ministry of Justice 2013b).

Since 2008, the market share of community sentences has dropped steadily, from 14 per cent to 10.5 per cent in 2013 (Ministry of Justice 2014b, Table A1.1). Although it is not entirely clear why the popularity of community sentences has waned in this period, an important factor has been the introduction (in 2005) of the SSO (in 2005, under the Criminal Justice Act 2003), which offered sentencers the possibility of combining a suspended custodial sentence with a range of possible community-based requirements. This sentence has proven extremely popular with sentencers looking for an alternative to immediate custody, and the SSO has therefore displaced a potentially large number of community sentences in recent years (Mair *et al.* 2007) (see Figure 3.1).

Meanwhile, recently published statistics indicate that the total annual caseload carried by the probation service increased by 39 per cent between 2000 and 2008, reaching a high of 243,434 offenders at the end of that period (Ministry of Justice 2014c). Since then, however, the probation caseload has fallen year on year, to 219,588 at the end of 2013 (see Figure 3.2).

There are a number of important points to emphasise here. The first is that the 'probation caseload' referred to above is something of a 'mixed bag'; it includes offenders on community sentences, but also those subject to SSOs with community-based requirements, as well as offenders whose custodial sentence includes a period of statutory supervision on licence post-release. Therefore, the probation caseload includes both ex-prisoners currently under supervision in the community on licence and some prisoners who have yet to be released but who are nonetheless allocated to a probation worker to prepare for release. One of the striking facts about the probation caseload, particularly since the implementation of the Criminal Justice Act 2003,[11] is the growing proportion of offenders on probation caseloads in the latter categories; that is, those subject to suspended sentences of imprisonment or pre- or post-release supervision. This trend will

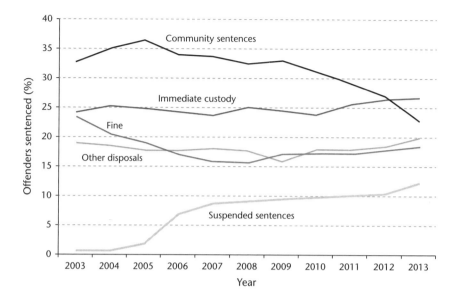

FIGURE 3.1   Sentencing outcomes for indictable offences at all courts, 2003–2013

Source: Ministry of Justice (2014b, Figure 5.2, p. 36). Available under the Open Government Licence.

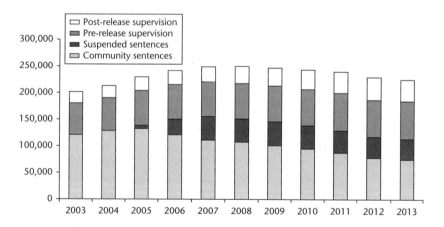

FIGURE 3.2   Number of offenders under Probation Service supervision (at end of December), 2003–2013

Source: Ministry of Justice (2014c, Figure 1.2, p. 12). Available under the Open Government Licence.

intensify when recent legislation[12] extending mandatory post-custodial supervision for sentences of less than 12 months comes into effect.

All of this means that the profile of 'community punishment' in England and Wales is changing, such that an increasing portion of it comprises quasi-custodial provision (i.e. supervision pre- and post-release from custody, or alongside a sus-pended sentence of imprisonment), whilst the portion that comprises stand-alone community sentences is reducing. It would appear, then, that attempts to rele-gitimate community punishment have not been entirely successful, and there are reasons to be concerned that the market share of community sentences may continue on a downward curve in the foreseeable future, as I shall discuss below.

A new crisis of legitimacy?

At the time of writing, community punishment is subject to a widely contested programme of reform known as 'Transforming Rehabilitation' (TR) (Ministry of Justice 2013c; see also National Audit Office 2014; Annison *et al.* 2014). The TR programme centres on the contracting out of the supervision of low- and medium-risk offenders to providers from the private and not-for-profit sectors, whilst the supervision of high-risk offenders remains in a shrunken public sector National Probation Service (NPS). Its other major strand is the extension of mandatory post-custodial supervision to short-term prisoners, as mentioned above. At the time of writing, probation staff have been recently allocated to roles in either the NPS or one of twenty-one new Community Rehabilitation Companies which are due to be sold off towards the end of 2014.

The principal rationale offered by the Ministry of Justice for this drastic pro-gramme of reform is economic: the costs to the public purse of reoffending by known offenders – particularly those released after short prison sentences – must be driven down, and this is to be achieved by creating a 'market' in community punishment, in which providers are incentivised by profit in a system of remuneration known as 'payment by results' (Hedderman 2013). Critics, however, argue that there is no evi-dence to support government forecasts of innovation, efficiency and effectiveness; nor is it fair to blame the probation service – which has had no statutory responsibility for the supervision of short-term prisoners – for this group's high reoffending rates. Indeed, the available evidence indicates that there have been, over the past 10 years or so, incremental reductions in reoffending by those subject to community sentences under the supervision of public sector Probation Trusts[13] (Ministry of Justice 2014d, Table 18a). It would therefore appear that a political ideology centred on the mar-ketisation of public services has won through, with little to back it up besides a purported 'lack of public confidence' in existing arrangements.[14]

In a recent newspaper headline, the Justice Secretary Chris Grayling was said to be responsible for 'murdering the probation service' (Leftly 2014). Having already been severed from their traditional roots in the profession of social work, probation workers and their representatives have found themselves woefully undefended in the struggle to maintain control over probation work. What we can tentatively say about the TR reforms is that they will significantly widen the net of community punishment (by introducing mandatory rehabilitative supervision to tens of thou-sands of short-term prisoners). We cannot, however, predict what the impact might be on sentencing practice and more broadly the perceived legitimacy of community sentences. How judges and magistrates will feel about passing community sentences to be managed by the new Community Rehabilitation Companies – at least some of which seem destined to fall into private ownership – remains to be seen (Allen 2013). The TR reforms are likely to normalise the idea of 'community punishment for profit' and the commodification of offenders as 'units' on a balance sheet (McCulloch and McNeill 2007; Robinson 2005). They may also drive large numbers of probation workers who, until now, have identified as public servants, out of the field. TR therefore offers a great deal of potential to deliver a new crisis of legitimacy for community punishment.

Reflections

The foregoing analysis seems to confirm much of what other analysts of the penal field and policy-making in England and Wales have sought to demonstrate – albeit that they have tended not to focus on the particular corner of the field occupied by community punishment (Lacey 2008; Cavadino and Dignan 2006; Cavadino *et al.* 2013; Tonry 2004). All of these accounts have drawn attention to the persistence of competing punishment narratives[15] and the chronic volatility of a penal field which has become less and less insulated from the adjacent political field. Whilst in this context ideas about evidence-based policy-making have not entirely lost their purchase, the influence of academics and others formerly recognised as 'experts' in the penal field has tended to wane in favour of lobbyists and 'think tanks' more closely aligned to the interests of particular political parties. Meanwhile, other influences have also been important and have contributed to the general volatility of the field. Economic hard times and calls for austerity across publically funded services have been one such influence. Another has been the rise of managerialism and with it the concept of 'risk' as a key organising principle in public and private domains.

As I have sought to demonstrate, the particular corner of the penal field occupied by community punishment has been deeply implicated in these various developments. Indeed, it is no exaggeration to say that, in the last 25 years, it has been in a state of almost constant flux. During this timeframe (1989–2014), the idea that we can identify distinct periods or phases in the development of community punishment has become untenable. This is not just because we cease to have a long-range view or because the pace and amount of change has intensified – although both are true (see Cavadino and Dignan 2006: Chapter 4). Rather, it is principally because the changes we can observe since the early 1990s have increasingly run in parallel, rather than in discrete, consecutive stages. Some of the time we have seen contradictions in the development of community punishments, as they have come to be pushed and pulled in a variety of directions under a range of different influences in and around the penal field. At other times, we have witnessed developments which have appeared to reflect a blending or 'braiding' (Hutchinson 2006) of different strategies and/or discourses. The picture, then, is rather complex and calls for a different approach from the traditional periodisation we see in most accounts of community punishment: one which can convey the very real variety of developments – both quantitative and qualitative – that are discernible from the perspective of the present.

I will conclude with a final observation about terminology in the English and Welsh context. I noted at the beginning of this chapter that the term 'punishment in the community' has specific origins in England and Wales in the penal policies of the early 1990s, and that the idea of 'community punishment' is therefore less controversial in this jurisdiction than it may be elsewhere in Europe. I would add, however, that 'punishment' is not, in the twenty-first century, entirely uncontentious (from the perspectives of at least some of those who work in the field); but neither is 'community'. Indeed, as it is applied to the penal field, 'community' has a somewhat vacuous character, tending to denote little more than a context outside the prison. As Bottoms (2008) has observed, recent years have seen a marked physical retreat of what we might loosely term 'probation work' from residential communities, as probation workers have increasingly based themselves in office locations, often some distance from the neighbourhoods in which their supervisees reside (see also Robinson et al. 2014; Phillips 2014). This, Bottoms argues, is a development to be regretted, for both instrumental and normative reasons. In England and Wales, then, community punishment may be very much alive in penal discourse, but is by no means an unproblematic notion.

Notes

1 The 1972 Act also empowered courts to attach supervision to certain suspended sentences.
2 The 'reparative' narrative outlined by Robinson et al. (2013) and in the introduction to this volume has played a less important role in England and Wales than it has elsewhere (e.g. in Scotland – see Chapter 10 of this volume).
3 Standard determinate sentences are custodial sentences of a fixed length (e.g. 10 weeks, 10 months, 10 years).
4 In May 1993 Michael Howard became Home Secretary and pursued a 'tough on crime' agenda, famously asserting in October 1993 in a conference speech that 'prison works'.
5 In 1997, a new 2-year training programme – the Diploma in Probation Studies – was introduced for those wishing to enter the probation service. This was revised again a decade later, but neither programme qualifies trainees to practise social work.
6 The creation of the Community Order prompted concerns that sentencers would be tempted to overload community sentences with multiple requirements, essentially setting them up to fail. However, recent statistics indicate that only about 13 per cent of Community Orders have three or more requirements, with an average of 1.6 (Ministry of Justice 2014a, Table A4.8).
7 The Crime (Sentences) Act 1997 removed the requirement for consent to a probation order.
8 Crime and Courts Act 2013.
9 These rationales are: the punishment of offenders; the reduction of crime (including its reduction by deterrence); the reform and rehabilitation of offenders; the protection of the public; and the making of reparation by offenders to persons affected by their offences.

10 In 1978 fines made up 85.8 per cent of sentences; in 2013 their use had dropped to just 67.8 per cent (Ministry of Justice 2014c, Table A1.1).

11 The Criminal Justice Act 2003 introduced the SSO and extended the length of licence periods for most prisoners.

12 Offender Rehabilitation Act 2014.

13 Electronic monitoring has been in the hands of private companies since it was introduced in the 1990s.

14 Although frequent, references in policy documents to poor public confidence in community sentences are rarely substantiated by research and, to the extent that public confidence is low, this is likely to reflect the low visibility and lack of public understanding of such sentences (Roberts and Hough 2005).

15 For example see the trio of contemporary penal strategies described by Cavadino *et al.* (2013: 6, 7). These are characterised as strategies A (highly punitive), B (managerialist) and C (human rights).

References

Allen, F. A. (1981) *The Decline of the Rehabilitative Ideal: Penal Policy and Social Purpose*. New Haven: Yale University Press.

Allen, R. (2013) 'Paying for justice: Prison and probation in an age of austerity', *British Journal of Community Justice*, 11(1): 5–18.

American Friends Service Committee (1971) *Struggle for Justice: A Report on Crime and Punishment in America*. New York: Hill and Wang.

Annison, J., Burke, L. and Senior, P. (2014) 'Transforming Rehabilitation: Another example of English "exceptionalism" or a blueprint for the rest of Europe?' *European Journal of Probation*, 6: 6–23.

Bottoms, A. E. (1995) 'The philosophy and politics of punishment and sentencing', in C. Clarkson and R. Morgan (eds) *The Politics of Sentencing Reform*. Oxford: Clarendon Press, pp. 7–49.

Bottoms, A. E. (2008) 'The community dimension of community penalties', *Howard Journal of Criminal Justice*, 47(2): 146–69.

Bottoms, A. E. and McWilliams, W. (1979) 'A non-treatment paradigm for probation practice', *British Journal of Social Work*, 9: 159–202.

Bottoms, A., Rex, S. and Robinson, G. (2004) 'How did we get here?', in A. Bottoms, S. Rex and G. Robinson (eds), *Alternatives to Prison: Options for an insecure society*. Cullompton, Devon: Willan, pp. 1–27.

Casey, L. (2008) *Engaging Communities in Fighting Crime: A Review (Casey Report)*. London: Cabinet Office.

Cavadino, M. and Dignan, J. (2006) *Penal Systems: A Comparative Approach*. London: SAGE.

Cavadino, M. and Dignan, J. (2007) *The Penal System: An Introduction*, 4th edn. London: SAGE.

Cavadino, M., Dignan, J. and Mair, G. (2013) *The Penal System: An Introduction*, 5th edn. London: SAGE.

Dignan, J. (2005) *Understanding Victims and Restorative Justice*. Maidenhead: Open University Press.

Duff, A. (2001) *Punishment, Communication, and Community*. Oxford: Oxford University Press.

Farrall, S. and Sparks, R. (2006) 'Introduction', *Criminology and Criminal Justice*, 6(1): 7–17.

Feeley, M. and Simon, J. (1992) 'The new penology: notes on the emerging strategy of corrections and its implications', *Criminology*, 30: 449–74.

Foucault, M. (1977) *Discipline & Punish*. London: Allen Lane.

Garland, D. (1985) *Punishment and Welfare*. Aldershot: Gower.

Garland, D. (1996) 'The limits of the sovereign state: strategies of crime control in contemporary society', *British Journal of Criminology*, 36(4): 445–71.

Garland, D. (1997) 'Probation and the reconfiguration of crime control', in R. Burnett (ed.) *The Probation Service: Responding to Change* (Proceedings of the Probation Studies Unit First Colloquium), Oxford: University of Oxford Centre for Criminological Research, pp. 2–10.

Garland, D. (2001) *The Culture of Control*. Oxford: Oxford University Press.

Harding, J. (2013) 'Forty years of community service', *Guardian*, 8 January.

Hedderman, C. (2013) 'Payment by results: hopes, fears and evidence', *British Journal of Community Justice*, 11(2/3): 43–58.

Home Office (1977) *A Review of Criminal Justice Policy 1976*. London: HMSO.

Home Office (1990) *Crime, Justice & Protecting the Public* (Cm 965). London: HMSO.

Home Office (2006) *Rebalancing the Criminal Justice System in Favour of the Law-Abiding Majority: Cutting Crime, Reducing Re-offending and Protecting the Public*. London: Home Office.

Hutchinson, S. (2006) 'Countering catastrophic criminology: Reform, punishment and the modern liberal compromise', *Punishment and Society*, 8(4): 443–67.

Jarvis, F. (1972) *Advise, Assist and Befriend: A History of the Probation and After-Care Service*. London: NAPO.

Kemshall, H. and Maguire, M. (2001) 'Public protection, partnership and risk penality: the multi-agency risk management of sexual and dangerous offenders', *Punishment and Society*, 3(2): 237–64.

Kemshall, H., Parton, N., Walsh, M. and Waterson, J. (1997) 'Concepts of risk in relation to organizational structure and functioning within the personal social services and probation', *Social Policy and Administration*, 31: 213–32.

Kendall, K. (2004) 'Dangerous thinking: A critical history of correctional cognitive behaviouralism', in G. Mair (ed.) *What Matters in Probation*. Cullompton, Devon: Willan, pp. 53–89.

Lacey, N. (2008) *The Prisoners' Dilemma*. Cambridge: Cambridge University Press.

Leftly, M. (2014) 'Chris Grayling is accused of "murdering the probation service"', *Independent*, Sunday 17 August.

Mair, G. (1997) 'Community penalties and the probation service', in M. Maguire, R. Morgan and R. Reiner (eds) *The Oxford Handbook of Criminology* (2nd edn). Oxford: Clarendon Press, pp. 1195–232.

Mair, G., Cross, N. and Taylor, S. (2007) *The Use and Impact of the Community Order and the Suspended Sentence Order*. London: Centre for Crime and Justice Studies.

Maruna, S. and King, A. (2008) 'Selling the public on probation: beyond the bib', *Probation Journal*, 55: 337–51.

McCulloch, P. and McNeill, F. (2007) 'Consumer society, commodification and offender management', *Criminology and Criminal Justice*, 7(3): 223–42.

McGuire, J. (ed.) (1995) *What Works: Reducing Reoffending*. Chichester: Wiley.

McNeill, F. (2006) 'A desistance paradigm for offender management', *Criminology and Criminal Justice*, 6(1): 39–62.

McWilliams, W. (1983) 'The mission to the English police courts 1876–1936', *Howard Journal of Criminal Justice*, 22: 129–47.

McWilliams, W. (1985) 'The Mission transformed: Professionalism of probation between the wars', *Howard Journal of Criminal Justice*, 24: 257–74.

McWilliams, W. (1986) 'The English probation system and the diagnostic ideal', *The Howard Journal*, 25(4): 241–60.

McWilliams, W. (1987) 'Probation, pragmatism and policy', *The Howard Journal*, 26: 97–121.

McWilliams, W. and Pease, K. (1990) 'Probation practice and an end to punishment', *The Howard Journal*, 29: 14–24.

Mews, A. and Coxon, C. (2014) *Updated Analysis of the Impact of the Intensive Alternatives to Custody Pilots on Re-offending Rates* (Ministry of Justice Analytical Summary). London: Ministry of Justice.

Ministry of Justice (2009) *Story of the Prison Population 1995–2009 England and Wales*. London: Ministry of Justice.

Ministry of Justice (2010) *Breaking the Cycle: Effective Punishment, Rehabilitation and Sentencing of Offenders*. London: TSO.

Ministry of Justice (2013a) *Story of the Prison Population 1993–2012 England and Wales*. London: Ministry of Justice.

Ministry of Justice (2013b) 'Radical overhaul of sentencing continues', Press Release 2 December 2013. Available online at www.gov.uk/government/news/radical-overhaul-of-sentencing-continues (accessed 19 June 2014).

Ministry of Justice (2013c) Transforming Rehabilitation: A Strategy for Reform. (May 2013).

Ministry of Justice (2014a) Offender Management annual tables 2013. Available online at www.gov.uk/government/publications/offender-management-statistics-quarterly-october-december-2013-and-annual (accessed 23 June 2014).

Ministry of Justice (2014b) *Criminal Justice Statistics 2013*. (15 May 2014).

Ministry of Justice (2014c) *Offender Management Statistics Bulletin*. (24 April 2014).

Ministry of Justice (2014d) *Proven Reoffending Statistics Quarterly Bulletin: October 2011-September 2012, England & Wales*. London: Ministry of Justice (31 July 2014). Available online at www.gov.uk/government/collections/proven-reoffending-statistics (accessed 23 June 2014).

National Audit Office (2014) *Probation: Landscape Review*. London: National Audit Office.

National Probation Service/Home Office (2001) *A New Choreography*. London: Home Office.

Nellis, M. (2010) 'Electronic monitoring: towards integration into offender management', in F. McNeill, P. Raynor and C. Trotter (eds), *Offender Supervision: New Directions in Theory, Research and Practice*. Cullompton, Devon: Willan, pp. 509–33.

Newburn, T. (2007) '"Tough on crime": Penal policy in England & Wales', *Crime and Justice*, 36: 425–70.

Padfield, N., Van Zyl Smit, D. and Dünkel, F. (2010) *Release from Prison: European Policy and Practice*. Cullompton, Devon: Willan.

Phillips, J. (2014) 'The architecture of a probation office: A reflection of policy and an impact on practice', *Probation Journal*, 61(2): 117–31.

Pratt, J., Brown, D., Brown, M., Hallsworth, S. and Morrison, W. (eds) (2005) *The New Punitiveness: Trends, Theories, Perspectives*. Cullompton, Devon: Willan.

Radzinowicz, L. and Hood, R. (1990) *The Emergence of Penal Policy*. Oxford: Clarendon Press.

Raynor, P. (1988) *Probation as an Alternative to Custody*. Aldershot: Avebury.

Raynor, P. (1997) 'Evaluating probation: a moving target', in G. Mair (ed.) *Evaluating the Effectiveness of Community Penalties*. Aldershot: Avebury, pp. 19–33.

Raynor, P. (2014) 'Consent to probation in England & Wales: How it was abolished, and why it matters', *European Journal of Probation*, 6: 296–307.

Raynor, P. and Robinson, G. (2009) *Rehabilitation, Crime and Justice*. Basingstoke: Palgrave Macmillan.

Raynor, P. and Vanstone, M. (2007) 'Towards a correctional service', in L. Gelsthorpe and R. Morgan (eds) *Handbook of Probation*. Cullompton, Devon: Willan, pp. 59–89.

Roberts, J. and Hough, M. (2005) *Understanding Public Attitudes to Criminal Justice*. Maidenhead: Open University Press.

Robinson, G. (2002) 'Exploring risk management in the probation service: contemporary developments in England and Wales', *Punishment & Society*, 4(1): 5–25.

Robinson, G. (2005) 'What works in offender management?', *Howard Journal of Criminal Justice*, 44(3): 307–18.

Robinson, G. (2008) 'Late-modern rehabilitation: the evolution of a penal strategy', *Punishment and Society*, 10(4): 429–45.

Robinson, G. (2013) 'What counts? Community sanctions and the construction of compliance', in P. Raynor and P. Ugwudike (eds) *What Works in Offender Compliance: International Perspectives and Evidence-Based Practice*. Basingstoke: Palgrave Macmillan, pp. 26–43.

Robinson, G. and McNeill, F. (2004) 'Purposes matter: examining the 'ends' of probation practice', in G. Mair (ed.) *What Matters in Probation*. Cullompton, Devon: Willan, pp. 277–304.

Robinson, G. and Ugwudike, P. (2012) 'Investing in toughness: Probation, enforcement and legitimacy', *Howard Journal of Criminal Justice*, 51(3): 300–16.

Robinson, G., McNeill, F. and Maruna, S. (2013) 'Punishment in society: The improbable persistence of probation and other community sanctions and measures', in J. Simon and R. Sparks (eds) *Sage Handbook of Punishment and Society*. London: SAGE, pp. 321–40.

Robinson, G., Priede, C., Farrall, S., Shapland, J. and McNeill, F. (2014) 'Understanding "quality" in probation practice: Frontline perspectives in England & Wales', *Criminology and Criminal Justice*, 14(2): 123–42.

Rose, N. (2000) 'Government and control', *British Journal of Criminology* 40: 321–39.

Tonry, M. (2004) *Punishment and Politics*. Cullompton, Devon: Willan.

Vanstone, M. (2004) *Supervising Offenders in the Community*. Aldershot: Ashgate.

von Hirsch, A. (1976) *Doing Justice: The Choice of Punishments*. Report of the Committee for the Study of Incarceration. New York: Hill and Wang.

Wong, K. (2013) 'Integrated offender management: assessing the impacts and benefits – holy grail or fool's errand?', *British Journal of Community Justice*, 11(2/3): 59–81.

Worrall, A. (1997) *Punishment in the Community*. Cullompton, Devon: Willan.

4

FRANCE

Legal architecture, political posturing, 'prisonbation' and adieu social work

Martine Herzog-Evans

Introduction

Each author of this volume was asked to present, explain and contextualise 'community punishment' in his/her jurisdiction. This Anglophone terminology immediately struck me as being problematic in the French context. In France, the word 'community' has a very negative connotation. It generates feelings of menace, as well as threat to the national unity and to the secular state. Numerous publications for instance have been recently released that pertain to this 'threat' (Landfried 2007; Dhume-Sonzogini 2007). In fact, in order to better reflect their disdain for the word 'community', French people tend to use an even more pejorative term: *'communautarism'* (Miclo *et al.* 2002; Lévy 2005; conversely, Germain and Lassalle 2008), which in French conveys the idea, perceived as negative, that various communities prefer to build their identity, lives and activities within their group, rather than feel that they are part of the French nation as a whole. In such a context, one prefers to use the word 'society' rather than 'community'. 'Society' has positive connotations, namely France's unity and the general interest of all France's inhabitants. This can be explained by the historical origin of the French Nation's foundation. It happened via the negation of local or regional communities, their languages, identity and culture (Broudig 1996; De Certeau *et al.* 2002). As a consequence, community sentences are usually labelled as 'alternative sentences' or as: *'restriction* of liberty sentences' (as opposed to *'deprivation* of liberty sentences'), the rather inelegant legal term. The supervisory component of community sentences is usually literally called *'open environment'* as opposed to *'closed environment'*, even if the term probation is currently gaining momentum.

My second difficulty with the request made for this chapter pertained to the use of the word 'punishment'. Even if punishment is one of the goals of sentences – along with, as we shall see, reinsertion – sentences are never called punishment, whether in the law or by academics or practitioners. The legal and practical term is '*peine*', that is indeed 'sentence', although '*peine*' also has the connotation of 'pain' and 'hardship'. Moreover, as we shall see below, when sentences are implemented, the principle of punishment leaves the scene and is replaced by the principle of reinsertion.

It is important to remember that France is a written law jurisdiction, where laws and other statutes are extremely detailed. In such a context, a legal rather than a pragmatic or evidence-based approach prevails, whereby laws are expected to solve crime issues, rather than programmes, where measures and obligations as laid down in the law are expected to address criminogenic needs rather than the modernisation or improvement of supervision. The current socialist Minister of Justice, Mme Taubira, has thus obtained the enactment of a new penal law (15 August 2014) with the goal of solving overcrowding and reoffending issues by creating a new sentence and by fast processing offenders out of prison virtually without support. This is the fourth law addressing reoffending since 2005!

Another trait is that France's state probation service is still relatively recently established (1949) compared to other jurisdictions, but in recent times has become extremely powerful since it merged with the prison services in 1999. It has now become a monopolistic and prisonised agency, which tends to spend too much time engaging in turf and corporate wars with other agencies (Herzog-Evans 2014b) and too little engaged in social work and care (de Larminat 2012). It is not punitive per se, but in many cases is essentially administrative, tick-boxing and insufficiently unsupportive of offenders' actual needs (de Larminat 2012; Dindo 2011). It has recently discovered 'evidence-based practices' but still has a superficial understanding of what they entail and, more importantly, of the considerable institutional and professional changes such an approach would require.

Care and social work was a very strong component of French supervision and reentry when the French ancestor of the 'Problem-Solving Court' (the *Juge d'Application des Peines*, JAPs; see Herzog-Evans 2014a) was created in 1945. For decades, JAPs worked in harmony with probation services and the third sector (Perrier 2013). In view of the aforementioned imperialistic probation services' evolution, these judges have become marginalised and their still very desistance oriented professional culture (Herzog-Evans 2014b) may well become extinct. It does not help that both these courts and probation services are exceptionally overloaded and that the French Justice budget is one of the poorest of modern Europe.

The current situation could not be more removed from the origins of French community sentences and measures (CSM).

Origins and history of French community sentences

The history of French CSM is a history of increased diversification of sentences and measures; and of agencies and practitioners.

Community sentences and measures

Notwithstanding fines, the first French alternative sentence, simple sentence suspension without supervision (*sursis simple*), was created in 1891 in a very favourable political context (Badinter 1992). It was also strongly influenced by the principle of individualisation of sentences best theorised by the hugely influential (Audren *et al.* 2013) Raymond Saleilles (1898). Prior to this France had created conditional release (*libération conditionnelle* – 1885). In 1912, with the influence of Edouard Julhiet who enthusiastically advocated American treatment methods for juveniles after spending 5 years in the United States (Julhiet 1906), the first law that truly adapted the treatment of juveniles was enacted. It created special jurisdictions for minors and stated that the main principle of juvenile justice was education. Individualisation can, however, also be punitive. The same era saw an Act (1854) allowing some offenders to be sent to the colonies for forced labour; another created a general prison regime of solitary confinement (1875) and yet another (1885) made deportation of recidivists mandatory.

The intense reform activity of the time was energised by the importation of ideas from the United States (in particular with regard to prisons). Ideas circulated to a great extent thanks to the creation of the General Society for Prisons (*Société Générale des Prisons*, 1896 – Kaluszynski 1996, 2001) and with the participation of French experts and practitioners at the World Prison Congresses that started taking place in the 1840s (Lucas 1872; Tanguy 2007). There was a general innovative excitement largely due to the new trust in applied sciences and technology (Kaluszynski 2013). The feasibility of the implementation of these reforms was made possible by an increased community participation in public matters. In particular, as in many other jurisdictions (Mair and Burke 2012), charities became organised (to a great degree under religious auspices) and started contributing heavily to offenders' support and, later, to their supervision. The so-called *Comités de Patronage* (Support Committees) were thus granted the responsibility for prisoners' reentry and would later be in charge of parolees. This intense and enthusiastic reform activity was also driven by politicians (and in particular Senator F. Béranger).

From the very beginning, reformers wanted to adapt sentences and release measures to offenders' level of risk and moral worth, which at the time was crudely understood as differentiating first-time offenders versus recidivists. To this rather rudimentary risk-based dichotomy, the response was essentially legal and took the shape of a diversification of sentences and measures which would increase during the twentieth century.

The two world conflicts subsequently put an end to reformers' enthusiasm (Carlier 1989). The renewed impetus of 1945 was the direct result of the war, which acted as a form of criminal justice clean slate. Indeed, a great number of the people who worked in the Ministry of Justice at the time were former members of the resistance and deportees, many of whom had endured France's appalling prisons or concentration camps. The first reform (Amor reform 1945) thus logically pertained to prisons (Castan *et al.* 1990). It also pertained to juveniles: the Ordinance of 1945 profoundly renewed the 1912 Act and created a children's judge (*juge des enfants*), who would be in charge of both juvenile offenders and minors in danger, the grounding principle being that both needed protection. In the 1950s another influence would be the New Social Defence movement led by Marc Ancel (1954).

A second wave of reforms thus took place in the 1950s. They all contributed to the diversification of CSM. First, with the creation in 1951 of 'semi-freedom', a measure 'under prison registry' (Herzog-Evans 2012, 2012–2013a, Title 43), whereby the person is under custody at night and over the week-end, but works or does other social (e.g. training) or health-related (e.g. drug treatment) activities during the day; second, with the creation of a new custodial suspended sentence with probation in 1958, at the same time when the new Code of Penal Procedure was enacted (see below). Parallel to the creation of this new sentence, state probation services were established.

The history of the suspended sentence with probation (*sursis avec mise à l'épreuve* – SME) is fascinating. In a jurisdiction which is instinctively suspicious of anything of an Anglophone origin, it nonetheless was an unashamed penal transfer from England. Indeed, in 1947, Paul Amor, the first director of the prison services to be appointed after WWII, tellingly used the word 'probation system' – in English – in a publication (Amor 1948). The main argument in favour of a suspended custodial sentence with probation was that it constituted a much needed intermediary sentence between a simple sentence suspension and custody and would increase scope for the individualisation of sentences. France opted for a suspended custodial sentence rather than a stand-alone probation order, as it was felt by policy-makers that both offenders and public opinion should understand that this was also a sanction (Perrier 2013).

From the 1970s to the 1980s, many more sentences and measures were created *inter alia*: remission (1972, 1979), sentences' suspension or fractionation (1975), community work (1983), SME plus community work (1983), electronic monitoring (EM – 1997), and socio-judicial supervision for sex offenders (1998). Two of these new sentences and measures (community work and EM) were, again, English or Anglophone penal transfers. Another interesting measure was the transformation of nineteenth-century former *chantiers extérieurs*, from mandatory construction work for prisoners into a sentence or release measure under prison registry, called 'placement in the community'. It is currently a form of re-entry measure for highly dissocialised offenders, who need a host of on-site interventions, and is therefore similar to North-American half-way houses and UK-approved premises.

Diversification affected both front-door and back-door measures. A prisoner can currently be released under medical sentence suspension, parole, semi-freedom, EM, placement in the community or a combination and/or succession. Indeed, the implementation of sentences (*application des peines*, including community sentences, release decisions, post-release supervision, breach and recall) has become an autonomous legal field, with a multitude of possibilities, bifurcations and procedures. A recent evolution (2000–2004) has consisted in attaching fair-trial rights (right to a hearing, defence, appeal…) to most decisions made in the implementation of sentences. This change has been labelled 'the judicialisation of sentences' implementation'. It has allowed courts of appeal and the Court of Cassation (France's supreme court for criminal justice, CJ, matters) to control local courts' decisions and to unify the application of laws, and it has contributed to the development of this legal field. Importantly, it has promoted a significantly more legitimate decision-making process. This movement has been influenced by a similar and parallel evolution in prison law (Herzog-Evans 2012–2013b, Chapter 3), which in turn has been influenced by prisoners' rights NGOs, European law, the incarceration of Very Important Persons and a vigorous doctrinal activity in the 1990s (Herzog-Evans 1994; Céré 1998; Péchillon 1999) along with the joint 'legal guerrilla war' that these NGOs and authors conducted (de Suremain 2014).

These changes were made in the context of very favourable public opinion: in the year 2000, following the high-profile publication of a book written by a general practitioner working in the Parisian prison of La Santé, which referred to famous politicians who had been detained there, the media spent months revealing and displaying the horrific conditions of French prisons (Vasseur 2000). Both the National Assembly and the Senate (Assemblée Nationale 2000; Sénat 2000) published very critical reports, the Senate calling this situation a 'humiliation for the Republic'. Now that they decide in the context of a formal hearing, judges (see below) can make rulings on the basis of a host of psycho-social and criminological factors as opposed to being fundamentally dependent on – and instrumentalised by – the prison services and their traditional focus on good order and behaviour (cf. Herzog-Evans 1994 and Herzog-Evans 2014b). Therefore, release measures and the obligations attached to them have become closer to the 'support narrative in which the release plan of the offender should address the multiple deficits of the offender' (Maruna and LeBel 2003: 95). Resocialising offenders has never been contentious in France, perhaps because public opinion is overall rather lenient on crime (Mayhew and van Kesteren 2002). Even if the 'right' side of the political fence typically advocates longer sentences for serious offenders and certain punishment for less serious ones, it has never gone as far as to contesting the principles of reinsertion and individualisation. As an example, even though, during the presidency of Nicolas Sarkozy, many punitive laws were passed, the Prison Act of 2009 then went farther than ever before in developing early release measures and even enshrined in the guideline article 707 of the Penal Procedure Code that all offenders *should* benefit from early release measures in order to facilitate their reinsertion.

The great diversity of sentences, measures and obligations, also exposes the French one-sided focus on rules and legal frameworks, rather than on programmes, supervision quality and outcomes.

To sum up, France had become until recently a leading jurisdiction in terms of human rights and fairness in decision-making, but was still very primitive regarding evidence-based practices. Moreover, the changes which occurred in 2000–2004 did not go down well with other state agencies.

Agencies

Before the Second World War, the prison services interacted with charities and other community agencies, but France had no state probation, nor any judicial participation in supervision. However, the great reformation spirit of the time also affected community supervision agencies. In 1945, the *juge des enfants* (literally Children's Judge), the descendant of the 1912 specialised courts, was created by the aforementioned Ordinance of 1945. Like judges in modern problem-solving courts, the *juge des enfants* was both a sentencing and a sentences' implementation judge. With adult offenders, however, a specialised sentences' implementation judge (JAP) was first experimented with in 1945. The generalisation of this approach was decided in 1958. Until 2000, however, JAPs were hybrids, midway between being 'super social workers' and judges. They made their decisions in a sentences' implementation commission (*commission de l'application des peines* – CAP) within the prison walls and surrounded by prison staff, which inevitably led to the aforementioned excessive focus on prison behaviour. Prisoners were not allowed in during the CAP, nor were any attorneys; JAPs' decisions could not be appealed.

Parallel to this, and respectively in 1946 and in 1949, 'social assistants' and 'educators', the 'Mrs Yes' and 'Mr No' (Perrier 2012: 187) of prison social work and reentry were created. In the community, Patronage committees were structured in 1946 and their missions regulated. It was only in 1958 that state probation services were given full competence over probation sentences, and later over other CSM (Perrier 2013). Probation officers (PO) remained educators and social assistants until 1993. In the community, POs worked within tribunals, in direct and quotidian contact with JAPs. However, in 1999, community and prison social work merged and was absorbed by the prison services. A new corps of PO (called Insertion and Probation Counsellor; Herzog-Evans 2013a) had been created in 1993 and progressively incorporated former social assistants and educators. Increasingly, lawyers rather than social workers would be recruited; progressively, prison culture and institutional organisation penetrated and permeated probation staff (Herzog-Evans 2014c). As they added their limited numbers to those of prison staff – and, importantly to prison services' colossal budget – they became significantly more powerful and monopolistic. Linked to the increased recruitment of lawyers (de Larminat 2012), this led to the gradual elimination of social work in probation and prison reentry (Herzog-Evans 2011).

The prison services' annexation of probation in 1999 coincided with the wider executive annexation of criminal justice. As politicians progressively became aware of the communication tool that crime issues represented, and supported by a typically Jacobin centralised culture, where separation of powers always implies that the executive is superior, prosecutors were increasingly put in charge of judicial activities. In France, prosecutors are not independent of the executive. Since the mid-1990s, prosecutors have thus been put in charge of out of court ('bifurcation') procedures such as transaction, mediation, warning or a form of plea bargaining that allows them to sentence offenders. An increased number of offenders are thus sentenced out of court – if not out of tribunals – by prosecutors (Danet 2013). Contrary to judges, prosecutors can be ordered to adopt managerial processing methods, to implement zero-tolerance policies or, conversely, when prisons are full, more tolerant practice and so on. French community sentences have thus increasingly become an executive affair and are therefore greatly dependent on the political ideologies of those in charge. The result of this shift is essentially that more cases are processed through the criminal justice system (CJS) than ever before. It has also led the prison services to issue a circular which radically changed the focus of probation services from reinsertion and resocialisation to the prevention of reoffending (Circular of 19 March 2008 pertaining to the missions and the methods used by probation services). This was done during the 'reign' of Mr Sarkozy, who, as mentioned previously, was elected based on a punitive agenda, therefore with public opinion behind him: the very same public opinion which had reacted strongly at the beginning of the new millennium, following the publication of Vasseur's book (2000; discussed above). The 'versatility' of French public opinion, which, according to General de Gaulle, permanently oscillated between a lenient and a punitive stance, was once again evident.

Contextualising changes

The principles that ground French community sentences can partly be explained by the aforementioned systemic changes. These changes are also the results of socio-political factors. In both cases, however, rules and policies have become rather blurry and contradictory, to the point where it has now become difficult to clearly identify whether French policies are mostly punitive or rehabilitative.

Grounding principles

It is only recently that the guiding principles of French sentences and release measures have been expressly mentioned in the law. This has been done for both front-door and back-door measures.

With regard to *sentencing*, it is in the new penal code of 1994 – which replaced the former 1810 Code – that article 132-24 was included. It first explained what criteria should guide courts when they pronounced sentences and, second, laid down the principles that should be balanced in doing so (Dréan-Rivette 2005, 2006). Article 132-24 has been amended and replaced by a new article, 130-1, of the penal code by the recent 15 August 2014 Act, which tellingly pertains to two opposite goals: 'the individualisation of sentences and [the] reinforce[ment of] the efficacy of penal sanctions'. However, the new law seems at first glance to place punishment in the driving seat. Whereas article 132-24 used to put the reinsertion of offenders on a par with the prevention of reoffending and did not mention punishment, the new article 130-1 first states, in section 1 (: 1), that sentences aim at punishing the author of the offence and then only, in a second section (: 2) that they also aim at facilitating offenders' amendment and their insertion or reinsertion.

The strict application of French legal interpretation principles indicate that what is first mentioned – here, punishment – prevails on what follows – here, reinsertion. Yet, in a rather contradictory fashion, another new article, 132-1, in turn insists on the need to individualise the sentence based on the circumstances of the offence, the offender's personality and his/her personal material, family and social circumstances. In short, the concept of punishment has thus been incorporated in the law, but individualisation remains the guiding principle for courts' decision-making.

The introduction of punishment was actually an attempt to respond to public opinion, as the Ministry of Justice (who drafted this law) was portrayed by the opposition as being too lenient with offenders. In spite of this guiding principle, however, France has not opted for a just-desert sentencing principle where only the offence is taken into consideration, but adapts sentences to the person's context and personality, well in line with Saleilles' doctrine (Saleilles 1898/2009).

The guiding principles for the *implementation of sentences* were first enumerated by the Constitutional Council (CC), in 1994, apropos of the constitutionality of the 'true life' Act (CC 20 January 1994, no. 93334 DC; van de Kerchove 2008). The Council stated that the aim of sentences' implementation was 'not only to protect society and ensure the offender's punishment, but also to facilitate his amendment and prepare him for his future reinsertion'. This rather obsolete terminology was not emulated when article 707 was incorporated as the opening article to the sentences' implementation part (5th) of the Penal Procedure Code (PPC; 2004 'Perben 2' Act). Paragraph 2 thus stated that 'sentences' implementation facilitates the insertion or reinsertion of convicted persons into society as well as the prevention of reoffending, whilst respecting the interests of society and the rights of victims'.

At first glance it seems that article 707 is very similar to article 130-1. However, there is one essential difference: it does not refer to punishment. It is thus plain that, when the time comes for sentences to be implemented, punishment is no longer a goal. The generally accepted idea is that one must then consider the future and, in particular, reinsertion and public – and victims' – safety. This happens the minute sentences are passed, as custodial sentences of up to 2 years can be immediately transformed by the JAP into CSM (art. 723-15 of the PPC). Similarly, article 707, paragraphs 3 and 4, states that offenders should never serve their custodial sentences fully and should be released early in order to be better prepared for their reentry. It is, however, important to note that article 707 has been entirely redrafted by the 2014 Act. Moreover, paragraph 3 now expressly states that prison conditions and overcrowding are the sole guiding principle for early release decisions. Following in the footsteps of its right-wing predecessor (recall the Prison Act 2009), the current government is now essentially concerned with managerial and financial considerations pertaining to prison space. This need is deemed so pressing that neither the previous right-wing government, nor the present left-wing one seem to have paid much attention to how public opinion would perceive such a philosophy.

However, the majority of the legal norms which lay down the *conditions* of early release measures still indicate that a release plan must be prepared which focuses on obvious resettlement needs such as employment, housing, treatment and family ties. Moreover, articles 132-44 and 132-45 of the Penal Code further validate the aforementioned 'support narrative' (Maruna and LeBel 2003: 95); a great number of the obligations which they list for CSM and release measures also address these needs. Importantly, though, French reentry judges use them sparingly (Herzog-Evans 2014b).

One will surely have noticed that the aforementioned guiding principles do not take victims into consideration; in fact article 707 has eliminated them from the guiding considerations for decision-making. Victims are barely tolerated in the CJS (Cario 2012), and reparation is only an indirect effect of punishment as the new paragraph IV of article 707 now states. It mostly takes the shape of damages, which strictly speaking are of a civil law nature. Even community work is usually invoked for its resocialising impact rather than for its reparative nature.

As explained above, the judicialisation of 2000–2004 has resulted in fair trial having become an important grounding principle of sentences' implementation. France no longer considered that these were executive issues where offenders' procedural rights could be ignored (Herzog-Evans 2012–2013a). This had very likely increased the legitimacy of the decisions made, but remained fragile, as we shall see.

As suggested above, French people have a tendency to believe that laws change reality. Unfortunately, in practice, the legal architecture laid down in articles 130-1, 132-1 and 707 meets a number of obstacles.

Given the quasi-zero-tolerance policies of the last years, more cases have been processed through the courts or via 'bifurcation' prosecutor-led procedures, as noted above. However, prosecutors' procedures have not been able to absorb all these new cases. A new obsession has become moving the docket (courts) and allocating cases (probation services) (Danet 2013), thereby transforming the CJS into a gigantic factory line. The sheer volume of cases is so considerable that practitioners' traditional culture of attending to details, thoroughness and quality is rapidly disappearing, in particular in big cities' tribunals (see, for JAPs, Herzog-Evans 2014b). JAPs are, for instance, graded by their chiefs of jurisdictions based on the number of cases they process, and pressured so that they tolerate that their partners only deliver mediocre work. POs have an official caseload of 90–100 offenders, but these figures do not take part-time work into consideration. In most services, the reality is closer to 130 cases and, in some jurisdictions (e.g. currently in Reims and Châlons), the number goes up to 200. France also has one of the least well-resourced justice systems in Europe (*Alternatives Economiques*, March 2011, no. 300). Most tribunals' meagre funds are spent by March or April of a fiscal year. France's managerialism is thus mainly a desperate attempt at managing poverty. As a consequence, sentences' implementation is increasingly perceived as being merely a 'back door' – therefore discreet – way of releasing offenders or not incarcerating them at all, when public opinion is not 'looking', after having led more people to the 'front door'.

Meanwhile, the overall intensity of social control has increased. More people than ever are processed through the CJS. Even if France is still rather lenient in terms of incarceration rates (Aebi and Marguet 2014: SPACE-II 2012), prison-sentence lengths have increased in the last years, although the vast majority of custodial sentences are only of up to 1 year (ibid.). At the same time, courts are still pronouncing very large numbers of alternative sentences (Aebi and Marguet 2014: SPACE-II 2012). France also created so-called safety measures in 2005 and 2008; that is, mandatory supervision and preventive detention for 'dangerous offenders' at risk of 'maxing out' on their sentences, because no court has taken the risk of releasing them early (van der Wolf and Herzog-Evans 2015). For most offenders serving a community sentence or measure, supervision is nonetheless surprisingly loose. Drug and alcohol tests are rare, predictable and unreliable; meetings with probation officers are equally infrequent (every month to every 2–3 months) and can be purely administrative in nature; there is no way of knowing what offenders are doing nor where they are between these meetings, and there is no collaboration with the police to try and learn more; and, in many cases, people have secured a CSM by providing counterfeited documents that could never be checked out. POs' caseloads, but also their institutional and professional culture (Herzog-Evans 2014c), generate an extremely unsupportive form of supervision and reentry (Herzog-Evans 2011) – but for the work done by the third sector (Herzog-Evans 2014d).

Adding to this is the overall lack of collaborative culture. JAPs have lost their historical ties with probation services since 1999 and, consequently, their relationships have suffered (Herzog-Evans 2014b). Since then, the embedding of the probation services in the prison services has considerably increased. Rather than 'polibation' (Nash 1999) French probation could best be labelled as 'prisonbation'. State probation services are now in a position to benefit from the considerable power attached to prison services and to perceive themselves as being in charge of a 'sovereign' mission (a term which is increasingly used to describe a mission that is of public interest and should, therefore, only be allocated to civil servants). As a result they tend to see other agencies as subcontractors or employees rather than as partners and as being the 'gendarmes' of their 'collaboration' with these other agencies (Herzog-Evans 2014d). Therefore, probation has acquired a higher status in French society, one that implies that it is an essential state public service, in sole charge of supervision. Prisonbation has also contributed – with the aforementioned recruitment of lawyers – at the expense of social work. The prison services headquarters have made clear that reinsertion is no longer the mission of probation services (Prison Services circular 2008) – in clear breach of the aforementioned legal principles (art. 707) – and, in 2010, issued a decree which has systematically deleted the label 'social worker' from the Penal Procedure Code (Herzog-Evans 2013a). This has occurred within the context of a new prison 'disciplinary governance' era (Herzog-Evans 2012–2013b), from 2002 onwards, which has taken place against the backdrop of the aforementioned new punitive age. For instance, prisoners in prisons for medium and long sentences had previously enjoyed the freedom to move around the prison premises; now, they were confined to their cell all day and were submitted to classification (Cliquennois 2008). Moreover, prison staff now had new military-like labels (captain, lieutenant. . .), although contradictory trends such as the development of prisoners' rights have also been at play (Chantraine 2010).

Socio-political factors

One must certainly not over-emphasise the links between welfare and crime policies (Downes and Hansen 2006). Such links are neither universal nor straight-forward. They nonetheless provide a rather useful analytical tool (Snacken and Dumortier 2012). France is still to a great extent a welfare society: its universal health coverage, albeit bankrupt and *de facto* partially privatised, is still up and run-ning. Moreover, French public opinion – in spite of what some politicians may think (Cavadino and Dignan 2006: 139) – is overall still extremely soft on crime (Mayhew and van Kesteren 2002). Furthermore, France does not have a typically English sensationalist press – a risk factor for punitive policies according to Tonry (2007). Even if, for Cavadino and Dignan (2006), France's specific context may be explained *inter alia* by its Catholicism, today Catholicism has little direct influ-ence. Quite the contrary, France's secular nature has become more important than ever and any religious reference is typically avoided. More convincing is the persis-tence of Marxism (Lacey 2008: 48 ff.) throughout the twentieth century as a strong political force. Even if the communist party and other extreme-left parties have now virtually disappeared, they have left a strong imprint on the French psyche. As a result left discourses and culture are still very much present and contribute to the high political polarisation of most issues, including crime policies. Lacey (2008) also suggests that political systems contribute to the nature of penal discourses and policies. Her dichotomy between liberal and corporate jurisdictions certainly rings true in France.

Penal policies have been at the forefront of most political elections and political discourses over the last few decades. In this jurisdiction, the tipping factor was 9/11 (Danet 2006). Another factor has been chronic unemployment (BBC 2014), a sit-uation which does not seem to be resolvable in the near future (Pisani-Ferry 2014), along with a 'diploma inflation' phenomenon (requiring high levels of qualifica-tion for unskilled work), which excludes offenders and other dissocialised people. Unable to solve the real problems faced by their population, politicians have jumped on the 'tough on crime' bandwagon. This was already visible at the beginning of the Petrol Crisis in 1974 and has become endemic since Nicolas Sarkozy's political leadership, first as a very active Minister of Interior (2002–2007), then as President (2007–2012).

Prior to this, crime was not as prominent in political discourse. Time was taken to discuss matters and prepare reforms: changes in sentencing and probation after the Second World War were spread from 1945 to 1958 and the merging of prison and probation in 1999 had been discussed for several years (Perrier 2013). The current times are an era of fast and frantic reforming, devoid of a clear compass. Both the Prison Act (2009) and the 2014 Act were only discussed once by the two parliamentary chambers thanks to an 'emergency' procedure, when twice is habitually the norm. In both cases, and increasingly so, traditional political frontiers have become blurry. For instance, whereas conservative-liberal Nicolas Sarkozy is indeed responsible for more than a dozen punitive penal reforms, his Prison Act created an extremely lenient prisoner-release system. Conversely, socialist François Hollande's government has just been responsible for the 2014 Act, which marks a clearly punitive turn, albeit confusingly, in CSM. Both presidents have in common the discovery of probation and sentences' implementation as a political propaganda vector. Both have mainly focused on legal changes, rather than on solving institutional issues or improving the very nature of supervision (Herzog-Evans 2014c, d). The future is therefore looking increasingly uncertain and, perhaps, desolate.

Recent and future changes

As this chapter is completed, a new law has been enacted. More penal changes are thus about to happen (they come into force in October 2014). During the parliamentary debates, the extent of the aforementioned turf wars has been on public display, and the most powerful camp has obtained decisive victories. The modest progress of evidence-based practices have to be analysed under these negative auspices.

Penal changes

As mentioned previously, France has just enacted yet another penal law (14 August 2014) – this will be the thirteenth of its kind since 2002 – tellingly labelled 'pertaining to the efficacy of penal sanction' – which reforms CSM; but the reality is that it emphasises factory-line penal processes. This law was promoted as yet another penal transfer; that is, the importation of the English probation order. The promoters of the new measure naively hoped that by replacing the previous importation of English probation in 1958 (SME) by a probation order disconnected from imprisonment, there would be less incarceration. This, as I immediately argued, was legally, factually and criminologically inexact (Herzog-Evans 2013b). Legally, because there would not magically be fewer breaches or fewer further offences, and these inevitably would be sanctioned by recall as with SME. Factually, because without a predetermined suspended imprisonment sentence to execute, JAPs would not legally be allowed to sanction offenders – whereas they can with SME. Indeed, the 2014 Act transfers this competence to another type of judge who has not supervised the offender and who does not have JAPs' desistance culture (Herzog-Evans 2014b). As I showed in a former research study, in nearly 100 per cent of the cases, JAPs first convoke (or summon) offenders to remind them of their obligations, but do not revoke the sentence or measure the first time around (ibid.). Another judge would not have the time nor the information and the culture to act likewise. Therefore, a greater number of people would be sent back to prison, contrary to what the government has said it wanted to do.

The Act is also criminologically delusional as it assumes, yet again, that reality can be transformed by laws and, in particular, that courts will inevitably prefer the new sentence to incarceration. The famous net-widening effect (Cohen 1985) has been ignored, even though the history of French penal reform could provide numerous examples. In particular, the prison services and governmental focus on EM in the 2000s had led to the reduction of the number of parole decisions and, even more so, of the much more supportive placement in the community. In other words, either the new sentence would be pronounced, but then it would be unlikely to compete with incarceration, or it would not, in particular because it was too similar to SME and did not change supervision's credibility and quality. Thus French law-reformers further ignore well-known decision-making factors in sentencing (Hough *et al.* 2003; Tombs 2004; Wandall 2008; Danet 2013; Boone and Herzog-Evans 2013) and in particular they have neglected the utmost importance of pre-sentence reports, which the government did not plan on developing – in practice they are rare (Brizais 2006).

Unfortunately, the parliamentary debates have revealed how removed from these facts and realities MPs are. They have spent a lot of time arguing about the definition of sentences' goals and have added to the chronic legal confusion by also creating the aforementioned two articles (art. 130-1 and 132-1 of the Penal Code). The debate has also revealed the high level of uncertainty as to the exact goals of the government and has showed that, in spite of considerable polarisation, in reality the left–right boundaries are more blurry than ever, the right taking ownership of amendment and reinsertion, and the left insisting it is also punitive. Whilst they have used precious parliamentary time thus posturing, MPs have spent no time discussing technical – but essential – legal details and have simply dismissed most of the amendments that have been presented against the Bill, which has thus retained most of its original punitive nature.

For indeed, behind the apparent decarceration discourse, the reality is that the new community sentences, measures and procedures are more punitive. As Robinson *et al.* have argued, CSM can indeed be punitive (Robinson *et al.* 2013: 327). In the French context these punitive adaptations take different shapes from those in England and Wales (Robinson, Chapter 3 of this volume). Firstly, the aforementioned August 2014 Act has not abrogated safety measures, even though the socialist party fiercely combated them when they were enacted in 2005 and 2008; quite the contrary, the 2014 Act has added yet another one to the original list (PPC, art. 706-136-1). Secondly, the development of probation can in fact correspond to the development of 'mass probation' (Phelps 2013; McNeill 2013) without necessarily reducing incarceration. Thirdly, probation can be painful (Durnescu 2011) and, in some instances, offenders prefer incarceration to supervision (May and Wood 2010).

This is undoubtedly often the case with 'measures under prison registry' (Herzog-Evans 2012); that is, community measures whereby the offender is still legally a prisoner. Such is the case for EM, semi-freedom and 'placement in the community'. It will also be the case with the new French probation order aptly called '*contrainte pénale*' (i.e. 'penal constraint'), as it is indeed significantly more constraining than previous sentences – something the National Human Rights Commission has deplored (Commission Nationale Consultative des Droits de l'Homme 2014). Such will also be the case with mandatory early release, which is revealingly called 'release under constraint' (*liberation sous contrainte*). Originally the Ministry of Justice Bill stated that prisoners would not have the right to refuse or appeal decisions thus made, even if the measure that was chosen for them was one of the most constraining ones (e.g. semi-freedom or EM). Luckily the parliament amended the law, and prisoners' consent will be asked and they will have a right to appeal decisions.

However, and fourthly, given the procedural context of the decision-making (CAP), prisoners will be judged essentially based on their prison behaviour rather than on their readiness for release or their reentry plan. Fifthly, there will not be a reentry plan, as the mass release of prisoners via this purely administrative procedure (which processes up to 100 cases in half a day compared with 6 to 15 per hearing) will make it impossible for both prisoners and probation services to prepare one – as is unfortunately already the case in practice given the current caseload (Tribunal de Grande Instance de Créteil 2014). In such an unsupportive and controlling context, prisoners' desistance and the prevention of reoffending are no longer the ultimate goals; nor are policymakers much concerned with public opinion. At best they are hoping that the public will be convinced by the punitive narrative and terminology also present in the 2014 Act – confusingly mixed with a decarcerating discourse. For indeed, politicians' and prison services' main objective is to free prison beds, no matter what the offenders' context, reality, vulnerability or level of support and agency are. The obsession of politicians and the prison services is first and foremost financial. As they are instrumentalising community sentences and particularly release measures (Snacken *et al.* 2010; Scheirs *et al.* 2014), they are emptying them of any 'support narrative' content.

As offenders will increasingly be released, supervised, sanctioned and recalled, without a fair trial (Herzog-Evans 2013b), and fast processed in administrative or administrative-like procedural contexts, the legitimacy of the CJS will be considerably reduced. Even if there is currently no empirical evidence that fair trial in supervision and release is linked to more legitimacy from the perspectives of the public or offenders (Herzog-Evans 2015), there are reasons to believe it is (Hough 2015). This regrettable trend is also fuelled by petty and counterproductive turf wars.

Turf wars and their consequences

Unlike its English–Welsh counterpart (Robinson, Chapter 3, this volume), French state probation has never been as powerful and as uncontested as today. Since 1999, and particularly since the aforementioned prison services circular of 2008, the probation service's corporatism (Cavadino and Dignan 2006; Lacey 2008) and intrinsic belief in its own superiority (see Johnson 1972) has reached unprecedented levels. Prison services' unions have always been extremely powerful (Carlier 1989, 2009) and their incestuous relationships with the headquarters is a well-known fact (Perrier 2013). Their desire to get rid of JAPs (Gentilini 2014) or at least reduce their power to that of a 'judge of the incident' (i.e. breach) is not new (Perrier 2013), but has been made greater with their own development and other more complex institutional reasons (Herzog-Evans 2014b: 146–200). Eliminating fair trial from the new 'penal constraint' implementation and marginalising it with offenders' release will allow probation services to downgrade JAPs' decision-making power and status, whilst giving more power to their opinion: they are members of the prison staff present during CAP meetings, where JAPs will become prison services' rubber-stamping puppets as they too often were in the recent past (Herzog-Evans 1994).

Probation also has issues with the third sector. When the aforementioned Bill was presented at the Senate, the chamber realised that state probation services would not have capacity to supervise all the offenders should penal constraint be a success. It was thus decided that supervision *could* be transferred to the third sector. Against all evidence, most unions presented a united front against this so-called probation privatisation. In reality, this was only optional, only applied to penal constraint, a sentence which, as mentioned previously, was very similar to SME, and article 740 of the PPC has stated since 1970 that the third sector could be in charge of SME. Importantly, the French term 'privatisation' implies that an activity is transferred to the for-profit sector, a description that certainly does not apply to under-funded 'associations'. Amidst this debate, state probation has accused the third sector of being incompetent, dangerous and costly for society as well as for offenders; every single one of these assertions being false. In fact, the third sector has *de facto* long been in charge of prisoners' reentry, of pre-sentence reports, of part of supervision, of community sentences and of many local programmes, and increasingly so as state probation has forsaken social work (Herzog-Evans 2014d). The third sector is highly professionalised and, rather than mainly hiring lawyers as state probation now mostly does, employs social workers and psychologists. At this point, state probation services are not in a position to claim that they are more competent, nor that they implement evidence-based techniques.

Evidence-based practices?

In order to try and end this rather low-spirited chapter on a more positive note, I would like to refer to the current criminological momentum which has gradually become apparent in French supervision since the 2008 prison circular. After having created home-grown programmes and an actuarial assessment tool designed to acculturate its staff, French probation services are now gradually becoming accustomed through various training sessions to desistance, the Good Lives Model, Risk–Need–Responsivity principles and Core Correctional Practices. So far, however, very little concrete implementation has followed. It is, however, positive that French probation services are now ready to catch up when, just a few years back, they were still rather oppositional (Herzog-Evans 2011; de Larminat 2012).

However, if local probation services are, as I predicted, particularly interested in desistance (Herzog-Evans 2011), their national headquarters are currently focusing mainly on the importation of Canadian actuarial tools. If assessment is part and parcel of modern probation, one might wonder whether this is not putting the cart before the horse when one-to-one supervision is yet to be structured and evaluated (Dindo 2011) and programmes are non-existent. Bearing in mind the 2014 Act, the 'prisonbation' nature, structure and culture of state probation, its monumental caseload and its consequences (unsupportive administrative supervision), there is a serious risk that evidence-based practices will reinforce its current shortcomings and failings. So far rather than calling into question current practices (e.g. desistance studies – NB: Farrall 2002; Farrall *et al.* 2014) and leading to more social work-influenced approaches, evidence-based practices appear to represent a modernisation of techniques rather than the probation revolution that France so desperately needs.

Conclusion

The narrative history of French CSM has been contrasted and fluctuating. France has never been fully at ease with the *punitive narrative*. Historically, it has attributed a punishment goal to sentencing, but not to the execution of sentences. However, a punitive relegitimation affecting the execution of sentences was briefly present during Nicolas Sarkozy's 10-year-long presence as the head of the state; yet this punitive discourse was schizophrenically withdrawn for the majority of offenders in 2009, as Europe was pointing a finger at France for violating prisoners' rights. The remaining result of this era is that many more cases are processed in the CJS.

A persistent *narrative* since the end of the nineteenth century has been that of the *individualisation of sentences*. Originally designed to better tailor the sentence to a person's circumstances, during Nicolas Sarkozy's governmental presence, it also rejoined the punitive narrative, as much effort was made to differentiate serious offences and criminals (treated harshly) from the wide majority (treated leniently). Differentiating is also linked to a general managerial trend in public services and in probation in particular (de Larminat 2012).

Another consistent *narrative* has been *rehabilitation* or rather, in French terms, *reinsertion*. It has been historically present since the conditional release law of 1885 and the suspended-sentence law of 1891. However, the prisonisation of probation services since 1999 has done much to reduce the importance of rehabilitation within probation.

Conversely, the *reparative narrative* is the most recent of all and only appeared in 2001 with the 15 June laws. Despite minimal progress, victims are nonetheless in practice still rather neglected by the CJS. If victims' rights were briefly instrumentalised during the more punitive era of Nicolas Sarkozy, there is a general fear that giving them too much might lead to more punitive decision-making. Many law reforms have thus been essentially declaratory. Such has recently been the case, once again, with the August 2014 law, which defines victims' rights in a general rule (article 707) and refers to restorative justice practices in yet another unspecific rule, but does not give victims any actual rights which they could truly use.

Managerialism is also a rather recent *narrative*, which also appeared in 2001 with a law on the efficacy of public services, which consists mainly in giving statistically measurable targets to the public. However, in CSM, the real pressure of managerialism has only been felt since the 2009 Prison Law, when the objective of release measures has gradually solely become the release of a greater number of prisoners, in a purely 'pipe draining' logic, without much regard for efficient rehabilitation and reentry, as the obsession is now to save space and money. Managerialism is also felt through another channel: probation services having merged with the prison services are now subjected to its quasi-military organisation and management.

The recent law of August 2014 has further blurred the grounding narratives of CSM. The current government, eager to please all sides of the public opinion spectrum, has designed a penal law that attempts to embrace all aforementioned narratives at the same time. On the surface, there is a legal and political human rights and reinsertion discourse. But the reality is one of prison overcrowding, prison disciplinary governance, measure-based unsupportive and abandoning reentry, mock and superficial evidence-based practices, administrative supervision, overloaded 'prisonbation' agents, an extremely poorly resourced CJS, managerial 'safety valve' (Robinson et al. 2013) or 'bathtub unplugging' offender processing in and out and back in and out of prison, and delegitimising justice by eliminating hard-earned fair trial and prisoners' 'voice' protections (Lind and Tyler 1988; also see de Mesmaecker 2014).

There is still hope, however, that practitioners and offenders will resist the current trend, as has been the case in the past with former reforms. But alternatively, the future could be worse than it is now and comprise mass probation and increasingly punitive CSM. Already France has a great number of CSM being pronounced. On 1 January 2014, probation services were, inter alia, supervising 141,107 people on SME, 36,588 on community work and suspended sentence with community work, and 6,428 on parole. These figures have increased consistently over the last years (contrasting respectively with, for January 2008: 121,700; 24,502; and 6,581; Direction de l'Administration Pénitentiaire 2014); whilst, at the same time, the increase in the prison population has also been consistent, reaching 67,310 in 2013 compared with between 61,000 and 63,000 in the year 2008 (Tournier 2014). Another risk is for JAPs to disappear in the future (Gentilini 2014) as prisonbation increases.

For French researchers, the challenge is to continue being the itching powder of the established order, whilst evaluating current practices. There is an urgent need for a 'blueprint' evaluation of current French practices and their outcome and for the evaluation of the upcoming changes.

References

Aebi, M. F. and Marguet, Y. (eds) (2014) *SPACE II, Annual Penal Statistics, Persons Serving Non-custodial Sanctions and Measures in 2012*. Council of Europe and University of Lausanne.

Amor, P. (1948) 'Le *probation system* ou système de l'épreuve surveillée', *Revue Pénitentiaire et de Droit Pénal*, pp. 6–26.

Ancel, M. (1954) *La Défense Sociale Nouvelle, un Mouvement de Politique Criminelle Humaniste*. Paris: Cujas.

Assemblée Nationale (2000) *La France Face à ses Prisons*. Report of the investigation commission on the situation in French prisons, vols I, II, no. 2521.

Audren, F., Chene, C., Matthey, N. and Vergne, A. (eds) (2013) *Raymond Saleilles et Au-delà*. Paris: Dalloz.

Badinter, R. (1992) *La Prison Républicaine*. Paris: Fayard.

BBC (2014) French unemployment at record high, January 27 – accessible at www.bbc.com/news/business-25922231, consulted 12 July 2014.

Boone, M. and Herzog-Evans, M. (2013) 'Decision-Making and Offender Supervision', in F. McNeill and K. Beyens (eds) *Offender Supervision in Europe*. Basingstoke: Palgrave McMillan, pp. 51–96.

Broudig, F. (1996) *L'interdiction du Breton en 1902. La IIIe République contre les Langues Régionales*. Coop Breizh: Spézet.

Brizais, R. (2006) *Enquête Sociale Rapide, Mission Evaluation des Mesures Socio-Judiciaires*. Citoyens et Justice.

Cario, R. (2012) *Victimologie. De l'Effraction du Lien Intersubjective à La Restauration Sociale*. Paris: l'Harmattan.

Carlier, C. (1989) *L'administration Pénitentiaire et son Personnel dans La France de l'Entre Deux-Guerres, vol. 1, L'impossible Réforme*. Ministère de La Justice, Direction de l'Administration Pénitentiaire; Service des Études et de l'Organisation, coll. 'Archives pénitentiaires', no. 9.

Carlier, C. (2009) 'Histoire des prisons et de l'administration pénitentiaire française de l'Ancien Régime à Nos Jours', *Criminocorpus* [online], *Varia*, uploaded 14 February, consulted 13 July 2014. http://criminocorpus.revues.org/246; DOI: 10.4000/criminocorpus.246.

Castan, N., Faugeron, C., Petit, J.-G., Pierre, M. and Zysberg, A. (1990) *Histoire des Galères, Bagnes et Prisons: XIIIe-xxe Siècles*. Paris: Privat.

Cavadino, M. and Dignan, J. (2006) *Penal Systems: A Comparative Approach*. London: Sage.

Céré, J.-P. (1998) 'Le contentieux disciplinaire dans les établissements pénitentiaires français à l'aune du droit européen', PhD Thesis, Pau.

Chantraine, G. (2010) 'French prisons of yesteryear and today', *Punishment and Society*, 12(1): 27–46.

Cliquennois, G. (2008) 'La réduction des risques et La responsabilisation dans La prise de décision en établissements pour peine', PhD Thesis in sociology, USL and EHESS, Brussels.

Cohen, S. (1985) *Visions of Social Control*. Cambridge: Polity Press.

Commission Nationale Consultative des Droits de l'Homme (2014) *Avis sur le projet relatif à La prévention de La récidive et à l'individualisation des peines*, Assemblée Plénière, 27 March 2014.

Danet, J. (2006) *Justice Pénale: le Tournant*. Paris: Le Monde-Folio.

Danet, J. (ed.) (2013) *La Réponse Pénale. Dix Ans de Traitement des Délits*. Rennes: Presses Universitaires de Rees.

De Certeau, M., Julia, D. and Revel, J. (2002) *Une Politique de La Langue*. Paris: Gallimard.

de Larminat, X. (2012) 'La probation en quête d'approbation. L'exécution des peines en milieu ouvert entre gestion des risques et gestion des flux'. Thèse Cesdip-Université de Versailles–Saint Quentin.

De Mesmaecker, V. (2014) *Perceptions of Criminal Justice*. Abingdon: Routledge.

de Suremain, H. (2014) 'Genèse de La naissance de La "guérilla juridique" et premiers combats contentieux', in Slama S. and Ferran N. (eds) *Défendre en justice la cause des personnes détenues*. Actes du colloque des 25 et 26 janvier 2013, Paris: La Documentation Française: 47–52.

Dhume-Sonzogini, F. (2007) *Liberté, égalité, communauté? L'Etat français contre le communautarisme*. Paris: Homnisphères.

Dindo, S. (2011) 'Sursis avec mise à l'épreuve: la peine méconnue. Une analyse des pratiques de probation en France'. Etude pour La Direction de l'administration pénitentiaire, bureau PMJ1, mai.

Direction de l'Administration Pénitentiaire (2014) *Statistiques trimestrielles de La population prise en charge en milieu fermé*. Bureau des Etudes et de La Prospective, Ministère de La Justice, no.136.

Downes, D. and Hansen, K. (2006) *Welfare and punishment in comparative perspective*, in S. Armstrong and L. McAra (eds) *Perspectives on Punishment: The Contours of Control*. Oxford, Oxford University Press. pp. 133–54.

Dréan-Rivette, I. (2005) *La personnalisation de La peine dans le code pénal*. Paris: l'Harmattan.

Dréan-Rivette, I. (2006) 'L'article 132-24 alinéa 2. Une perte d'intelligibilité de La loi pénale?', *Actualité juridique pénal*. 117–18.

Durnescu, I. (2011) 'Pains of probation: Effective practice and human rights', *International Journal of Offender Therapy and Comparative Criminology*, 55(4): 530–45.

Farrall, S. (2002) *Rethinking What Works with Offenders*. Cullompton, Devon: Willan.

Farrall, S., Hunter, B., Sharpe, G. and Calverley, A. (2014) *Criminal Careers in Transition. The Social Context of Desistance from Crime*. Oxford: Oxford University Press.

Gentilini, A. (2014) Le juge de l'application des peines: vers une disparition?', in F. Ghelfi (ed.) *Le Droit de l'Exécution des Peines. Espoirs ou Désillusion*. Paris: l'Harmattan, pp. 107–20.

Germain, L. and Lassalle, D. (eds) (2008) *Communautés, Communautarisme: Aspects Comparatifs*. Paris: L'Harmattan.

Herzog-Evans, M. (1994) 'La gestion du comportement du détenu. L'apparence légaliste du droit pénitentiaire'. PhD thesis Criminal Law, Poitiers (later published: La Gestion du Comportement du Détenu. Essai de Droit Pénitentiaire. Paris: l'Harmattan, 1998).

Herzog-Evans, M. (2011) 'Desisting in France: What probation officers know and do. A first approach', *European Journal of Probation*, 3(2): 29–46.

Herzog-Evans, M. (2012) 'The six month limit to community measures "under prison registry": a study of professional perception', *European Journal of Probation*, 4(2): 23–45.

Herzog-Evans, M. (2012–2013a) *Droit de l'Exécution des Peines*. Paris: Dalloz.

Herzog-Evans, M. (2012–2013b) *Droit Pénitentiaire*. Paris: Dalloz.

Herzog-Evans, M. (2013a) 'What's in a name: Penological and institutional connotations of probation officers' labelling in Europe', *Eurovista*, 2(3): 121–33.

Herzog-Evans, M. (2013b) 'Récidive et surpopulation: pas de baguette magique juridique', *Actualité Juridique Pénal*, March: pp. 136–9.

Herzog-Evans, M. (2014a) 'Is the French *juge de l'application des peines* a Problem-Solving Court?', in M. Herzog-Evans (ed.) *Offender Release and Supervision: The Role of Courts and the Use of Discretion*. Nijmegen: Wolf Legal Publishers.

Herzog-Evans, M. (2014b) *French Reentry Courts and Rehabilitation: Mister Jourdain of Desistance*. Paris: l'Harmattan.

Herzog-Evans, M. (2014c) 'Explaining French probation: social work in a prison administration', in I. Durnescu and F. McNeill (eds) (2013) *Understanding Penal Practice*. Abingdon: Routledge, pp. 63–76.

Herzog-Evans, M. (2014d) 'French third sector participation in probation and reentry: Complementary or competitive?', *European Journal of Probation*, 6(1): 42–56.

Herzog-Evans, M. (ed.) (2015) *Offender Release and Supervision: The Role of Courts and the Use of Discretion*. Nijmegen: Wolf Legal Publishers.

Hough, M. (2015) 'Legitimacy and executive release: a procedural justice perspective', in M. Herzog-Evans (ed.) *Offender Release and Supervision: The Role of Courts and the Use of Discretion*. Nijmegen: Wolf Legal Publishers.

Hough, M., Jacobson, J. and Millie, A. (2003) *The Decision to Imprison: Sentencing and the Prison Population*. London: Prison Reform Trust.

Johnson, T. J. (1972) *Professions and Power*. London and Basingstoke: Macmillan.

Julhiet, E. (1906) *Les Tribunaux pour Enfants aux Etats-Unis*. Paris: Arthur Rousseau.

Kaluszynski, M. (1996) 'Production de La Loi et Genèse des Politiques Pénales en France sous La IIIème République'. Rapport pour le GIP Justice/CNRS, October.

Kaluszynski, M. (2001) 'La réforme des prisons sous La troisième République. Une co-gestion d'acteurs publics et privé', *Revue Française d'Administration Publique*, no. 99, July to September: pp. 393–403.

Kaluszynski, M. (2013) 'La science pénitentiaire comme science de gouvernement. Espaces juridiques, réseaux réformateurs et savoirs experts en France à La fin du XIXe siècle', *Revue d'Anthropologie des Connaissances*, 7(1): 87–111.

Lacey, N. (2008) *The Prisoners' Dilemma. Political Economy and Punishment in Contemporary Democracies*. Cambridge: Cambridge University Press.

Landfried, J. (2007) *Contre le communautarisme*. Paris: Armand Colin.

Lévy, L. (2005) *Le Spectre du Communautarisme*. Paris: Editions Amsterdam.

Lind, E.A. and Tyler, T. R. (1988) *The Social Psychology of Procedural Justice*. Dordrecht: Kluwer Academic/Plenum Publishers.

Lucas, C. (1872) 'Examen critique du congrès international pénitentiaire de Londres', Monograph.

Mair, G. and Burke, L. (2012) *Redemption, Rehabilitation and Risk Management. A history of probation*. Abingdon: Routledge.

Maruna, S. and LeBel, T.P. (2003) 'Welcome home? Examining the "reentry court" concept from a strengths-based perspective', *Western Criminology Review*, 4(2): 97–107.

May, D. C. and Wood, P. B. (2010) *Ranking Correctional Punishments. Views from Offenders, Practitioners, and the Public*. Carolina: Academic Press.

Mayhew, P. and Van Kesteren, J. (2002) 'Cross-national attitudes to punishment?', in M. Hough and Julian V. Roberts (eds) *Changing Attitudes to Punishment. Public Opinion, Crime and Justice*. Cullompton, Devon: Willan, pp. 63–92.

McNeill, F. (2013) 'Community Sanctions and European Penology', in T. Daems, D. Van Zyl Smit and S. Snacken (eds) *European Penology?*. Oxford: Hart Publishing, O nati International Series in Law and Society, pp. 171–91.

Miclo, F., Grossmann, R. and Adler, A. (2002) *La République Minoritaire: Contre le Communautarisme*. Paris: Michalon.

Nash, M. (1999) 'Enter the "polibation officer"', *International Journal of Police Science and Management*, 1(4): 360–8.

Péchillon, R. (1999) *Sécurité et Droit du Service Public Pénitentiaire*. Paris: LGDJ.

Perrier, Y. (2012) 'Insertion et probation: retour sur une histoire', in P. Mbanzoulou, M. Herzog-Evans and S. Courtine (eds) *Insertion et Désistance des Personnes Placées sous Main de Justice. Savoirs et Pratiques*. Paris: l'Harmattan, pp. 181–98.

Perrier, Y. (2013) *La probation de 1885 à 2005. Sanctions et Mesures dans La Communauté*. Paris: Dalloz.

Phelps, M. (2013) 'The paradox of probation', *Law and Policy*, 35(1–2): 51–80.

Pisani-Ferry, J. (2014) *Quelle France dans Dix Ans? Les Chantiers de La Décennie*. France Stratégie, Report to the President of the Republic, June.

Robinson, G., McNeill, F. and Maruna, S. (2013) 'Punishment *in* Society: The Improbable Persistence of Probation and Other Community Sanctions and Measures', in J. Simon and J. Sparks (eds) *The Sage Handbook of Punishment and Society*. London: Sage, pp. 321–40.

Saleilles, R. (1898) *L'individualisation de La Peine*: *Étude de Criminalité Sociale*. Paris: Germer Baillière et Cie, Félix Alcan (in English: *The Individualization of Punishment*. Bibliobazaar, reprinted 2009).

Scheirs, V., Beyens, K. and Snacken, S. (2014) 'Who's in charge? Conditional release in Belgium as a complex bifurcation practice', in M. Herzog-Evans (ed.) *Offender Release and Supervision: The Role of Courts and the Use of Discretion*. Nijmegen: Wolf Legal Publishers.

Sénat (2000) *Prisons: Une Humiliation pour La République*. Report of the Investigation Commission on detention conditions in French prisons, no. 449, vols I, II, Paris.

Snacken, S., Beyens, K. and Beernaert, M. A. (2010) 'Belgium', in N. Padfield, D. Van Zyl Smit and F. Dünkel (eds) *Release from Prison. European Policy and Practice*. Cullompton, Devon: Willan Publishing, pp. 70–103.

Snacken, S. and Dumortier, S. (eds) (2012) *Resisting Punitiveness in Europe? Welfare, Human Rights and Democracy*. London: Routledge.

Tanguy, M. (2007) *Le congrès pénitentiaire international de Stockholm*, Histoire pénitentiaire, vol. 6, Travaux et Documents, Direction de l'Administration pénitentiaire, Ministère de la Justice.

Tombs, J. (2004) *A Unique Punishment. Sentencing and the Prison Population in Scotland*. Edinburgh: The Scottish Consortium on Crime and Criminal Justice.

Tonry, M. (2007) 'Determinant of penal policies', in M. Tonry (ed.) *Crime, Punishment, and Politics in Comparative Perspective*. Chicago: Chicago University Press, pp. 1–48.

Tournier, P. V. (2014) Nouvelles series pénales temporelles (NSEPT) Actualisées au 1er Octobre 2013, Université Paris Panthéon-Sorbonne.

Tribunal de Grande Instance de Créteil (2014) 'Les obstacles à l'aménagement des peines. L'impact des courtes périodes de détention sur La mise en oeuvre des aménagements de peine', report, 11 March.

Van de Kerchove, M. (2008) 'Le sens de La peine dans La jurisprudence du Conseil constitutionnel français', *Revue de Sciences Criminelles et de Droit Pénal Comparé*, pp. 805–24.

Van der Wolf, M. and Herzog-Evans, M. (2015) 'Supervision and detention of dangerous offenders in France and the Netherlands: a comparative and human rights' perspective', in M. Herzog-Evans (ed.) *Offender Release and Supervision: The Role of Courts and the Use of Discretion*. Nijmegen: Wolf Legal Publishers.

Vasseur, M. (2000) *Médecin-Chef à La Prison de La Santé*. Paris: Le Cherche Midi.

Wandall, R. (2008) *Decision to Imprison. Court Decision-Making Inside and Outside the Law*. Aldershot: Ashgate.

5

'DER RESOZIALISIERUNGSGRUNDSATZ'

Social reintegration as the dominant narrative for community punishment in Germany?

Christine Morgenstern

Introduction

'*Resozialisierung*', best translated into English as 'social reintegration',[1] as the most important aim of punishment has not really been contested in Germany since the 1970s. Within the Criminal Justice System the *Resozialisierungsgrundsatz* serves as the overarching principle for sentencing, for the execution of sentences and for dealing with offenders once the sentence has been served. It equally claims validity for all types of sanctions and measures, custodial or non-custodial (or, as in German usage, 'ambulant'). Accordingly, the question whether an intervention serves or is contrary to this aim can often be found as the leading argument in judicial decisions, and in criminal policy debates new developments are usually measured against the principle.

But the commitment to resocialization often seems to be formal and superficial; the shape and content of the concept have remained vague (Cornel 2009; Hassemer 2002; Lüderssen 1991). Interpretations differ not only between the disciplines and professional groups involved (criminology, law, social work), but also within these groups. This is partly due to the fact that in the last decades other penal adaptations that have been characterized as influential for shaping particular community sanctions – managerial, punitive and reparative adaptations (Robinson *et al.* 2013) – can be found in Germany just as elsewhere. Many discussions, however, are prison related: '*Resozialisierung*' is defined as the main aim of executing a prison sentence in the German Prison Act, while, in a quite 'un-German' way, an act that regulates the execution of community sanctions does not even exist. This chapter concentrates on the development and existing contours of social reintegration as a 'penal strategy' (Robinson 2008) with regard to community punishment and considers where the conceptualization has been weak and vulnerable to other influences and penal adaptations.

Some theoretical foundations

The constitutional basis

The relatively unchallenged status of the principle of resocialization is based on a decision from 1973 by the Federal Constitutional Court.[2] In the relevant passage of the judgment, the court argued that:

> from the point of view of the offender, this interest in resocialization accrues from his constitutional rights in terms of article 2 (1) in conjunction with article 1 of the Basic Law. Viewed from the perspective of the community, the principle of the social state requires public care and assistance for those groups in the community who, because of personal weakness or fault, incapacity or social disadvantage, were adversely affected in their social development; prisoners and ex-prisoners also belong to this group. Not least, resocialization serves the protection of the community itself: it lies in its distinct interest that the offender will not re-offend.
>
> *(All translations provided by the author*
> *unless indicated otherwise)*

So the idea that social reintegration should be the end towards which the penal system should strive has its foundation in a constitutional principle – the principle of the 'social state' (Sozialstaatsprinzip, Art. 20 (3) Basic Law). The 'social state' corresponds roughly with the notion of the 'welfare state', including the constitutional obligation for the state to cater for social security and social justice. The second constitutional leg is an individual human rights position: the respect for human dignity and the right to develop the personality freely (Art. 1 and 2 Basic Law). The principle of resocialization as legal entitlement consists of both negative fundamental rights against state infringements (the right to be left alone) and positive rights to state action.

Penal theory

The German criminal justice model can be seen as standing in the neoclassic, liberal continental tradition: It is characterized by the principles of individual responsibility, minimum (penal) intervention and proportionate punishment. The penal sanction is limited by the principle of culpability (or guilt principle, *Schuldgrundsatz*), again rooted in the constitutional guarantee to protect human dignity (Hörnle 2013). But equally modern or utilitarian approaches, taking into account empirical perspectives, namely the offender's personality and needs, were of great importance for its development (prominently represented by von Liszt 1883).

Today, both approaches are combined in various forms. With his influential *dialektische Vereinigungstheorie*, Roxin (1966) presented a combination model that attributes different aims to different stages of the criminal justice process. In the first tier, represented by the criminal law with its description of the offence and the sanctions that can be imposed, all citizens are addressed and the aim is general prevention. In the sentencing stage, as the second tier, retribution (within the limits of the guilt principle mentioned above) is dominant. In the execution of sentences, as the third tier, the only aim that needs to be pursued is special prevention with a focus on reintegration, although it is also possible to consider risks. Even if the question of how exactly to combine the approaches mentioned (and integrate, for example, a restorative approach) is disputed ceaselessly, Germany is a good example of the 'relative autonomy' between the aims of *imposing* and *enforcing* penal sanctions (van Zyl Smit and Snacken 2009: 76).

Terminology

'Punishment'

Our editors entrusted us with the task of reflecting on their choice of title for this book. Indeed both parts of the term 'community punishment' require some comment in the German context.

State reactions to criminal offences in Germany are applied in a so-called two-track system: the Penal Code provides the first track for penal sentences (*Strafen*), the most commonly used being the day fine, followed by suspended and unsuspended prison sentences. The second track contains 'measures of correction and security' (*Maßregeln der Besserung und Sicherung*).[3] Only the first track is designed as punishment; the aim of the second is exclusively preventive. That means that 'measures' are intended to incapacitate or support the offender who, according to judicial assessment, poses a risk to society. They are ordered instead of or in addition to a penal sentence.

Some measures are designed exclusively for those not or not fully held criminally responsible, namely the mental hospital order (sec. 63 Penal Code) and the custodial addiction treatment order (sec. 64 Penal Code). Other measures, however, can be applied to both criminally responsible and criminally irresponsible offenders. The most prominent and problematic amongst them is preventive detention (*Sicherungsverwahrung*) for a long or even indefinite period after the completion of the initial sentence. Its ambulant equivalent that is of special interest here is the 'supervision of conduct order' (*Führungsaufsicht*), sometimes also translated as 'intensive supervision'.

Most legal scholars insist on the important difference between penalties on the one hand and preventive measures on the other – the latter are not supposed to be punishment and therefore not subject to the same legal constraints, such as sentence proportionality or the prohibition on retrospective imposition. This view is also taken by the Federal Constitutional Court. This doctrinal discussion is beyond the scope of this chapter (for a discussion, see Drenkhahn *et al.* 2012). It nevertheless is interesting in two ways: First, the European Court of Human Rights in 2009 did not endorse this opinion in the case of preventive detention; its line of argument was roughly: this intervention looks like prison, feels like prison, is enforced in prisons, so whatever you call it, we call it a penalty.[4] Whether it would take the same stance with regard to the intensive supervision order, however, is not clear. Supervision practice will be described in more detail below. For the moment it can be said that the differences between the execution of a 'normal' probation order as attached to a suspended sentence and an intensive supervision order following longer terms of imprisonment in practice are small enough to include it in this contribution.

Second, when discussing and justifying the two-track-approach, it has been argued that the existence of the (severe) preventive measures contributes to the relatively low imprisonment rate observed in Germany. According to three leading German scholars, Hassemer (2006), Albrecht (2013a) and Hörnle (2013), it functions as a 'safety valve' (Albrecht 2013a: 213) that allows the judiciary to stick to moderate, proportionate sentences, because if an ongoing risk is observed such a preventive measure will or can follow. They argue and justify their view with reference to the small numbers of those in preventive detention (the measure is applied in roughly 100 cases per year; currently almost 450 persons are in preventive detention). It 'characterizes a penal system that exposes a few offenders to extreme (indeterminate and possibly lifelong) measures of security in exchange for routine sentence application in the first track of criminal sanctions' (Albrecht 2013a: 221; see also Hörnle 2013: 205). None of them mentions that intensive supervision has developed at a virtually exponential rate (see below). Apart from depriving their arguments of much of their persuasiveness, this omission reflects perfectly well the introductory observations by our editors that community punishment still is not represented well enough in scholarly research and that the simple but misleading equation punishment = prison continues to be assumed.

'Community'

The use of the label 'community' often serves, as the editors pointed out in the Introduction, to avoid the term 'non-custodial'. In Germany to this end sanctions and measures enforced *extra muros* often are called 'ambulant' measures. This neutral and therefore handy expression, however, is wide and may include, for example, financial sanctions such as the German day fines, which do not comprise any conditions or obligations that need to be supervised.

'Community' also conveys the notion of the offender remaining part of a community – and the community being in one way or another involved in the implementation 'to assist offenders to develop meaningful ties in the community, to become aware of the community's interest in them and to broaden their possibilities for contact and support', as the European Rules for Community Sanctions and Measures put in their No. 46 (Council of Europe 1992). The German Constitutional Court as quoted above points in the same direction. The placement in the community with a (possible) involvement of the community in Germany can be found in several types of sanctions that involve supervision by a state authority with or without the involvement of a third-sector agency and possibly also volunteers from the community.

Summing up, the term 'community punishment' fits the German discussion, because it includes state reactions to a crime, addresses (adult) offenders held responsible for their crime and involves a significant restriction on the offender's liberty through the imposition of conditions and obligations that are imposed as the result of a conviction.

Community punishment in practice

Development and current scope

The main types of community punishment[5] for adults that involve supervision today are (regardless of their legal classification):

- the suspended prison sentence with a probation order or under other conditions (*Strafaussetzung zur Bewährung*);
- the conditional release from prison after serving part of a sentence (*Strafrestaussetzung zur Bewährung*);
- the intensive supervision order (*Führungsaufsicht*) that is implemented after the full completion of a prison sentence;
- community service (*gemeinnützige Arbeit*) in case of fine default to avoid fine-default detention.

For young offenders under 18 years old and in many cases also for young adult offenders under 21, a special juvenile justice system exists. It has a distinct sanction system and, at least partly, distinct agencies that implement these sanctions. This chapter will therefore for the most part concentrate on the system for adults over the age of 21.

A suspended sentence was introduced for the first time in the Juvenile Justice Act of 1923 to enable 'the convict to earn the remission of his sentence by good conduct during a probationary period' (Sec. 10 JJA 1923), but no probation service existed at that time. This practice for juveniles was later discontinued under the Nazi-Regime. In 1953, the possibility to suspend sentences of imprisonment under conditions or without conditions was (re)introduced in the Penal Code for adults and in the JJA 1953. Initially only prison sentences up to nine months could be suspended, and suspension was not possible for most recidivists.

With the major penal reform of 1969 the scope was significantly expanded. Since then, sentences of up to 1 year of imprisonment must be suspended, when 'there are reasons to believe that the sentence will serve as a sufficient warning to the convicted person and that, even without the effect of serving of the sentence, he will commit no further offences' (sec. 56 (1) PC). Up to 2 years of imprisonment may be suspended in special cases of a positive criminal prognosis (sec. 56 (2) PC). The parliamentary material for this expansion, which fell in a time of liberal penal policy-making, generally speaks of the 'offending citizen' and the need for his 'social adjustment'. A suspension of a prison sentence is not 'an act of mercy but an important tool of modern criminal policy'. It is argued that experiences made abroad show that a suspension is suitable not only for first time offenders but also for more difficult offenders, provided that they receive support and guidance that are 'a special form of ambulant treatment that is often successful and can avoid negative consequences of imprisonment' (Deutscher Bundestag 1969a: 10).

Statistics show that today 77 per cent of all prison sentences of up to one year are suspended, but also almost 73 per cent of those up to 2 years. Initially this option was used quite reluctantly with only 8 per cent in 1975. As recently as 1990 only half of all prison sentences between 1 and 2 years were suspended (Heinz 2012). The reason for the courts' ever increasing trust in both options can probably be seen in the relatively low rates of revocation that for many years have been around 30 per cent. Two thirds of them are revocations due to new offences, but they do not necessarily lead back to prison (Heinz 2012). The story of suspended sentences therefore is told as a success story, partly confirmed also by recent studies on recidivism (see below).

As a result, in Germany the overall percentage of unsuspended prison sentences is small compared to many other countries.[6] Table 5.1 shows also the number of custodial *measures*, which has significantly risen, but because of low absolute numbers has not changed the sentencing landscape dramatically. The sentence pattern therefore has remained relatively stable for decades.

This does not, however, mean that 95 per cent of those sentenced never see a prison from the inside, because some of those who get their suspension revoked as well as those who do not pay their fines may finally end up in prison. Nevertheless, criminal punishment in Germany for the by far largest part takes place 'on the streets'.

To assess their development over time, the four types of community punishment mentioned above need to be explained further. Prison sentences may be suspended with the sole condition not to reoffend within a period of between 2 and 5 years. They can also be suspended under conditions, either under conditions that are intended as legal restraints with a certain punishing, according to the law

TABLE 5.1 Sentences in Germany, 1980–2012

	Adults convicted	Fine		Suspended prison sentence		Unsuspended prison sentence		Custodial measures under sec. 63, 64 PC
	n	n	%	n	%	n	%	n
1980	599,832	494,114	82.4	68,878	11.5	35,972	5.9	805
1990	615,089	512,343	83.3	69,705	13.2	32,749	6.4	1058
2000	638,893	513,336	80.3	84,552	13.2	40,753	6.4	879
2010★	704,802	575,068	81.9	92,073	13.1	37,661	5.3	3026
2012★	682,206	560,377	82.1	85,436	12.5	36,373	5.3	3034

★Since 2007 the statistics comprise data from the whole of Germany; before, only West Germany was included.

Source: Statistisches Bundesamt, Strafverfolgungstatistik.

'compensating', effect (*Auflagen*). Also directives (*Weisungen*) can be attached that are intended to support and guide offenders with criminogenic needs. *Auflagen* are the payment or other forms of compensation to the victim, the payment of a fixed sum of money to the state treasury or a charity, or community service. In about two-thirds of all suspensions, this kind of condition is added to the suspension, usually consisting of a financial obligation of the second kind (Heinz 2012). *Weisungen* may consist of obligations to follow instructions that relate to the convict's residence, education, work or leisure, or to the ordering of financial affairs; to report to the court or another authority; not to have contact with the victim or other persons; not to keep certain objects; or to pay alimony. With the consent of the convict, the directive may also consist of medical and/or addiction treatment. Part of the non-exhaustive catalogue of supportive directives is also the probation order: according to sec. 56d PC, 'the court shall place the convicted person under the supervision and guidance of a probation officer for all or part of the operational period if this appears necessary to prevent him from committing offences'. Typically it shall do so if the suspended prison sentence is longer than 9 months and the convicted person is younger than 27 years old. With this provision, which has been included in the Penal Code since 1953, the legislator followed the suggestions to legally introduce the Probation Service that had been founded in 1951. The development was influenced by experiences in other countries, namely the United Kingdom (Mutz 2008).

Our second type of community punishment is the suspension of the latter part of a prison sentence (*Strafrestaussetzung*). The same conditions may be applied as for the initial suspension. All prisoners are eligible for release when they have served two-thirds of their sentences; in the case of life sentences, they are normally eligible for release after 15 years. The release depends on a positive prognosis; according to sec. 57 PC, release must be 'accounted for with regard to public security interests' and the prisoner must consent. Those imprisoned for the first time and serving a sentence of a maximum of 2 years may be released after having served half of their term, but this option is rarely used (Heinz 2012).

The modalities of actually suspending a sentence in practice seem to have undergone a change in recent years. Figure 5.1 shows, in the columns, the actual number of ongoing probation orders at the end of the year, while the curve shows the prison sentences pronounced. Both cannot be correlated directly. However, the figure illustrates the longitudinal development. Fewer prison sentences have been passed in recent years, both unsuspended and suspended, while the number of probation orders attached to suspended sentences has become increasingly popular and shows an unbroken upward trend. The increase is exclusively caused by the growth of initial probation orders, while the number of parole cases with such an order has remained relatively stable. In his thorough analysis of the German sentencing practice, Heinz (2012) argues that, because of the shift from custodial to ambulant, and in particular to informal sanctions, those actually receiving a (suspended) prison sentence represent a more and more difficult clientele in terms of criminal records, as well as in terms of social needs. This can be shown by the share

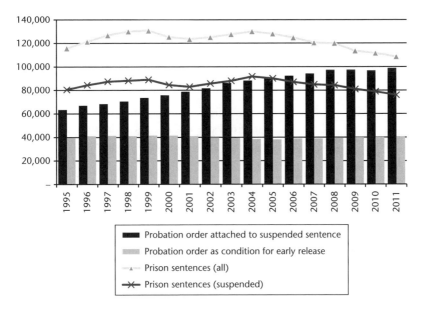

FIGURE 5.1   Probation orders in West Germany

of probationers who have been imprisoned or under probation supervision before. This, on the other hand, shows a consistent willingness of German judges to rely on non-custodial options.

A third group of persons that are punished in the community are those under intensive supervision. They are a heterogeneous group: both mentally ill offenders that are conditionally released from a psychiatric hospital and those who have served their prison sentence in full are targeted. The underlying aim is to prevent recidivism from offenders that are deemed both 'dangerous and endangered' (Deutscher Bundestag 1969b: 35), meaning that they pose a risk for the public but also need support to address social and criminogenic needs. The measure was introduced in 1975 but has its roots in an earlier police supervision which provided no room for reintegrating or supporting activities. Various sub-types exist; the type in question here addresses offenders that have been held criminally responsible. Again: legally this is not a punishment but a 'measure', but may, in my view, be seen as an additional penalty for those not eligible for parole. According to sec. 68f PC, the 'supervision of conduct order' must, in principle, be applied after all prison sentences of at least 2 years that have been fully served; for some sex offences this term is only 1 year. If it can be expected, however, that without supervision relapse will not occur, the court can decide not to order it. The supervision normally lasts between 2 and 5 years.

The formal control of the order is exerted by the court and the person concerned is assigned to a probation officer. Other actors are the 'supervising institutions' (which in most Federal States, *Länder*, are part of the regional court administration and employ judges and probation officers) and, in special cases, the recently introduced forensic psychiatric clinics. The mixture of roles and the complicated collaboration of actors are characteristics of this type of order. In a noteworthy wording, sec. 68 PC prescribes that the 'probation officer and the supervising institution are, in mutual agreement, standing by the convicted person to help and support him'. Usually one or more concrete directives are attached to the order. The court can choose from 12 possibilities, some more controlling, some more supporting. Apart from the classic ones addressing housing, money or work-related problems, several new directives have been introduced more recently.

In 1998, 2007 and 2010, major reforms have intensified control, but, to a lesser extent, also support tools. Since 1998, for certain serious sex offences, the supervision may last for an indefinite period, possibly for a lifetime. In 2007 the so-called therapy directive was introduced. There is still no possibility to order a coercive therapy; psychotherapy, alcohol or drug treatment and similar forms are only possible when the person concerned consents. But the supervisee must at least regularly see a therapist if ordered to do so. In that way reluctant offenders should be motivated to try a therapy. In the same reform the directive not to consume alcohol or drugs was included in the catalogue. Also the forensic-psychiatric clinics, usually attached to a (private) mental hospital, were introduced to provide tools and drop-in places for crisis situations. In 2010 electronic monitoring of certain violent or sex offenders was introduced under certain restrictive conditions. One feature of this type of order is that serious violations of the directives constitute offences (sec. 145a PC). Since breach procedures may not simply reinstitute the original prison sentence, as it is already fully served, this was deemed necessary as a means of control for the probation service. The offence can be punished with a prison sentence: before 2007, up to 1 year; now, up to 3 years.

The fourth group of offenders under supervision by the probation service or, more often, third-sector providers, are those carrying out community service. Most of them are doing this work for defaulting on fine payments. Estimates show that between 5 and 7 per cent of all fines lead to fine-default detention and that numbers, probably because of increasing social problems for some of the clientele, have risen (Albrecht 2013b). While the Penal Code only allows for imprisonment for fine default (sec. 43 PC), since the 1980s the *Länder* one after another have introduced the possibility of avoiding detention by doing community work. The modalities differ, and 1 day of fine-default detention equals 3–6 working hours, depending on the *Land* and the nature of work. In some regions special programmes have been established to reach out to those clients that, often because of multiple social problems, neither pay their fine nor manage to organize their community service. These programmes, but also a generally increased willingness of the enforcing authorities to accept applications to work instead of serving fine-default detention have helped to at least alleviate the problem (Dünkel 2011).

Exactly how many people are clients of the Probation Service or other agencies and supervised in the community is hard to tell, because federal probation statistics cover only certain aspects and still only compile data for West Germany. No comprehensive data at all exist on the number of people carrying out community service for fine default. On the contrary, and well in line with the over-representation of prison issues in research and policy, comprehensive prison statistics are available. They show a constant decrease both in stock and flow since 2005. While much ado is made about this development (Albrecht 2013a) and even the media take notice (the *Süddeutsche Zeitung*, 23 January 2014, titled '*Resozialisierung: Im Knast sind viele Zellen frei*' [Resocialization: There are many empty cells in the clink]), the full correctional picture is not painted, as Figure 5.2 shows.

Correctional population in Germany 2004: ca. 254,700

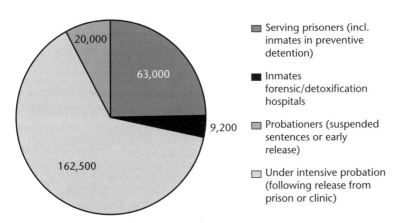

Correctional population in Germany 2012: ca. 274,000

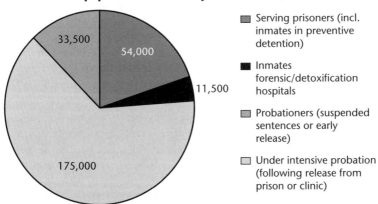

FIGURE 5.2 Correctional population, 2004 and 2012

Source: Author's estimates on the basis of Federal Statistics; AG Psychiatrie der Obersten Landesgesundheitsbehörden (2012: 15); Grosser and Maelicke (2009: 185); and Reckling (2014).

And who is doing the supervision and probation work? While third-sector providers take a role in supervising community service, provide resettlement services and, to a lesser extent, also provide special services such as psychiatric and psychological aftercare, it is usually the Probation Service. As indicated, the numbers of probation orders attached to suspended sentences and the numbers of intensive supervision orders have risen dramatically. Only scant statistics, however, exist for the number of professional probation officers. According to Heinz (2012), relying on data provided by the Ministries of Justice, the caseload per probation officer was on average 74 (in 2003) and 82 (in 2006). Volunteers do have a role in the execution of probation supervision, but usually only in supplementary functions. A recent evaluation in Baden-Württemberg showed that the number of clients has increased far more than expected. The caseload in 2006 was 96 and in 2011, 78, achieved mainly by employing more probation workers and to a lesser degree by involving the volunteers more actively (Dölling *et al.* 2014).

Key moments and problems

The most important moment for the criminal justice system in its current form was 1969, when the reformed Penal Code was adopted and earlier developments, such as the introduction of the Probation Service in 1953, were significantly strengthened. A lot less important than one might expect was the political change that took place in 1990 and the years after the German reunification. It is true that the 1990s were dominated by rising crime and prison rates, partly as reaction to the political and social overthrow in Germany and its Eastern neighbours, which influenced the penal climate (Dünkel and Morgenstern 2010). The Eastern *Länder* were busy building up functioning administrative and judicial systems, among them the probation services. These new *Länder* did not entirely copy the Western model as they all opted for a unified criminal justice social service for adults (instead of having separate services for probation, court aid, victim–offender mediation etc.). But no influences of former practices in the German Democratic Republic (GDR) can be traced; everything was modelled on existing practices in West Germany. A probation system in the strict sense did not exist in the GDR; all was supposed to be regulated by 'the collective'. This meant, for example, that bigger companies, all state-owned, employed social workers that dealt with social problems of all sorts, among them ex-prisoners. The strong interdependency between state, company and social workers, however, was something that after reunification was met with deep suspicion. Some of these social workers later successfully took part in the setting up of a functioning, professional probation service Western style in the Eastern part of Germany (Loy 2010). However, the work of volunteers in probation or prisoner resettlement is less frequent in East Germany (Stelly and Thomas 2009).

In the 1990s the existing sanctioning system came under pressure from various sides. A long and comprehensive debate by practitioners, scholars and politicians led to almost nothing: neither were the possibilities to suspend prison sentences extended (despite many suggestions by experts to do so), nor was community service established as a sentence in its own right. The latter had been advocated to better avoid fine-default detention; but the reform also was to be sold as useful and painful at the same time under the slogan '*Schwitzen statt sitzen*', 'sweating instead of serving' (Morgenstern 2002). There was also a widespread scepticism against electronic monitoring, which was generally rejected as unsuitable and constitutionally problematic (Groß 2012). Only the State of Hessen showed early (and still unbroken) enthusiasm when it introduced electronic monitoring in 2000. It serves mainly as a directive for suspended sentences there, first in a pilot, but, since 2004, as a regular option. A second Federal State, Baden-Württemberg, piloted electronic monitoring between 2009 and 2013. After a change of government, however, no regular scheme was introduced.

No reformatory efforts affecting the sanction system as such have been seen since, other than a small and recent debate around driving bans as sentences in their own right. This is supposed to replace fines for those 'who do not feel them hard enough' (as spelled out in the Coalition Agreement between the current governing parties; CDU and SPD 2013: 146). This driving ban would be entirely punitive; it would not, however, represent community punishment involving supervision as of interest here.

A distinct penal reform of the year 1998 (introducing the 'Act on the Prevention of Sexual Offences and other Dangerous Criminal Acts'), however, marked a significant toughening up of (some) sentences and practices: It was mainly directed at expanding prison sentences for sex and violent offences, but also lead to the expanded forms of intensive supervision discussed above. During a recent conference the role of the media in the reintegration of offenders was discussed. A journalist (Lakotta 2014) from one of the leading German quality journals, *Der Spiegel*, pointed to the 'unholy alliance' between politics and (some) media by quoting the former chancellor Schroeder. In an interview with a tabloid newspaper in 1998, he had said that the only possibility to deal with certain sex offenders was 'Wegsperren für immer' ('lock 'em up forever'). This catchy remark has become a slogan, has been quoted in nearly every publication dealing with penal policy ever since and certainly had profound and long-lasting implications for the overall penal climate.

The year 2007, as well as the above-mentioned reform of the intensive supervision order that boosted its use, also saw the first privatization of a probation service, in Baden-Württemberg. While privatization as transfer of State responsibilities to private institutions and in particular to commercial companies is a constitutionally contested issue, it is not uncommon – one German prison operates nearly fully privatized, as do most private forensic-psychiatric hospitals. Nevertheless the move to privatization, more precisely to contracting with the private Austrian company Neustart, seemed to mark a new era for probation and was met with a lot of criticism. Neustart for the last 50 years provided for all criminal justice social work in Austria. The company is a for-profit organization; it is, however, working 'for the public good' (*gemeinnützig*), so that it profits from certain tax reductions but must reinvest all profits in the enterprise. The contract was prepared in 2002 under the clear requirement of a lean criminal justice administration and organizational reform. The private company was expected to provide a better quality service (measured for example in revocations) delivered more efficiently – meaning with less costly staff than expensive public servants. Also volunteers have been recruited more actively than before. A recently published evaluation report shows mixed results with regard to performance and (cost) efficiency (Dölling *et al.* 2014), but the plans of the new government of Baden-Württemberg to resocialize the service (i.e. put it back in state hands) have been withdrawn for the time being.

The last key moment for community punishment came in December 2009, when, as a consequence of the above-mentioned verdict of the European Court of Human Rights in the case of M., nearly 100 persons, all of them with the label 'still very dangerous', had to be released from preventive detention. Apart from the public outcry, the media hysterics and the problems for probation services and other institutions dealing with this situation, this led to a broad reform not only of preventive detention, but also of ambulant forms of securing, controlling and – if at all possible – reintegrating dangerous offenders. For the intensive supervision order this brought in 2011 electronic monitoring as an additional directive and the final breakthrough for electronic monitoring (and its provider Elmotech). It is applied now in the whole of Germany, with a central institution for the monitoring in Hessen. According to preliminary results of an ongoing evaluation study, only a few offenders are affected, but their number is rising quickly, from 31 at the end of 2012 to 68 in February 2014 (Baur and Kinzig 2013).

Additionally the intensive supervision order in recent years has been closely linked to preventive schemes by the police, intensifying the control aspect. Indications can be found that the willingness of the responsible probation officers to exert more control may have increased: until recently only very few offences of breaching supervision directives have been prosecuted, because a prosecution depends on an application by the 'supervising institution'. So far this has been very unpopular because of the consequences for the relationship between probation officer and client. The crime statistics now show a rise from 700 cases in 2009 to over 1200 in 2012, the conviction statistics, from 200 in 2009 to 537 in 2012 (Baur and Kinzig 2013). A recent legislative proposal was labelled 'Draft Act to strengthen the Probation Service and offender aid' (Bundesrat 2014), although its sole aim is to enable probation workers to give information on acutely dangerous behaviour with the risk of grave offences of clients directly to the police. Due to data protection rules, this up to now has to be done via the court or the monitoring institution in cases of an intensive supervision order.

Social reintegration as a penal strategy

Putting the principle into practice

By now, the concept of resocialization 'German style' may have become clearer in its restrictive or defensive function. It implies that state interventions must avoid desocialization by custodial sanctions or inappropriately demanding community sanctions (for example obligations that are problematic for family and work life), and the state must provide certain precautions against undue stigmatization by media coverage or disclosure of criminal records. Less clear, however, is the positive approach: must the state – within the criminal justice system – (only) support a life without new offences or must it support the full social participation in society of a convicted person? This last point is still very much debated amongst criminal law scholars with a narrow approach and those who are more practice oriented. As a proponent of the first position, Fabricius (1991) argues that the concept aims solely as 'socialisation towards the ability to know right from wrong' and in that way is also a defence against a state that wants to extort more. Cornel (2009) on the contrary rejects this as a purely normative argument disregarding the close connection between social exclusion, stigmatization, offending and reoffending. While it was true that those responsible for putting the resocialization principle into practice are part of the criminal justice system and therefore also 'perform retributive tasks' (Cornel 2009: 51), they also must offer support that addresses material and social conditions of living, psycho-social issues etc. While the latter is true, there is a certain risk to limit the principle of social reintegration to those who are perceived as disintegrated and losing sight of those who are apparently fully integrated because they have a family, a job etc. – namely white collar offenders. To discuss how far the concept fits for them as well goes beyond the aim of this chapter and seems to be a nearly untouched question in the German discussion.

In any case the responsible actors and their practices need to be looked at, and special consideration must be given to the role and status of the probation service. In Germany, probation officers and other criminal justice social workers are professional social workers or social pedagogues. They usually complete six semesters of training at a university of applied sciences and receive a degree of social work or social pedagogy. Up to this moment no specialization in criminal justice social work has taken place; usually this happens during the mandatory one-year on-the-job training (Mutz 2008). Although the *Länder* have different regulations for details, this broad framework is valid for the whole of Germany and has not changed. It can thus be said that the 'social work imprint' comes first and criminal justice constraints follow later.

One of these constraints in the last decade or so is an intensified preoccupation with risk assessment and management, fuelled by the discussions about those released from preventive detention and other dangerous, mostly sex or violent offenders. Looking at thematic issues of the German probation journal *Bewährungshilfe*, but also the themes of the main conference of the German Probation association *DBH, Fachverband für Soziale Arbeit, Strafrecht und Kriminalpolitik*, a focus on this topic can be found. The coming conference, for example, will be entitled 'Risk and the Probation Service' and will deal with new schemes of 'risk-oriented probation work' that have been or currently are introduced in all *Länder* (Grosser and Maelicke 2009). British and Canadian influences are strong, as both the Level of Service Inventory – Revised (LSI-R; Andrews and Bonta 2003) and Offender Assessment System (OASys, as used by the English–Welsh National Offender Management Service) served as models for German versions of risk-oriented case management (Mutz 2012).

Since another and connected preoccupation is evidence-based work (Grosser and Maelicke 2009), a look at the available evidence is also necessary. While thorough evaluation studies for individual programmes are rare (Cornel 2009; Dessecker 2012), some general statistics on success rates exist. As mentioned above, the data of the probation statistics show that the initial experiment of the legislator in 1969 to expand the scope of suspended sentences and the experiment of judicial practice to use this instrument were successful: the remission rate – meaning the share of those who get their sentence remitted when the probation period has elapsed without revocation – is constant at around two-thirds since 1990. Even though courts may assume that more clients have criminogenic needs and therefore impose more probation orders – and therefore more control by probation officers – to suspended sentences, nothing has changed (Dünkel 2008; Heinz 2012). Additional insight is provided by the German Recidivism Study. According to the second version, which generally confirmed the first (Jehle et al. 2013: 188–91), 56 per cent of those with suspended sentences without a probation order did not reoffend, while 33 per cent of those with a probation order did not reoffend in a 6-year follow-up period. Only 25 per cent of the latter group, however, received an unsuspended prison sentence for the new offence. In a relatively recent 'memorandum' for the German Probation Association, however, this way of measuring success was questioned and it was also asked how the results can be connected to ever rising caseloads, and what criteria for success according to the self-concept of the service would be appropriate (van Heek and Marks 2006).

Many probation workers therefore seem to be a lot less confident about their work results and the circumstances under which they have to perform their duties. First of all, many report grave role conflicts, but they also feel that the demands of the criminal justice system differ from their professional views (Böttner 2004). But as they are more concerned with the positive, socially supportive approach to resocialization they also notice increasingly bleak living circumstances of their clients, as well as growing inequalities in society. Comprehensive studies on lifestyles and problems of probation clients are relatively old (Cornel 2000; Engels and Martin 2002) and could therefore not consider the reform of the German social systems in the years 2003–2005. These reforms are based on the 'Agenda 2010' by the *Schroeder*-led government formed by the Social Democrats and the Greens: its main objectives were to promote economic growth and reduce unemployment, but it also brought serious cuts in the social welfare system, in particular for the long-term unemployed. While the agenda may have worked for the overall economic climate and indeed decreasing unemployment rates, growing percentages of people living in precarious socio-economic conditions as well as growing inequalities in German society cannot be ignored. This has also been conceded in the last governmental report on poverty and wealth using data for the 'at-risk-of-poverty rate' and the Gini-index (BAS 2013).

These developments are considered a major challenge to the principle of the social state and are a constant topic for debate, in particular for those professions dealing with a socially disadvantaged clientele (Butterwegge 2013). The studies quoted showed that nearly 60 per cent of all probation clients left school without graduation, the vast majority were without work and the average level of debt was high. While no new studies dedicated to service users have been conducted since, the German Probation Association held its 2012 annual conference under the heading 'Crisis of social justice'. From the material published (DBH–Fachverband für Soziale Arbeit, Strafrecht und Kriminalpolitik 2013) it becomes quite clear that this crisis is also a dominant concern for every day probation work.

Results of one of the studies mentioned also pointed to a group that could not even be reached by supportive probation work: foreigners, which in 1999 formed ca. 8 per cent of the population were strongly over-represented amongst those convicted (22 per cent) and sentenced with an unsuspended prison sentence (26 per cent). They, however, only formed 17 per cent of the probation population. The suspected reason is that foreign convicts less often receive suspended sentences with probation orders, 'because they are either expelled after the conviction or because language problems seem to make successful probation supervision impossible' (Engels and Martin 2002: 22).

As a final point in this section, a relatively recent and ambivalent development should be mentioned: It seems that the belief in rehabilitative treatment of offenders is experiencing a renaissance. As indicated, the legislator had to react to doubts raised by the Federal Constitutional Court and needed to legitimize both preventive detention and supervision of conduct orders as preventive – and not punitive – measures. It did so by stressing their rehabilitative functions. A focus here is on therapeutic interventions, offered for example by the forensic-psychiatric clinics, but also by intensified efforts by probation officers (Morgenstern and Hecht 2011). Whether this evocation of the rehabilitation ideal actually mirrors a genuine belief in those interventions or aims at disguising more punitive and/or risk-oriented policies is not entirely clear; in any case it increases once again the expectations and pressure on practitioners.

Adaptations or a transformation of the Resozialisierungsgrundsatz?

So even if resocialization as an aim of penal sentences and measures seems to be carved in stone and the word rolls off even conservative tongues easily, it may be that the concept has changed, transformed or been pushed aside over time. It remains my task therefore to examine the developments described above in terms of the penal adaptations suggested in the introduction of this book, which, in fact, can all be found in German penal policy and practice.

A strong argument has been made that the German penal practice has also had its 'punitive turn' (for an account in English language: Sack 2013). Others have opposed this general assessment (Heinz 2012; Dünkel and Morgenstern 2010). For community punishment in Germany, some punitive developments indeed have been indicated in this chapter: Judges tend to order more conditions and obligations attached to suspended sentences and in particular to intensive supervision orders. The argument for strengthening community service was that it is a punishment that truly can be felt, which makes offenders 'sweat'. In particular for the supervision of conduct order, a serious tightening up in quantity and quality can be seen: more offenders are affected, and the intensity of supervision has increased greatly. While the existing possibility of punishing the breach of directives in the PC has always been criticized as alien to the system of supposedly supporting conditions, its use now has increased. All penal policy-making with regard to serious (sex) offenders happened in the shadow of the 'lock 'em up and throw away the key' remark by the then-chancellor, a philosophy that could very well have served as carte blanche for punitive reforms.

The strong positions of the German Constitutional Court and the European Court of Human Rights has so far only had a direct (and moderating) impact on imprisonment and preventive detention. But, with regard to community punishment, the ordinary judiciary seems to counteract harsher penal policy intentions; the overall use of non-custodial options has not changed, more rather than less problematic clients have been included without this producing more revocations. As regards penal policy, community service as a tough option has not been introduced; instead many *Länder* seek to increase its use to reach out to more fine defaulters and to those with serious social problems. Some of the additional conditions attached to suspended sentences, but also to the supervision of conduct order, may have been added for supportive rather than punitive purposes.

German penal policy and practice, however, seems to be obsessed with *risk*. The bulk of cases where a prognosis is needed, in particular to address the question of whether it is reasonable to suspend the prison sentence, is solved without much ado in everyday practice. However, in more serious cases, in particular the conditional release of potentially dangerous sex and violent offenders, risk assessment has become a real issue. For many of these decisions the courts rely on (psychiatric) experts, which results in complicated, often delayed, shared decision-making (Morgenstern 2015). On the ambulant side, the supervision of these released offenders involves more agencies, including the police, an increased use of risk-focused assessment tools and ultimately more control.

Some of these developments have intended or unintended punitive effects. Its origins, however, rather seem to be the political fear of grave cases of recidivism and more generally the characteristics of politics and judicial practice in the 'risk society' (Beck 1986). This tendency to apply techniques that aim at controlling or mitigating risks leads to the 'managerial adaptation' that in recent years had, also in Germany, profound impact on community punishment. The focus on managerial concerns is best illustrated by highlighting again two aspects: in Baden-Württemberg the best way to make the probation service more efficient seemed to be privatization, and most of the structural changes related to different risk allocation and recording practices, as well as to involving more voluntary probation workers (Dölling *et al.* 2014). This turn to managerial approaches is also reflected in studies of community punishment: older studies (and one recent small study) have taken into account the offender's view, choosing interviews with offenders as an appropriate means to assess their 'typical social circumstances and typical needs' (Engels and Martin 2002; with a similar approach: Cornel 2000; Kawamura-Reindl and Stancu 2010). Current comprehensive studies, in contrast, have tended to concentrate on questions of standards, organization and overall performance of supervision work (Dölling *et al.* 2014; Fachkommission der Freien und Hansestadt Hamburg 2010). Here, offenders' views are merely one element in an assessment of the quality of work by the probation service (which ultimately is measured against revocation rates). The inclusion of the user view in the study by Dölling *et al.* (2014: annex 35) confirmed another issue raised above: clients do not rate success in the same way as policymakers and researchers. While the 636 clients surveyed reported no progress in most of the concrete areas in which social problems are usually located (namely work, housing, personal relationships and health), two-thirds of them felt that their 'general life situation' had improved since they were 'with a probation officer'. This means that probation work is successful from the probationers' points of view, even if it cannot be measured by the usual categories that are managerial 'benchmarks'.

The editors of this volume finally suggest the reparative adaptation as influential for the legitimation of community punishment. Again, this development can be found in Germany as well: the *Täter–Opfer-Ausgleich* (Victim–Offender Mediation) probably was the most discussed 'alternative option' in the early 1990s. These discussions did have profound impact on practice and policy, but it hardly reached beyond juvenile justice and the pre-trial phase. Since both areas are outside the scope of this chapter, the reader must be directed to other sources, for example to a brief overview in the English language in the Second Periodical Report on Crime and Crime Control (Federal Ministry of Justice 2006: 82–6).

Outlook

Is, after all, social reintegration the dominant narrative for community punishment in Germany? Yes, it is. While it has been shaped and influenced by all of the discussed adaptations, it is the only narrative in the linear sense since the 1970s and thus has persisted as the dominating concept. But the concept has not persisted untouched. In particular risk aspects have influenced it, as may be seen in current parliamentary material for the reform of preventive detention and the supervision of conduct order. While the word '*Resozialisierung*' can be found many times, it is always – with a 'utilitarian justification' of rehabilitative efforts that focus on criminogenic needs and thus on risk (Robinson 2008) – serving a secondary function: 'measures to reduce dangerousness of the offender are not only in the resocialisation interest of the offender, but also in the security interest of the public' (Deutscher Bundestag 2012: 12). This may not be a general deformation, but it certainly affects the group of dangerous (sex) offenders. For this group, and increasingly for other violent offenders, the diagnosis of a 'bifurcated system' (Dünkel and Morgenstern 2010; Albrecht 2004) remains true as the control aspects of community sanctions, in particular as realized in the supervision of conduct order, by far outweigh the supportive functions. To a lesser extent this observation is also valid for foreign offenders. They often do not profit from the general readiness to reintegrate offenders back into society, not even when they have lived in Germany for a long time.

A fresh wind may blow into matters of resocialization following new initiatives to draft a 'Resocialization Act'. This mainly is an initiative by a penal reform group (*Ziethener Kreis*),[7] striving for a uniform and principled approach for the implementation of both custodial and ambulant sanctions under the principle of resocialization, which in particular seeks to link criminal justice agencies and regional social welfare providers. Preparatory works for such an act have been undertaken on behalf of the Ministry of Justice of the *Land* Brandenburg, partly by the same experts. Looking at them, it becomes clear that the authors are pursuing a combined approach to resocialization, a 'double programme', including 'expectations to the offender to conform to the norms. On the other hand it is expected of society to make offers to the offender that compensate for social disadvantage and individual deficits' (Arbeitsgruppe Resozialisierungsgesetz 2011). Against the background of growing social injustices and failing social inclusion of various groups, this seems indispensable and an affirmation of the ever-true remark by one of the most influential German penologists, that 'the best criminal policy is a good social policy' (von Liszt 1883: 3).

Notes

1 I will therefore use 'resocialization' and 'social reintegration' synonymously throughout this chapter.
2 The full German version of the so-called Lebach decision can be found in the official collection of the FCC decisions as BVerfGE 35, 202. The Court developed its position in response to a post-prison situation where the possible obstacle to resocialization came from the media. Three men had robbed an army depot, killing four soldiers. A public TV operator planned a documentary about this spectacular crime. The broadcast was scheduled to coincide with the release of one of the offenders from prison. He sought injunction against the publication of his name and picture, claiming a right to a new start after serving his sentence. In the judgment the court gave priority to the protection of the ex-offender's privacy over freedom of expression or information. It evaluated the opposing rights and was of the opinion that, in view of the circumstances of the case, such an intensive invasion of privacy and in fact the whole life of the ex-offender would take place that the freedom of expression must give way to the protection of privacy.
3 I prefer this translation (Drenkhahn *et al.* 2012). Other translations exist; in the quasi-official translation on behalf of the German Ministry of Justice, Bohlander (2008) uses 'measures of rehabilitation and incapacitation', which is an interpretation rather than a translation.
4 M. v. Germany (2010) 51 E.H.R.R. 41.
5 More comprehensive descriptions of the German Probation System as well as the main features of sentencing and types of sanction already exist in English (Mutz 2008; a short description is also included in the DOMICE project, available at: www.domice.org; as for research, see Dessecker 2012, www.offendersupervision.eu) (websites last accessed 27 March 2015).

6 Measured against the number of all cases prosecuted, it is even lower: Despite the official prevalence of the principle of legality, the Public Prosecution Service in Germany widely uses discretionary methods to discontinue proceedings. For adults, currently one third of all criminal proceedings are discontinued without or under conditions (Heinz 2012). These conditions are mostly of a financial nature. Only some of them involve supervision because they consist of community service or victim-offender mediation, but since they are not 'punishment' but pre-trial solutions, they will not be discussed here.

7 See, for more information, www.rsf.uni-greifswald.de/duenkel/publikationen/internet/ ziethener-kreis.html (accessed 27 March 2015).

References

AG Psychiatrie der Obersten Landesgesundheitsbehörden (2012) Psychiatrie in Deutschland – Strukturen, Leistungen, Perspektiven. Bericht an die Gesundheitsministerkonferenz 2012 mit Tabellenanhang. Available online at: www.gesunde.sachsen.de/ download/Download_Gesundheit/Anlagen_GMK-Bericht_2012_der_AG_Psychiatrie_ der_AOLG.pdf (accessed 26 May 2015).

Albrecht, H.-J. (2004) 'Security gaps: responding to dangerous sex offenders in the Federal Republic of Germany', *Federal Sentencing Reporter*, 16: 200–7.

Albrecht, H.-J. (2013a) 'Sentencing in Germany. Explaining long-term stability in the structure of criminal sanctions and sentencing', *Law and Contemporary Problems*, 7: 211–36.

Albrecht, H.-J. (2013b) '§43 StGB', in U. Kindhäuser, H.-U.Paeffgen, U. Neumann (eds) *Nomos Kommentar zum Strafgesetzbuch*, 4th edn, vol. 2. Baden-Baden: Nomos.

Andrews, D. A. and Bonta, J. (2003) *The Psychology of Criminal Conduct*. Cincinnati, OH: Anderson.

Arbeitsgruppe Resozialisierungsgesetz (2011) *Empfehlungen für ein brandenburgisches Resozialisierungsgesetz*. Available online at: www.mdj.brandenburg.de/sixcms/media.php/4055/ Empfehlungen%20f%C3%BCr%20ein%20Brandenburgisches%20Resozialisierungsgesetz. pdf (accessed 27 March 2015).

Baur, A. and Kinzig, J., (2013) 'Evaluation der Führungsaufsicht, ein Werkstattbericht', DBH-Fachtagung zur Führungsaufsicht, Kassel, 11–12 March 2013. Conference paper published online at: www.dbh-online.de/fa/Baur_Kinzig_Kassel_2013 (accessed 27 March 2015).

Beck, U. (1986) *Risikogesellschaft. Auf dem Weg in eine andere Moderne*. Frankfurt a. M.: Surhkamp.

Böttner, S. (2004) *Der Rollenkonflikt der Bewährungshilfe in Theorie und Praxis*. Baden-Baden: Nomos.

Bohlander, M. (2008) *The German Criminal Code: A Modern English Translation*. Oxford: Hart Publishing.

Bundesministerium für Arbeit und Soziales, BAS (2013) The German Federal Government's 4th Report on Poverty and Wealth. Executive Summary. BAS: Berlin.

Bundesrat (2014) 'Entwurf eines Gesetzes zur Stärkung der Bewährungshilfe und der Straffälligenarbeit", BT-Drs. 18/2012.

Butterwegge, C. (2013) 'Die Krise der sozialen Gerechtigkeit und die Entwicklung des Wohlfahrtsstaates', in DBH-Fachverband für Soziale Arbeit, Strafrecht und Kriminalpolitik (ed), *Krise der sozialen Gerechtigkeit*. Köln: DBH.

CDU and SPD (2013) *Deutschlands Zukunft gestalten. Koalitionsvertrag zwischen CDU, CSU und SPD*. Berlin. Available online at: www.cdu.de/sites/default/files/media/dokumente/koalitionsvertrag.pdf (accessed 27 March 2015).

Cornel, H. (2000) 'Probanden der Bewährungshilfe für Jugendliche und Heranwachsende', *Bewährungshilfe*, 47: 302–21.

Cornel, H. (2009) 'Zum Begriff der Resozialisierung', in H. Cornel, G. Kawamura-Reindl, B. Maelicke and B.-R. Sonnen (eds) *Resozialisierung*. Baden-Baden: Nomos.

Council of Europe (1992) Recommendation (92)16E 19 October 1992 on the European rules on community sanctions and measures. Council of Europe: Strasbourg.

DBH–Fachverband für Soziale Arbeit, Strafrecht und Kriminalpolitik (ed) (2013) *Krise der sozialen Gerechtigkeit*. Köln: DBH.

Dessecker, A. (2012) 'Research on offender supervision practice in Germany: a review'. Available online at: www.offendersupervision.eu/wp-content/uploads/2013/04/Practising-OS-in-Germany-Nov-2012.pdf (accessed 27 March 2015).

Deutscher Bundestag (ed) (1969a) Erster Schriftlicher Bericht des Sonderausschusses für die Strafrechtsreform, BT-Drs. V/4094. Bonn.

Deutscher Bundestag (ed) (1969b) Zweiter Schriftlicher Bericht des Sonderausschusses für die Strafrechtsreform, BT-Drs. V/4095. Bonn.

Deutscher Bundestag (ed) (2012) Entwurf eines Gesetzes zur bundesrechtlichen Umsetzung des Abstandsgebotes im Recht der Sicherungsverwahrung, BT-Drs. 17/9874. Berlin.

Dölling, D., Hermann, D. and Entdorf, H. (2014) *Evaluation der Bewährungs- und Gerichtshilfe sowie des Täter-Opfer-Ausgleichs in Baden-Württemberg. Abschlussbericht*. Heidelberg: Universität Heidelberg; Frankfurt: Universität Frankfurt.

Drenkhahn, K., Morgenstern, C. and Van Zyl Smit, D. (2012) 'What is in a name? Preventive Detention in Germany in the Shadow of European Human Rights Law', *Criminal Law Review*, 25: 167–87.

Dünkel, F. (2008) 'Rechtliche, rechtspolitische und programmatische Entwicklungen einer Sozialen Strafrechtspflege in Deutschland', in DBH-Fachverband für Soziale Arbeit, Strafrecht und Kriminalpolitik/Justizministerium Mecklenburg-Vorpommern (ed) *Kriminalpolitische Herausforderungen. Bewährungs- und Straffälligenhilfe auf neuen Wegen*. BoD: Norderstedt.

Dünkel, F. (2011) 'Ersatzfreiheitsstrafen und ihre Vermeidung. Aktuelle statistische Entwicklung, gute Praxismodelle und rechtspolitische Überlegungen', *Forum Strafvollzug*, 60: 143–53.

Dünkel, F. and Morgenstern, C. (2010) 'Deutschland', in F. Dünkel, T. Lappi-Seppälä, C. Morgenstern and D. Van Zyl Smit (eds) *Kriminalität, Kriminalpolitik, strafrechtliche Sanktionspraxis und Gefangenenraten im europäischen Vergleich*. Mönchengladbach: Forum Verlag, pp. 3–23.

Engels, R. and Martin, M. (2002) *Typische Lebenslagen und typischer Unterstützungsbedarf von Klientinnen und Klienten der Bewährungshilfe*. Berlin: Institut für Sozialforschung und Gesellschaftspolitik.

Fabricius, D. (1991) 'Mindestanforderungen an eine resozialisierende Sozialtherapie', *Monatsschrift für Kriminologie und Strafrechtsreform*, 74: 197–209.

Fachkommission der Freien und Hansestadt Hamburg (2010) Optimierung der ambulanten und stationären Resozialisierung in Hamburg. Available online at: www.dbh-online.de/service/RESO-KOMM_Endbericht_04-03-2010.pdf (accessed 27 March 2015).

Federal Ministry of Justice (ed) (2006) *Second Periodical Report on Crime and Crime Control in Germany*. BMJ: Berlin. Available online at: www.uni-konstanz.de/rtf/ki/Second_Periodical_Report_on_Crime_and_en.pdf (accessed 27 March 2015).

Groß, K.-H. (2012) 'Section 56c StGB', in W. Joecks, K. Miebach (eds) *Münchener Kommentar zum Strafgesetzbuch*, 2nd edn, vol. 2. München: C. H. Beck.

Grosser, R. and Maelicke, B. (2009) 'Bewährungshilfe', in H. Cornel, G. Kawamura-Reindl, B. Maelicke and B.-R. Sonnen (eds) *Resozialisierung*. Baden-Baden: Nomos.

Hassemer, W. (2002) 'Darf der strafende Staat Verurteilte bessern wollen?' in C. Prittwitz and M. Barumann (eds) *Festschrift für Klaus Lüderssen*. Baden-Baden: Nomos.

Hassemer, W. (2006) 'Sicherheit durch Strafrecht', *HRRS-Strafrecht*, 7: 130–41.

Heinz, W. (2012) *Das strafrechtliche Sanktionensystem und die Sanktionierungspraxis in Deutschland 1882–2010*. Available online at: www.uni-konstanz.de/rtf/kis/Sanktionierungspraxis-in-Deutschland-Stand-2010.pdf (accessed 27 March 2015).

Hörnle, T. (2013) 'Moderate and non-arbitrary sentencing without guidelines: the German experience', *Law and Contemporary Problems*, 7: 189–210.

Jehle, J.-M., Albrecht, H.-J., Hohmann-Fricke, S. and Tetal, C. (2013) *Legalbewährung nach strafrechtlichen Sanktionen*. Berlin: Bundesministerium der Justiz.

Kawamura-Reindl, G. and Stancu, L. (2010) 'Die Beziehungsqualität zwischen Bewährungshelfern und ihren jugendlichen und heranwachsenden Probanden', *Bewährungshilfe*, 57: 133–50.

Lakotta, B. (2014) 'Three days in Warnemünde. Reflections from different points of view – the journalist', paper presented during the final conference of the Justice Cooperation Network (JCN): The reintegration of high-risk offenders, Warnemünde, 3–5 September 2014 (unpublished conference paper).

Loy, T. (2010) 'Deutsche Einheit: Bewährung im Kollektiv', *Der Tagesspiegel*, 14 October 2010. Available online at: www.tagesspiegel.de/berlin/deutsche-einheit-bewaehrung-im-kollektiv/1956518.html (accessed 27 March 2015).

Lüderssen, K. (1991) 'Krise des Resozialisierungsgedankens im Strafrecht?' *Juristische Arbeitsblätter*, 24: 222–8.

Morgenstern, C. (2002) *Internationale Mindeststandards für ambulante Strafen und Maßnahmen*. Mönchengladbach: Forum Verlag.

Morgenstern, C. (2015) 'Conditional release in Germany – who decides? And who really does?', in M. Herzog-Evans (ed) *Offender Release and Supervision: The Role of Courts and the use of Discretion*. Nijmegen: Wolf Legal Publishers, pp. 109–35.

Morgenstern, C. and Hecht, A. (2011) 'Rechtstatsachen zur Führungsaufsicht im kriminalpolitischen Kontext', *Bewährungshilfe*, 58: 177–95.

Mutz, J. (2008) 'Germany', in A. van Kalmthout and I. Durnescu (eds) *Probation in Europe*. Nijmegen: Wolf.

Mutz, C. (2012) *Der Englische National Offender Management Service und die Deutsche Bewährungshilfe*. Tübingen: Universitätsbibliothek Tübingen.

Reckling, K. (2014) Weiterer Anstieg der Zahlen zur Führungsaufsicht. Available online at: www.dbh-online.de/unterseiten/themen/fuehrung.php?id=494 (accessed 26 May 2015).

Robinson, G. (2008) 'Late-modern rehabilitation: the evolution of a penal strategy', *Punishment and Society*, 10: 429–45.

Robinson, G., McNeill, F. and Maruna, S. (2013) 'Punishment in society: The improbable persistence of probation and other community sanctions and measures', in J. Simon and R. Sparks (eds) *Sage Handbook of Punishment and Society*. London: Sage.

Roxin, C. (1966) 'Sinn und Grenzen staatlicher Strafe', *Juristische Schulung*, 6: 377–87.

Sack, F. (2013) 'Social structure and crime policy: The German case', *Punishment and Society*, 15: 367–81.

Stelly, W. and Thomas, J. (2009) 'Freie Straffälligenhilfe unter Veränderungsdruck – Ergebnisse einer repräsentativen Befragung', *Forum Strafvollzug*, 58: 87–90.

Van Heek, A. and Marks, E. (2006) 'Inhaltliche und konzeptionelle Aspekte', in A. Bickel, A. Van Heek, G. Kastenhuber, N. Lippenmeier, E. Marks, T. Quadt, T. Rensmann, W. Thörner and H. Wegener (eds) *Denkschrift zur Lage und Zukunft der Bewährungshilfe in Deutschland*. Available online at: www.dbh-online.de/service/denkschrift_06.pdf (accessed 27 March 2015).

Van Zyl Smit, D. and Snacken, S. (2009) *Principles of European Prison Law and Policy*. Oxford: Oxford University Press.

Von Liszt, F. (1883) 'Der Zweckgedanke im Strafrecht', *Zeitschrift für die gesamte Strafrechtswissenschaft*, 3: 1–47.

6

COMMUNITY PUNISHMENT IN THE NETHERLANDS

A history of crises and incidents

Miranda Boone

Introduction

Both the title and the structure of this contribution can be understood as a response to one of the questions posed to authors in the introduction to this book, namely: *Have there been moments of crisis in respect of the legitimacy of punishment in the community? What happened?* The approach adopted in this chapter is responsive to the central topic of legitimacy in this volume. At various times during its existence, 'community punishment' in the Netherlands has been under a lot of pressure or has had to respond to general crises occurring in society. The use of community punishment has had to be relegitimized or has found new sources of legitimacy in its contribution to the solution of these problems. These moments have had a major influence on the shape and magnitude of community punishment in society today.

Following a general introduction on the emergence of community punishment in the Netherlands, the incidents and crisis that will be discussed are: the shock that the introduction of community sentences brought to the probation service; the immense expansion of community service orders and the responses to that; public disquiet concerning 'lenient' sentences; the disclosure of high recidivism rates; public outrage concerning reoffending while under supervision; and economic crises and cutbacks. In the final section of the chapter, the history of community punishment in the Netherlands will be analysed in the light of the four narratives the editors of this book distinguish in their introduction and in an earlier article (Robinson *et al.* 2013), although these will be easy to recognize in what precedes. In this section the remaining questions will also be answered: Does 'punishment in the community' make sense conceptually in the Netherlands (for the sake of consistency the term will be structurally used in this chapter, but it remains an open question)? And if an understanding of community punishment contributes to an understanding of 'the penal climate' in the Netherlands, how does it do so?

The introduction of community punishment in the Netherlands

The history of community sentencing in the Netherlands started in the mid-1960s, when prison sentences were heavily criticized. Two points of criticism were stressed in particular. First, exclusion and stigmatization were seen as harmful side-effects of the prison sentence that qualified it as an inhuman reaction that should only be used very selectively. Second, whilst it was generally recognized that both society and the offender profited from rehabilitation, there was great disappointment concerning the rehabilitative potential of the custodial sentence. This prompted initiatives to develop alternatives to imprisonment. Enhancing the use of financial penalties was also investigated (Commissie Vermogensstraffen 1969, 1972), as well as increasing the use of suspended sentences (Mulder and Schootstra 1974).

Community punishment as an alternative to custody was applied for the first time in the Netherlands in 1971, when three steel workers who had committed a violent offence were ordered to undertake 'unpaid labour in the public interest' instead of being sentenced to prison. The rather wide sentencing discretion of judges in the Netherlands allowed for this decision. However, in 1979 a governmental committee on alternative sanctions advised that a start be made with community service orders on a more systematic (but experimental) basis. These experiments obtained an important impulse from the lack of prison capacity, a problem that started to grow at the beginning of the 1980s. Besides contributing to more humane and effective sentencing, alternatives to prison sentences were also considered now as a remedy against the shortage of cells. After a few years of experiments with several judicial measures, unpaid labour was introduced in 1989 as a third formal sentence (besides custodial and financial penalties) in the Penal Code for adults. The sentence was called *Dienstverlening* (the provision of services), a term which was defined in the law as 'unpaid labour to benefit the community.' Unpaid labour could be imposed instead of a 'considered' non-suspended prison sentence of 6 months at most. This complicated formulation was chosen to guarantee the substitutional character of the penalty. The judge in question first had to determine the length of the prison sentence and then had to decide whether this sentence could be replaced by a community service order. The choice of a formal sentence had as a consequence that most of the other juridical possibilities were ruled out. For example, community service orders could no longer be imposed as a condition of pre-trial detention or as an out-of-court settlement by the Public Prosecutor as had been possible during the experiments with this sentence. The reason for this is that (formal) sentences can only be imposed by a judge after a hearing in court.

In 2001 the legal framework for community sentences changed, primarily to enable growth. By that time, community sentences were no longer exclusively seen as a possible substitute for prison sentences, but as autonomous sentences in their own right that were, in terms of their severity, placed between prison sentences and fines. This change of character was illustrated by the change of terminology: they now became '*taakstraffen*', a phrase that emphasizes the effort the offender has to make. A task sentence could consist of a community service order or a training order or a combination of both. This change of status for community service also resulted in an adaptation of the legal framework. In the 2001 Bill, task sentences became 'autonomous sentences', meaning that they were no longer exclusively meant as an alternative to prison sentences. It was emphasized in the Green Paper preceding the new Bill that 'in cases where offenders had been given the benefit of the doubt in the past and were punished by a suspended sentence because there was no alternative thereto, they may be sentenced to a community service order from now on' (Ministry of Justice 1996, p. 30). So, a judge no longer had to impose a community service order instead of a prison sentence of a certain duration; he could now impose a community service order and determine a period of detention if the offender failed to carry out the community service order in a satisfactory manner. Furthermore, 'the prosecution modality' was introduced, giving the prosecutor the possibility to require a community sentence as a condition of an 'out of court settlement'.

Probation under pressure

The introduction of community service orders in the Dutch sanction system as such and the choice of the organization that had to execute them resulted in the first crisis that will be discussed in this chapter, a crisis within the probation service (*Reclassering*). The outcome of that crisis has had an immense impact on both the shape of community sentences and on the probation service itself. To understand that crisis and its influence, it is necessary to give some historical background information on the probation service.

The Dutch Fellowship for Moral Reformation of Prisoners (*Nederlandsche Genootschap voor Zedelijke verbetering van Gevangenen*), was founded in 1823 by the merchants Willem Hendrik Suringar, John Leonard Nierstrasz and Willem Hendrik Warnsinck. They were inspired, in particular, by the ideas about prison reform of John Howard, who had visited prisons in most countries in Western Europe and had presented his shocking findings in the book *The State of the Prisons* (Howard 1977). The aim of the Society was to promote the moral improvement of (ex-)prisoners, an aim that was truly remarkable at a time when the penal system was still fully based on deterrence. It was hoped to achieve that objective by visiting prisoners and by offering them assistance after discharge. In practice, however, the focus of the Society's activities was on prison visiting and it was mainly occupied by organizing education and meaningful work in prison (Boone 2009b). Around the turn of the century, a shift of paradigm occurred in the criminal justice system that had a major influence on the development of the Society. The conception of man as a free and responsible individual was slowly replaced by a much more deterministic view. The modern direction in penal law was born and brought many changes, including a much higher profile for the probation service (as it was called by then). Under the influence of these new ideas, the legal possibilities for early release expanded. In a departure from previous practice, a number of conditions could be attached to the decision to release a person. Also in 1915 the possibility of a conditional sentence was included in the Criminal Code. Probation was closely involved in the implementation of both measures. Probation councils advised on the application of suspended sentences by writing advisory reports for the judge and supervised the conditions that were attached to the suspended sentence and early release decision. This greater interference was rewarded by governmental subsidy and a legal basis for probation work in the law (Boone 2009b).

After the Second World War, the probation service underwent professional development. The professional education of probation workers had become a condition for government subsidy, a measure that resulted in the disappearance of voluntary workers and the education of probation workers as social workers in so-called social academies (institutions for the training of social workers). These academies fostered the typical anti-authority mentality of this era. In addition, they were taught that a professional relationship with the client needed a basis of trust, a condition that was difficult to combine with judicial tasks that require enforcement. In this period, the probation service fully identified itself with its clients. The organization was very much influenced by the School of Utrecht with its delinquent-centred way of thinking (Moedikdo 1976). The idea was to understand the offender as a whole person and not just as a perpetrator of a crime (Janse de Jonge and Kelk 1992).

The changing attitude towards crime and the criminal complicated the already difficult relation with central government and the position of the probation service in the criminal justice system even more, though this was a relationship that had always been difficult given the independent character of the probation service (Janse de Jonge 1991; Heinrich 1995). The causes of crime were no longer sought in the individual psychological circumstances of the offender, as had been the case in the modern era (Boone 2012), but rather in the structure of society and social circumstances, an analysis that asked for much broader action than could be justified by the more limited goals of the Ministry of Justice (Heinrich 1995). Nevertheless, the Ministry did accept the more autonomous position of the probation service in the first instance, resulting in a decrease of supervision tasks and an increase in means available for care and assistance. For example, to give probation officers full freedom in the shape of the contact with their clients, the range of possible conditions that could be linked to conditional release was reduced to only one, namely, probation contact, whatever form that might take.

Bearing this preceding period in mind, one can imagine that the involvement of the probation service with the implementation of community sentences came as a shock for the organization and most probation workers. The organization was bitterly divided on the issue. In an early letter to the Secretary of Justice, the organization agreed on organizing and supervising unpaid labour, but refused to control and report failures to the prosecution service (Boone 2000). Persisting in this refusal, however, would have been the starting point of the dismantling of the organization (Heinrich 1995, p. 255). Full dependence on governmental subsidies left any counter-offensive without much chance of success (Heinrich 1995). The involvement with community service can be seen as the starting point of increasing governmental interference in probation; a development that has gathered a great deal of momentum and meant that the probation service has changed from a social-welfare organization into one fully managed by 'production numbers'.

A more 'business-like' way of working has become most visible in the far-reaching automatic data processing systems that were implemented around the last turn of the century. One of them is a registration system, called the Client Follow System (*Client Volg Systeem, CVS*) in which all activities that are undertaken with probation clients are recorded. Even more radical has been the transformation of the service into an output-guided organization. For this operation it was necessary to classify all probation activities under a restricted number of probation 'products' that the Ministry of Justice was prepared to pay for. This operation resulted in the definition of eleven products, excluding many activities that were also important in the eyes of probation officers such as, for instance, offering assistance inside prison, attending cases of clients in court hearings or visiting a demoralized client to give them support. Subsidy is totally based on the output system. Each year an agreement is made between the probation service and the Ministry of Justice on the numbers of products supplied per year. Those numbers may not be exceeded. The probation service is paid by the number of products produced in 1 year, multiplied by its cost price. These agreements influence the whole organization, of course. Production numbers are passed on to the different departments and on a more informal level also to individual probation officers (Boone 2005).

Expansion

In the early years after its official introduction in the sanction system, the implementation of unpaid labour increased dramatically. In the first year of its existence (1981) only 213 unpaid labour penalties were enforced; at the end of the 1980s the number reached the respectable total of 6,000, while this figure tripled to around 20,000 in the 1990s and doubled again in the period until 2005. However, since 2006 the number of community service orders has been decreasing, in line with the general trend of decreasing punishment (Van Swaaningen 2013; Boone and Van Swaaningen 2013). Even so, 30 per cent of all sentences imposed by a court or judge consist of a community service order (Kalidien and Heere-de Lange 2012, Table 6.7). In an earlier article, I argued that the increased use of the community service order has always been considered a good thing, regardless of its outcomes (Boone 2005, 2010). Although the risk of net-widening was clearly rejected at the time of the introduction of community service orders, at a later stage it was more or less encouraged, because community sentences were no longer seen as direct alternatives to prison sentences, but as intermediate sanctions (Morris and Tonry 1990) that could also replace *less* severe sanctions. Community sentences were seen as an appropriate tool to address a perceived lack of criminal justice enforcement (Boone 2005, 2010). Expansion has been visible in particular at the lower end of the sentencing tariff; this is explained partly by the intensifying fight against social security fraud (Poort and Zengerink 2009). There have been clear exceptions to this rule, however, in particular at times when prison capacity has been low. For example, in the period between 2001 and 2008, a scarcity of prison cells resulted in more intensive uses of community service for violent offences (Kalidien and Heere-de Lange 2012, Table 6.11). In general, however, the gradual decrease in the number of hours imposed, and in particular the halving of the number of community service orders of more than 120 hours, suggests growth in the imposition of community sentences for less serious offences (Kalidien and Heere-de Lange 2012, Table 6.12).

The expansion of community service has had at least three important consequences. First, in addition to private projects in government or public organizations such as health care services and residential homes for the elderly, group projects and placements were started to accommodate the increased use of community service orders. The 'mirror-model' that had been strived for in the experimental period, meaning that a link should exist between the crime and the content of the order, had to be relinquished for that reason (Boone 2000). The need for quantitative growth and cut backs on the probation service (see below) also resulted in the introduction of separate community service order units in the probation organization in 2003. From that time, the supervision of community service orders was no longer integrated with the other tasks of probation, in particular individual aid and support. Reducing the provision of support for offenders on supervision can therefore be seen as a third consequence of the quantitative growth of community sentences. It is striking that in the annual report of the probation service it is openly acknowledged that growth can only be realized with less support. It is mentioned with pride, however, that the probation service has proven itself a reliable partner of the prosecution service and the judiciary (SRN 2004, p. 4). The Implementation of Sanctions Inspectorate (*Inspectie voor de Sanctietoepassing*, ISt) of the Department of Justice, meanwhile, has been critical of the support the general probation service can offer, but was more positive on the small-scale units of the two probation organizations specializing in homeless and addicted people (ISt 2005, p. 4). Also other studies or advisory bodies have recommended a more intensive level of support and supervision for these specific groups (Lünneman et al. 2005; Raad voor de Strafrechtstoepassing en Jeugdbescherming, RSJ 2005). These recommendations resulted in new initiatives from the probation service to combine community service orders with a more intensive level of counselling for specific groups, with the aim being to reduce recidivism rates (Poort and Zengerink 2009; Poort and Eppink 2009).

Footballers and opera singers

An aspect that is central to the question of community sentencing and its legitimacy is the public acceptance of community punishment. In the history of community punishment in the Netherlands, this is a recurring issue that finally resulted in the exclusion of recidivists and more serious offenders from community service. Political and societal debate on this issue has always been preceded by certain incidents.

In 1995, a famous international footballer caused a fatal car accident while exceeding the speed limit by 40 km per hour. Two weeks later he committed another traffic offence, this time without casualties. He received a community service order of 240 hours for both incidents. Two years later another celebrity, this time a famous opera singer, was responsible for a comparable road traffic accident. He was drunk at the time of the accident and he also received a community service order of 240 hours. Both cases led to an overwhelming amount of media attention. The general opinion was that a community service order was much too lenient a punishment for crimes such as these and that it was only because of the status and fame of the offenders that they escaped prison.

A television documentary on the community service order in 2007 probably had an even more negative impact on the public acceptance of the community service order, reporting that community service orders were also being imposed for serious offences such as murder and rape. Fierce debates followed on the internet and in the media. Members of Parliament asked the Minister of Justice to exclude this possibility by law. A study demonstrated that the programme makers had used unreliable data, for example formal definitions of crimes that did not correspond to the seriousness of the actual offences (Klijn *et al.* 2008). The study proved that the commotion resulting from the television programme was not the result of reliable facts. Nonetheless, the result of the continuing debate was that a Bill was passed in which recidivists and those committing (serious) violent and sexual offences were categorically excluded from 'stand-alone' community service orders (meaning community service orders without an accompanying sentence), a far-reaching restriction of the traditional sentencing discretion of the Dutch judiciary.

More rigorous studies on public acceptance of community sentences shows much broader acceptance of community punishment, however. Van der Laan (1993) concluded that broad support existed in Dutch society for community sentences. In this study seven cases were presented to a representative sample of 1,027 persons. Even in the more serious cases, for example public violence with moderate injury, tax fraud and drink-driving causing serious casualties, a substantial part of the sample supported a community service order or a behavioural intervention (63 per cent for the violent offence, 33 per cent for the tax fraud and 38 per cent for drink-driving causing serious injury) eventually combined with a fine. A similar, more recent study also found relatively high support for the community service order, including for more serious offences that are excluded from community service orders as a result of the new legislation, for example sexual assault (Ruiter *et al.* 2011).

Unveiling recidivism rates and 'What Works'

In 2005, the first outcomes of the 'recidivism monitor' were published (Wartna *et al.* 2005a, 2005b). The recidivism monitor was developed in the 1990s by researchers of the Scientific Research and Documentation Centre of the Department of Justice (Wetenschappelijk Onderzoek en Documentatiecentrum, WODC) and is based on the data of the Judicial Documentation system in which criminal records are registered. In 2005 two publications appeared that were based on data from the recidivism monitor: *Recidivecijfers 1997* (*Recidivism rates*, by Wartna *et al.* 2005a) and *Door na de gevangenis* (*Continuation after prison*, by Wartna *et al.* 2005b). The publications caused some unrest, because they proved that rates of recidivism after serving a sentence were extremely high. More than 70 per cent of the offenders on whom a prison sentence was imposed turned out to be arrested again within 7 years, and more than half within 2 years. Also half of the offenders who were sentenced to a community service order or a conditional prison sentence had committed another offence within 7 years.

The results had a catalysing effect on the efforts of Dutch policymakers to reduce recidivism. From the end of the 1990s onwards, an approach had become popular in the Netherlands that was mainly established by the Canadian scholars Andrews and Bonta and their colleagues, known as the 'What Works' or the Risk–Need–Responsivity (RNR) model. Based on a meta-analysis of a number of rehabilitation programmes, Andrews *et al.* (1990a, 1990b) came to the conclusion that the effectiveness of a programme for a particular offender depends on the risk that he will reoffend (the risk principle), the extent to which the programme can address the needs that resulted in his criminal behaviour (the need principle) and the responsivity of the particular programme to the offender (the responsivity principle). In 2002 a Dutch version of 'What Works', 'Pushing Back Recidivism' (*Terugdringen Recidive*), was introduced in the Netherlands. As with its Canadian and British counterparts, it aimed to treat offenders on a more scientific basis, mainly based on the work of the Canadian scholars. The programme consisted of three components: 1) A screening of all probationers and almost all detainees to assess their levels of risk, criminogenic needs and responsivity issues as described in the What Works literature; 2) The application of behavioural, cognitive interventions that had a demonstrable and positive effect on recidivism; and 3) An ambitious aftercare program for ex-detainees, aiming to prepare them for their return into society with regard to four major fields: income, housing, identity papers and care.

'Pushing Back Recidivism' radically changed the method of working in both prison and probation services, and it changed the way they cooperated. The risk screening became fully decisive for the rehabilitation programme that was offered to prisoners and probation clients. Not volunteering for a risk assessment or a negative risk assessment had serious consequences. For prisoners it resulted in reduced opportunities for leave or for detention phasing. For defendants assessed as high-risk offenders, it increased the chances of a prison sentence or intensive supervision instead of a community service order or conditional sentence.

An important aim of the programme was to enhance the effectiveness of behavioural interventions. For that reason, all interventions offered in the context of a penal sentence had to be approved by an accreditation panel before they could eventually be subsidized from state funds. Despite the numerous interventions that were applied to prisoners and probationers at the time of the installation of the panel, it took a long time before a reasonable number of interventions was (provisionally) acknowledged. At the time writing, 28 interventions have been provisionally recognized by the panel.

An interesting and new aspect of this reform programme was that its implementation was defined as the responsibility of the municipalities and no longer as a first concern of the prison. The Secretary of Justice of the time simply stated that ex-prisoners should be considered as normal citizens for whom his department did not have a special responsibility. Nobody could really disagree with this statement, although it primarily had a financial motive, of course. The implication of this statement for the probation service was that it did not have a specific responsibility for ex-prisoners either, and the organization was more or less dismissed from the task for which it had been established: preparing prisoners for their return to society. Special prison officers were assigned or educated to guarantee a 'warm transfer' of prisoners to the community and, in the communities, special offices were to be opened for this category of 'citizens' (although they were often hard to find) (RSJ 2009). The main goals of the aftercare programme are to provide detainees with valid identity papers, housing, an income, insight into debts and realization or continuation of care. The programme focuses on regional collaboration between penitentiary institutions, municipalities and social partners, such as housing corporations and care institutions. It is recognized that detention of prisoners close to their hometown is a condition for success, but realization of this condition contrasts with other developments, in particular closure of prisons and the construction of a very large prison in the Upper North of the Netherlands (Duijvenbooden and Pattje 2010).

Despite the radical changes it caused, 'Pushing Back Recidivism', was introduced in the Netherlands without too much resistance, in the first instance. After a while, some critical voices were heard, however, partly based on new theoretical approaches about the effectiveness of sentencing, in particular Desistance and the Good Lives Model. Critics questioned the theoretical basis of the RNR model and wondered if not *what works*, but *why things work* should be the central question in the search for more effective sentences (Rovers 2008; Nelissen 2008). They argued that in the research that is the basis of the RNR model the focus was too much on the internal validity of programmes, while the important role of external factors, of the motivation of the participants or of the interaction between trainer and participant were neglected (Nelissen 2008; Rovers 2008; Boone and Poort 2002).

The criticism was fed by lack of evidence of success. The reform programme was carefully scrutinized in a recent study by Bosma *et al.* (2013). They found that, of the 40,000 prisoners who enter prison each year, only 5,000 fulfil the requirements of Pushing Back Recidivism, which can be explained by the large numbers of prisoners in the Netherlands who serve a prison sentence of less than 6 months and for whom participation in accredited interventions is impractical. Of the prisoners who fulfil the requirements of the reform programme, only around 40 per cent really participate in it. It is not clear what the reasons are for non-participation or for premature drop-out. Even more remarkably the number of behavioural interventions that have been implemented through the years has remained very low, with only 700 interventions implemented on average on a yearly basis. In 2011, for example, of the 2,067 candidates that completed the programme, 718 were actually involved in behavioural intervention. Assuming that every participant is involved in one intervention (although in practice one participant can be involved in more interventions) this would mean that a maximum 35 per cent of all participants were actually involved in behavioural interventions. This is a rather disappointing outcome, since behavioural interventions form the heart of the RNR approach. This could be justified perhaps if the majority of the participants in the Push Back Recidivism programme were low-risk offenders deemed inappropriate for behavioural interventions. This does not seem to be the case, however. Research shows the opposite, namely that criminogenic factors occur more frequently in the group excluded from the interventions than in the group who receive interventions (Fischer *et al.* 2012).

Jesse, Savannah and the intensification of supervision

Despite the fact that the probation service has supervised offenders since its existence, supervision has only been defined and professionalized as such relatively recently. A direct precursor of this development was the massive public and media attention that was attracted by several offences committed by ex-offenders while they were still under some form of supervision. In particular the case of Julien C., an offender who murdered an eight-year-old boy in 2006 while he was under supervision, caused a lot of negative publicity for the probation service. The murder of a 73-year-old man on his own boat and the rape of a young girl by mentally ill offenders on parole leave in 2005 really put the Dutch system of gradual release of mentally ill offenders serving a forensic-psychiatric measure under pressure.

The public anger resulting from these and other incidents forced the probation service to professionalize its supervision task, an operation that was called 'Redesign Supervision' (*Redesign Toezicht*). Supervision is now defined as 'controlling the conditions imposed by one of the organizations involved in the criminal justice system and stimulating and motivating the persons under supervision to comply' (Poort 2009, p. 8). Conditions can be be applied in several judicial modalities, but are mostly applied as special conditions of a suspended sentence or release order. Several other variances are possible, however, for example suspension of pre-trial detention or conditional treatment for mentally ill offenders in a non-custodial setting (*conditional tbs*). To encourage the judge to apply more conditional sentences and to increase the legal certainty for offenders, the main conditions that can be added to a conditional sentence have been explicitly enumerated in the law since 2009. Before the new legislation, many requirements were brought under the generally formulated condition of 'other conditions concerning the behaviour of the convict', a formulation so vague that it was seen as a breach of the principle of legality.

Since the introduction of Redesign Supervision, the probation service has distinguished three levels of supervision: which one will be applied depends on the recidivism risk that the offender presents. Further, two main supervision tasks are distinguished: control (surveillance) and support. Control tasks are described in detail in one of the manuals of the probation service. The amount of required contact is specified for every level of supervision, and this is also true for the number of times the probationer has to report to probation and the number of home visits the probation officer has to pay. In similar detail the manual describes what has to happen should the probationer violate one of the rules; in what circumstances a warning has to be given; and when the prosecutor (who is formally responsible for the execution of sentences) has to be notified. In several comments on Redesign Supervision, it was noted that almost no attention was paid to support as the other aspect of supervision. Support is still described in much less detail than control, but from several sources it is possible to discern what it can contain. It is described as a systematic and particular method to motivate and enable a person to live a responsible life (Krechtig *et al.* 2012, pp. 17, 21). It is assumed that this can be achieved by helping the supervised person with practical issues such as work, education or care, but also by giving him or her the opportunity to take part in a behavioural intervention.

In recent years, however, the upper time limits on periods of supervision have been extended. In the case of a conditionally suspended sentence, the maximum duration of supervision is 3 years. However, where there is judged to be a serious risk that another violent or sexual offence may be committed, the supervision period can now be extended to 10 years. In the case of conditional release from a hospital order for mentally ill offenders (*tbs measure*), a person can be supervised for a maximum of 9 years (this used to be 3 years). Currently, a Bill, which is already accepted in the Lower House and is now waiting to be discussed in the Upper House of the Dutch Parliament, proposes lifelong supervision for the most serious categories of offenders.

In addition to these increases in the duration of supervision, the number of people under some form of supervision has also increased dramatically due to the measures described above. While in 1995, 6,000 people were supervised by the probation service on a daily basis, this number increased to 18,000 in 2010; more than 21,000 people were supervised by the probation service on 1 December 2014. More than two-thirds of them are supervised in the context of a suspended sentence.

Further cutbacks and electronic monitoring

A form of community punishment that has not been discussed yet is electronic monitoring. In the Netherlands, electronic monitoring has been in use since 1995. Currently, it is being applied in several modalities, most notably as a condition for the suspension of pre-trial detention, as a special condition of a conditional prison sentence, as a special condition of conditional release and in the context of penitentiary programmes. Despite the many legal possibilities, the use of electronic monitoring has remained remarkably stable through the years, with around 300 persons tagged on a daily basis. Unless it is legally prescribed, electronic monitoring is only imposed in a minority of the cases in which it potentially could be added to a conditional sentence or conditional suspension of preventive detention. In particular practical objections seem to stand in the way. Officers of the criminal justice system are not aware of the legal and technical possibilities, and often there is not enough time to prepare a plan for electronic monitoring or there are technical objections that stand in the way (Inspectie voor de Sanctietoepassing 2007).

That said, the intended cutbacks in the prison service have recently brought a new momentum to the debate on electronic monitoring. In 2013, the master plan of the Dutch prison service for the years 2013–2018 was published. It describes the intended changes in the prison system aimed at reducing the expenditure by up to 340 million euros in 2018 (Ministry of Justice 2013). Electronic detention is presented as one of the important instruments for realizing these cuts, and a Bill on electronic detention is proposed in the same period as the master plan of the Dutch Prison Service (DJI). Two modalities are mentioned. The first is the 'back-door modality', to be applied after half of the prison sentence has been served but before eligibility for conditional release. The second is the 'front-door modality', which is meant to be a substitution for any prison sentence shorter than 6 months, unless the possibility for electronic detention is explicitly ruled out in the verdict. The second proposal caused a wave of criticism. In the political arena the dominant opinion was that electronic monitoring was far too mild an alternative to detention. Therefore electronic monitoring was not considered acceptable as an alternative to short prison sentences. Most of the Advisory Committees that commented on the Bill were positive about electronic monitoring as an alternative to short prison sentences, but only if it would become an autonomous sentence imposed by the judiciary. As a result of this discussion, the Secretary of State decided to withdraw the second variant. He concluded: 'The introduction of electronic monitoring, which would be imposed by a judge as a principal sentence, does not sufficiently meet the requirements to substitute for short-term prison sentences and, conse-quently, to reduce reoffending' (cited in Boone and Van Hattum 2014, p. 2182). More enthusiasm existed for the back-door modality, although several concerns were expressed in relation to this modality as well, in particular concerning the replacement of the existing system of gradual release from prison by electronic detention and the exclusion of certain groups of detainees from electronic detention as a result of contra-indications and conditions that would be required (RSJ 2013; Boone and Van Hattum 2014). It was also emphasized by several Advisory Com-mittees and other commentators that 'bare detention' without support or guidance was not advisable and that the principle of rehabilitation should be a central con-cern (RSJ 2013). In September 2014, the electronic detention bill was rejected by the Upper House, mainly based on the arguments mentioned above. An adapted proposal is expected soon.

In the meantime, the use of electronic monitoring is rising, due to the intro-duction of a virtual helpdesk (i.e. a digital information point) (Digitaal Loket Electronische Controle) in October 2013. The purpose of this helpdesk is to make it easier for different actors in the criminal justice chain, such as public prosecutors, magistrates and probation workers, to request electronic monitoring advice. Ultimately, the desk should serve to increase the application of electronic monitoring (Reclassering Nederland, 4 November 2013). The requester needs to go through several steps. She/he has to indicate the type of crime committed (violent crime, property crime, sexual offence) and the specific crime profile (for example, domestic violence). Subsequently, the desired type of monitoring needs to be indicated (restriction to a location or exclusion from a location). This information helps to identify which of the eleven applications of electronic monitoring would be most appropriate. When the electronic monitoring request is completed, an electronic monitoring specialist at the probation service investigates the possibility and desirability of applying electronic monitoring in the specific case. Since the introduction of the digital helpdesk, the number of applications of electronic monitoring has increased significantly. It is unclear, however, the extent to which this increase can be ascribed to the addition of electronic monitoring in cases in which supervision without it would have been applied beforehand, or whether it represents replacement of imprisonment by electronic monitoring.

Discussion

In their contribution to the *Sage Handbook of Punishment & Society*, Robinson *et al.* (2013) explain the different faces of community sanctions and measures in contemporary society with reference to four narratives: rehabilitative, punitive, managerial and reparative. In my story of crisis and incidents in the Netherlands, the reparative narrative has not appeared as an important storyline. Although the welfare approach promoted by Louk Hulsman certainly paved the way for community punishment in the Netherlands in the 1970s, by contributing to the growing resistance to custody, followers of the welfare approach have subsequently turned their backs on community punishment, primarily because it seems to pose a serious threat of net-widening. Although a reparative approach has recently become more influential in the Dutch criminal justice system (but predominantly in the sense of giving the victim a stronger position in the penal process), this has not yet had much influence on the shape of community sentencing. The victim and his or her perceived interest does influence the decision-making process regarding community sentences (Boone and Herzog-Evans 2013), but not so much in the forms that community sentences take or the ways they are carried out. I fully agree, however, that community sentences do have a major reparative potential (or maybe even value; but this has yet to be systematically researched), if not to the victim in particular then to society in general. This reparative function is also clearly visible in the more prominent role volunteers have been playing in probation work recently, for example in the role volunteers have in the Circles of Support and Accountability (COSA) that are used as a relatively successful intervention for sexual offenders (Höing and Vogelvang 2012).

The other narratives distinguished by Robinson *et al.* are, however, all clearly visible in the developments sketched in this chapter, but in a typical Dutch mix.

Starting with the rehabilitative narrative, the preceding sections should have made clear that the history of community punishment in the Netherlands is closely connected to post-war developments in the probation service. The forced role of the probation service in the implementation of community service had a side-effect that the community service order was fully framed as a 'more humane and rehabilitative' alternative to prison sentences, although it was already clear by that time that net-widening had been an issue in all of the countries in which community service had already been introduced (Boone 2000). This rehabilitative frame could also not prevent the probation service from suffering an identity crisis, in particular because the execution of sentences soon became its main task and the embedding of community sentences in the organization was accompanied by a reorganization that aimed to change the probation service into a 'more business like organisation' (Boone 2005). These changes confronted the probation service with a crisis of legitimacy. If supporting the welfare of the suspect or offender was no longer to be the main aim of the Service, the question was: What legitimized its existence? Why should an independent probation service continue to exist and not simply become a service of the Justice Department?

The answer to those questions can be read in successive annual reports: since 2003 the probation service has characterized itself as an organization that works for the benefit of society. Its main aim is to enhance the safety of society, not to support the well-being of suspects or offenders, although these objectives can sometimes be aligned of course. Reducing recidivism and contributing to the safety of society are measurable aims; however, by totally identifying itself with these aims, the probation service has forced itself into the position that it can only justify its activities and interventions by referring to its assumed effectiveness in terms of reducing recidivism. This position does not give much room for the argument that activities can also be very useful even when they do not lead to a (direct) reduction of recidivism (and possibly also do not contribute to the credibility of community sentences *as* punishment). From this point of view, it is also difficult to start a reasonable discussion concerning the question of what risks should be accepted by a society that wants to give room for community punishment alongside custodial sentences. When it is assumed that community punishment should contribute to the safety of society, not lead to less safety, every crime committed by an offender who is supervised in the community is framed as a failure of the probation service and a disqualification of community punishment. Although, in general, the media is not very interested in community punishment as a social phenomenon (contrary to prison), media attention is intense whenever an offence is committed by an offender under supervision.

It must be admitted, however, that, despite these concerns, probation work has been evaluated relatively positively in the context of effective sentencing. A remarkably positive evaluation of the effectiveness of community service compared with short prison sentences put community service provisionally beyond suspicion (Wermink *et al.* 2009). Also, in a more recent study, community service orders and supervision were considered as much more effective in terms of reducing recidivism compared with imprisonment (Zebel *et al.* 2013). On the other hand, what

Robinson *et al.* (2013) call the instrumental version of the rehabilitative narrative makes community punishment inherently vulnerable. It is questionable for example whether behavioural interventions will survive, now that their contribution to the safety of society has been shown to be limited.

One of the main characteristics of punishment from a doctrinal point of view is that it is generally considered as an evil (Jonkers 1991). In other words: to legitimate the use of community measures *as punishment, these have to be perceived as punitive by the general public.* From this point of view it is defensible that prison is still defined as punishment, despite the fact that, for example, a homeless person may *perceive* a stay in prison as rather comfortable in winter-time or that a small minority of the public still thinks prison is comparable to a hotel. Conceiving of punishment as a measure that is considered as an evil by the majority of the people, however, also enables us to argue, for example, that particular sentences should be abolished or only applied to a limited category of offenders or offences, in case it is massively contested as an evil. So, the question of whether the concept of community *punishment* makes sense in the Dutch situation (see the Introduction), is strongly connected to the punitive narrative. It is interesting to look at the development of community sentences in the Netherlands from this point of view. To make community service orders more acceptable to the general public, several aspects have been added to them. The work has become more demanding, for example, and has begun to be executed in group projects or carried out in high-visibility orange jackets.

Furthermore, training orders, which were considered predominantly as rehabilitative interventions, have been abolished as autonomous sentences and redefined as conditions of suspended sentences. Electronic monitoring has very recently been rejected by Parliament as an autonomous sentence, because it is considered to be too mild as an alternative to detention. So, the question of whether 'community punishment' is an appropriate term in the Dutch context can only be answered with an equivocal 'yes', at least from a legal and normative point of view. Community sanctions (and note the term 'sanctions' is deliberately used instead of 'punishment') are often not imposed *as* punishment, because these are (considered to be) not accepted as punishment in political discourse. How far these normative, political choices are built on empirical solid ground can be contested, since they are mostly inspired by media coverage and invalid research, while more robust empirical research points to much broader acceptance of community punishment by the general public. On the other hand, it has to be admitted that, where community sanctions are accepted by the general public, this is mostly on the basis of a rehabilitative and not a punitive narrative (Ruiter *et al.* 2011).

Without doubt, the most striking narrative in the Dutch context is the managerial one, understood as developing systematic strategies to meet the aims of criminal justice in a highly cost-effective way (Bottoms 1977; Simon and Feeley 1992). Despite the fact that both the effectiveness and punitive weight of community punishment are constantly contested, community punishment is applied on a large scale in all phases of the criminal justice system, mostly on less dangerous categories of offenders (Boone 2010); however, exceptions do exist in the release phase, in which more severe categories of offenders are supervised for a much longer period of time than they used to be. The Dutch system has been extremely effective in managing this quantitative growth. Highly advanced data-processing systems have been developed and have resulted in a probation service that is substantially driven by output numbers. Much effort has been put into better cooperation among the different organizations involved in the imposition and execution of (community) sentences (called 'chain' partners, although it is disputed whether the judiciary is also part of 'the chain'; Boone 2009a). Levels of control and supervision are described in detail, as are the responses when requirements are violated. To understand these organizational changes from a managerial perspective, it is not enough to look at their contribution to the more formal or classical aims of punishment such as rehabilitation, retribution, reparation or preventing crime. These changes sometimes simply don't contribute to these aims and definitely do not do so in a cost-effective manner. They do serve the credibility of the criminal justice system, however – or at least they are supposed to do so, a characteristic that has been recognized as an important aim of community punishment in an early stage of its development (Boone 2010). That authorities lose their credibility when they do not (visibly) respond to crime has been the dominant political view since the 1990s, and community punishment can often be characterized as a satisfying response from both a proportional and a financial perspective. The managerial responses to the crises and incidents described in this chapter can also be partly understood as efforts of the organizations and individuals involved in the imposition and execution of community sentences to enhance their credibility.

Thus we come to the final question mentioned in the introduction of this book: what does the understanding of community punishment in the Netherlands contribute to an understanding of the penal climate in general? The question is not so difficult to answer. Insight into the practice of community punishment in the Netherlands shows one side of a very bifurcated penal climate (Cavadino and Dignan 2006; Boone 2012; Boone and Van Swaaningen 2013). It shows a society that strongly rejects all forms of visible crime and inconvenience, but accepts that some categories of offenders get away with a relatively mild punishment as long as the rest of society is not compromised. It also shows a society with strong attachments and beliefs in rehabilitation, both among the people working in the criminal justice system and among the general public. These ambitions, however, are pursued for limited categories of offenders; what happens to ('dangerous') others is beyond the scope of this chapter.

References

Andrews, D. A., Ivan Zinger, Robert D. Hoge, James Bonta, Paul Gendreau and Francis T. Cullen (1990a) 'Does correctional treatment work? A clinically-relevant and psychologically informed meta-analysis', *Criminology*, 28: 369–404.

Andrews, D. A., J. Bonta and R. D. Hoge (1990b) 'Classification for effective rehabilitation; rediscovering psychology', *Criminal Justice and Behaviour*, 17: 19–52.

Boone, M. (2000) *Recht voor Commuun Gestraften, Dogmatisch-Juridische Aspecten Van Taak-straffen en Penitentiaire Programma's*. Deventer: Gouda Quint.

Boone, M. (2005) 'Community justice in a safety culture: probation service and community justice in the Netherlands', in J. Winston and F. Pakes (eds), *Community Justice. Issues for Probation and Criminal Justice*. Cullompton, Devon: Willan, pp. 300–20.

Boone, M. (2009a) 'Ketenpartner of geketend. Rechterlijke bemoeienis met de tenuitvoer-legging Van sancties', *Proces*, 2: 65–75.

Boone, M. (2009b) 'Reclassering', in E. R. Muller and P. C. Vegter (eds), *Detentie. Gevangen in Nederland*. Alphen aan den Rijn: Kluwer.

Boone, M. (2010) 'Only for minor offences, Community service in the Netherlands', *European Journal of Probation*, 2(1): 22–40.

Boone, M. (2012) *Our own Rascals First: Inclusion And Exclusion in the Use of Sanctions*. The Hague: Eleven International Publishers.

Boone, M. and W. van Hattum (2014) '"Promoveren en degraderen" Van gedetineerden', *Nederlands Juristenblad* 31: 2179–84.

Boone, M. and M. Herzog-Evans (2013) 'Offender Supervision and Decision-Making in Europe', in F. McNeill and K. Beyens (eds), *Offender Supervision in Europe*. New York: Palgrave Macmillan, pp. 51–96.

Boone, M. and R. Poort (2002) 'Wat werkt (niet) in Nederland? De What Works principes toegepast op het programma-aanbod Van de Reclassering', *Justitiële Verkenningen*, 8: 48–63.

Boone, M. and R. Van Swaaningen (2013) 'Regression to the mean: punishment in the Netherlands', in V. Ruggiero and M. Ryan (eds) *Punishment in Europe*. New York: Palgrave Macmillan, pp. 33–57.

Bosma, A., M. Kunst and P. Nieuwbeerta (2013) 'Rehabilitatie in Nederlandse gevangenis-sen. Wat is de stand Van zaken ten aanzien Van het programma Terugdringen Recidive', *Tijdschrift voor Herstelrecht*, 12(3): 3–19.

Bottoms, A. (1977) 'Reflections on the renaissance of dangerousness', *Howard Journal of Penology & Crime Prevention*, 16: 70–96.

Cavadino, M. and J. Dignan (2006) *Penal Systems. A Comparative Approach*. London: Sage.

Commissie Vermogensstraffen (1969) *Interimrapport*. The Hague: SDU.

Commissie Vermogensstraffen (1972) *Eindrapport*. The Hague: SDU.

Duijvenbooden, K. Van and W. Pattje (2010) *Stand Van zaken Implementatie Samenwerk-ingsmodel Nazorg binnen het Gevangeniswezen en binnen gemeenten*. The Hague: Ministerie Van Justitie/VNG.

Fischer, T. F. C., W. J. M. Captein and B. W. C. Zwirs (2012) 'Gedragsinterventies voor volwassen justitiabelen. Stand Van zaken en mogelijkheden voor innovatie'. The Hague: Boom | Lemma Uitgevers, WODC.

Heinrich, J. (1995) *Particuliere Reclassering En Overheid in Nederland sinds 1823*, diss. Groningen. Arnhem: Gouda Quint.

Höing, M. and B. Vogelvang (2012) COSA in Nederland: eerste ervaringen. Een onderzoek naar de proefimplementatie Van *een* nieuwe aanpak voor de re-integratie Van veroordeelde zedendelinquenten, *Tijdschrift voor Herstelrecht* 12(2): 60–9.

Howard, John (1977) *The State of the Prisons in England and Wales*. Abingdon: Professional Books.

Inspectie voor de Sanctietoepassing (2005) *Uitvoering Werkstraffen Reclassering*. The Hague: Inspectie voor de Sanctietoepassing.

Inspectie voor de Sanctietoepassing (2007) *Uitvoering Elektronische Detentie*. The Hague: Inspectie voor de Sanctietoepassing.

Janse de Jonge, J. A. (1991) *Om de Persoon Van de Dader: Over Straftheorieen en Voorlichting Door de Reclassering*. Arnhem: Gouda Quint.

Janse de Jonge, J. A. and C. Kelk (1992) *Met Schuld Beladen, De Kern en Actuele Betekenis Van het Werk Van G.Th. Kempe over Straf En Reclassering*. Arnhem: Gouda Quint.

Jonkers, W. H. A. (1991) 'De strafrechtelijke straf: inhoud, grondslag, doeleinden', in W. H. A. Jonkers (ed), *Penitentiair Recht*. Arnhem: Gouda Quint.

Kalidien, S. and N. De Heere-de Lange (eds) (2012) *Criminaliteit en Rechtshandhaving 2011: Ontwikkelingen en Samenhangen*. The Hague: Boom Juridische uitgevers.

Klijn, A., F. v. Tulder, R. Beaujean, T. v. d. Heijden and G. Rodenburg (2008) *Moord, doodslag, taakstraf? Een Zembla-uitzending nader bekeken*. The Hague: Raad voor de Rechtspraak.

Krechtig, L., M. Lans, A. Andreas and A. Menger (2012) *Begeleiding bij Toezicht. Handboek Reclassering*. HU/KSI: Utrecht.

Laan, P. H. v. d. (1993) 'Het publiek en de taakstraf: een maatschappelijk draagvlak voor de taakstraf', *Justitiële Verkenningen*, 19(9): 89–100.

Lünneman, K. D., W. M. E. H. Beijers, M. E. Wentink, J. Junger-Tas and S. Tan (2005) *Werkstraffen: Succes Verzekerd? Succes-en faalfactoren bij werkstraffen Van meerderjarigen*. Utrecht: Verwey-Jonker Instituut.

Ministry of Justice (1996) *Beleidsnota taakstraffen 'Voor straf werken en leren'*. Kamerstukken II 1995/96, 24 807, nos 1–2.

Ministry of Justice (2013) *Masterplan DJI 2013–2018*, Kamerstukken II 2012–2013, 24 567, no. 535.

Moedikdo, P. (1976) 'De Utrechtse school Van Pompe, Baan en Kempe', in C. Kelk, M. Moerings, N. Jörg and P. Moedikdo (eds), *Recht Macht En Manipulatie*. Utrecht/Antwerpen: het Spectrum.

Morris, N. and M. Tonry (1990) *Between Prison and Probation: Intermediate Punishments in a Rational Sentencing System*. New York: Oxford University Press.

Mulder, G. E. and H. Schootstra (1974) *De voorwaardelijke veroordeling: prae-advies*. Zwolle: Tjeenk Willink.

Nelissen, P. (2008) 'Interventie op basis Van bevindingen uit de levensloopcriminologie: een nieuw paradigma voor verbetering?', *Proces*, 3: 78–88.

Poort, R. (2009) *Fundamenten voor toezicht. Over de grondslagen voor de ontwikkeling Van reclasseringstoezicht*. Utrecht: Reclassering Nederland.

Poort, R. and K. Eppink (2009) *Een literatuuronderzoek naar de effectiviteit Van de reclassering*. The Hague: BJu Legal Publishers.

Poort, R. and J. Zengerink (2009) 'De reclassering en de werkstraf', *Sancties*, no. 3: 158–68.

Raad voor de Strafrechtstoepassing en Jeugdbescherming (2005) *De tenuitvoerlegging Van werkstraffen*. The Hague: RSJ.

Raad voor Strafrechtstoepassing en Jeugdbescherming (2009) Doorpakken. Maatschappelijke re-integratie en nazorg voor ex-gedetineerden, Advies 17 September.

Raad voor de Strafrechtstoepassing en Jeugdbescherming (2013) *Advies over het 'conceptwetsvoorstel tot wijziging Van de Penitentiaire beginselenwet en het Wetboek Van Strafrecht in verband met de herijking Van de wijze Van tenuitvoerlegging Van vrijheidsbenemende sancties en de invoering Van elektronische detentie' Van 2 mei 2013*.

Reclassering Nederland (2013) *Lancering loket elektronische controle*.

Robinson, G., F. McNeill and S. Maruna (2013) 'Punishment *in* Society. The Improbable Persistence of Probation and Other Community Sanctions and Measures', in J. Simon and R. Sparks (eds), *Sage Handbook of Punishment & Society*. London: Sage Publications, pp. 321–40.

Rovers, B. (2008) 'Ze deugen nergens voor: het belief-effect in justitiële jeugdinterventies', in H. Moors and B. Rovers (eds) *Geloven in Veiligheid: Tegendraadse Perspectieven*. The Hague: Boom Juridische Uitgevers, pp. 73–112.

Ruiter, S., J. Tolsm, M. de Hoon, H. Elffers and P. Van der Laan (2011) *De burger als rechter. Een onderzoek naar geprefereerde sancties voor misdrijven in Nederland*. The Hague: Boom Lemma Uitgevers.

Simon, J. and M. M. Feeley (1992) The new penology: notes on the emerging strategy of corrections and its implications, *Criminology*, 30(4): 449–74.

Stichting Reclassering Nederland (SRN) (2004) *Krachtig op koers*, jaarverslag 2003.

Swaaningen, R. Van (2013) 'Reversing the punitive turn', in T. Daems, S. Snacken and D. Van Zyl Smit (eds) *European Penology*. Oxford: Hart, pp. 339–60.

Wartna, B. S. J., N. Tollenaar and M. Blom (2005a) *Recidive 1997: Een cijfermatig overzicht Van de strafrechtelijke recidive Van volwassen en jeugdige daders*. The Hague: WODC.

Wartna, B. S. J., N. Tollenaar and A. A. M. Essers (2005b) *Door na de gevangenis; Een cijfermatig overzicht Van de strafrechtelijke recidive onder ex-gedetineerden*. The Hague: WODC.

Wermink, H., A. Blokland, P. Nieuwbeerta and N. Tollenaar (2009) 'Recidive na werkstraffen en na gevangenisstraffen, een gematchde vergelijking', *Tijdschrift voor Criminologie*, 51(3): 211–28.

Zebel, S., D. L. Alberda and B. S. J. Wartna (2013) 'Recidive na een reclasseringscontact. Overzicht en analyse Van de terugval Van personen na beëindiging Van een toezicht of een werkstraf in de periode 2002–2009', The Hague: Boom/Lemma, WODC.

7

CONTINGENT LEGITIMACY

Community sanctions in Northern Ireland

Nicola Carr

Introduction

The trajectory of community sanctions and measures in Northern Ireland shares some common characteristics with England and Wales, with similar origins, in the form of court missionaries, and the same foundational legislation passed in the UK parliament – the Probation of Offenders Act (1907). However, the development of community-based sanctions and measures, and the institutions that administered them in Northern Ireland were different for a number of reasons. From its earliest stages their contours have been shaped by the wider political context. This has included a strong focus on internal security following partition of the island of Ireland in the early part of the twentieth century and the impact of the violent 30-year civil and political conflict known as the 'Troubles' from the late 1960s into the late 1990s. The ongoing transition from conflict and the attention towards reform of the criminal justice system have also impacted on the role of the probation service. During this period there has been an increased focus on risk and public protection, and an increase in the numbers of people under the Probation Board for Northern Ireland's (PBNI) care or supervision.

This chapter considers the legitimating discourses that have been drawn upon to support the use of community sanctions and measures in Northern Ireland over time. In the earliest stages redemption and reform were legitimating narratives. In the course of the political conflict, a community-based presence grounded on neutrality provided a powerful legitimating rationale in a context where State legitimacy and the role of criminal justice agencies in particular were highly problematic. In the period of transition from conflict, public protection, claims of greater effectiveness and lower costs when compared with prison have been employed as rationales to advocate the use of community sanctions. These claims have been linked to an overarching aim of penal reductionism, particularly in relation to a government policy objective to reduce the use of short prison sentences.

As indicated by the title, this book explicitly addresses the concept of 'community punishment'. It is important to note that the term 'community punishment' bears a particular resonance in Northern Ireland, usually taken to refer to punishment beatings and attacks by paramilitary groups. Historically paramilitaries have been involved in 'policing' of local communities in the context of legitimacy deficits in State-administered justice (Feenan 2002; Monaghan 2004). In the period since the ceasefires of the main paramilitary organizations (mid-1990s onwards), the numbers of punishment beatings and attacks have declined, but they continue to cause concern (PSNI 2014).[1] Perhaps for this reason, in Northern Ireland (unlike in England and Wales), the concept of 'punishment in the community' has never found favour in relation to community sanctions and measures.

This chapter draws on a small amount of existing literature on the history of probation in Northern Ireland and primary research exploring the context of probation practice during the Troubles. It draws on an oral history of probation comprising interviews with 19 retired or serving probation officers and managers who had worked in the service in a period collectively spanning from 1969 to the present. Findings from the initial stages of this research were reported in Carr and Maruna (2012).[2]

Early years – redemption and the 'fledgling chick'

Previous accounts of the early years of probation in Northern Ireland describe a nascent and underdeveloped institution (O'Mahony and Chapman 2007; Fulton and Parkhill 2009). In the first decades of the twentieth century, probation officers were located primarily in the main urban centres – Belfast and Derry/Londonderry – and were drawn from the ranks of Christian missionary groups. Fulton and Parkhill's (2009) historical account records that in its early stages probation, as an alternative sanction to imprisonment, was used mainly for less serious offending and 'deserving cases' – that is, those who were considered by the Courts to be 'redeemable'.[3] This emphasis on redemption legitimized the alternative sanction, sitting well with the religious orientation and a focus on temperance. The influence of the temperance movement, which had attained widespread support in Ireland and transcended the dual traditions (Catholic and Protestant), meant that many cases referred to probation by the courts involved people whose offending was linked to alcohol use (Fulton and Webb 2009).

Despite the introduction of the UK Probation of Offenders Act (1907), in the early years probation services did not develop in the same fashion in Northern Ireland as in England and Wales. According to O'Mahony and Chapman (2007: 156):

> the early development of probation in Northern Ireland was hampered by a series of ineffective mechanisms that were put in place to establish the service, persistent problems over funding and a general lack of 'professional status' for the service or probation officers at the time.

Following partition of Ireland under the Government of Ireland Act (1920), responsibility for criminal justice was devolved to the Northern Ireland parliament. However, as Fulton and Parkhill (2009) note, internal security was a preoccupation and a consideration of alternatives to prison or a penal-welfarist approach were not high on the agenda. In such circumstances: 'The fledgling probation chick was largely left to fend for itself' (Fulton and Parkhill 2009: 15).

A government committee established to consider legislation in relation to children and young people following the enactment of the Children and Young Persons Act (1933) in England and Wales also examined the role of probation services.[4] The Lynn Committee (1938) made recommendations for the development of the probation service in Northern Ireland, including the expansion of its role, the development of specific training and for probation officers to be employed directly by the Ministry for Home Affairs (O'Mahony and Chapman 2007). However, the outbreak of war put a hold on developments and further legislation was not enacted until the Probation Act (Northern Ireland) 1950. In 1950 the Ministry for Home Affairs took on responsibility for probation and in the following years the numbers of people subject to probation supervision expanded but remained at relatively low levels (Fulton and Carr 2013).

Until the mid-1960s probation remained the only supervised community sentence available to the court. The Treatment of Offenders (Northern Ireland) Act 1968 provided a legislative basis for the post-release supervision for long-term prisoners, and in 1976 the community service order was introduced as an alternative sanction to imprisonment.[5] The Northern Ireland legislation was modelled on the Criminal Justice Act 1972 (England and Wales). Described by one commentator as representing 'a smorgasbord of penal purpose' (Thorsvaldson 1982, cited in Pease 1985: 57), the legitimation for the community service order was provided in light of its reparative veneer and the fact that it was a cheaper sanction than imprisonment (Pease 1985). The impetus for the introduction of this measure in Northern Ireland appears to be a direct effect of policy transfer.

Until the early 1970s, community-based sanctions remained a relatively underdeveloped part of the criminal justice system. This was in part related to the institutional structures. The administration of probation came under the remit of the Ministry of Home Affairs, and probation officers were employed as civil servants. As this respondent, who joined the service under a graduate trainee scheme in the 1970s, described it, the organization was considered relatively staid and conservative:

> In those days the Probation Service was pretty under-developed, and when I got a job they would have pulled anyone off the street if they had a degree. You know, in those days probation officers were sort of people who had been either good Protestants or good Catholics, you were recommended by the church. . . it was very conservative. It was very much civil service.
>
> *(PHI01)*

At this time, the probation officer's role was still traditionally aimed towards 'advising, assisting and befriending', and the typical clientele referred by the courts were young people and persistent offenders involved in relatively low-level offending:

> There wasn't a lot of offending behaviour work or anything, it was just – what's your problem, how can we help? You were advising, assisting and befriending in those days. . . I would have had mostly probationers and mostly young ones.
>
> *(PHI01)*

> The courts saw us, when they put someone on probation the idea was that we would help that person stay out of trouble, and that was [in] the sixties and the beginning [of the] seventies.
>
> *(PHI02)*

As the testimonies of probation officers who served in this period illustrate, the role and function of probation was largely framed in penal-welfarist terms (Garland 1985). There was recognition of need and provision of help, but little emphasis on the 'diagnosis' of causal factors or engagement with the person's offending per se. Probation as a penal sanction was a somewhat marginal endeavour reserved for young people and less serious offending.

Probation and the political conflict – 'neutral and useful'

The emergence of a new generation of professionally trained staff in the 1970s and the escalation in civil and political conflict marked a critical turning point in the development of community sanctions and measures in Northern Ireland. Perhaps somewhat paradoxically, during the periods of most intense violence, probation established a presence in communities which were considered no-go areas by other criminal justice agencies (Carr and Maruna 2012). This was linked to the neutrality stance adopted by staff and advanced through their union, the National Association of Probation Officers (NAPO), and through the focus placed on community-based work, which was initiated and supported by the new generation of staff. This respondent who worked as a probation officer during this period explains:

> one of the things I thought from a community perspective was that people like probation officers should be visible. Whereas most probation work as you know is invisible. It's in offices and stuff. I wanted to be seen and known as the probation officer of the area, and so I would have gone to community meetings and resident meetings and things like that and would have done a lot of things like at difficult times of year, would have hired a mini-bus to take groups of kids, not all of whom would have been on probation, but maybe brothers or sisters. So I think what I thought was that we need to be seen as being useful, not as sort of clinical practitioners but as a resource to the community, and it wouldn't have just been me that did that. So I think that, that as we go

on, I think that that was an important thing was that we were sort of neutral politically, we didn't take a stand sort of one way or the other. Now, there's problems with that as well as advantages, but also that we were useful. It was important to be seen to be useful.

(PHI01)[6]

This sense of having a visible presence and being useful was important in achieving legitimacy in communities that were experiencing high levels of violence and in which criminal justice agencies were viewed with mistrust. The 'neutrality' stance adopted by probation was initially motivated by the introduction of mandatory sentences under 'Emergency' legislation[7] for young people involved in 'riotous behaviour'. However, as this respondent outlines, this crystallized into a position where probation officers would not work with individuals involved in 'politically motivated' offending in anything other than a voluntary capacity:

the Tory government at that time introduced legislation that anyone who was arrested for riotous behaviour, there was lots of rioting going on and a lot of young people were getting involved, would get a 6-month Borstal sentence, it was Borstal in those days. Automatic, mandatory, it was a bit like you hear about knife crime, you get a mandatory, it was the same idea. So there was a mandatory sentence, but the law also said that if you were a juvenile you had to have a Social Enquiry Report prepared by a Probation Officer. So we would be going out and doing social background etc. knowing that this guy is going to get 6 months, so we just said – this is stupid. Now at first it was just a contradiction – this is stupid, what's the point? But then we sort of started to debate it within the union and realised that there were sort of some principles about this that we were being asked to treat people who were breaking the law out of political motivation and we were asked to sort of pathologise in some way this sort of behaviour; to see it as a sort of personal issue, a personal problem. And that led us on to think that there was something unethical about assessing and supervising people on statutory orders who were committing offences out of political reasons. That brought us into conflict then with the law and with the courts. But we went to the national union, it became national policy because obviously occasionally Irish people were being arrested in England for politically motivated [crimes], and it would have been adults as well so it would have been issues like parole supervision, so it became a national policy [in the National Association for Probation Officers – which served England, Wales and Northern Ireland].

(PHI01)

The stance on politically motivated offending grounded in a clear principle also had more pragmatic effects. It meant that unlike other criminal justice workers (such as the police or prison officers), probation staff were not considered 'legitimate targets' by paramilitary organizations and no probation officer was killed in the course of the conflict. Other areas of the criminal justice system had been mobilized in an attempt to contain the conflict (e.g. the prisons were used for internment without trial) (McEvoy 2001). However, given its more liminal role, probation was more 'off the radar' and its 'neutral' and 'useful' position meant that it could function in what was a highly dysfunctional context:

> we were a bit sort of off the radar, we weren't that important. So obviously you had you know judges, police officers, prison officers, magistrates were all getting killed. So I think we were saying, and obviously what you had in those days was the Diplock Courts[8], the whole criminal justice system was being adjusted to deal with serious political offences, the courts, the police were adopting new approaches, the courts were, the prisons obviously were, so everybody were adapting to this political situation. And I suppose we thought that if we kept working with politicals eventually our practice would become much more oriented towards that and therefore that would not only be unethical, but dangerous. So I think going back to that earlier point about it being useful, I think that our strategy during the Troubles was (a) we're neutral and (b) we're useful.
>
> *(PHI01)*

The motion regarding 'politically motivated offending' was brought by the Northern Ireland Branch to NAPO's Annual National Conference in 1975, where it was passed and became a national policy. The role of the NAPO branch in Northern Ireland during this period was critical; according to a number of respondents it provided leadership and a rallying point for staff and an outlet for the newer generation of graduates.

> I would say in many ways NAPO managed probation, the union was very strong, all of the bright people were in NAPO. The managers were old dinosaurs, who were civil servants so the bright people were in NAPO and we had a huge amount of influence.
>
> *(PHI01)*

NAPO also acted as a bulwark when the Northern Ireland Office placed pressure on probation staff to acquiesce on their stance, going so far at one point to threaten to fire probation staff:

> the Northern Ireland Office[9] [who] refused to accept that we needed to act and work in a different way *even* as they saw the prison service being colonised into being anti-terrorist and fighting a war. But it was a matter of whether the organisation could exist or not because we had to have the confidence of the community of going about our business.
>
> *(PHI02)*

In a curious way therefore the political conflict provided a creative space for probation to develop during this period. Its adaptation was to try to be 'useful' and this 'usefulness' was to be present in local communities and to provide practical assistance where possible. In this way the Probation Board invoked neutrality as a powerful legitimating discourse within communities and civil society. In so doing it distinguished itself from other parts of the criminal justice system. In practical terms this involved providing assistance where possible, including diverting young people from areas at times of high tension – for example through the provision of outward-bound activities:

> I think there would have been a lot of talk about IT, intermediate treatment[10] and I remember there was a lot of people going over to Liverpool for focus on football and that. It was a very male-dominated environment then, but the idea was again you had the Troubles and internment; it was about trying to help divert young people away.
>
> *(PHI08)*

At times the role also involved providing assistance to young people who were under paramilitary threat. In some cases this involved facilitating young people leaving Northern Ireland to avoid punishment beatings or shootings.[11] As one probation officer recalled it, 'paramilitaries' shootings and beatings, paramilitary punishments were just part and parcel of working' (PHI09), particularly with young men involved in car crime.

In the accounts of probation officers who worked during the periods of most intense political conflict, these exceptional circumstances generated the possibility for innovations that may not have occurred otherwise. As this respondent puts it, while neutrality provided a 'space', the political context also provided a 'camouflage' that allowed for innovation and resistance within probation:

> So I think that sort of political neutrality gave you space to do that and also the fact that the camouflage of being in Northern Ireland meant that some of the more reactionary, in my opinion, stuff that was coming from England could be blocked, and we could sort of say, that doesn't work over here, we're different.
>
> *(PHI01)*

Community and contingent legitimacy

The community-based aspect of probation practice in Northern Ireland, which developed in the 1970s and 1980s, was also linked to the development of community governance structures in areas that were bearing the brunt of the Conflict. A range of community groups established in this period and funded through various initiatives provided a network for probation to link in with and to support.

> Lord Melchett was... one of the Ministers of State and this must have been, I would say, sometime in between '78 and '82/'83, around about then, he

came in and we had [the] 'Making Belfast Work' initiative and because we worked in communities like that we were seen as people who had something to contribute... It was a whole political thing but nevertheless you were contributing. You think you were contributing very importantly so you had that kind of community development strand, that kind of community involvement which I think served us well.

(PHI04)

The voluntary sector was also strong, with organizations such as Extern, the Quakers and NIACRO (Northern Ireland Association for the Care and Rehabilitation of Offenders) playing important roles (Fulton and Parkhill 2009). At the risk of painting a somewhat romanticized version of probation's role during this period, it is important to note, however, that probation's presence within some communities was contingent on the approval of paramilitaries. While one could argue that this was a particular sort of legitimacy, it also meant that the capacity to challenge activity such as paramilitary punishments of young people accused of involvement in offending or anti-social behaviour was muted. To take a position on such issues was to risk taking a political stance and to risk 'crossing the line' in terms of neutrality.

I think a lot of us, some went through the Troubles with those sort of unspoken rules that you couldn't make public or explicit but you knew that if you got on the wrong side of the paramilitaries seriously you couldn't do the job you wanted to do. You would have to retreat back into a big office in the centre of town and get people to come down from Anderstown to see you, whereas we had an office in Anderstown, an office in the Falls.[12]

(PHI01)

The dividend of being able to function and to be present in communities necessitated such adaptations, but the price was that some of the sectarian hatred that fuelled the hostilities was not addressed. Probation was avowedly non-sectarian (as was reflected in the composition of its workforce),[13] but it was not *anti*-sectarian, as this probation officer outlines:

we realised that by taking a non-sectarian stance, it was hard to take an anti-sectarian stance. It's like being non-racist rather than anti-racist, you know the only thing I would be proud of you know was I believe that the Probation Service wasn't sectarian. But it was passively non-sectarian as opposed to actively non-sectarian. If you know what I mean?

(PHI01)

The grounding of probation in communities that occurred in this period also informed changes to its administrative structures. In 1979 the government appointed a Children and Young Persons Review Group to consider the delineation of child welfare and justice services and the future organizational structure of the Probation Service.[14] The report of the review (more commonly referred to as the *Black Report*), recommended the establishment of a community-based board to manage probation. The Northern Ireland Office would retain budgetary responsibility for probation, but the new structure would operate at a distance, allowing for a greater degree of autonomy and more community involvement:

> if the Service is to enjoy fully the confidence of the community, which will be essential if it is to carry out its work successfully, we consider that this can be better achieved if the community participates directly in the management of the Service.
>
> *(Report of the Children and Young Persons*
> *Review Group 1979: 53)*

This recommendation eventually led to the enactment of the Probation Board of Northern Ireland (Order) (1982), which established probation as a non-departmental public body (NDPB). The Board, which was appointed from the community, led by a Chairperson and Deputy Chair and comprised of 10–18 board members, directly employed probation staff, meaning that probation officers now became public servants rather than civil servants (Fulton and Parkhill 2009). However, the core duties of the probation officer as set out in the 1982 Order remained largely unchanged from those articulated in the Probation of Offenders Act (1907):[15]

a. to supervise the persons placed under their supervision and to advise, assist and befriend those persons;

b. to enquire in accordance with any direction of the court into the circumstances or home surroundings of any person with a view to assisting the court in determining the most suitable method for dealing with him, and

c. to perform such other duties as may be prescribed or imposed by or under any statutory provision or as the Probation Board may direct.

(Schedule 4, Probation Board of Northern Ireland
Order, 1982)

The establishment of the Board and the development of new administrative structures represented a new era for probation. While continuing its community-based role, it further developed this base by providing funding for a range of local organizations and partnerships. Notably a fifth of probation's entire budget was directed towards such initiatives during this period (O'Mahony and Chapman 2007). Significantly by 2009 this proportion had reduced to just 7 per cent (McCaughey 2009). A focus on group-based approaches, at times responding to specific concerns (such as joy-riding) (Chapman 1995), led to the development of programmes that were precursors to the emergence of a stronger focus on evidence-based practice (Chapman and Hough 1998). Indeed one of the earlier programmes developed by probation in Northern Ireland – STAC (Stop Think and Change), was highlighted as an exemplar in the review of effective offender supervision by the probation inspectorate of England and Wales (Underdown 1998).

Conflict transformation and policy emulation

During the 1990s the role of the Probation Board expanded with the introduction of new legislation, and the organization's future role was considered in a review of the criminal justice system undertaken as part of the peace process. The Criminal Justice Review (2000), which followed from the Belfast (Good Friday) Agreement in 1998, considered all aspects of the criminal justice system (with the exception of policing, which was dealt with in a separate report),[16] including the courts, youth justice, probation and prisons. Its recommendations led to the establishment of a separate service to administer the youth justice system and the introduction of a restorative justice model as the primary response for dealing with youth offending (Doak and O'Mahony 2011). While probation retained responsibility for certain categories of young people (i.e. a small number made subject to probation orders or community service orders), its role in working with young people had become much more marginal.

Legislation establishing a separate Youth Justice Agency and placing restorative justice within a statutory framework as the primary response to youth offending was enacted in 2002. The restorative-based youth–conference model adopted in Northern Ireland was a direct response to the legitimacy deficit in the administration of justice in the period of Conflict (Doak and O'Mahony 2011). While not without its difficulties (for a discussion see McAlister and Carr 2014), it has been hailed as an international success (Jacobson and Gibbs 2009). It is notable that while restorative justice has formed a central underpinning rationale and legitimating discourse for the *youth* justice system, it is has not received anywhere near such currency within the adult criminal justice system, specifically in relation to community sanctions and measures. Some possible reasons for this include the marginalization of PBNI's role with young people and the move towards work with 'higher risk' offenders.

From the 1980s onwards, probation had reoriented its work more towards adults. The introduction of key legislation expanded its mandate (Criminal Justice (Northern Ireland) Order 1996) and saw more 'hard end' or serious offending coming under its remit. The account below reflects this shift and also notes that work in which probation had previously been centrally involved had increasingly been devolved to voluntary sector agencies:

> The end of the work which a lot of us we felt was very useful was the kind of advocacy. . . It's now done by the voluntary sector so we kept the hard end of the job and all the very nice bits went to the voluntary sector so they do. . . I'm sure it's not nice all the time, but you know what I mean, they do all the floating support, all that personalized support, and all that has gone to the

voluntary sector and that may well be that's the right way, but it has meant that people have much more now… and of course it had to be, and of course big, big change to dealing with adult offenders.

(PHI04)

Reflecting this changing role, the Criminal Justice (NI) Order (1996) marks a shift in the orientation of community sanctions and measures in this period. The legislation articulates that community sentences such as probation should serve a rehabilitative function, but with the underpinning aim of 'protecting the public from harm'.[17] Framed in these terms the individual is the locus of intervention, but the wider public is also the potential benefactor. The concept of 'community' which provided an important legitimating discourse for PBNI as a penal-welfarist organization now becomes a more diffuse 'public'. And as others have noted, invariably the offender subject is outwith this 'public' who are in need of protection (Nash 2000; Robinson and McNeill 2004).

This shift in emphasis on the role of community sanctions in Northern Ireland in the mid-1990s parallels developments in England and Wales, where the traditional focus aimed at the rehabilitation of the individual had come under sustained criticism for a variety of reasons, including whether such endeavours were proportionate or effective (Mair and Burke 2012; Robinson *et al.* 2013). Whereas probation in Northern Ireland cannot have been said to have experienced 'a collapse of a rehabilitative ideal' – largely because rehabilitation had not been a dominant discourse within a society and a criminal justice system that was beset by violent conflict – this movement towards a more risk-focused, public-protection role was clearly influenced by wider penal trends. These developments also coalesced with a period of conflict transformation and the consequent changing dynamics of political authority and questions regarding the proper role of a functioning state.

The Criminal Justice Review (2000) also considered community sanctions and in particular the relationship between the Prison Service and the Probation Board. As part of its deliberations, it explored the possibility of greater integration between the Northern Ireland Prison Service (NIPS) and the Probation Board under a unified 'correctional service' (Blair 2000). This was informed by developments in England and Wales. In 1998 the Home Office had published a report, 'Joining Forces to Protect the Public', which had advocated closer cooperation between prisons and probation and which prefigured the influential Carter Report (2003), which led to the establishment of the National Offender Management Service (NOMS) (Mair and Burke 2012). In Northern Ireland, however, such an amalgamation was not considered possible, one of the main obstacles being that the prison service would be required to undergo it own reforms and restructuring in the post-conflict era. As the Review Report observed:

there is a very real danger that the Prison Service with its larger staff, larger budget and higher profile would tend to dominate… We would be concerned that the community ethos and credibility achieved by the Probation Service might be put at risk if such an amalgamation took place.

(Criminal Justice Review 2000: 304)

Pointing to the credibility (or legitimacy) achieved by the Probation Board based on its grounding in the community, the contrast made with the prison system, while perhaps not directly intended, is evident. The prisons, having been 'colonised into being anti-terrorist and fighting a war' (PHI02), had become highly contentious battlegrounds over the course of the Troubles (McEvoy 2001). The policy of 'criminalization' – that is, the denial of political legitimacy through the removal of 'special category' status for prisoners convicted of conflict-related offences (Gormally *et al.* 1993) – pursued in the prisons from the mid-1970s until 1981, directly contrasted with the route taken by probation. And it had led to devastating effects. Ten men died on hunger strike in the Maze/Long Kesh prison in protest (Beresford 1987). And, between 1974 and 1993, 29 prison officers were killed by paramilitaries.[18]

Prisoners convicted of conflict-related offences were released as part of the peace agreement secured in 1998 (McEvoy 1998), and this process was well underway by the time the Review reported. The need for the prison service to downsize and become reoriented towards a less securitized model was noted by the Review, and this formed part of the rationale for its conclusion that an amalgamation of probation and prisons was not feasible. The desirability of a closer working relationship between these two agencies was, however, articulated and, as O'Mahony and Chapman (2007: 171) observe, the Criminal Justice Review 'signalled the intention of the government to take a stronger lead in criminal justice policy than previously'.

Post-conflict – A new 'normal'?

The period of the transition from conflict has seen an ongoing process towards 'normalization' of the criminal justice system. Here the use of this term is understood to mean that the focus has increasingly turned towards tackling 'ordinary' offending rather than conflict containment.[19] This is not intended to downplay the significant legacy issues that remain in the post-conflict era, including continued paramilitary activity and ongoing difficulties within the prisons (Owers *et al.* 2011; CJINI 2013a, 2013b; Horgan 2013), but rather to convey the overall shift in emphasis within the criminal justice system. As mentioned previously, for the PBNI this process had begun with the introduction of the Criminal Justice (Northern Ireland) Order (1996), which saw a movement towards a public protection function. Further legislation introduced in the 1990s and 2000s relating to the management of sex offenders, domestic violence offences and the release of life-sentenced prisoners further underlined this shift.[20]

With the expansion of PBNI's role and the increased emphasis on risk and public protection, greater attention was paid towards standardization and systemization. The introduction of practice standards by PBNI in 2000 set out guidelines for the preparation of pre-sentence reports and supervisory arrangements for the various community sanctions supervised by the Probation Board. These 'core standards' have been periodically revised and have become increasingly expansive, detailing risk-assessment practices, multi-agency interactions, breach processes etc. (PBNI 2012). The rationale for the increased formalization and proscription of practice has clearly been informed by a managerialist approach which has emphasized the need for greater accountability and efficiency, but which has invariably led to increased bureaucratization.

Within PBNI this has also been influenced by a need to be accountable to the public whom it has an articulated responsibility to protect. Indeed in the Foreword to the practice standards, accountability and the public protection role are identified as reasons for expanding the reach of proscription (PBNI 2006). The Foreword notes that the standards have been informed by a number of factors, including:

> increasing demands for protection of the public from crime and its effects...
> the outcomes of four years of monitoring practice and periodic internal audits;
> a raft of recommendations which reflect the findings of successive external
> reviews and inspections.
>
> *(PBNI 2006: i)*

The public protection trope therefore serves an important legitimating role for probation both institutionally and symbolically providing a means to demonstrate utility, accountability and efficiency. Linking to the risk, need and responsivity model (RNR) of offender supervision which also gained currency in this period (Ward and Maruna 2007), it also provides an organizing framework through which the work of community sanctions can be quantified and through which resources can be allocated (McCulloch and McNeill 2007). Critically also it provides the means through which the organization of probation must be accountable to its funder – the State.

While clearly representing an increased bureaucratization of work, for some these developments signalled a 'coming of age' for PBNI and a greater relevance of the organization within the wider criminal justice system:

> There are probably more systems, protocols and processes in place and in doing
> that we probably had to become quite sort of like at times it would probably
> have felt quite bureaucratic, but I think it needed it. It was like coming into
> the twenty-first century, we had to and also because of the changes in our
> own society and the influences from the national criminal justice and that
> system.
>
> *(PHI07)*

> I think that we have developed and matured greatly over the . . . years that I can
> recall in it. The introduction of standards, the introduction of a process, our
> role within the criminal justice system, we are now very much central within

the criminal justice system, no longer are there debates about getting a slice of the cake, getting reports written, I mean we are our role in looking at how we are working with sex offenders, high-risk offenders, domestic violence, victims, restorative justice . . .

(PHI09)

The focus on higher-risk offences, manifest in increased attention paid towards sexual offending, parallels the development of risk-based orthodoxies and similar governance frameworks in England and Wales (see McAlinden 2012). Multi-agency Sex Offender Risk Assessment and Risk Management Arrangements (MASRAM) involving probation, police, prisons and social services were introduced in Northern Ireland in 2001 (McAuley 2010). These were superseded by Public Protection Arrangements Northern Ireland (PPANI), which were also given a legislative basis, and their ambit was extended to include violent offences. The introduction of 'public protection' legislation (Criminal Justice (Northern Ireland) Order 2008), also mirrored legislation previously introduced in England and Wales (Bailie 2008).[21] The 2008 Order introduced extended and indeterminate custodial sentences which allow courts to sentence a person to longer or indeterminate periods in custody based on an assessment of 'dangerousness'. While such sentences are only applicable to certain categories of offences and the court must make the ultimate adjudication on dangerousness, such an adjudication is informed by the assessments submitted to the court by probation (amongst others). The establishment of the Parole Commissioners for Northern Ireland has also further involved PBNI in decisions about release from custody, emphasizing a risk-management role and shifting more of probation's work towards post-custodial supervision.[22]

These shifts in the orientation of probation practice have been influenced by wider contexts that have led to penal expansionism both within prisons and in the numbers subject to supervision in the community. Facilitated by a prisoner release scheme, prison numbers declined markedly following the peace agreement (early 2000s), but have risen in recent years. A recent analysis of the growth in the Northern Ireland prison population between 2009 and 2013 links this to a higher number of custodial sentences, driven in part by greater numbers coming before the courts, an increase in sentence lengths and higher numbers of recalls to prison (DoJ 2014a).[23]

Data on probation in Northern Ireland also shows that the number of people subject to community sanctions and measures has risen markedly in recent years. The number of people subject to supervision on an annual date rose from 2,969 at year end 2000–2001 to 4,468 in 2012–2013, an increase of approximately one-third.[24] The breakdown in the number of people under the supervision of PBNI on 30 June 2014 included more than half who were subject to a community sentence (2,591) and over a third who were the subject of a combined custodial–community sanction (1,688) such as a Custody Probation Order (CPO) or a Determinate Custodial Sentence (DCS) (PBNI 2014).[25] For example, a DCS allows the court to sentence a person to a period of imprisonment followed by a period of supervision in the community. The court specifies the length of both elements at the point of sentencing. This form of sanction has become increasingly popular, with numbers rising when compared with stand-alone community sanctions.

Determinate Custodial Sentences were introduced alongside public protection sentences in the Criminal Justice (Northern Ireland) Order (2008). They have been legitimated on the basis of an offender/risk-management approach, grounded in the rationale that the offender (as a risk bearer) should be managed throughout their time in prison and in their transition back into the community. The rise in the use of DCSs illustrates the attractiveness of melding prison and community disposals and suggests that, rather than providing an alternative to custody, community punishment is increasingly seen as custody's adjunct. Recalls to prison and the shift towards greater numbers under post-custodial supervision further underlines the increasingly porous boundary between prison and community.

Conclusion

The administration and legitimation of community sanctions and measures in Northern Ireland have been profoundly shaped by the political context. Moving from a marginal position within the criminal justice system in the first half of the twentieth century, probation was viewed as an alternative to custody for 'redeemable cases'. In the 1950s the administrative arrangements for supervising probation orders were formalized. Probation officers were brought under the ambit of a government department and further legislation was enacted. During the period of most intense political conflict and anchored in a commitment to be 'neutral and useful', probation officers remarkably established a presence in communities. In the period of conflict transformation grounded in a new legislative mandate, the range of community sentences expanded, as did the organization which administered them. Probation officers continued their community-based presence, but in a move towards more generalized legitimacy became increasingly focused on evidence-based practice, reflecting wider penal trends (McNeill and Robinson 2013; Robinson et al. 2013).

While once a case could be made about the 'special' context of Northern Ireland as a block against some of the more negative vagaries of policy transfer, the move towards 'normalization' has made this more difficult. As this former probation officer observes:

> gradually over the years in Britain, following on [sic] America, was the notion of our job was to control offenders in the community, almost to the extent now where people will talk about the sense of total supervision, prison in the community. Probation has moved with that. Again it's a different discussion as to whether probation could have, whether that was right, and whether probation could have resisted that, but certainly the origins of being allowed by

the courts to help offenders has become much more secondary to controlling the behaviour of offenders in the community.

(PHI02)

In Northern Ireland, as in other countries, community sanctions and measures have served mutable purposes and have employed varying rationales over time – redemptive, rehabilitative and risk oriented. For reasons outlined at the outset, 'punishment' within the community has not featured as a legitimating discourse. Of course this is not to say that community sanctions and measures do not have a punitive effect marked by increasing strictures and the emphasis placed on public protection. The 'paradox of probation' (Phelps 2013) in this context is that, in the 'post-conflict' era, the numbers coming under the penal gaze – both in the community and the prisons – have risen exponentially in recent years. Here the boundaries between these sites of penality have become increasingly porous. Changes in political authority evident in the re-establishment of a local legislature and the devolution of policing and justice powers to the Northern Ireland Assembly in 2010 point to a shift in the relationship between government and its citizenry.

However, it is notable that under this new dispensation community sanctions and measures have been somewhat marginalized within a political discourse that has focussed on other aspects of the criminal justice system – notably prisons and the youth justice system, which have been the subject of two substantial reviews (Owers *et al.* 2011; Youth Justice Review 2011). While the Prison Review noted areas for further collaboration between the Prison Service and PBNI, its main focus was on the pressing need for prison reform in a system which was criticized for being highly costly and overly securitized (Owers *et al.* 2011; CJINI 2013a, 2013b). In this context the contrast between prisons and more effective and cheaper community-based sanctions has fostered a penal reductionist legitimating rationale, advocating the greater use of community sanctions (CJINI 2013c; DoJ 2011, 2013), and calling for increased expenditure in this area (McCaughey 2009, 2012).

However, the question of budgets remains a vexed one. Government spending on community sanctions remains comparatively low, and further spending cuts have recently been announced (DoJ 2014b).[26] In response the PBNI issued a statement warning that a reduced budget will negatively impact on public safety and reoffending rates (Patterson 2014). Perhaps characteristically media coverage in response focussed on the 'threat' of unsupervised sex offenders.[27]

As McNeill and Dawson (2014) note, changing political contexts undoubtedly shape the symbolic and material character of penality. Despite the historically problematic and unsettled character of this particular State and the specific 'limits of sovereignty' within it (Garland 1996), it is notable that within a new political dispensation attention is increasingly focussed towards offenders as a 'suitable enemy' (Christie 1986). As other contributions to this book make all too clear, the perils of legitimation of community sanctions via this route have been well documented and, for that reason, the position of community sanctions in Northern Ireland seems likely to remain insecure.

Notes

1 During 2013 and 2014 the police recorded 70 casualties as a result of paramilitary-style attacks. However, these are likely to be significant under-reports due to fears and/or poor relationships with the police (PSNI 2014).

2 Throughout the chapter this full set of interviews (19) is denoted 'probation history interviews' (PHI), each with a relevant interview number.

3 Fulton and Parkhill's (2009) historical overview was undertaken to mark the centenary of the passage of the foundational legislation and the twenty-fifth anniversary of the establishment of its current administrative structure (the Probation Board for Northern Ireland).

4 The committee published its report: 'Report on the Protection and Welfare of the Young and the Treatment of Young Offenders' (1938). The committee was chaired by Sir Robert Lynn, and the report is more commonly referred to as the 'Lynn Report'.

5 The Treatment of Offenders (Northern Ireland) Order 1976.

6 Some of the quotes that appear in this text have previously been published in Carr, N. and Maruna, S. (2012) 'Legitimacy through neutrality. Probation and the conflict in Northern Ireland,' *Howard Journal*, 51,5: 474–87. Permission to reproduce these quotes has kindly been granted by the publishers John Wiley and Sons.

7 The enactment of 'Emergency Provisions' legislation outlawed membership of 'prohibited' organizations and provided for summary conviction for imprisonment for a range of associated offences. Northern Ireland (Emergency Provisions) Act, 1973; Northern Ireland (Various Emergency Provisions) (Continuance) Order, 1974.

8 Diplock Courts refer to non-jury courts, which were introduced in Northern Ireland under Emergency Legislation in 1973 for certain scheduled offences (i.e. terrorist-related offences). They are named after Lord Diplock, who chaired the parliamentary commission that proposed their introduction to counter potential 'fear of intimidation' of jury members by paramilitary organizations (Report of the Commission to Consider Legal Procedures to Deal with Terrorist Activities in Northern Ireland; Diplock 1972).

9 The Northern Ireland Office (NIO) was established following the imposition of 'Direct Rule' in 1972. Direct rule of Northern Ireland affairs by Westminster was initially viewed as a temporary measure (McKittrick and McVea 2001). Led by the Secretary of State for Northern Ireland, the NIO retained its primary role until the re-establishment of a local legislature following the Belfast (Good Friday) Agreement. It retained responsibility for policing and justice powers until 2010, when these powers were devolved to the local legislature.

10 Intermediate Treatment was a term used in this period to describe work with young people outside of the custodial setting. The objective of intermediate treatment was articulated as 'seeking to improve the quality of life through providing community-based opportunities' (Powell 1982: 573) Much of what was commonly delivered was activity based rather than specifically focused on offending.

11 Historically, in Republican communities, punishment beatings, exiles, shootings and executions involved the regulation of behaviour in the absence of an accepted form of policing. During the course of the conflict, paramilitary 'policing' of communities was linked to a legitimacy deficit in state-administered criminal justice (Feenan 2002; Monaghan 2004). In Loyalist communities, the emergence of paramilitary regulation from the early 1970s was initially viewed as an adjunct or assistance to the police. However,

over time, particularly with a growing sense of disenfranchisement within working-class Loyalist communities, the role of paramilitary 'punishments' has similarly been linked to deficits in state legitimacy (Monaghan 2004).

12 Anderstown, a Belfast suburb, and The Falls Road in West Belfast, are communities which experienced a high degree of violence during the Troubles.

13 Unlike other agencies within the criminal justice system probation was notable for the equivalent representation of Catholics and Protestants in its workforce.

14 The Review Group was appointed in 1976 by the Minister of State for Health and Social Services to review legislation and services relating to the care and treatment of children and young persons under the Children and Young Persons Act (Northern Ireland) 1968, the Adoption Act (Northern Ireland) 1967 and the Probation Act (Northern Ireland) 1950, 'taking into account developments in these fields in Great Britain' (Report of the Children and Young Persons Review Group 1979: 1). The reason that the role of probation was considered in a report that focused primarily on young people was because work with young people appearing before the courts including the provision of assessment formed a 'substantial part' of probation's role at this time (ibid., 1979: 52).

15 And other preceding legislation: Probation Act, Northern Ireland (1950).

16 Policing was dealt with separately in the Patten Report (1999), and its recommendations led to the disbandment of the Royal Ulster Constabulary (RUC) and the formation of a new police force – the Police Service for Northern Ireland (PSNI) (Ellison and Mulcahy 2001). The fact that policing was considered separately reflected the contentious nature of this area.

17 The legislation outlines that the purpose of supervision on a probation order is as follows: the supervision of the offender by a probation officer is desirable in the interests of – (a) securing the rehabilitation of the offender; (b) protecting the public from harm from him or preventing the commission by him of further offences (Part 10, 1, Criminal Justice Order (NI), 1996).

18 Following the ceasefires of the main paramilitary organizations (in 1994) one prison officer has subsequently been killed. In 2012, David Black, a prison officer was murdered on his way to work. His murder has been attributed to dissident Republicans: www.theguardian.com/uk/2012/nov/12/david-black-new-ira-prison-officer.

19 This echoes the term 'ODC' (ordinary decent criminals) used to refer to the general offending population, that is, those not convicted of conflict-related offences (Dwyer 2007).

20 See for example: Sex Offender Act (1997); Sexual Offences Act (2003); Sexual Offences (Northern Ireland Order) 2008; Life Sentence (Northern Ireland) Order 2001; Family Homes and Domestic Violence (Northern Ireland) Order, 1998; Domestic Violence Crime and Victims Act (2004).

21 Criminal Justice Act (2003).

22 The Criminal Justice (Northern Ireland) Order 2008 also provided that the Life Sentence Review Commissioners (LSRC), established as an independent body following a recommendation of the Criminal Justice Review (2000), be renamed the Parole Commissioners for Northern Ireland. Prior to the establishment of the Life Sentence Review Commissioners in legislation (Life Sentences (Northern Ireland) Order, 2001), a non-statutory body comprising of officials within the Northern Ireland Office had fulfilled aspects of this function. However, the advent of the Human Rights Act, 1998 and compliance with the European Convention of Human Rights entailed that each prisoner should be entitled to have his or her case reviewed periodically by an independent body.

23 The prison population in September 2009 was 1,437; in September 2013 it was 1,858 (DoJ 2014a).
24 Personal communication with PBNI, 27 June 2013.
25 There were 4,538 people subject to probation supervision on 30 June 2014; in addition to those cited above, the remaining numbers constituted those on licences (including Life Licences and Sex Offender Licences) and those subject to 'Public Protection Sentences', that is, Extended or Indeterminate Custodial Sentences. Twenty-seven per cent of the Probation caseload were in custody, and probation's involvement pertained largely to pre-release work (PBNI 2014).
26 In 2014–2015 the budget allocation for PBNI was £18.4 million compared with £102.8 million for the Northern Ireland Prison Service (NIPS).
27 BBC Northern Ireland, 11 December 2014: 'Sex offenders: Probation Board for Northern Ireland issues warning on budget cuts'. Available at: www.bbc.com/news/uk-northern-ireland-30427028 (accessed on: 19 December 2014).

References

Bailie, R. (2008) 'Criminal Justice (Northern Ireland) Order 2008', *Irish Probation Journal*, 5: 20–2.
Beresford, P. (1987) *Ten Men Dead. Story of the 1981 Irish Hunger Strike*. London: Harper Collins Publishers.
Blair, C. (2000) *Prisons and Probation. Research Report 6. Review of the Criminal Justice System in Northern Ireland*. Belfast: Criminal Justice Review Group.
Carr, N. and Maruna, S. (2012) 'Legitimacy through neutrality. Probation and the conflict in Northern Ireland', *Howard Journal*, 51(5): 474–87.
Carter, P. (2003) *Managing Offenders, Reducing Crime*. London: Strategy Unit.
Chapman, T. (1995) 'Creating a culture of change: a case study of a care crime project in Belfast', in J. Maguire (ed.) *What Works in Reducing Reoffending*. Chichester: Wiley.
Chapman, T. and Hough, M. (1998) *Evidence-Based Practice: A Guide to Effective Practice*. London: Her Majesty's Inspectorate of Probation.
Children and Young Persons Review Group (1979) *Report of the Children and Young Persons Review Group (Black Report)*. Belfast: HMSO.
Christie, N. (1986) 'Suitable enemy', in Herman Bianchi and René Van Swaaningen (eds) *Abolitionism: toward a non-repressive approach to crime*. Amsterdam: Free University Press.
CJINI (Criminal Justice Inspection Northern Ireland) (2013a) *Report on an Announced Inspection of Ash House, Hydebank Wood Women's Prison*. Belfast: CJINI.
CJINI (Criminal Justice Inspection Northern Ireland) (2013b) *Report on an Announced Inspection of Hydebank Wood Young Offenders Centre*. Belfast: CJINI.
CJINI (Criminal Justice Inspection Northern Ireland) (2013c) *An Inspection of Community Supervision by the Probation Board for Northern Ireland*. Belfast: CJINI.
Criminal Justice Review Group (2000) *Review of the Criminal Justice System in Northern Ireland*. Belfast: Criminal Justice Review Group.
Department of Justice (DoJ) (2011) *Consultation on a Review of Community Sentences*. Belfast: DoJ.
Department of Justice (DoJ) (2013) *Strategic Framework for Reducing Reoffending. Towards a Safer Society*. Belfast: DoJ.
Department of Justice (DoJ) (2014a) *Prison Population Review. A Review of the Factors Leading to the Growth in Prisoner Numbers between 2009 and 2013*. Belfast: DoJ.

Department of Justice (DoJ) (2014b) *Department of Justice Consultation on 2015–16 Draft Budget Proposals*. Belfast: DoJ.

Diplock, Lord (1972) *Report of the Commission to Consider Legal Procedures to Deal with Terrorist Activities in Northern Ireland*. London: HMSO.

Doak, J. and O'Mahony, D. (2011) 'In search of legitimacy: restorative youth conferencing in Northern Ireland', *Legal Studies*, 31(2): 305–25.

Dwyer, C. (2007) 'Risk politics and the "scientification" of political judgement', *British Journal of Criminology*, 47(5): 779–97.

Ellison, G. and Mulcahy, A. (2001) 'The policing question in Northern Ireland', *Policing and Society*, 11(3–4): 243 –58.

Feenan, D. (2002) 'Justice in conflict: paramilitary punishment in Ireland (North)', *International Journal of the Sociology of Law*, 30(2): 151–72.

Fulton, B. and Carr, N. (2013) 'Probation in Europe: Northern Ireland'. Available at: www.cepprobation.org/uploaded_files/Probation-in-Europe-2013-Chapter-Northern-Ireland.pdf (accessed on: 12 March 2014).

Fulton, B. and Parkhill, T. (2009) *Making the Difference. An Oral History of Probation in Northern Ireland*. Belfast: PBNI.

Fulton, B. and Webb, B. (2009) 'The emergence of probation services in North-East Ireland', *Irish Probation Journal*, 6(1): 32–48.

Garland, D. (1985) *Punishment and Welfare: A History of Penal Strategies*. London: Ashgate.

Garland, D. (1996) 'The limits of the Sovereign State: Strategies of crime control in contemporary society', *British Journal of Criminology*, 36(1): 445–71.

Gormally, B., McEvoy, K. and Wall, D. (1993) 'Criminal justice in a divided society: Northern Ireland prisons', *Crime and Justice*, 17: 51–135.

Home Office (1998) *Joining Forces to Protect the Public: Prisons–Probation. A Consultation Document*. London: Home Office.

Horgan, J. (2013) *Divided We Stand: The Strategy and Psychology of Ireland's Dissident Terrorists*. Oxford: Oxford University Press.

Jacobson, J. and Gibbs, P. (2009) *Making Amends: Restorative Justice in Northern Ireland*. London: Prison Reform Trust.

Mair, G. and Burke, L. (2012) *Redemption, Rehabilitation and Risk Management. A History of Probation*. London: Routledge.

McAlinden, A. (2012) 'The governance of sexual offending across Europe: Penal policies, political economies and the institutionalization of risk', *Punishment and Society*, 14(2): 166–92.

McAlister, S. and Carr, N. (2014) 'Experiences of youth justice: Youth Justice discourses and their multiple effects', *Youth Justice*, 14(3): 241–54.

McAuley, W. (2010) 'The public protection arrangements in Northern Ireland', *Irish Probation Journal*, 7(1): 85–93.

McCaughey, B. (2009) Presentation to Assembly Committee on Devolution of Policing and Justice: Probation Board for Northern Ireland. Official Hansard Report Session: 2008/09. 24 February 2009.

McCaughey, B. (2012) 'Probation Board for Northern Ireland: Key issues and priorities'. Northern Ireland Assembly Justice Committee. Official Hansard Report Session 2012/12. 14 June 2009.

McCulloch, T. and McNeill, F. (2007) 'Consumer society, commodification and offender management', *Criminology and Criminal Justice*, 7(3): 223–42.

McEvoy, K. (1998) 'Prisoners, the Agreement, and the political character of the Northern Ireland Conflict', *Fordham International Law Journal*, 22(4) 1539–75.

McEvoy, K. (2001) *Paramilitary Imprisonment in Northern Ireland: Resistance, Management and Release*. Oxford: Oxford University Press.

McKittrick, D. and McVea, D. (2001) *Making Sense of the Troubles*. London: Penguin.

McNeill, F. and Dawson, M. (2014) 'Social solidarity, penal evolution and probation', *British Journal of Criminology*, 54(5): 892–907.

McNeill, F. and Robinson, G. (2013) 'Liquid legitimacy and community sanctions', in A. Crawford and A. Hucklesby (eds) *Legitimacy and Compliance in Criminal Justice*. London: Routledge, pp. 116–37.

Monaghan, R. (2004) '"An Imperfect Peace": Paramilitary "Punishments" in Northern Ireland', *Terrorism and Political Violence*, 16(3): 439–61.

Nash, M. (2000) 'Deconstructing the Probation Service – the Trojan horse of public protection', *International Journal of the Sociology of Law*, 28(3): 201–13.

O'Mahony, D. and Chapman, T. (2007) 'Probation, the state and community – delivering probation services in Northern Ireland', in L. Gelsthorpe and R. Morgan (eds) *Handbook of Probation*. Cullompton, Devon: Willan, pp. 155–78.

Owers, A., Leighton, P., McCrory, C., McNeill, F. and Wheatley, P. (2011) *Review of the Northern Ireland Prison Service. Conditions, Management and Oversight of all Prisons*. Belfast: Prison Review Team.

Patten, C. (1999) *The Patten Report – A New Beginning: Policing and Northern Ireland*. The Report of the Independent Commission on Northern Ireland. London: HMSO.

Patterson, W. (2014) 'Proposed cuts will fundamentally change how probation supervise and rehabilitate offenders', PBNI Press Release. Available at: www.pbni.org.uk/site/Content. aspx?x=6HzjOZy9Euw=&z=re3CTZjVrrI=#sthash.0PTNR6i5.dpbs (accessed on: 20 December 2014).

Pease, K. (1985) 'Community Service Orders', *Crime and Justice*, 6: 51–94.

PBNI (2006) 'Northern Ireland Probation Practice Standards'. Available at: www. pbni.org.uk/archive/Guide%20to%20Information/What%20are%20our%20priorities/ ServiceStandards/NI%20Standards.pdf (accessed on: 23 November 2014).

PBNI (2012) 'Best Practice Framework Incorporating Northern Ireland Standards'. Available at: www.pbni.org.uk/archive/Guide%20to%20Information/What%20are%20our%20 priorities/ServiceStandards/PBNIstandards_v1%2004.10.12.pdf (accessed on: 02 September 2014).

PBNI (2014) *PBNI Caseload Statistics (Quarter 1 2014–2015)*. Available at: www.pbni. org.uk/archive/pdfs/About%20Us/Statistics%20and%20Research/Caseload%20Statistics/ Caseload%20Trends%20Report_30%20June%202014_Internet%2022.07.14.pdf (accessed on: 14 August 2014).

Phelps, M. S. (2013) 'The paradox of probation: Community supervision in the age of mass incarceration', *Law and Policy*, 35(1–2): 51–80.

Powell, F. (1982) 'Justice and the young offender in Northern Ireland', *British Journal of Social Work*, 12(6): 565–86.

PSNI (Police Service of Northern Ireland) (2014) *Police Recorded Security Situation Statistics. Annual Report covering the period: 01.04.13–31.03.14*. Belfast: PSNI.

Robinson, G. and McNeill, F. (2004) 'Purposes matters: The ends of probation', in G. Mair (ed.) *What Matters in Probation Work*. Cullompton, Devon: Willan, pp. 277–304.

Robinson, G., McNeill, F. and Maruna, S. (2013) 'Punishment *in* society: The improbable persistence of probation and other community sanctions and measures', in J. Simon and R. Sparks (eds) *The Sage Handbook of Punishment and Society*. London: Sage, pp. 321–40.

Thorsvaldson, S. (1982) *Crime and Redress: An Introduction. Proceedings of the National Symposium on Reparative Sanctions.* Vancouver: Ministry of Attorney General cited in Pease, K. (1985) 'Community Service Orders', *Crime and Justice*, 6: 51–94.

Underdown, A. (1998) *Strategies for Effective Offender Supervision.* London: HM Inspectorate of Probation.

Ward, T. and Maruna, S. (2007) *Rehabilitation.* London: Routledge.

Youth Justice Review Team (2011) *A Review of the Youth Justice System in Northern Ireland.* Belfast: Department of Justice.

8

THE EVOLUTION OF PROBATION SUPERVISION IN THE REPUBLIC OF IRELAND

Continuity, challenge and change

Deirdre Healy

Scholars across the Anglophone world have expressed disquiet about the current direction of policy and practice with respect to community sanctions and measures. Concerns centre on their reinvention as community punishments and the resulting emphasis on surveillance, risk management and social control. Given its geographical location between the UK and the USA, the Republic of Ireland could be expected to follow a similar trajectory, yet probation supervision in this jurisdiction has changed little over time. This chapter charts its evolution from the foundation of the Irish state to the present day and explores the contexts that either inhibited or facilitated change at critical turning points. The discussion concludes with a series of reflections on the narratives that underpin contemporary policy and practice.

Emergence: 1900–1959

The early history of probation supervision was shaped by the principles and practices of nineteenth century philanthropy, as well as the informal police court missionary system (Guerin 2005). These voluntary practices were given a legislative basis by the Probation of Offenders Act 1907, which encouraged probation officers to 'advise, assist and befriend' the person under supervision, a maxim that was operationalised through the provision of social casework to offenders (O'Dea 2002). The 1907 Act permitted judges to sentence convicted individuals to a period of probation supervision or, alternatively, to make a finding of guilt but not proceed to a conviction. Under the latter provision, no supervision is imposed and judges can either dismiss the charge or conditionally discharge the offender. The 1907 Act was subsequently amended by the Criminal Justice Administration Act 1914, which allowed additional conditions to be attached to probation orders, for example a prohibition on alcohol consumption. The 1914 Act also permitted the state to authorise voluntary agencies to provide offender rehabilitation services on its behalf and to recognise staff employed by these agencies as assistant probation officers. It is noteworthy that both acts of the UK parliament came into being before Ireland gained independence in 1922, but remained in force for over 100 years. Their longevity highlights the crucial part played by Ireland's colonial past in the long-term development of probation. The legitimising narrative behind the probation order was also imported from Britain. Consequently, early probation officers were concerned with the quasi-religious task of saving souls (see McWilliams 1985).

The Irish judiciary also devised two common-law practices that remain in use today.[1] Adjourned supervision is used when judges are unsure whether the offender can fulfil the conditions of a probation order. The offender is placed under supervision and a probation report is submitted to the court after a set period of time. Because the sanction has no legal basis, there is no limit on the duration of the supervision period or the penalty that can be applied for non-compliance (this disposal will be given a statutory basis if the Criminal Justice (Community Sanctions) Bill is enacted; see below). Adjourned supervision is intended to provide offenders with an opportunity to show remorse and make amends (Osborough 1981). Its introduction reflects the significance that judges attach to their independence, evidenced in the following case extract: 'It is not open to a judge [...] to fetter the exercise of his judicial discretion through the operation of a fixed policy' (*People (DPP) v WC [1994] 1 ILRM 321*). Secondly, the suspended sentence allowed judges to defer the imposition of a custodial sentence (the sanction was subsequently given a statutory basis by the Criminal Justice Act 2006; see below). Suspended sentences were introduced to deal with particular classes of offender, including first-time offenders whose offences were committed in mitigating circumstances, political offenders who agreed to rescind their paramilitary membership and offenders whose specific needs could not be managed within the prison system (Osborough 1982). Contemporary accounts suggest that judges use suspended sentences primarily for the purposes of deterrence (Maguire 2010).

Further progress with regard to probation supervision was halted by the political and civic turbulence that preceded the establishment of the Irish Free State in 1922.[2] Many of the men who might otherwise have become involved in social reform were embracing nationalist politics, while women with an interest in this field were being encouraged to join religious orders (McNally 2007; Kearney and Skehill 2005). Post-independence, the Catholic Church exerted a major influence on the evolution of probation supervision. The Church wielded substantial political power during the first half of the twentieth century, and senior officials played important advisory roles in government decision-making, including decisions related to social policy (Ferriter 2007). Catholic social policy was informed by *Quadragesimo Anno*, a papal encyclical issued by Pope Pius XI in 1931, which posited that the state should not assume responsibility for functions that could be delivered by non-state bodies (McNally 2007). As a result, the development of social work practices, including probation, constituted a bipartite process whereby professional, state-run services operated alongside voluntary, charitable services (Kearney and Skehill 2005). Fahey (2007) concluded that the Church's intervention delayed social reform, because Church-run services were primarily concerned with promulgating the Catholic faith rather than achieving social justice. On a more positive note, the Church's contribution meant that Catholic communities received a level of service provision that would not have been possible on the basis of state resources alone.

A perusal of political debates reveals that these values permeated political attitudes towards probation supervision. For example, Gerald Boland, then Minister for Justice,[3] rejected calls to increase the number of probation officers on the grounds that 'better results would obtain if a number of volunteers, working without financial reward in a spirit of charity, could be organised to assist the regular probation officers' (Dáil Debates, 5 May 1942, cited in Guerin 2005: 94). In addition, John Charles McQuaid, then Archbishop of Dublin,[4] was personally thanked in the Dáil (Irish parliament) for his contribution to the recruitment of volunteer probation officers and for his work with juvenile offenders (McNally 2007). Unsurprisingly, this philosophy limited possibilities for expansion, with the result that just four probation officers and a chief probation officer were employed by the Probation Service in the 1940s (McNally 2007). Their work was augmented by a variety of charitable organisations, including the Society of St. Vincent de Paul, the Legion of Mary and the Salvation Army (O'Dea 2002). Although the Catholic Church subsequently lost its hegemonic position in Irish society, it is notable that external agencies continue to play a prominent role in the delivery of probation services. In 2013, the Probation Service provided funding to 61 community-based organisations at a cost of €10.572 million, which represented 28 per cent of its total budget (Probation Service 2014).

The wider socio-cultural context inhibited the growth of probation supervision in other, less subtle ways. At this time, a variety of custodial institutions designed to contain and treat socially problematic individuals was operating in the Irish state. By 1951, around 1 per cent of the population was incarcerated at a range of sites, including reformatory and industrial schools, psychiatric institutions, Magdalene laundries[5] and prisons (O'Sullivan and O'Donnell 2007). It is likely that the existence of these institutions fostered a coercive mentality among politicians, policymakers and the public, and militated against the expansion of community-based approaches (Seymour 2013). Indeed, as the numbers of children sent to industrial and reformatory schools declined, religious orders complained to the Department of Education that too many children were being placed on probation rather than sentenced to detention (Raftery and O'Sullivan 1999).

The political context also delayed progress in relation to probation practice. The Fianna Fáil party, which remained in power for much of the 1930s and 1940s, was led by Eamon de Valera, whose vision for Ireland is encapsulated in a famous speech, where he described his dream of 'a people who valued material wealth only as a basis of right living, of a people who were satisfied with frugal comfort and devoted their lives to things of the spirit' (re-printed in Ferriter 2007: 363). In reality, the people of de Valera's Ireland experienced high levels of material deprivation, gender inequality, unemployment and emigration (Ferriter 2005). In spite of these difficulties, de Valera's charismatic personality ensured that the period was characterised by political stability but, as Lee (1989) noted, there is a fine line between stability and stagnation.

Politicians' and policymakers' cautious and pragmatic approach to criminal justice matters resulted in a prolonged period of stagnation (Rogan 2012). Political lassitude was facilitated by low crime rates, an uninterested public, a conservative bureaucracy and an absence of debate within the media, the church or academia (Rogan 2011; Kilcommins *et al.* 2004). In addition, judicial commitment to classical models of punishment acted as a buffer against the adoption of the penal welfare philosophy which was revolutionising probation practice elsewhere (Kilcommins *et al.* 2004). Attitudes towards probation supervision were apathetic at best, and contemporary accounts suggest that they played a peripheral role within the criminal justice system. For example, Molony (1920–1923: 126) advocated greater use of probation but acknowledged that this recommendation would not 'evoke any particular enthusiasm'. Twenty years later, Fahy (1943: 76) estimated that six full-time probation officers were supervising an average of 200 cases each and, not surprisingly, concluded that the use of probation at that time was 'far from satisfactory'.

Finally, the fact that the first probation officers were female may partly explain why the Probation Service remained marginalised. At that time, women had few rights and were viewed primarily as wives and mothers, a characterisation that was enshrined in the Irish Constitution (Ferriter 2005). It is unlikely that an organisation with a wholly female workforce would be held in high esteem in a society with significant levels of gender inequality. In this regard, it is noteworthy that the first male probation officer was appointed in 1937 and then promoted to senior probation officer over his longer-serving female colleagues in 1938 (McNally 2007). Writing in a contemporary context, Worrall and Mawby (2013) have argued that the feminisation of probation work may have contributed to its declining status in England and Wales, where vestigial patriarchal values still exist.

Professionalisation: 1969–1979

As religious vocations declined, professional social workers were recruited to manage the transition from institutional to community care and from voluntary to statutory service provision (Kearney and Skehill 2005). During this period, the Probation Service was transformed from a largely voluntary service into a structured, professional organisation (Guerin 2005). Although day-to-day work altered very little, McNally (2007: 21) characterised this period as 'a major break with the past' due to these structural changes.

Following decades of neglect, the Probation Service became the subject of two official reviews. An Inter-departmental Committee on Juvenile Delinquency, the Probation System, the Institutional Treatment of Offenders and their Aftercare (1962) recommended *inter alia* the establishment of the Service on a professional basis, the introduction of a management structure, the development of prison-based probation services and the expansion of volunteer probation services (McNally 2007). Rogan (2011: 97) described this report as a 'watershed' in light of its commitment to penal welfare ideals. A second internal review of the Service, conducted in 1969, recommended further expansion in the use of alternatives to custody and laid the foundations for a modern probation service (McNally 2009). These reviews, in conjunction with a government commitment to job creation in the public sector, led to an increase in probation officer numbers to 47 by 1973 (McNally 2007; O'Dea 2002). Probation officers also began to supervise prisoners on temporary release under the Criminal Justice Act 1960, later amended by the Criminal Justice (Temporary Release of Prisoners) Act 2003. In addition, the Probation Service was re-structured in 1979 and renamed the 'Probation and Welfare Service' (PWS), a title which emphasised its social work credentials.

To a certain extent, this era can be characterised as the golden age of penal welfarism, because rehabilitative ideals became fashionable among politicians, policymakers, the judiciary and the media (Rogan 2012). The welfarist agenda was driven primarily by several key individuals operating in a receptive socio-political environment where any ideas deemed socially progressive were highly valued (Rogan 2011). Key actors included the then Minister for Justice Charles Haughey[6] and a newly recruited cohort of civil servants who favoured innovation, action and reform. The emphasis on rehabilitation may therefore have been inspired mainly by a desire to modernise the state rather than by a commitment to the penal welfare ideology. Despite these developments, penal welfarism never became the dominant penal philosophy (Kilcommins *et al.* 2004) and the Probation Service remained 'woefully under-developed' (Ferriter 2005: 587). Nevertheless, the adoption of penal welfare values represented an important advance in official thinking, because the state had previously regarded all foreign innovations with suspicion (Ferriter 2005). Ironically, the absence of rigorous intellectual debate ensured that the Nothing Works mentality never captured the Irish criminological imagination (McNally 2007).

Notwithstanding this dynamic but short-lived period of modernisation, the public service was primarily viewed as a barrier to reform during this period. For instance, the then Director of the Institute of Public Administration criticised 'the formidable nature of the inertia and opposition to change [. . .] within the system' (cited in Lee 1989: 550). The Devlin report, which was commissioned to investigate the performance of the public sector, noted that public servants' preoccupation with day-to-day activities inhibited their ability to formulate innovative and strategic policies (Public Services Organisation Review Group 1969). The authors of the report also criticised the policy of promoting public servants on the basis of seniority rather than merit, claiming that this generated a dearth of talent and expertise at senior levels. The report's recommendations were never implemented, primarily because public servants claimed that they were too busy to make the changes (Lee 1989)! It is likely that public service inertia also militated against innovation in the field of criminal justice. In addition, the Probation Service did not have a formal management structure until the 1970s, which meant that any new initiatives were introduced by staff on an *ad hoc* basis rather than as part of a coherent policy plan (McNally 2009).

As Rogan (2011) observed, certain individuals played pivotal roles in the development of Irish penal policy. The dominant figure in the history of probation is Martin Tansey, who acted as Principal Probation Officer for almost 30 years (McNally 2009). In a posthumous memorial lecture, Sean Aylward (2008: 2), then Secretary General of the Department of Justice, Equality and Law Reform, described Tansey as a 'committed Christian' and 'iron realist' who was concerned with rehabilitation, communitarian principles and the alleviation of social injustice. Tansey's long service at the head of the organisation ensured that it experienced an extended period of stability in terms of its ethos, values and activities. In fact, probation officers' duties 'as defined in the 1907 Act remained the founding and enduring definition of probation work' throughout this period (Guerin 2005: 84).

Crisis: 1980–2005

By the 1980s, Ireland was 'a country in crisis' economically, politically and culturally (Ferriter 2005: 695). Unemployment was rising, heroin addiction had taken hold in deprived communities and crime was increasing. A sense of chaos permeated the prison system as policymakers struggled to cope with the challenges of overcrowding and deteriorating prison conditions. Rehabilitation came to be regarded as an unaffordable luxury, and grand reform projects were abandoned because of budgetary constraints, lack of leadership and a turbulent political climate (Rogan 2012). In this context, the government published the Whitaker Report, a landmark investigation of the penal system which advocated increased use of existing non-custodial options, the establishment of a community-service scheme and the use of imprisonment only as a last resort (Committee of Inquiry into the Penal System 1985). However, its recommendations came at a 'politically inconvenient' time (Rogan 2011: 169) and were never fully implemented (IPRT 2007a).

That said, the Probation Service appeared to benefit from the sense of crisis, at least in the short term, because its remit was expanded with the introduction of the community service order (see the Criminal Justice (Community Service) Act 1983). Its purpose was to provide offenders with opportunities to repair harm to the community and achieve reintegration (Walsh and Sexton 1999). It must be noted, however, that the order was introduced primarily to alleviate prison overcrowding and thus did not represent a commitment to increase the use of community sanctions (Rogan 2011). The legislation was borrowed from England and Wales and slightly amended, leading John Kelly TD to describe it as 'a British legislative idea taken over here and given a green outfit with silver buttons to make it look native' (cited in Kilcommins *et al.* 2004: 182). Community service orders can be imposed on people over the age of 16 who must complete between 40 and 240 hours of unpaid work in the community. Since community service is a direct alternative to custody, judges must specify a default period of detention at sentencing. Non-compliance is an offence that is punishable either by a fine or a revocation of the order. On revocation, judges may impose the sanction that would otherwise have been imposed had the order not been made. Around this time, the judiciary also developed a practice of inserting review dates into prison sentences but this has since been discontinued (see Bacik 2001). On the review date, judges could suspend the remainder of the sentence if they deemed the prisoner's conduct to be satisfactory and place the released prisoner under probation supervision. The practice was intended to provide prisoners with an incentive to participate in rehabilitation programmes and ensure that they served a minimum sentence.

By the 1990s, the Probation Service was experiencing its own crisis. Caseloads had increased, but funding remained static, leading O'Dea (2002: 640) to lament that 'hopelessly inadequate staffing levels have seriously undermined the capacity of the PWS [Probation and Welfare Service] to deliver services'. Similarly, Kilcommins et al. (2004: 260) noted that the organisation remained the 'poor relation within the penal system' due to its sparse resources relative to the prison system and its limited use by the judiciary. Although the government agreed to increase staffing levels in 1999 following strike action by probation officers, the promised recruitment never occurred (O'Dea 2002). In 2000, management capped caseload numbers and asked judges to limit their requests for reports and supervision orders (CAG 2004). The number of probation officers was later increased from 148 in 1997 to 266 in 2008 (Healy 2009).

Changing socio-political attitudes created additional challenges for the organisation. The murders of journalist Veronica Guerin and Garda Jerry McCabe in 1996 heightened public fears about crime and triggered a shift towards a populist and punitive political agenda (Kilcommins et al. 2004). During the 1997 election campaign, the Fianna Fáil party adopted a punitive rhetoric to capitalise on public fears and ultimately won the election on a law-and-order platform. Although the punitive shift was short-lived, it left an enduring mark on penal policy. The election coincided with a period of unprecedented economic growth, known as the Celtic Tiger, during which time the economy grew by an average of 7.5 per cent per annum (Kirby 2010). Healthy public finances fuelled expansion of the Court Service, An Garda Síochána (Ireland's police force) and the prison system. The Probation Service budget also increased, albeit marginally and from a very low base. Its funding levels peaked in 2007 at €59 million, which compares poorly to a budget allocation of €397 million for the Irish Prison Service that year (Healy 2009). The adoption of a punitive narrative, coupled with a political preference for visible, 'quick-fix' solutions, meant that the penal welfare narrative – which was still being employed to legitimise probation work – was at odds with prevailing political ideals (see Table 8.1 for an overview of trends in the use of probation supervision).

Nevertheless, an Expert Group was commissioned to examine the work of the Probation Service. They recommended a 'significant shift in policy to facilitate the increased use of a much greater range of non-custodial sanctions' and advised inter alia that the government should: update probation legislation; introduce a broader menu of community sanctions; expand research capacity; establish the organisation as an autonomous agency with its own Director; appoint an inspector of probation services; and provide the organisation with sufficient resources to carry out its functions (Expert Group 1999: 8). Later that year, opposition parties criticised the government for its failure to implement the recommendations of the Expert Group (Dáil Debates, 2 March 1999). This report and its aftermath highlight ongoing political apathy towards probation and paint a portrait of a neglected and under-resourced organisation operating within an archaic legislative framework (for detailed discussions of the challenges faced by community sanctions during this period, see Seymour 2006; Healy and O'Donnell 2005). It is likely that chronic under-resourcing, coupled with political and judicial apathy, undermined the Service's capacity (and possibly willingness) to expand.

Five years later, a value-for-money report by the Comptroller and Auditor General (2004) revealed that little had changed. The report, which covered the period from 1995 to 2002, concluded that the effectiveness of probation work could not be properly evaluated due to the absence of meaningful statistical data and the lack of clear and quantifiable performance indicators. At that time, statistical information was still collected manually and stored in paper files, which led to significant delays in the publication of annual reports. This stasis highlights the political indifference that existed towards the managerial values that were transforming probation practice in other jurisdictions. In general, Irish politicians and policymakers favour informal and flexible policy approaches, because they believe that citizens are suspicious of authoritarian styles of leadership (Hamilton 2013). One former minister even described managerialism as 'repugnant to the Irish psyche' (Hamilton 2013: 161).

In spite of these difficulties, several new orders expanded the remit of the Probation Service to include greater numbers of serious offenders, including prisoners. For example, two intensive probation schemes which operated according to 'What Works?' principles were established in Dublin and Cork to work with serious offenders (O'Dea 2002). In addition, suspended sentences were given a statutory basis by the Criminal Justice Act 2006 which allowed the courts to partially or fully suspend a prison sentence and permitted judges to attach probation supervision as a condition if deemed appropriate. Finally, the Sex Offenders Act 2001 introduced post-release supervision for sex offenders. John O'Donoghue, then Minister for Justice,[7] stated that the aims of post-release supervision were 'to help the offender maintain self-control over his or her offending behaviour and, second, to provide external monitoring of his or her post release behaviour and activities' (Dáil Debates, 6 April 2000). His comments indicate that its purpose was not to facilitate access to rehabilitation, but to manage the potential risks posed by sex offenders to the public. These developments signal a fledgling interest in international innovations, particularly practices related to risk management, public protection and evidence-based programmes. Furthermore, the legitimising discourses that underpin the initiatives contain echoes of the 'managerial' and 'new rehabilitation' narratives that have been used to legitimise probation practice in other Anglophone countries (see Introduction).

Consolidation: 2006 to date

The managerial narrative has become increasingly salient in contemporary discourse. For example, the Probation Service's (2008) *Strategy Statement* included terms such as efficiency, effectiveness, planning, governance and value for money. In addition, the organisation introduced a computerised case tracking system and established the *Irish Probation Journal* in conjunction with the Probation Board for Northern Ireland. These developments, which reflect a growing preoccupation with data collection, cost-efficiency, and research, were inspired by a wider public-sector reform programme that was initiated in the mid-1990s by a group of senior civil servants who believed that the managerial approach would ensure fiscal rectitude after the economic crisis of the 1980s and address under-performance within the public sector (Collins *et al.* 2007). However, the findings of three recent reports suggest that the managerial rhetoric does not always reflect the reality of probation work.

The first report, which examined the performance of community-based rehabilitation programmes, criticised the lack of quantifiable objectives, the failure to implement effective information systems and the absence of evaluative research (Petrus 2008). The second examined the Community Service Scheme and established that it was operating at just a third of its full capacity (Petrus 2009). The authors also expressed concern about the dearth of operational data, claiming that this could impinge on the Service's ability to manage the Scheme and evaluate its performance. Despite their concerns, they concluded that community service orders constituted a cost-effective alternative to imprisonment. More generally, a recent review of the Department of Justice and Equality found that the organisational climate consisted of a 'closed, secretive and silo-driven culture' (Independent Review Group on the Department of Justice and Equality 2014: 8). The report identified other organisational weaknesses, including lack of leadership, poor management practices, limited oversight and accountability, an absence of targets and performance measures, antiquated IT systems and a failure to develop formal relationships between agencies. Taken together, the findings of these reports suggest that the managerial narrative operates primarily at a symbolic level (although it must also be noted that the Probation Service has since addressed some of the issues identified by the reports, particularly those relating to data quality).

Nonetheless, the managerial rhetoric ensured that the Probation Service became a politically attractive entity after the onset of recession in 2008. The government recently introduced several initiatives in an effort to increase the use of community service orders. For instance, the Fines Act 2010 allowed judges to sentence people who default on the payment of a fine to community service instead of prison. Discussing the rationale behind the Act, Dermot Ahern, then Minister for Justice,[8] stated:

> The traditional policy of imprisonment is no longer viable or socially desirable. It also places a significant financial burden on the State and uses prison places

that should be available for serious criminals. The proposals in my amendments will result in fewer offenders failing to pay fines as who would want a receiver knocking on the door, in front of neighbours, and removing property?

(Dáil Debates, 3 March 2010)

This statement suggests that the Act was inspired by the need to promote the use of cost-effective disposals in an era of economic austerity, as well as a strange combination of compassion and deterrence. In addition, the Criminal Justice (Community Service) Amendment Act 2011 was introduced to encourage judges to consider imposing a community service order as an alternative to prison sentences of 12 months or less. Former minister Alan Shatter's[9] comments highlight potential financial savings to the state, but also stress the reparative benefits of community service orders for offenders and society:

[Community service] delivers at a national, community and individual level. Financial benefits will accrue to the Exchequer from the significantly lower costs associated with community service as compared to imprisonment. The community obtains a measure of reparation and the benefit from unpaid work. Community service allows offenders to remain in work or education, maintain links with family and community and deliver reparation for the offence for which they have been convicted.

(Dáil Debates 7 April 2011)

Finally, the Community Return Programme, which was launched by the Probation Service and the Irish Prison Service in 2011, allows prisoners serving sentences of between 1 and 8 years to apply for early release to perform community service under the supervision of the Probation Service. Applicants must have served at least half of their sentence and be assessed as suitable by prison staff. To date, 548 prisoners have participated in the programme which has a 90 per cent compliance rate (Probation Service 2014). In a speech to the Prison Officers' Association, Alan Shatter (2013) highlighted its rehabilitative ethos, stating that the programme has 'a very positive impact on the resettlement and reintegration prospects of prisoners'. A recent evaluation found that, despite some challenges, the majority of participants experienced a range of benefits that enhanced their willingness and ability to desist, including the addition of structure to their daily lives, the acquisition of transferable employment skills and the opportunity to enact pro-social roles within their communities (Probation Service/Irish Prison Service 2014). The Irish Prison Service and the Probation Service (2013) also produced a joint strategy which aims to facilitate prisoner reintegration though integrated sentence planning and the provision of resettlement programmes. These advances in prisoner reintegration policy and practice were facilitated by the appointment to senior positions of policymakers with an interest in community sanctions and measures, such as Michael Donnellan, who served as Director of the Probation Service before being appointed as Director General of the Irish Prison Service in 2011.

Although the initiatives appear to have been driven by a political commitment to increase the use of community sanctions, it is more likely that they were inspired by the need to increase cost efficiencies during a time of economic austerity. For this reason, the accompanying discourse could be characterised as an 'austerity narrative' rather than a managerial narrative. Imprisonment is an expensive option at a cost of €65,404 per space (Irish Prison Service 2013), and the community service scheme had significant spare capacity, which meant that an increase in its use would not require additional resources. Nevertheless, the IMPACT Trade Union, which represents probation officers, queried the expansion of workloads at a time when resources were dwindling (Williamson 2012).[10] Ultimately, the effect of the initiatives on sentencing practices was marginal, and the number of community service orders handed down by the courts has been declining since 2011 (Probation Service 2014). Overall, community sanctions represent a small proportion of sentences (for example, probation and community service orders constituted less than 4 per cent of the sentences handed down by the District Court in 2013 (Court Service 2014).

The Probation Service has traditionally deployed a penal welfare narrative to justify its existence, and this narrative remains dominant in contemporary discourse. The organisation's most recent strategy statement emphasised penal welfare goals, such as rehabilitation and social inclusion, in a language that reflects an enduring faith in rehabilitation, for example, the statement that 'offenders can change their behaviour and through our purposeful intervention we can help them to achieve their potential as citizens' (Probation Service 2012: 4). Strong welfarist sentiments are also evident in the following description of probation work offered by Vivien Guerin (2011: 21), the current Director of the Probation Service, which emphasises the value of professional relationships:

> that enable [probation officers] to engage with, motivate and help offenders as clients, and as their own primary change agents, to change and live better lives and avoid reoffending; while monitoring and overseeing how they behave, and holding them to account.

Nevertheless, there are signs that the Probation Service is beginning to shift away from its penal welfare roots. In 2006, its name was changed from the 'Probation and Welfare Service' to the 'Probation Service'. In addition, the organisation established a number of offending behaviour programmes, including *Choice and Challenge* and the *Sex Offender Risk and Management* (SORAM) programme. The vocabulary of the new rehabilitation is also making inroads into policy statements. For example, a concern with holding offenders accountable is evident in the statement that 'offenders must accept personal responsibility for their behaviour and where possible, make good the harm they do' (Probation Service 2012: 4). Similarly, victims' needs are prioritised in the promise to 'respect the interests and rights of victims of crime, in our work with offenders' (Probation Service 2012: 4). Finally, the use of the term 'offender' instead of 'client' throughout the document indicates changing attitudes towards people under supervision.

Like the managerial script, the new rehabilitation narrative appears to operate primarily at a symbolic level. The longevity of the 1907 Act has ensured that probation officers continue to 'advise, assist and befriend' people under their supervision (although this act will shortly be replaced with new legislation; see below). Clinical judgement remains a key skill and the majority of probation officers are trained social workers who use social casework techniques in their day-to-day work with offenders (Seymour 2013). In addition, many of the rehabilitation programmes funded by the Probation Service focus on welfarist needs, such as employment and substance abuse, rather than so-called criminogenic risk factors. That being said, recent studies highlight a growing tension between new and traditional modes of practice which may signal the beginnings of a cultural shift towards a hybridised welfare–risk model (Bracken 2010).

The punitive narrative is almost entirely absent from current discourse, but there is some evidence to suggest that it is beginning to infiltrate policy and practice, for example, the removal of the term 'welfare' from the title of the Service and the growing concern with victims and public protection (Healy 2009, 2012b). Electronic monitoring was also introduced in 2013, albeit on a limited scale (see the Criminal Justice Act 2006). At the same time, the content, nomenclature and structure of community sanctions have changed little over time and community sanctions have not been given a 'punitive bite' to make them appear harsher to a fearful public. Moreover, the term 'punishment in the community' does not make conceptual sense in a jurisdiction where the penal welfare model remains dominant (although it must be recognised that welfare-oriented sanctions can be perceived as punitive by their recipients).

Finally, the reparation narrative has always been an inherent feature of probation practice but has gained ground in recent years due to the popularity of restorative justice. There are currently two restorative justice programmes for adult offenders, namely the Nenagh Community Reparation Project and Tallaght Restorative Justice Services, which dealt with 445 cases in 2013 (Probation Service 2014). In addition, the Probation Service (2013a) published a strategy that aims to strengthen the restorative elements in its day-to-day practice and increase the use of restorative programmes more generally.

Trends in the use of probation supervision

There is limited information available about the use of probation supervision during the early years of its existence. When Fahy (1943: 79) attempted to obtain official statistical information, he encountered secrecy, evasion and a 'point blank refusal' from the Department of Justice. McNally (2007) reported that 188 probation orders were made in 1908, the first year of operation, with the figure rising to 258 by 1914. Although the legislation did not impose any restrictions by age, gender or offence type, he found that the majority of probationers during this early period were young males. The Probation Service did not begin to publish official statistical data until 1980. Table 8.1 shows trends in the use of probation supervision and prison committals for selected years between 1980 and 2012. The use of probation supervision increased significantly over time. However, the figures suggest that the community service order is not fulfilling its role as an alternative to custody, since the number of prison committals also increased dramatically during this period. Despite this, Ireland has not witnessed a generalised shift towards the up-tariffing of community sanctions, primarily because the individualised sentencing model precludes the development of universally agreed sentencing norms, policies and practices.

Probation supervision has attracted minimal attention from scholars over the years. As a result, little is known about the characteristics, experiences and outcomes of people under supervision (see Carr *et al.* (2013) for an in-depth review of existing research). The first – and only – socio-demographic survey of probationers was conducted by Hart (1974), who analysed patterns of reconviction among 150 young people on probation. He found that 58 per cent were reconvicted within the follow-up period, a disappointing outcome that he attributed to high caseloads and limited contact between probation officers and clients. The likelihood of reconviction was also increased by a range of social and psychological factors, including previous convictions, poverty, dysfunctional parental relationships, poor educational attainment and emotional difficulties.

More than 20 years later, Walsh and Sexton (1999) reviewed a representative sample of community service orders and found that the typical recipient was a young male with multiple social problems and a history of committing minor offences. The study documented high levels of compliance, with 80 per cent of

TABLE 8.1 Probation supervision 1980–2012 (selected years)

Year	Probation order	Adjourned supervision	Community service order	Other[a]	Total committals to prison
1980	479	642	–	–	2,317[b]
1984	1,326	583	–	–	3,284
1988	1,257	1,341	1,080	–	3,814
1992	1,039	1,062	1,745	–	4,756
1996	1,280	1,815	1,386	–	–
2000	1,345	2,625	998	116	–
2004	1,878	5,623	843	79	10,657
2008	2,676	2,045	1,413	356	13,557
2012	1,742	1,695	2,569	1,436	17,026

[a] The 'other' category includes suspended sentences (part or full), post-release supervision orders, supervision of life-sentence prisoners, young persons' probation orders and supervision of sex offenders in the community. Caution is advised when interpreting trends in this category, because the data relate to different combinations of sanctions.
[b] The 1980 figure includes people sentenced to penal servitude.

Source: Taken from Annual Reports of the Probation Service 1980–2012; Annual Reports of the Irish Prison Service 1980–2012; O'Donnell et al. (2005, Table 3.2).

orders completed satisfactorily. Recent surveys reveal that a significant proportion of people under probation supervision experience problems with homelessness (Seymour and Costello 2005) and substance abuse (Horgan 2013). However, recidivism rates are comparatively low. Official figures show that approximately 41 per cent of people sentenced to probation or community service reoffend within 3 years (Probation Service 2013b).

Further insights into probation philosophies and practices can be gleaned from investigations of the supervision experience. Healy's (2012a, 2012b) interviews with repeat adult offenders who were under supervision between 2003 and 2004 found that the majority were satisfied with the experience. In particular, they appreciated the use of welfarist approaches, including practical assistance with social problems, strong working relationships and opportunities to discuss personal problems. Given the recent changes that have occurred in probation practice, additional research is required to explore contemporary supervision experiences (although see Seymour 2013, on young people's experiences of community sanctions).

Reflections

The Probation Service has experienced many turning points in its 100-plus years of existence, but its overall trajectory is characterised by continuity rather than change. Indeed, the survival of penal welfare ideals constitutes one of the most remarkable events in its history. This section explores the contextual factors that influenced the evolution of probation supervision, focusing in particular on the cultural, political, socio-economic, judicial and international factors that enabled the organisation to maintain structural and ideological continuity over time.

The organisational culture of the Probation Service contributed to stability in several ways. First, the absence of a formal management structure in its early years meant that innovations were rare and any improvements that did occur were initiated by proactive probation officers rather than management (McNally 2009). Second, senior positions within the organisation have, for the most part, been held by former probation officers who worked their way up the ranks. As a result, administrators are acculturated to existing norms and tend to favour the status quo. Third, studies suggest that civil servants are typically conservative and resistant to change (Lee 1989; Independent Review Group on the Department of Justice and Equality 2014). Although its organisational culture has not been examined in detail, it is likely that this characterisation also applies to the Probation Service. In fact, probation officers have shown a willingness to take industrial action to preserve the integrity of their work and have opposed the introduction of techniques that they perceive to be in conflict with the penal welfare ethos. Resistance to change may be beneficial in this instance, because the values and practices associated with the new rehabilitation model have been widely criticised (O'Ciardha and Ward 2013). Fourth, the diffusion of responsibility for offender rehabilitation services to external agencies, combined with weak inter-agency relationships, makes it difficult to implement systemic change.

The political climate also fostered continuity, albeit primarily through neglect. Politicians have traditionally adopted a conservative approach to penal policymaking which, apart from a brief flowering of interest in penal welfarism during the 1960s and 1970s, resulted in a prolonged period of stagnation (Rogan 2011). Even when politicians flirted with punitiveness during the 1990s, the pragmatic nature of Irish politics ensured that a deep-rooted antipathy towards probation supervision never took hold. Political apathy also meant that the Probation Service did not have to adopt populist policies or faddish treatment methods to justify its existence. More negatively, it has resulted in the progressive marginalisation of probation work. Although the Probation Service never encountered serious ideological threats to its legitimacy, it could be argued that the organisation always existed on the edge of crisis due to chronic underfunding, outmoded legislation and delayed modernisation. In fact, Guerin (2005) claimed that it survived at times only through luck and the dedication of a small group of advocates.

The socio-economic climate both helped and hindered the evolution of probation supervision. On the one hand, the dominance of the Catholic Church ensured that the Probation Service experienced limited growth during the first half of the twentieth century. On the other hand, the communitarian structure of Irish society fosters strong public support for welfare provision (Svalfors 2012) and community sanctions (IPRT 2007b). In addition, the background conditions associated with the rise of the new penology, such as loss of faith in rehabilitation and a rising fear of crime, are not entrenched (Kilcommins et al. 2004). Interestingly, the economy appears to have exerted the most profound effect on the status of probation supervision. The Probation Service tends to thrive during recessionary periods as governments seek to reduce public expenditure, but contracts during prosperous times, when politicians favour costlier, punitive measures.

The judiciary have also played a key role by determining the extent to which probation supervision is imposed on offenders. In practice, community sanctions are rarely used and judges seem to be resisting current political pressure to increase their numbers. Their reticence may be partly explained by a preference for classical theories of crime which conflict with penal welfare ideals (Healy and O'Donnell 2010). Individualised sentencing models allow significant autonomy in decision-making and this is not the first time that judges have used their independence to subvert policies perceived to be in conflict with their penal philosophy. For example, many resisted the introduction of sentencing tariffs on the grounds that they would lose their discretion to tailor sentences to the unique characteristics of the offender and the offence (Maguire 2010). Despite their apparent antipathy, the judiciary have contributed to the development of community sanctions and measures by introducing innovations, such as adjourned supervision.

Finally, probation policy and practice has been influenced by international developments, at least to some extent. During the 1960s and 1970s, policymakers and politicians embraced the penal welfare philosophy, even though enthusiasm for the approach was beginning to wane elsewhere. More recently, the adoption of standardised risk-assessment tools, offending behaviour programmes and managerial rhetoric suggests that a modicum of policy transfer is occurring between Ireland, the USA and Britain. Practice has also been influenced somewhat by European initiatives, including the European Rules on Community Sanctions and Measures (1992), the Council of Europe Probation Rules (2010) and the Council Framework Decision on the Application of the Principle of Mutual Recognition to Judgments and Probation Decisions with a View to the Supervision of Probation Measures and Alternative Sanctions (2008). Political support for EU membership has traditionally been strong, suggesting that a 'Good European' narrative may be at play here. For the most part, though, political preoccupation with local matters engenders a reluctance to embrace foreign innovations (Kilcommins *et al.* 2004).

End of an Era

The Probation Service has operated within the framework of the Probation of Offenders Act 1907 for over a century, but this phase of its history is coming to a close. On 5 February 2014, Alan Shatter, then Minister for Justice, published the Criminal Justice (Community Sanctions) Bill, which, if enacted, will replace the 1907 Act. Its provisions are not radical but will remove anachronisms from the system; introduce new sanctions such as reparation orders, which require offenders to make payments into a fund for victim services; and place several existing practices, including adjourned supervision, on a statutory footing. The probation order remains largely unchanged, but the famous edict to 'advise, assist and befriend' has been replaced with a new description of the probation officer's duties which will be to 'establish a positive relationship with the person in order to supervise, guide and assist.' Although many of the provisions reflect penal welfare ideals, such as the emphasis on rehabilitation and the requirement that all probation officers possess a social work qualification, others resonate with a managerial philosophy; for example the requirement that offenders' potential risk to the public should be considered in the imposition and implementation of community sanctions.

It is difficult to make predictions about the future of the Probation Service, but three possible scenarios can be put forward. In the first, probation practices stay largely the same and the work of the organisation remains invisible to policymakers, politicians and the public. Although the community service order is currently enjoying a period of popularity due to its status as a cost-effective alternative to custody, political interest may dissipate once the economic crisis recedes. This scenario is the most consistent with its history to date. Alternatively, the Probation Service could experience a more dystopian outlook. The introduction of programmes and sanctions for serious offenders may lead to greater media scrutiny, which could ultimately threaten its perceived legitimacy. Indeed, media commentators have already begun to question the use of community sanctions with serious offenders (Maguire and Carr 2013). This is of concern, since media coverage of crime and criminal justice is believed to have contributed to a rise in punitiveness in other jurisdictions (Cheliotis 2010). Finally, probation work may gain recognition as an effective and humane alternative to custody. Although this is perhaps the least likely scenario, the onset of recession has prompted a renewed interest in issues relating to social justice, equality and welfare (Healy 2012b).

Conclusion

This chapter explored the evolution of probation supervision in the Republic of Ireland and identified the critical turning points, contextual factors and philosophical values that shaped its development. The findings challenge dominant academic narratives in the history of probation supervision in several ways. For example, Ireland has not (yet) experienced the phenomenon of 'mass supervision' (Phelps 2013), since the numbers under supervision remain significantly lower than the number of committals to prison. In addition, the work of the Probation Service does not bear the hallmarks of the 'culture of control' (Garland 2001), nor has it been shaped very much by the theories and practices associated with the 'new rehabilitation' (Robinson 2008). Instead, probation work continues to be legitimised primarily through a penal welfare narrative, although an austerity narrative tends to become salient during times of economic crisis. It is hoped that this case study will contribute to a greater understanding of the development of community sanctions and measures by highlighting an alternative trajectory within their history.

Notes

1 Although their exact origins are not publicly recorded, both are believed to have existed at least since the foundation of the State.
2 Ireland became a fully fledged Republic in 1949.
3 September 1939 to February 1948.
4 1940–1971.
5 Magdalene laundries housed criminal and so-called fallen women and were run by religious orders. Since 1922, approximately 10,000 women spent time in one of these laundries (Inter-departmental Committee 2013).
6 October 1961 to October 1964.
7 June 1997 to June 2002.
8 May 2008 to January 2011.
9 March 2011 to May 2014.
10 The Probation Service budget was reduced from €59 million in 2007 to €38 million in 2013 (Probation Service 2008, 2014).

References

Aylward, S. (2008) 'Diversity in the criminal justice system', Irish Association for Criminal Justice Research and Development's Inaugural Martin Tansey Memorial Lecture, 21 May 2008.

Bacik, I. (2001) 'Sentencing – *People (DPP) v Padraig Finn*', *Irish Criminal Law Journal*, 11(1): 22–5.

Bracken, D. (2010) 'Differing conceptions of risk and need in Irish probation officers', *Irish Probation Journal*, 7: 108–18.

Carr, N., Healy, D., Kennefick, L. and Maguire, N. (2013) 'A review of the research on offender supervision in the Republic of Ireland and Northern Ireland', *Irish Probation Journal*, 10: 50–74.

Cheliotis, L. (2010) 'The ambivalent consequences of visibility: Crime and prisons in the mass media', *Crime Media Culture*, 6(2): 169–84.

Collins, N., Cradden, T. and Butler, P. (2007) *Modernising Irish Government: The Politics of Administrative Reform*. Dublin: Gill and Macmillan.

Committee of Inquiry into the Penal System (1985) *Report [The Whitaker Report]*. Dublin: Stationery Office.

Comptroller and Auditor General (2004) *Report on Value for Money – The Probation and Welfare Service*. Dublin: The Stationery Office.

Court Service (2014) *Annual Report 2013*. Dublin: Stationery Office.

Expert Group on the Probation and Welfare Service (1999) *Final Report*. Dublin: Stationery Office.

Fahey, T. (2007) 'The Catholic Church and social policy', in B. Reynolds and S. Healy (eds) *Values, Catholic Social Thought and Public Policy*. Dublin: CORI (pp. 143–63).

Fahy, E. (1943) 'Probation of Offenders', *Hermathena*, LXII: 61–82.

Ferriter, D. (2005) *The Transformation of Ireland 1900–2000*. London: Profile Books.

Ferriter, D. (2007) *Judging Dev*. Dublin: Royal Irish Academy.

Garland, D. (2001) *The Culture of Control: Crime and Social Order in Contemporary Society*. Oxford: Oxford University Press.

Guerin, V. (2005) 'The development of social work in probation', in N. Kearney and C. Skehill (eds) *Social Work in Ireland: Historical Perspectives*. Dublin: IPA (pp. 77–106).

Guerin, V. (2011) 'Defining what we do: The meaning of "supervision" in probation', *Irish Probation Journal*, 8: 6–27.

Hamilton, C. (2013) 'Punitiveness and political culture', *European Journal of Criminology*, 10(2): 154–67.

Hart, I. (1974) *Factors Relating to Reconviction among Young Dublin Probationers*. Dublin: Economic and Social Research Institute.

Healy, D. (2009) 'Probation matters', *Irish Jurist*, XLIV: 239–57.

Healy, D. (2012a) *The Dynamics of Desistance: Charting Pathways Through Change*. Abingdon: Routledge.

Healy, D. (2012b) 'Advise, assist and befriend: Can probation supervision support desistance?' *Journal of Social Policy and Administration*, 46(4): 377–94.

Healy, D. and O'Donnell, I. (2005) 'Probation in the Republic of Ireland: Context and challenges', *Probation Journal*, 52(1): 56–68.

Healy, D. and O'Donnell, I. (2010) 'Crime, consequences and court reports', *Irish Criminal Law Journal*, 20(1): 2–7.

Horgan, J. (2013) *Drug and Alcohol Misuse among Young Offenders on Probation Supervision in Ireland: Findings from the Drugs and Alcohol Survey 2012*. Dublin: Probation Service.

Independent Review Group on the Department of Justice and Equality (2014) *Report*. Dublin: Stationery Office.

Inter-departmental Committee to Establish the Facts of State Involvement with the Magdalen Laundries (2013) *Report*. Dublin: Stationery Office.

Irish Penal Reform Trust (2007a) *The Whitaker Report Twenty Years On: Lessons Learned or Lessons Forgotten*. Dublin: IPRT.

Irish Penal Reform Trust (2007b) *Public Attitudes to Prison*. Dublin: IPRT.

Irish Prison Service (2013) *Annual Report 2012*. Dublin: Stationery Office.

Irish Prison Service and Probation Service (2013) *Joint Irish Prison Service and Probation Service Strategic Plan 2013–2015*. Dublin: Stationery Office.

Kearney, N. and Skehill, C. (2005) 'Introduction', in N. Kearney and C. Skehill (eds) *Social Work in Ireland: Historical Perspectives*. Dublin: IPA (pp. 1–12).

Kilcommins, S., O'Donnell, I., O'Sullivan, E. and Vaughan, B. (2004) *Crime, Punishment and the Search for Order in Ireland*. Dublin: IPA.

Kirby, P. (2010) *Celtic Tiger in Collapse: Explaining the Weaknesses of the Irish Model*. Basingstoke: Palgrave Macmillan.

Lee, J. (1989) *Ireland 1912–1985 Politics and Society*. Cambridge: Cambridge University Press.

Maguire, N. (2010) 'Consistency in sentencing', *Judicial Studies Institute Journal*, 2: 14–54.

Maguire, N. and Carr, N. (2013) 'Changing shape and shifting boundaries – the media portrayal of probation in Ireland', *European Journal of Probation*, 5(3): 3–23.

McNally, G. (2007) 'Probation in Ireland: A brief history of the early years', *Irish Probation Journal*, 4: 5–24.

McNally, G. (2009) 'Probation in Ireland, Part 2: The modern age', *Irish Probation Journal*, 6: 187–228.

McWilliams, W. (1985) 'The mission transformed: Professionalisation of probation between the wars', *Howard Journal of Criminal Justice*, 24(4): 257–74.

Molony, T. (1920–1923) 'The prevention and punishment of crime,' *Journal of the Statistical and Social Inquiry Society of Ireland*, XIV(2): 117–32.

O'Ciardha, C. and Ward, R. (2013) 'Theories of cognitive distortions in sexual offending: What the current research tells us', *Trauma, Violence and Abuse*, 14(1): 5–21.

O'Dea, P. (2002) 'The Probation and Welfare Service: Its role in criminal justice', in P. O'Mahony (ed.) *Criminal Justice in Ireland*. Dublin: Institute of Public Administration.

O'Donnell, I., O'Sullivan, E. and Healy, D. (2005) *Crime and Punishment in Ireland 1922 to 2003: A Statistical Sourcebook*. Dublin: IPA.

Osborough, N. (1981) 'Deferment of imposing sentence', *Irish Jurist*, 2: 262–70.

Osborough, N. (1982) 'A Damocles sword "guaranteed Irish": The suspended sentence in the Republic of Ireland', *Irish Jurist*, 2: 221–56.

O'Sullivan, E. and O'Donnell, I. (2007) 'Coercive confinement in the Republic of Ireland: The waning of a culture of control', *Punishment and Society*, 9(1): 27–48.

Petrus Consulting (2008) *Value for Money and Policy Review Report on Projects Funded by the Probation Service*. Dublin: Probation Service.

Petrus Consulting (2009) *Value for Money and Policy Review of the Community Service Scheme*. Dublin: Probation Service.

Phelps, M. (2013) 'The paradox of probation: Community supervision in the age of mass incarceration', *Law and Policy*, 35(1/2): 51–80.

Probation Service (2008) *Strategy Statement 2008–2010*. Dublin: Stationery Office.

Probation Service (2012) *Strategy Statement 2012–2014*. Dublin: Stationery Office.

Probation Service (2013a) *Restorative Justice Strategy*. Dublin: Stationery Office.

Probation Service (2013b) *Probation Service Recidivism Study 2008–2013*. Dublin: Probation Service.

Probation Service (2014) *Annual Report 2013*. Dublin: Stationery Office.

Probation Service/Irish Prison Service (2014) *Community Return: A Unique Opportunity: A Descriptive Evaluation of the First Twenty-Six Months*. Dublin: Stationery Office.

Public Services Organisation Review Group (1969) *Report* [*The Devlin Report*]. Dublin: Stationery Office.

Raftery, M. and O'Sullivan, E. (1999) *Suffer the Little Children: The Inside Story of Ireland's Industrial Schools*. Dublin: New Island Books.

Robinson, G. (2008) 'Late-modern rehabilitation: The evolution of a penal strategy', *Punishment and Society*, 10(4): 429–45.

Rogan, M. (2011) *Prison Policy in Ireland: Politics, Penal Welfarism and Political Imprisonment.* Abingdon: Routledge.

Rogan, M. (2012) 'Rehabilitation, research and reform: Prison policy in Ireland', *Irish Probation Journal*, 9: 6–32.

Seymour, M. (2006) *Alternatives to Custody in Ireland.* Dublin: IPRT.

Seymour, M. (2013) *Youth Justice in Context: Community, Compliance and Young People.* Abingdon: Routledge.

Seymour, M. and Costello, L. (2005) *A Study of the Number, Profile and Progression Routes of Homeless Persons before the Court and in Custody.* Dublin: Stationery Office.

Shatter, A. (2013) 'Address', The Annual Conference of the Prison Officers' Association, 2 May 2013. Available at: www.justice.ie/en/JELR/Pages/SP13000162 (accessed 25 November 2014).

Svalfors, S. (2012) *Welfare Attitudes in Europe: Topline Results from Round 4 of the European Social Survey.* Available at: www.europeansocialsurvey.org/docs/findings/ESS4_toplines_issue_2_welfare_attitudes_in_europe.pdf (accessed 25 November 2014).

Walsh, D. and Sexton, P. (1999) *An Empirical Study of Community Service Orders in Ireland.* Dublin: Stationery Office.

Williamson, D. (2012) 'Probation staff raise resource concerns over community return scheme', *IMPACT* Press Release 4 May 2012. Available at: www.impact.ie/12/05/04/Probation-staff-raise-resource-concerns-over-community-return-scheme-.htm (accessed 25 November 2014).

Worrall, A. and Mawby, R. (2013) *Doing Probation Work: Identity in a Criminal Justice Occupation.* Abingdon: Routledge.

9

ROMANIA

Empty shells, emulation and Europeanization

Ioan Durnescu

Introduction

This chapter will analyse the development of community sanctions and measures in Romania from the beginning of modern times until today. Two moments seem particularly important in this story: the changes after the Romanian Revolution (in 1989) and the modernization and Europeanization that took place especially after 2009, when the new Penal Code was adopted. In the final section, some comments are made on the questions of how and why most of the transformations in the penal sphere took place.

Romanian penal and civil law followed the French and the German traditions from its modern inception. The modern history of Romania started in 1859, when two of the most important provinces – Moldova and Tara Romaneasca – were united to form the Romanian Principalities. In 1865 the penal laws in both principalities were unified under the first modern Penal Code. In 1866 the German Prince Carol Hohenzollern-Sigmaringen was proclaimed as ruler and, in 1881, as King of the Romanian Principalities. The solution of a foreign ruler appeared in order for the Romanian unification process to benefit from the support of the largest powers in Europe: France and Germany. The political unification was completed in 1918, when the third large province – Transylvania – joined Romania.

Ever since that moment, the relationships between the Romanian elite and these two European powers have been very close. Particular attention was dedicated to France, since probably it was easier for the Romanian elite to speak French (Romanian and French are both Latin languages). Many artists, scientists and writers went to Paris to study (e.g. Haricleea Darclee, Constantin Brancusi, George Enescu, Mircea Eliade, Eugen Ionescu and Emil Cioran). Some of them returned to Romania and assumed public positions where they could use their French experiences. The France–Romania special relationship was also reflected in the military sector.

The army general Henri Mathias Berthelot was the head of the French mission in Romania that helped the Romanian army to resist the German invasion in 1917.

It came naturally, based on this close relationship, that Romania imported many institutions and practices from France. This massive importation even created, back in those times, a sort of cultural resistance that criticized the 'empty forms' brought over from France. This phenomenon was criticized by a number of members of the elite (e.g. Maiorescu, Eminescu, Kogalniceanu). The main criticism was that the new forms imported from Western Europe did not fit the Romanian context. As some of them suggested, it was difficult, for instance, to build up an industrial elite in an agricultural country.

Belonging to the continental tradition of law, Romania based its sentencing on written laws and the Constitution. The principle of *'nulla poena sine lege'*[1] is at the heart of the Romanian judicial practice. According to many penal writers (Dongoroz *et al.* 1969; Bulai 1997; Mitrache 2003), since 1968 sanctions have been divided into two main categories: penal law sanctions and penal sanctions. The difference between these two is that penal sanctions are the only ones that have a complex role combining the functions of deterrence, re-education and prevention. They are called 'punishments' (in Romanian, *pedepse*). The penal law sanctions have a more rehabilitative and preventive role. Their punitive bite is close to null, at least in theory. Penal law sanctions are educative measures and safety measures: 'educative' measures are those that can be imposed on juveniles (e.g. supervised freedom or detention in a re-education centre); 'safety' measures, which are intended to prevent further offences, can be applied to someone who has committed an offence (e.g. internment in a hospital for mental health).

Due to these definitions, in the Romanian context at least, the concept of community sanctions and measures is more comprehensive than that of 'community punishment'. As shown above, at least theoretically, educative measures available for juveniles are not considered as punishments, but as measures. Furthermore, conditional release is not defined as a punishment in the Romanian legislation, but as a modality of individualizing the implementation of the prison sentence. Aiming first at rehabilitation, conditional release can also thus be defined as a measure rather than as a punishment.

Therefore, although I understand partly the reasons for calling all sanctions punishments, since in one way or another they all imply a punitive bite, I would also call for a more nuanced distinction between the primary aims of these sanctions. Based on the Romanian traditions, these distinctions seem important and carry both symbolic and instrumental value. For instance, according to the new Penal Code adopted in 2009 (Ministry of Justice 2009), there are no punishments provided for juveniles, but only educative measures. In spite of the fact that all the educative measures have a punitive message, the way they are defined and implemented should take a more educative and rehabilitative role. Furthermore, as they are educative measures, they are not mentioned in the criminal record. As mentioned above, conditional release and deferred sentence are good examples in this area. As they are regulated, they are not penal sanctions but penal measures that individualize the way a prison sentence is implemented. Thus they reflect rehabilitative or managerial intentions rather than punitive ones.

Inception

As an example of early policy transfer, the first modern prison law was adopted in 1874 under the advice of Ferdinand Dodun de Perrieres (Ciuceanu 2001), a French expert sent by the Ministry of Justice of France. According to Sucila-Pahoni (unpublished work), Ferdinand Dodun de Perrieres was also general director of the Prison Department between 1862 and 1876.

In terms of community sanctions and measures, this law had the merit of regulating conditional release for the first time in the Romanian Principalities. It should be noted that the 'conditional release' concept was still under debate at the European level when it was introduced in the Romanian Principalities. The decision to introduce conditional release was based on moral grounds: prisoners who made an effort to become 'better people' should be rewarded with early release (Ciuceanu 2001). It is important to note here that conditional release was made available only for juveniles and not for adults. Juveniles were considered more amenable to reform and therefore re-educative interventions were justified.

Another element that was introduced in the same law was the Société du Patronage (see also the chapter by Herzog-Evans in this book), who were responsible for the 'moral reform' of prisoners. Briefly, these voluntary organizations were set up around each penitentiary institution to visit prisoners and assist them after release. As suggested by Vanstone (2008, 2009), these societies were very popular in the Netherlands, Belgium, France and Switzerland. Based on some comments published in the newspapers or made in different official speeches at that time, it seems that these societies were not very significant in the life of prisoners in Romania, not even after such societies received more official recognition in law in 1908. According to Szabo (2010), the main reasons for the limited influence or impact of these organizations was lack of funding and lack of interest from public institutions. To some extent these reasons sound valid even today. However, one can observe that the Romanian legislation included these modern forms of sanctioning or rehabilitation. Unfortunately, there was a big distance between aspiration and reality.

The next normative act that regulated the sanctioning system was the Penal Code of 1936 – known as Carol's Code (after the name of the king). According to this act, the main punishments for common crimes were: forced labour for life, forced labour from 5 to 25 years and imprisonment from 3 to 20 years. Apart from these sanctions available for ordinary crimes, the Code also established sanctions for political crimes and misdemeanours (in Romanian, *delicte*). All of them were organized around imprisonment and fines.

The only measure or sanction that resembled a modern community sanction in this Code was conditional release. This measure could be applied to imprisonment or to forced labour under strict conditions. It is interesting to note here the interest in the victim. When deciding on the conditional release, the court could oblige the convicted person to reside in a different locality from the one where the victim lived or could oblige the offender to pay reparations to the victim if he/she had not done so until that moment in time.

Near to each penitentiary institution a supervisory committee was established, led by a judge from the county court. The role of this committee was to advise the court on the prisoner's transition from one prison regime to another and on the conditional release. This committee was also responsible for supervising offenders on conditional release. Besides this committee, the societies of patronage were established by the Code to help juveniles and adults released on conditional release to reintegrate back in society.

These two organizations were meant to work like probation services in relation to prison and conditional release. As mentioned by Constantinescu-Mion (a former head of the General Society of Patronage) and Dianu (former head of the Prison Service at the beginning of the twentieth century), the reintegration activity was to be focused on finding employment, financial assistance and negotiating the relationships between the ex-prisoners with the community (cited by Szabo 2010). Due to the limited involvement of the state and of the charitable organizations, these plans were, however, only dreams.

With only small changes, the Penal Code was in force up to 1968, when a new Code was adopted. Although the 1968 Code was drafted in the Soviet era, it was considered by penologists to be quite modern and in line with international trends (Mitrache and Mitrache 2003). The main punishments available were life imprisonment, imprisonment from 15 days to 30 years and fines. Conditional release was maintained in the new Code and was available for those who served two-thirds of their term of imprisonment (for sentences up to 10 years) or three-quarters of the prison sentence (for those with longer sentences). The measure could be applied to those who were 'hard workers, disciplined and provided solid evidence of reform'. One novelty of this Code was the introduction of the conditional suspension of the sentence that could be applied to fines or prison sentences of up to 3 years. The only obligation of the convicted person was not to commit further offences during the period of the suspension. There was no organization in charge of supervising offenders as there were no concrete obligations to fulfil. As it was configured, the conditional suspension of the execution of the prison sentence was a form of warning for the offender. However, if during the period of suspension the person did reoffend, then he/she could be required to serve the old sentence and then the new one for the second offence.

Juveniles could be sentenced to imprisonment or educative measures. The Code mentions explicitly that imprisonment could be applied only if the educative measures 'would not be enough to reform the juvenile'. As for adults, prison sentences of up to 3 years could be suspended conditionally. The educative measures were: warning, supervised freedom, internment in a re-education centre and internment in a medico-educative centre.

At this time, the only community-based measure was 'supervised freedom', which could be imposed on a juvenile for up to 1 year. During this time frame, the parents supervised the juvenile. The school or the work place was also informed about this measure in order for them to contribute to the 'juvenile re-education'.

Apart from these community sanctions and measures available for juveniles and adults, the 1968 Code provided also for some ways of replacing the penal response with some administrative measures, such as sending the case to a community organization or placing the person under an organization (or workplace) warranty. Once an offender was placed in this form of placement, his colleagues would supervise him or her until the sentence was considered served. Sometimes, workers with political responsibilities were to take up this task and therefore the 'rehabilitation' also included a political component. These measures were at the prosecution's or the court's discretion, but were only permitted for offences punishable with up to 6 months' imprisonment. Since the tariffs provided by the Code for offences were very high these options were not used extensively. Most offences were punishable by between 1 and 5 years of imprisonment.

An important moment in the evolution of the community-based sentences came in 1977, when Decree no. 218/1977 (State Council of the Socialist Republic of Romania 1977) was adopted. The Decree was adopted for two reasons.: first, to reduce the number of prisoners; and, second, because the political leaders wanted to demonstrate to international partners that Romania was committed to human rights. According to the explanatory memorandum, this decree aimed at 'increasing the role of socialist organizations, community organizations and the people in enhancing legality and re-education through work of people who broke the law'. The main measure promoted by this decree was to replace imprisonment of up to 5 years with work. The act made it almost impossible for juveniles to be sentenced to imprisonment. The only measure available for them was to be 'under the surveillance of the organizations where they go to school or work'. During this measure they had to follow some very strict rules of behaviour, and families and peers had to observe them closely. Only in exceptional cases could juveniles be sentenced to internment in re-education centres for up to 5 years. According to Dianu (1997), this massive deinstitutionalization led to a fall in prison sentencing from 66 per cent of all sentences passed in 1976 to 29.4 per cent in 1979, for both juveniles and adults. In other words, if previous judicial practice was structured around the prison sentence, after this Decree was adopted, sentencing practice became more community oriented. However, it is not yet clear how and with what impact peer and family supervision was functioning.

In terms of community sentencing, the Code of 1968 together with Decree no. 218/1977 remained in force without much amendment until the Romanian Revolution in 1989. Due to the fact that more and more companies became private, the obligation to be supervised by workplace colleagues became outdated and impracticable. The new managers would not allow these practices under their coordination.

Prior to 1989, the development of community sanctions and measures was based on different reasoning depending on each historical moment and each transformation. It seems that the first community-based sentences or measures (that is, through the patronage societies) were imported from France and Belgium to Romania, sometimes without any consideration given to the local context. This created resistance or at least led to a general non-application of those foreign dispositions of the law. But, on the contrary, other dispositions such as conditional release became very popular and were quite widely used in judicial practice. As conditional release was not accompanied by any form of supervision, we can assume that the rationale for such a success was that this device would help to decrease the prison population. Later, penal transformations seemed to take place either in response to the needs of the mass industrialization that took place after the Second World War or as a consequence of international pressures. The community elite clearly sometimes saw penal policy as a tool for seeking international prestige.

Contextualizing change after 1989

Based on Durkheim, Weber and Marx, Cavadino and Dignan (2006) suggest a possible framework for understanding penal change within a society; they refer to this as a radical pluralist model. This model is based on the assumption that society is constructed in and through the multiple interactions between different groups and interests. As this is close to the social constructivist model suggested by the editors in the introductory chapter to this book, the radical pluralist model will be used to explain the penal transformations that took place after 1989[2] (see Figure 9.1).

Economy

In the context of the transitions that followed the fall of the Berlin Wall in 1989, and subsequently the Romanian Revolution, Romania suffered multiple and rapid transformations. One of the most visible ones was the unemployment rate, which increased from 3 per cent in 1991 to 11.8 per cent in 1999 (Institutul Naţional de Statistică 2015). At the same time, social inequality increased from 0.24 in 1989 to 0.35 in 2001 (expressed in the Gini coefficient; Zamfir 2004). All these changes and also the anomie that characterizes any transition period led to an increase in the volume of crime. Whilst in 1990 Romania had 160 convictions per 100,000 inhabitants, in 1997 this indicator had risen to 496 convictions per 100,000 inhabitants.[3]

The incarceration rate increased from 171 prisoners per 100,000 inhabitants in 1992 to 200 per 100,000 in 1998 (International Centre for Prison Studies 2008). As one of the senior civil servants of the Prison Department mentioned, the annual cost per one prisoner place became higher than the average salary in Romania.[4] Observations like this created among the public and the political elite a sufficient critical mass to support the development of alternatives to prison. Thus, in 1992 the Penal Code was amended to introduce a new form of suspension called 'suspended sentence under supervision'. This community measure was introduced to replace imprisonment of up to 4 years. During the period of suspension, the convicted person had to follow some supervisory measures (e.g. to meet the judge on

FIGURE 9.1 An explanatory framework for the development of community sentences
and probation service in Romania

Source: Adapted from Durnescu (2008).

a regular basis or to advise of any change in residence) and fulfil some obligations
(e.g. to undertake some activities or to attend school or vocational training, or not
to visit certain places). Although these measures were promoted as credible alternatives to imprisonment, they were not used as frequently as expected, mainly due to
the lack of an enforcement infrastructure. There was no dedicated organization
to supervise offenders in the community. Judges and police had other institutional priorities that limited their capacity to allocate proper resources to offender
supervision.

Penal law

As mentioned in the previous sections, different penal regulations assumed or
enabled the existence of community supervision even before 1989. After 1989,
in the context of a steep increase in the prison population, the Romanian authorities started to promote alternatives to incarceration. As already noted above, the first
one was the introduction of a new form of suspension – suspended sentence under

supervision — after the French model of *sursis avec mise a l'epreuve*. Although the intention was to encourage judges to pass fewer prison sentences, in the absence of a real infrastructure to implement it, this new form of executing the prison sentence was not very popular. On the contrary, the courts kept imposing the conditional suspension that had existed before. As a consequence, the numbers of prison sentences were not altered much at all.

The necessary implementation infrastructure was developed later, in 2000, when a Governmental Decision (no. 92/2000) was adopted to set up the probation system. The aim of the probation system (available for both juveniles and adults) was described from the first article: 'to reintegrate offenders who are kept in liberty by the court and supervise the way they follow the obligations imposed upon them'. The main reasons for setting up this system were mentioned in the explanatory note: to implement community-based penal sentences, to supervise and assist offenders and to comply with the European Union (EU) and the Council of Europe standards. The 'positive results of the experimental centres' were also mentioned in the background document. These centres had been set up in 1997 in different locations in Romania to test different elements of the new institution (e.g. pre-sentence reports and post-release care). In setting up and running these centres, a crucial role was played by the Department for International Development of the UK Government, which funded two consecutive technical assistance projects to support the development of probation in Romania (see Durnescu and Haines 2012). A few twinning projects funded by the European Commission followed up these projects. Therefore, the influence of the UK Probation Service was long-lasting and significant. However, as suggested by Durnescu and Haines (2012), the probation service adapted its principles and core activities to the local context. To give only one example, due to the strong judicial tradition in Romania, the probation counsellors were not allowed to make recommendations in their pre-sentence reports, as was the case in England and Wales. They were expected only to provide a criminological analysis of the factors that contributed to the development of the offending behaviour. It was only the judge who could assess these factors and decide the best course of action.

Judicial practice

One of the main activities promoted by the UK project was to organize seminars, conferences and study visits. One of the privileged target groups for these activities was judicial staff: judges and prosecutors. Most of these events were organized together with magistrates from England, the Netherlands and other countries with established probation systems. This exposure to new and modern approaches to addressing recidivism led to a change in the judicial perception regarding prison and its alternatives. Whereas in the 1990s the judicial practice was quite prison-centric, in early 2000 magistrates started to demand more community sanctions in the Penal Code. Joint workshops and seminars where vignettes were used in sentencing exercises enabled Romanian judges to understand that their sentencing practices were maybe too punitive and therefore they started to think in new ways. Although judges are independent in their daily practice, they still need to belong to a professional body or community. The perceptions of the foreign magistrates regarding Romanian sentencing could not leave the Romanian judges indifferent. In a survey conducted in 2002, 94 per cent of the presidents of the courts suggested that the Penal Code should incorporate more community sanctions (Haines *et al.* 2002). The Council of Europe and Western partners promoted the same conclusion: Romanian penal practice was too punitive (with prison being used too much and for too long) and Romania needed new alternatives to prison.

The changes in the penal law together with transformations in judicial mentalities led to sentencing practice that was less prison-centric. If in 1999 imprisonment was imposed in 51.8 per cent of cases, this started to decrease dramatically after 2000, when the probation service was set up (imprisonment's share of disposals dropped to 50.1 per cent in 2000, to 40 per cent in 2001 and to 40.5 per cent in 2003). At the same time, the use of suspended sentences under supervision increased from 0.6 per cent (of all sentences) in 2000 to 2.4 per cent in 2004. Some of the potential prison sentences were converted into simple suspended sentences (with no supervision) or non-custodial measures for juveniles.

More generally, the introduction of a probation service in Romania was part of a wider decarceration movement, which included changes in preventative arrest procedures, different treatment of drug users and so on. All these changes together created the basis of a major decrease in the prison population from 228 per 100,000 in 2001 to 132 per 100,000 in 2010.

Europeanization and European institutions

Decarceration was also the message of the Council of Europe and European Commission. Indeed, Romania was admitted to the Council of Europe in 1993 and adopted the European Convention of Human Rights in 1994.

The influence of the Council of Europe is obvious from looking at the explanatory notes of many recent penal laws. Recommendations such as R(80)11 on preventative arrest and R(92)16 on the European Rules regarding Community Sanctions and Measures are very often mentioned in these documents as reasons to adopt new approaches. Laws or ministerial orders mention the same recommendations. For example, when the probation experimental centres were set up by ministerial orders, Recommendations (87)3 (Council of Europe 1987) on European Prison Rules and (92)16 (Council of Europe 1992) were constantly mentioned.

Another important institution that contributed to the development of community sanctions and institutions in Romania was the European Commission. From the beginning of the accession process in 1999, the European Commission published an evaluation report each year. One of the recurring statements in these reports concerned 'justice reform and a better human rights approach through setting up a probation system'. At the same time, the probation service was presented as a solution to prison overcrowding. The European Committee for Prevention of Torture and Inhumane or Degrading Treatment or Punishment (CPT) also recommended that Romania should reduce prison overcrowding.

Furthermore, two large twinning projects funded by the EU were dedicated to developing and consolidating the probation system in Romania. Therefore the pressure of European institutions and standards was quite decisive in promoting alternatives and setting up a probation system. In this respect, the role of the European Commission seemed very important, because it pushed Romania from two different directions. On one hand, in the country report the need to reduce the prison population and set up a probation system was mentioned every year. On the other hand, it provided technical assistance to accomplish this aim via the various instruments. The twinning instrument was the preferred method of achieving these ends. In a twinning programme one country is paired with one or (at most) two other countries to solve a problem. In the Romanian case, the National Offender Management Service from England and Wales won both twinning contracts. The way a twinning programme is designed makes the beneficiary almost dependent on the lead partner. In most cases, experts are brought in from the lead country and study visits are organized, and so on. Country reports (crucial in the accession process), twinning projects and nowadays Framework Decisions[5] make Europe more and more unified in the penal response to crime.

People and personalities

Savelsberg (1999, cited in Cavadino and Dignan 2006) observed that if the legislative process is based on bureaucratic procedures it tends to be more stable. By contrast, if the process is based on people, it tends to be more unstable and dynamic. It seems that Romania is closer to the second type of country where personalities can promote penal change if they have enough political support. In most cases, public debate or expert consultations are tokenistic processes undertaken to satisfy the legal formal requirement. In this context, it is not a surprise that most reforms have been associated with different personalities or Ministers of Justice (e.g. Stanoiu Code and Predoiu Code).

The inception and the early development of a probation system in Romania is associated with the name of a former minister of Justice – Mr. Valeriu Stoica. After visiting the Probation Service in London, meeting the Lord Chancellor and discussing options with different Romanian and foreign experts, the Minister decided to promote Governmental Decision 92/2000, which set up the probation system in Romania. The main reason he made this decision may be that he was convinced by the utility of such a service within the criminal justice system.

It seems that this practice is not new in Europe. Different personalities played a crucial role in promoting community sanctions and measures or community based institutions in Europe: Jules Lejeune in Belgium, Lucy Bartlett in Italy, Edouart Juhliet in France and Howard Vincent in the UK (Vanstone 2008).

Modernization and Europeanization

In 2009 a new Penal Code[6] was adopted in Romania (Law no. 286/2009). To quote from the Explanatory Note, the objectives of the new Penal Code are:

- to create a coherent legislative framework that avoids duplications with other special laws,
- to simplify the regulations and promote a more unified practice,
- to respond to all the Constitutional and international obligations,
- to transpose in the domestic legislation the legislation adopted at the European Union level,
- to harmonize the Romanian Penal Code with other regulations at the EU level to support the mutual recognition.

Three out of five objectives of the new law are associated with legislation and judicial practice at the European level. Regarding the sanctioning system, the initiators stated that they aimed at 'creating a flexible and diversified mechanism to allow the application of the most efficient measures'. The new Swiss Code, the Spanish Code and also the French Penal Code are mentioned as the main sources of inspiration. The new Penal Code incorporates demands coming vertically from the EU level, but also horizontally follows models and examples from other jurisdictions.

Indeed, although the main punishments are maintained from the old Code (life imprisonment, imprisonment and fines), the means of individualized implementation are more diverse. Organized on a scale of seriousness, these modalities are:

- Discharge – which can be applied if the offence is not very serious and the offender has good chances of rehabilitation with no punishment. However, the court will warn the offender of the consequences of continuing a criminal career.
- Deferred sentences – which can be applied to replace a fine or 2 years of imprisonment. During the deferral period, the offender will have to follow all the supervisory measures (e.g. to visit the probation service, to accept home visits from the probation officer, to announce any change in the domicile or the workplace). Attached to these measures, the court may also impose a series of obligations such as: to undertake a course or vocational training, to undertake community service between 30 and 60 days, to undertake rehabilitation programs organized by the probation service and so on.
- Suspended sentences – which can be applied to replace up to 3 years of imprisonment. The measures and the obligations are the same as those available for the deferred sentence, with the only difference being that those sentenced to imprisonment with suspended sentence must undertake community service between 60 and 120 days.

– Conditional release – which can be applied to those who have served two-thirds of a prison sentence if the sentence is up to 10 years or three-quarters of a prison sentence of between 10 and 20 years. If the remaining part of the sentence is longer than 2 years, the inmate will be supervised by the probation service. During the conditional release period, the inmate will have to comply with some supervisory measures. The court can also impose obligations when deciding the conditional release. As another novelty, in implementing some obligations, the police can use some new technologies. This regulation may be the 'foot in the door' for electronic monitoring in Romania. It might be possible that in the near future Romanian police will be able to use electronic monitoring. The idea seems to be supported by the rationale that only electronic means can effectively supervise someone on house arrest or released under judicial control. Therefore, the introduction of electronic monitoring in Romania might be justified by pragmatic reasons.

The sanctioning system for juveniles has been even more comprehensively reformed. According to the new Penal Code, imprisonment cannot be applied to juveniles. Instead, the only custodial educational measures are internment in an educative centre and internment in a detention centre. Besides these measures, the court can order civic-education supervision, weekend confinement and daily assistance. All these measures involve the probation service as the implementation agency. Civic education means an obligation for the juvenile to attend a course on how to behave as a decent citizen. The other three measures involve courses or programmes that juveniles will have to attend under probation service supervision.

When introducing the new sanctioning system for juveniles, the legislator stated that it took into consideration different UN rules (e.g. The Beijing Rules and The Riyadh Rules) (UN General Assembly 1985, 1990) and the Council of Europe recommendations 2003/20E and 2008/11 (Council of Europe (2003, 2008). When commenting on the educative measures, the legislator also mentioned as a source of inspiration the French (from 1945) and the Spanish law (from 2000).

If we look at how the community sanctions and measures are implemented in Romania, we can note sustained attention to training and to practice tools and techniques. In the last few years, there has been a constant consideration given to programmes, assessment tools and skills that need to be used by probation staff during supervision sessions. A new one-to-one programme is available (SEED) to probation counsellors, thanks to the National Offender Management Service in England and Wales. A risk-assessment instrument is about to be adopted. A pre-release programme delivered in partnership between prison and probation staff has been implemented in almost all prisons in Romania. Based on these developments we can conclude that, at least at the implementation level, rehabilitation is the dominant form of adaptation. The organizational interest in developing tools, manuals and procedures speaks also of a strong orientation towards managerialism.

All these devices are meant to standardize the work, make probation staff more accountable and promote a more professional face of the probation system. In order to deliver these interventions in a more effective way, the Probation Department was reformed into an independent National Department for Probation under the authority of the Ministry of Justice. It is expected that this change will help the organization make its own decisions and plans for development without any interference from other institutions and organizations.

Conclusion

Based on the account provided above, it can be concluded that penal changes in Romania were introduced as a result of a complex interaction between internal and external forces. In some cases, the external forces were stronger and did not pay enough attention to the local particularities. There were occasions when different institutions were adopted from abroad with no articulation to the local context. This made some Romanian scholars complain about so-called form without any content, or empty shells. A good example in this respect was the patronage society, which, although it was introduced in 1874, never became very active, even after a special law on this subject was adopted.

In other cases, outside forces were moderated and adapted to the local context. After the Second World War, the influence of the United Nations and the Council of Europe has increased in the legislative process of Romania. In many cases this vertical influence was complemented by some horizontal influences from abroad. This trend has became more visible in the latest Penal Code, where the influence of the French, the Spanish and the Swiss Codes are openly acknowledged.

Besides these external influences, some internal factors seemed to play an important role, either in initiating change or in shaping some sanctions in one way or another. Local 'champions' or economic factors played important roles, especially after the 1990s, when Romania became an open society. The role of the civil servants might have been crucial in some decisions, but that is very difficult to assess.

Almost all forms of adaptation mentioned in this book's introductory chapter – managerial, punitive, rehabilitative and reparative – can be found in the Romanian context, especially the first three of them. The reparative narrative is only beginning to appear in new legislation. For instance, before deciding on conditional release, the court must check whether the civil obligations imposed on the offender were fulfilled. Sometimes these forms of adaptation appear separate: different reforms were introduced to support different aims of punishment. When patronage societies were introduced, the only rationale was the rehabilitative one; inmates needed to be morally saved and supported after release. In some other cases, the rationale was not that straightforward and not based on only one narrative. If we take conditional release as an example, in the last Penal Code we will see that its introduction might be justified by the need to provide supervision to those with long sentences (emphasizing the managerial goals of the punishment), but, if we compare it with the previous situation where there was no supervision for any released prisoner, this reform can be seen as having a punitive effect; at least this is how some Romanian prisoners seem to look at it. As noted by Durnescu (2011), being subject to penal supervision involves significant 'pains of probation'.

If we take a historical perspective, we can observe that community-based penalties have developed both in terms of volume and in the range of their application. In general terms, we can confirm that community-based penalties are on an expansionist trajectory. If at the beginning of the last century Romania had only a limited number of community penal options, now the new Penal Code provides for many. Furthermore, these options are available for many categories of offenders. An interesting trend in this respect is that not all the community measures are meant to be purely rehabilitative. Conditional release, for instance, begins to look like a managerial tool for addressing systems-related needs to reduce the prison population.

Furthermore, if we analyse the new Penal Code we can note that the Government applies different rationales to different groups of offenders. For first-time or low-risk offenders, the Code opens a wide range of alternatives to custody (e.g. deferred sentence or suspended sentence); but, for the prisoners with long prison sentences, the Code provides automatic supervision by the probation service, emphasizing the punitive and managerial message. By contrast, for those committing more than one offence or for recidivists, the new Penal Code provides a very punitive response in the form of long prison sentences.

How all these provisions will be reflected in judicial practice is still difficult to estimate, but prison *and* probation overcrowding is one very likely outcome. As a whole, the new penal policy in Romania looks quite moderate, with a high number of non-prison options and with relatively low prison tariffs for the most common offences. However, as noted above, persistent and prolific offenders are subject to some very severe provisions – long prison sentences, supervision upon conditional release etc. These measures might work against the desistance process some of them would like to embark on.

From a Romanian perspective, it becomes obvious that, apart from the main four narratives, Europeanization is an important driver of change. As illustrated in this case, the European influence can initiate or shape penal transformations. It is possible sometimes that the only real reason for a penal reform to take place may be a European demand. Of course, this is possible in a country where criminal justice is very low on the public agenda and where the relationship with Brussels is not defined as a partnership but as subordination.

For the time being, the main concern is how to make the new Penal Code work effectively. There are still many challenges that judges and probation counsellors need to solve. For the medium- and long-term future, we can expect further developments in the field of community sanctions and measures. As the current legislation already states that electronic tools can be used to ensure effective surveillance, it can be anticipated that electronic monitoring will be on the public agenda soon. Due to the way it is defined in the Penal Code and the Penal Procedure Code, it seems that if and when electronic monitoring will be regulated it will not be under the probation service umbrella. It is rather the police and the prison service which will take over this task.

As community measures and sanctions (or penal policy in general) are not high on the public agenda, Romania has not yet experienced any legitimacy crisis. However, as the probation service will start working with parolees (and therefore with a different level of risk), it is possible that in the future issues such as high-profile recidivists committing serious crimes while under probation supervision will appear. This might be an important moment, when the legitimacy of probation supervision will be seriously questioned for the first time.

As mentioned above, by using the four forms of adaptation model suggested in the introductory chapter, comparative analysis of criminal justice acquires an analytical tool to answer the 'why' question: why some penal transformations take place and fail to take place in different historical and cultural contexts. The focus on legitimizing narratives addresses mainly the motivations and perhaps the desired outcomes of a penal change. As illustrated in this chapter, for a deeper understanding of these changes, other questions might also be useful: for example, we might ask *how* these transformations took place and what were the factors contributing to them. By introducing these questions into the discussions, the comparative analysis becomes more complex and the predictive power of the analysis might increase.

Notes

1 'No punishment without law'.
2 Some of these arguments were also used by Durnescu (2008).
3 Available at: http://statistici.insse.ro/shop/index.jsp?page=tempo3&lang=ro&ind=JUS104A.
4 Statement made by Sorin Dumitrascu, Deputy Director of the Prison Department, available at: www.fsanp.ro/2013/08/mass-media-despre-penitenciare/.
5 For the impact of the Framework Decisions, see also Morgenstern and Larrauri (2013).
6 Due to some political and economic factors, this Code came into force only on 1 February 2014.

References

Bulai, C. (1997) *Manual de Drept Penal. Partea Generală*. Editura All: Bucureşti.
Cavadino, M. and Dignan, J. (2006) 'Penal policy and political economy', *Criminology & Criminal Justice*, 6(4): 435–56. DOI: 10.1177/1748895806068581.
Ciuceanu, R. (2001) *Regimul Penitenciar din România 1940–1962*. Institutul Naţional pentru Studiul Totalitarismului: Bucureşti.
Council of Europe (2003) 'Recommendation Rec(2003)20E of the Committee of Ministers to member states concerning new ways of dealing with juvenile delinquency and the role of juvenile justice', available at: https://wcd.coe.int/ViewDoc.jsp?id=70063.
Council of Europe (2008) 'Recommendation CM/Rec(2008)11 of the Committee of Ministers to member states on the European Rules for juvenile offenders subject to sanctions or measures', available at: https://wcd.coe.int/ViewDoc.jsp?id=1367113&Site=CM.

Council of Europe (1987) 'Recommendation Rec(87)3E (replaced by Rec(2006)2) on the European Prison Rules', available at: https://wcd.coe.int/ViewDoc.jsp?id=955747.

Council of Europe (1992) Recommendation Rec(92)16 of the Committee of Ministers to member states on the European Rules regarding Community Sanctions and Measures', available at: http://pjp-eu.coe.int/documents/3983922/6970334/CMRec+%2892%29+16+on+the+European+rules+on+community+sanctions+and+measures.pdf/01647732-1cf7-4ea8-88ba-2c041bc3f5d6.

Dianu, T. (1997) *Non-custodial Sanctions: Alternative Models for Post-communist Societies*. Nova Science: New York.

Dongoroz, V., Kahane, S., Oancea, I. and Fodor, I. (1969) *Explicaţii Teoretice ale Codului Penal Roman*. Editura Academiei Republicii Socialiste România: Bucureşti.

Durnescu, I. (2008) 'O istorie a probatiunii in Romania', in Schiaucu, V. and Canton, R. (eds) *Manual de Probatiune*. Ed. Standard: Bucharest, pp. 8–25.

Durnescu, I. (2011) 'Pains of probation: effective practice and human rights', *International Journal of Offender Therapy and Comparative Criminology*, 55(4): 530–45.

Durnescu, I. and Haines, K. (2012) 'Probation in Romania, archaeology of a partnership', *British Journal of Criminology*. DOI: 10.1093/bjc/azs026.

Governmental Decision no. 92/2000. Available at: www.legex.ro/Ordin-92-2000-21062.aspx.

Grand National Assembly [Romania] (1968) The Penal Code of 1968. Available at: www.monitoruljuridic.ro/act/codul-penal-din-21-iunie-1968-emitent-marea-adunare-nationala-publicat-n-buletinul-oficial-nr-79-38070.html.

Haines, K., Willie, A., Lazar, C. and Durnescu, I. (2002) *Opiniile Judecatorilor Referitoare La Sistemul de Reintegrare Sociala si Supraveghere*, vol. I, no. 8/2002, Edit. Didactica si Pedagogica: Bucuresti.

Institutul Naţional de Statistică (2015) Anuarul Statistic al României (1991–2004). Available at: http://statistici.insse.ro/shop/index.jsp?page=tempo3&lang=ro&ind=JUS104A.

International Centre for Prison Studies (2008) *Prison Brief*. King's College: London.

Ministry of Justice [Romania] (2009) The Penal Code of 2009. Available at: www.just.ro/LinkClick.aspx?fileticket=Wpo7d56II/Q=.

Mitrache, C., and Mitrache, C. (2003) *Drept Penal Român – Partea Generală*, ediţia a II-a revăzută şi adăugită. Editura Universul Juridic: Bucureşti.

Morgenstern, C. and Larrauri, E. (2013) European norms, policy and practice, in McNeill, F. and Beyens, K. (eds) *Offender Supervision in Europe*. Palgrave Macmillan: Croydon, pp. 125–54.

Romanian Parliament (1936) The Penal Code of 1936. Available at: http://lege5.ro/Gratuit/heztqnzu/codul-penal-din-1936.

State Council of the Socialist Republic of Romania (1977) Decree no. 218/1977. Available at: www.legex.ro/Decretul-218-1977-642.aspx.

Sucila-Pahoni, C. (unpublished) *A critical look over the Prisons Law from 1874*. available at: http://crisia.mtariicrisurilor.ro/pdf/2012/009_C%20Sucila.pdf.

Szabo, A. (2010) Patronagiul infractorilor şi alte măsuri de asistare: 1874–1936. Începuturile probaţiunii în România, *Revista de Asistenţă Socială*, 9(3): 7–20.

United Nations General Assembly (1985) 'United Nations Standard Minimum Rules for the Administration of Juvenile Justice ("The Beijing Rules")'. Available at: www.un.org/documents/ga/res/40/a40r033.htm.

United Nations General Assembly (1990) 'United Nations Guidelines for the Prevention of Juvenile Delinquency (The Riyadh Guidelines)'. Available at: www.un.org/documents/ga/res/45/a45r112.htm.

Vanstone, M. (2008) The international origins and initial development of probation: an early example of policy transfer, *British Journal of Criminology*, 47(3): 390–404.

Vanstone, M. (2009) The engineer, the educationalist and the feminist writer: national champions and the development of probation in Europe, *European Journal of Probation* 1(2): 89–96.

Zamfir, C. (2004) *O analiză critică a tranziției. Ce va fi 'după'*. Polirom: Iași.

10

REDUCTIONISM, REHABILITATION AND REPARATION

Community punishment in Scotland

Fergus McNeill

Introduction

Scotland has a relatively long history of provision of prisoner aftercare and of probation services (or at least probation-like services), dating back to the nineteenth century. However, whether we can accurately refer to these services as delivering 'community punishment' is a more complex question, and one to which I will return in due course after having reflected on the foundations of these services, on key aspects of their development and on their current position and prospects. I will try to weave throughout this account attention to the questions set by the editors in the Introduction: questions which centrally concern the narratives and discourses through which attempts have been made – and still are being made – to legitimate community punishment both as a social practice and a social institution (Robinson *et al.* 2013).

Perhaps the simplest place to begin is with a brief account of the range of forms of community punishment (or more neutrally, community sanctions) that exist in Scotland today, and with some information about their uses. Since financial penalties are excluded from the ambit of this analysis (on which, see Munro and McNeill 2010), there are three legal contexts in which community sanctions and measures can be imposed in Scotland today. Scottish public prosecutors (called Procurators Fiscal) can impose certain direct measures in lieu of prosecution which involve an element of intervention and/or supervision; but they do so rarely, and since these measures are offered in lieu of prosecution (whether that possibility is deferred or waived entirely), they are not properly considered punishments and so I exclude them from the discussion here.[1] After a successful prosecution, Scottish judges (called 'sheriffs' in our intermediate courts) can impose a range of community sanctions, and prisoners in Scottish prisons can be released under a range of different forms of licence.

The forms of community sanction available to Scottish judges are limited in number, but they nonetheless provide a wide range of different forms of intervention. Since the passage of the Criminal Justice and Licensing Act 2010, the main community sanction is the Community Payback Order (CPO). Despite its name (which might imply a central focus on unpaid work or community service), the CPO replaced not just community service orders but also probation orders and supervised attendance orders (an alternative to fines). The CPO is like the Community Order in England and Wales inasmuch as there are many possible conditions that a judge can attach to it. These include conditions requiring people to submit to supervision, to undertake unpaid work (or other activities), and/or to participate in offending behaviour programmes, mental health treatment and alcohol or drug treatment. Requirements related to residence, conduct or compensation may also be imposed. The only other community sanctions available are Drug Treatment and Testing Orders (DTTOs) and Restriction of Liberty Orders (RLOs) (which impose electronically monitored curfews). In 2012–2013, there were 17,254 court cases in which community orders were imposed in Scotland; 14,924 were CPOs, 621 were DTTOs and 910 were RLOs (the balance was made up of probation orders, community service orders and supervised attendance orders imposed in cases where the offence predated the 2010 Act; these are sometimes referred to as 'legacy orders').[2]

With respect to post-release licences, since the passage of the Prisoners and Criminal Proceeding Act 1993, all prisoners who have served sentences of over 4 years are released on parole licence (if they succeed in gaining early release between the halfway and two-thirds points in their sentences) or on non-parole licence (if they are released automatically at the two-thirds point). The standard terms of these licences are very similar, requiring licensees to 'be of good behaviour' (that is, not to offend) and to submit to social work supervision for the remainder of their sentence, as well as limiting their mobility in various ways. In certain circumstances, more extended periods of post-release supervision can be imposed – including on shorter-term prisoners – usually where there are significant concerns about public safety. Those who have served life sentences are subject to licence conditions for life (although the conditions related to social work supervision can be lifted after 10 years). In 2012–2013, a total of 1,001 new cases involving release licences were commenced, and the total caseload of such licences amounted to 2,431. In addition, a further 3,731 people were receiving some form of voluntary throughcare service (most of these being short-sentence prisoners not subject to mandatory post-release supervision).[3]

Although the numbers of commencements of court-imposed orders or release licences in a given year are not the same as the number of people subject to them (since some people may be subject to multiple orders and some orders or licences last longer than a year), as a rough estimate we can say that about 20,000 people are subject to some form of community sanction in Scotland.[4]

Of course, while the legal scaffold around such sanctions and the extent of their use are important, neither tells us much about the *character* of these sanctions.

Whether or not they are legally imposed as punishments, the extent to which and ways in which they are experienced as punishment by those subject to them is also influenced by the social practices that instantiate them. These practices are, in turn, shaped by the institutional contexts in which they are rooted. In Scotland, community sanctions are implemented almost exclusively by professionally qualified *social workers* working within and for *local* authorities (though a wider network of practitioners in state, private and third-sector organisations also play important roles). These twin influences – social work and localism – have been and remain important in shaping debates about community punishment in Scotland, even if, as we will see below, both have also been regularly contested. Certainly, Scottish criminal justice social workers tend to disavow punishment as an explicit aim of their practice; as we will see below, their central preoccupation has been and remains rehabilitation (see McGuinness 2014). Whether and to what extent their dispositions and intentions moderate or influence the penal bite of community sanctions is, however, another question – and very much an open one (see McNeill 2009).

Foundations and early development of Scottish probation

Though voluntary societies created to provide aid to 'discharged prisoners' have a slightly longer history,[5] the limited available sources for probation history in Scotland suggest that probation emerged in the context of Victorian and Edwardian concerns about the 'demoralising' effects of imprisonment and in particular its iatrogenic effects on *civic* well-being (McNeill 2005; McNeill and Whyte 2007, Chapter 1).

These concerns were felt especially strongly in Scotland's biggest city, Glasgow (then known as the 'second city of the [British] Empire'), where very high rates of imprisonment for fine default were a particular concern. In 1905, Glasgow was amongst the first parts of Scotland (and of the UK) to establish a recognisable probation service. A brief history of this service, published in 1955 by the Glasgow Probation Area Committee, is intriguing, both for what it conveys about the origins of probation and for what it reveals about the concerns of the service in the mid-1950s.

The history begins by contrasting the (1950s) idea of the individual reformation of the offender with earlier times, '[when] punishments for offenders against the law were uniformly severe. There was but slight consideration for the individual; the law set the penalty, no matter who the offender or what the circumstances of the offence' (City of Glasgow 1955: 7).

Unusually, the origins of Glasgow's probation service do not appear to have been directly associated with religious ideals or church organisations. Rather, they were linked to public concern about the excessive use of custody, especially for fine-defaulters. This narrative – about the utility of probation as a means of *penal reductionism* – as we will see, is perhaps the central recurring theme in the history of community punishment in Scotland.

In Glasgow, probation emerged largely because of the efforts of a local councillor (Bailie John Bruce Murray), who had visited the USA to explore the operations of various probation and parole services there. In the Glasgow history, this American connection is stressed to the exclusion of any significant reference to the development of probation in England and Wales. On 14 December 1905, a special committee of the Glasgow Corporation recommended that the Chief Constable select police officers for each District Police Court to act, in plain clothes, as probation officers of the court. By 1919 there were eleven (male) police officers working as probation officers and five women probation officers.

Just as religious ideals are absent in the official account of probation's origins in Glasgow, so there is no mention of charitable or civil society organisations. This is doubtless a misrepresentation (as both police court missionaries and discharged prisoners' aid societies did exist in parts of Scotland, including in Glasgow, from the mid-nineteenth century); it may reveal a conscious or subconscious desire to dissociate 'professional', 'scientific' probation from its earlier 'amateur', religious forms. Certainly, in locating probation at the outset within the police service, the Glasgow initiative appears to have pre-empted later state ownership of probation (see McNeill and Dawson 2014). Perhaps predictably, the initial emphasis was primarily on supervision itself rather than on providing care or treatment; in the early days, there was no methodology of reform other than the putative deterrent effects of the order and its robust supervision. We can perhaps assume that the supervision was often very robust, given the liveliness of debates about the abolition of corporal punishment in the 1930s; probation officers gave evidence to the Young Offenders (Scotland) Committee of 1925 on both sides of the argument – with women officers playing a key role in the (eventually) successful abolition movement (Mahood 2002).

The Glasgow history, despite the praise that it reserves for some of the early police-probation officers, implicitly characterises their model of practice as being limited, noting that it was the Probation of Offenders (Scotland) Act 1931 that (following the report of a Departmental Committee set up by the Secretary of State to review the Protection and Training of Children and Young Offenders) 'completely revolutionised the Probation Service in Glasgow and the idea of *treatment, training and reformation* of Probationers superseded that of supervision' (City of Glasgow 1955: 11, emphasis added).

As well as creating local services by establishing probation committees in each local authority, the 1931 Act created a Central Probation Council to advise the Secretary of State for Scotland. It expressly prohibited the appointment of police officers as probation staff, indicating both that this may have been a common practice in Scotland beyond Glasgow and that it had fallen out of favour.

The Glasgow history was clearly written by advocates of a treatment model and this is apparent in the history that they construct. The authors' views of the significance of the new 'scientific' approaches to the treatment of offenders are evidenced, for example, in their assertion that treatment must be an individualised process following on from some kind of selection. Their discussion of selection reflects the assumption that only some offenders are 'reclaimable'. The language of scientific practice continues in the description of the officer as someone who, through interviewing and home visiting,

> *studies* the habits and surroundings of the Probationer and, by the impact of his personality, ever-ready advice and the force of example, tries to *influence* the offender towards the *normal* in life and conduct. The Probationer is helped to sustain *natural* relations with his fellows – relationships of employment, of friendships and of home ties.
>
> *(City of Glasgow 1955, p. 8, emphases added)*

It is not difficult to discern in these sorts of claims the emergence of a new legitimising narrative: it was no longer merely the case that probation could offer a means of avoiding the harms of imprisonment – now it could also promote the development of more virtuous and productive lives through the application of the new sciences of criminology, psychiatry, psychology and social work (Rose 1989). In other words, a *rehabilitative narrative* had emerged by the middle of the century to complement and buttress the *reductionist narrative*.

Following the Second World War, the Criminal Justice (Scotland) Act 1949 created new duties for the service and its officers, including the provision of 'social reports' on those aged 17–21 years and pre-trial reports on children (previously provided by Education Authorities). Indeed, a Scottish Office promotional booklet, *The Probation Service in Scotland: Its Objects and Its Organisation* (1947) shows that, by then, the courts used probation orders predominantly for children rather than adults. In 1932, in courts of summary jurisdiction, probation orders accounted for 950 out of the 9,173 disposals made in respect of children and young people (10.35 per cent), but only 1,117 out of 71,073 disposals involving adults (1.57 per cent). In 1945, the use of probation with juveniles had risen to 2,557 of 18,983 cases (13.47 per cent), but the use of probation for adults had fallen to just 513 of 58,764 cases (0.87 per cent). No adult probation orders at all were made in 1945 in 19 of the 51 probation areas. It is not clear precisely how or why probation had become, in effect, a measure for juveniles, but it seems plausible that it was partly accounted for by the increasing 'feminisation' of the service, particularly during the war years (when many male officers were engaged in war service). More generally, perhaps Scottish judges considered supposedly caring or rehabilitative responses to offending (however 'scientific') as more fitting for children than for adults.

Nonetheless, and evidencing the durability of reductionist aspirations for probation, later versions of *The Probation Service in Scotland* (revised and reissued in 1955 and in 1961) attempted to promote the use of probation, especially with adult offenders. These later documents offer greater guidance to judges on the kinds of cases for which probation might be appropriate: that is, in the middle ground between 'minor offences committed by those with clean records and good home backgrounds, and grave offences where there would be an undue risk in allowing the offender to remain at liberty' (Scottish Office 1955: 6; 1961: 6).

These booklets also reveal an increasingly modern and recognisable preoccupation with performance (perhaps even a proto-managerialism), albeit expressed in terms of the numbers of probation disposals rather than the outcomes of supervision. Though the absolute numbers of orders rose unevenly from 3,666 in 1951 to 4,558 in 1959, probation's share of the increasing number of disposals in the same period declined from 3.76 per cent to 2.87 per cent. Probation continued to be a much more popular disposal option for juveniles than adults: the proportion of juvenile cases involving crimes (as opposed to less serious offences) leading to probation orders fluctuated between 26.7 per cent and 34.5 per cent during 1951–1959; the corresponding figures for adults varied between 4.3 per cent and 8.0 per cent.

The emergence of criminal justice social work

The publication of the Kilbrandon Report (1964) revolutionised juvenile justice in Scotland by removing children in trouble from the criminal courts. Kilbrandon's most significant and enduring legacy is the Scottish Children's Hearings system, a system that firmly established the pre-eminence of a welfare-based approach to children in trouble predicated on social education principles (Moore and Whyte 1998). More significantly in the context of this discussion, the report also led to the integration of probation services within the new generic social work departments. Though this could be read as a logical extension to adult offenders of Kilbrandon's welfarist, social educational approach, some veterans suggest that the disbandment of the probation service was (also) a pragmatic manoeuvre occasioned both by the low numbers of adult probation cases and by the need for the comparatively well-trained probation staff to join and shape the new social work departments.

With respect to the legitimation of community sanctions, the Kilbrandon reforms provided *both* continuity and change. The continuity resided in the retention of both an essentially reductionist approach (for example, with respect to children and young people, the resulting Social Work Scotland Act of 1968 enshrined a 'no unnecessary order' principle of minimum necessary intervention) and a refreshed commitment to rehabilitation. The refreshment of rehabilitation was perhaps subtle: Kilbrandon's philosophy argued for *social* education rather than explaining and addressing offending purely in terms of individual or familial pathologies. In essence, the rehabilitative narrative shifted from one focused on a treatment model to one premised on social–psychological ideas (on which see Johnstone 1996).

Nonetheless, the dissolution of Scottish probation services represented a major organisational rupture and proved to be traumatic. By the late 1970s, academics, judges and professionals were expressing concerns about the viability of criminal justice services within generic social work departments (Marsland 1977; Moore 1978; Nelson 1977). When, in 1989, the Scottish Office introduced

ring-fenced funding for most criminal justice social work services, this was interpreted by some as recognition that work with offenders had fallen into a state of
comparative neglect, despite the successful piloting and then rolling out of community service by 1979 (see McIvor 2010). The new Scottish Office investment in
criminal justice social work did represent a response to a crisis of legitimacy, but this
was not an existential or philosophical crisis, it was an organisational one. Unlike in
some other Anglophone jurisdictions, the problem in Scotland was not cast around
ideas and practices of rehabilitation and their effectiveness (see Martinson 1974;
Allen 1981); rather, it concerned the near complete failure to *implement* these ideas
and practices after the demise of the probation services.

An organisational failure called for an organisational response. In this context
it is not surprising to detect the rise to prominence of a new *managerial* narrative.
That said, as I have noted above, in Scotland at least, managerialism (if it means a
preoccupation with systems, efficiency, outputs and outcomes) has a much longer
history than we tend to assume. From its inception, Scottish probation was intended
to produce both *systems effects* (on sentencing and imprisonment) and *individual
effects* (on those subject to it) – and both policymakers and practitioners have always
been concerned to gather evidence about and to analyse these effects.

That said, in the late 1980s and early 1990s (just as in the 1900s), the concern
with systems effects became predominant. In the context of a political crisis occasioned by prison overcrowding, riots and suicides, the new central government
funding was unequivocally an investment in a reductionist strategy of decarceration. Indeed, the now centrally funded (but still locally organised) criminal justice
social work services looked set to follow the 'alternatives to custody' model that
had already taken root in England and Wales (see Robinson, this volume). The
first objective of the *National Objectives and Standards* was 'to enable a reduction
in the incidence of custody... where it is used for lack of a suitable, available community-based social work disposal' (Social Work Services Group 1991a:
Section 12.1). But, unlike in England and Wales, probation in Scotland was not
required to negotiate the ideological traverse towards punishment in the community. Rather, a focus on *reducing reoffending* was seen as critical to the credibility
of community sanctions, on which reduction in the use of custody was thought
to depend. Both reducing reoffending and reducing the use of custody were to
be achieved (as in the mid-twentieth century) by the appliance of science (now
packaged in the form of 'what works?' research; see SWSG 1991b); the novel development was the introduction of managerialised discipline (for example, standardised
procedures and interventions, and performance measurement) through which these
'enhanced' techniques could be applied. Late-modern managerialism had indeed
arrived in Scottish penality, but on at least one authoritative account, that managerialism was perhaps intended to enhance both professionalism and welfarism rather
than to displace them (McAra 1999).

By the mid-to-late 1990s however, a growing emphasis on public protection on both sides of the border coincided with the introduction of significantly
higher risk populations of offenders to social work caseloads, partly because of

new arrangements for the post-release supervision of long-term prisoners (referred to in the Introduction). As in other jurisdictions (see, for example, Boone, this volume), scandals occasioned by serious further offences by people subject to supervision played a part in provoking this change. Subsequently, advances in both the rhetoric and the practice of risk management and public protection were rapid (see McIvor and McNeill 2007; Weaver and McNeill 2010). For example, in *The Tough Option* (Scottish Office 1998), it was declared both that 'Our paramount aim is public safety' and that the pursuit of reductions in the use of custody 'must be consistent with the wider objective of promoting public and community safety' (Section 1.2.3). *The Tough Option* also revisited the organisational arrangements for criminal justice social work. Although it openly debated centralisation of criminal justice services, ultimately it led merely to the creation of mechanisms for cooperation across local authority areas in a series of 'groupings'. But this was not to be the last time that reorganisation and, in particular, centralisation became a policy preoccupation.

Community punishment and devolution

The restoration in 1999 of the Scottish Parliament (which had been dissolved in 1707) has had profound but sometimes paradoxical effects on Scottish criminal justice. The terms of the Act of Union in 1707 had preserved the separate Scottish legal system. When 'law and order' became a key site of UK political debate in the 1980s, Scottish criminal justice was somewhat protected by its unusual constitutional position. In effect, a quasi-colonial administration through the Scottish Office of the UK Government lacked both (UK) parliamentary time and (Scottish) political and constitutional authority to drive through populist punitive reforms. Civil servants, senior law officers and a variety of professional and academic experts were able to maintain a constraining influence upon penal policymaking (McAra 2008). The creation of a Scottish Parliament with authority over criminal justice (save for a few areas related to national security) opened up the possibility of legislating for change. Perhaps, more importantly, it opened up space for political debate about – and political capacity building around – questions of crime and justice.

The result, according to McAra (2008), was a 'de-tartanisation' of Scottish criminal and youth justice policy – and a form of 'hyper-institutionalism' as the Scottish Parliament and Executive engaged in a frenzied period of debate, leading to a proliferation of new policy initiatives, plans, laws and 'quangoes'. Though many competing narratives were at play in the new penal politics in Scotland post-devolution, the traditional reductionist narrative was pushed further to the margins even than it had been in *The Tough Option* (1998). Indeed, 5 years later, in the 2003 election campaign, the Labour party manifesto adopted an almost expansionist tone:

> We will set up a single agency – the Correctional Service for Scotland – staffed by professionals and covering prison and community based sentences

to *maximise* the impact of punishment, rehabilitation and protection offered by our justice system.

(Scottish Labour 2003: emphasis added)

In fact, although the proposed organisational changes were clearly in a more corrective direction and doubtless were intended at least in part as a 'tough on crime' manoeuvre, it is hard to cast them as straightforwardly punitive. The vision of the then First Minister (Jack McConnell) for the future of criminal justice in Scotland retained rehabilitation among his three 'R's ('Respect, Responsibility and Rehabilitation'). In an important speech, McConnell (2003: 11) argued that,

> There is a balance to be struck. A balance between protection and punishment – and the chance for those who have done wrong to change their behaviour and re-engage with the community as full and productive members. If we don't get that balance right then the system will fail through lack of confidence and trust. Our justice service depends absolutely on ordinary people... we need them to be tolerant of the offender who returns to the community because they believe the person truly has been punished and has made amends and they are now ready to give him or her their second chance.

This determination to stress the responsibilisation of the 'offender', but to balance it explicitly with notions of tolerance and inclusion, had been evident in Scottish penal policy at least since the introduction of the national standards (SWSG 1991a) (and arguably for over 100 years). The same theme had underpinned the third of the *Criminal Justice Social Work Services: National Priorities for 2001–2002 and Onwards*, which was to 'Promote the social inclusion of offenders through rehabilitation, so reducing the level of offending' (Justice Department 2001: 3). In this context, rehabilitation was cast as the means of progressing towards two compatible and interdependent ends: not only the reduction of reoffending, but also the social inclusion of offenders. This reading of rehabilitation remains entirely consistent with Kilbrandon's welfarist, social educationalist philosophy (discussed above), which implicitly recognised both the *intrinsic* worth of promoting the social inclusion of offenders and its *instrumentality* in reducing offending.

Moreover, although McConnell's speech seemed to suggest that punishment was to be seen as a morally necessary prelude to reintegration, in Scotland (unlike England and Wales) there was evidence of a continuing, if more qualified, commitment to penal reductionism. This was reflected in the second of the *National Priorities*: to 'Reduce the use of unnecessary custody by providing effective community disposals' (Justice Department 2001: 3). Though the second and third priorities (reductionism and inclusion through rehabilitation) were increasingly subordinated to the first priority of contributing to 'increased community safety and public protection' by reducing re-offending (Justice Department 2001: 3), some recognition of some interdependencies between these objectives remained.

After a heated debate about the merits and demerits of establishing a single correctional service, the Management of Offenders Act 2005 represented another compromise solution – and another reorganisation (see McNeill and Whyte 2007). Scotland's 32 local authorities retained criminal justice social work, but eight Community Justice Authorities were established to develop and implement multi-agency and multi-authority strategies for reducing reoffending, and a new National Advisory Body on Offender Management (note the imported and quite un-Scottish terminology) was created to advise the Minister of Justice and to review these strategies.

However, the new system had little time to become established before the election of a Scottish Nationalist Party (SNP) minority government in 2007. The SNP government was re-elected (as a majority government) in 2011. Few commentators would dispute that these nationalist administrations have changed the tone and tenor of penal political debates in Scotland. With respect to sentencing and sanctions, their initial move was to appoint an independent commission to examine the use of imprisonment. The resulting McLeish report (Scottish Prisons Commission 2008) *Scotland's Choice* was unequivocal that Scotland's comparatively high use of imprisonment was undesirable and unsustainable, and that different choices were both possible and necessary (see McNeill 2011). Amongst many far-reaching proposals, the commission suggested the creation of the new, single community sentence: the 'Community Payback Order'. As the name suggests, this order was intended to place a new emphasis on reparation, although the report famously made a place for rehabilitation in its contentious claim that 'One of the best ways of paying back is by turning your life around' (Scottish Prisons Commission 2008: 33). The commission's (and subsequently the government's) intention was for this new order to displace custody as the default sanction in Scotland.

What is perhaps most interesting about these recent developments is that, although they reproduce probation's founding reductionist narrative (a sort of penal Hippocratism: 'When punishing, aim to do the least harm to society that you can'), they seek to allow *reparation and redress* their places amongst the necessary objectives of community sanctions; and implicitly they link legitimacy and credibility to reparation and redress rather than merely to rehabilitation and reducing reoffending.[6] In that sense, it may now (finally) make sense to talk about 'punishment in the community' in Scotland – but probably only if we make clear that 'punishment' need not be 'merely punitive' in Duff's (2001, 2003) sense. The pains of reparative effort are both legitimated and legitimising in this discourse, but they must be constructive rather than destructive; integrative rather than exclusionary; capacity building rather than incapacitating. This is not to say, however, that Scottish social work practitioners are ready to own reparation (far less 'punishment') rather than rehabilitation as their primary objective. Indeed, a recent ethnography of the implementation of the CPO by criminal justice social workers suggests that reparation remains a relatively marginalised aspect of their discourses and practices. Speed and visibility (of community sanctioning) emerge as more important aspects of their accounts of the implementation of the CPO rather than reparation itself, and, in their own direct practice, rehabilitation tends to remain centre stage (see McGuinness 2014).

Practitioner ambivalence about this new discourse stands at odds with the enthusiasm of the Scottish Government in its reform efforts. Seeking to account for that enthusiasm requires an analysis of the relationships between debates about constitutional change in Scotland and the adaptation and legitimation of community sanctions.

Constitutional change, community punishment and nation building

In 2000, a year after Scotland had secured its devolved Parliament, I argued in a conference paper that Scottish criminal justice had not suffered the effects of the 'crisis of state sovereignty' that Garland (1996) had identified in his discussion of the UK and the USA. In the 1980s and 1990s, the Scottish crisis was constitutional. It was not so much that the British state, under the pressures of globalisation, was failing and therefore seeking to 'bulk up' its legitimacy by flexing its muscles in the penal sphere. Rather, from the perspective of many Scots, the British state was *already* a failing state in political and constitutional terms. The central issue was not crime; it was politics. More specifically, it was the inability of UK political institutions to reflect and represent the values and aspirations of the Scottish electorate. Consequently, crime and punishment had relatively low political salience during the period when centre-left Scotland was struggling with the depredations of Thatcherism.

As I have already noted, following McAra (2008), devolution settled the constitutional crisis temporarily and changed the salience and dynamics of penal politics. Between 1999 and 2007, for many in the criminal justice system, benign neglect had never looked so attractive. But the 2007 election of the Nationalists raised the spectre of constitutional change once again. Although this did not lead to an immediate diminution of interest in criminal justice and penal policy, it did inaugurate a new sort of penal politics. As with all other areas of policy, the Nationalists sought to shift the question from 'What's wrong with Scotland?' to 'What might Scotland look like if we were independent?' To borrow the language of the Good Lives Model of Offender Rehabilitation (see Ward and Maruna 2007), the Nationalists switched from an avoidant, risk-averse politicking, to one that focused on approach goals, new narratives, the language of possibility. In every area of policy, including penal policy, the answers to the second question needed to be positive in order for the Nationalists to secure their prize: independence.

Although at first sight reparation seems at odds with this discursive shift – since it implies repairing what is broken – in fact the message of reparation is also that repair is possible. Indeed, one might construct reparation as a process aimed at *social reformation* or at least the reformation of civic social relations; and that is exactly the sort of narrative that the Nationalists needed. Political and social reformation was and is, after all, their raison d'être.

Conclusions: Lessons from a successful failure

At the same time as developing their response to *Scotland's Choice* (Scottish Prisons Commission 2008), the Scottish Government was involved in a parallel consultation about the development of new national outcomes and standards for criminal justice social work services (Scottish Government 2010[7]). Shortly after the passage of the Criminal Justice and Licensing Act 2010, and in preparation for the implementation of the CPO, I wrote a briefing paper for criminal justice social workers, exploring the connections between these two parallel developments (McNeill 2010). In particular, I aimed to give some substance to the notion of community payback – seeking to articulate its (potentially) reparative rather than its (potentially) punitive character. The new national outcomes and standards articulated a practice model based on four 'R's: reparation, rehabilitation, restriction and reintegration. Drawing the two sources together, I suggested the conceptual relationship between the four 'R's as shown in Figure 10.1.

Here, the primary task for criminal justice social work has become reparation, since the offender making reparation is seen as a pre-requisite of reintegration as a citizen and a member of the community. But it is recognised that, for some people, the most appropriate form of reparation might include rehabilitative activities – 'paying back by working at change' – and indeed rehabilitation might also be a necessary process to navigate where criminogenic or social needs represent significant barriers to reintegration. In some more serious cases, some measure of restriction might also be required for public protection. Though submitting to some forms of restriction is not reparative in itself, it might be a necessary part of allowing reparation and/or rehabilitation to take place safely in the community. Equally, in some cases, neither rehabilitation nor restriction will be required – here the reparation might be through apology (although this was not formally addressed in the 2010 Act), through financial compensation or through unpaid work.

Whatever the merits or demerits of this model, it neglects the crucial fifth 'R' – *reductionism* – an objective that was oddly absent from the new national

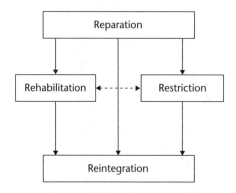

FIGURE 10.1 The four R's

outcomes and standards even though it was the central concern of *Scotland's Choice* (Scottish Prisons Commission 2008). Given that, as the Justice Secretary, Kenny MacAskill often expressed political commitment to reducing the prison population, it would be wrong to read too much into this omission, but it remains an important omission. The same omission is notable in the second phase of the Scottish Government's 'Reducing Reoffending Programme'.[8] Indeed, it is also obvious that the title and content of this key policy programme affecting community punishment stresses *rehabilitative and reintegrative* rather than *reparative* narrative themes, despite the arguments in *Scotland's Choice* (Scottish Prisons Commission 2008).

That said, talk and action are different things. Whatever the shifts in legitimation strategies and narrative reconstructions of community sanctions, to the extent that this is a history of reframed attempts at penal reductionism, it is also a history of successful failure. The success rests in the fact that community sanctions have (since the 1990s) established themselves as a significant and expanding feature of the penal landscape. Yet their failure is apparent in the analysis in *Scotland's Choice* (ibid. 2008); Scottish judges are still choosing to impose more and longer custodial sanctions than many of their European colleagues – at least insofar as this can be judged by relative imprisonment rates.

To give substance to this somewhat depressing conclusion, between 1977 and 2008–2009 (the peak year), Scotland witnessed a near nine-fold increase in the imposition of community sanctions and measures (from just over 2,000 to about 18,000, and this figure excludes post-release supervision).[9] Not only have the numbers of people under such supervision increased, so has the range of conditions to which people can be subject. As we have seen, this remarkable growth has been achieved partly through Government investment in ring-fenced funding (since 1991) of the criminal justice social work services delivered by local authorities, through the implementation of national objectives and standards, and through the development of social work education and training.

However, although rates of reconviction of those subject to community sanctions have declined (especially relative to those receiving custodial sentences), over the same period the number of custodial sentences in Scotland has *increased rather than decreased*, from about 10,000 to about 16,000. This puzzling simultaneous rise in *both* community *and* custodial sentences is largely explained by the dramatic decline in the use of financial penalties – from around 160,000 in 1977 (and 180,000 by 1983) to about 70,000 by 2008–2009 (and less than 60,000 in 2012–2013) (see Figure 10.2). Though it would take more detailed research to establish the precise relationships between the fates of the three main sorts of penalties (financial, supervisory and custodial), *prima facie* it seems that probation's growth has, for the most part, displaced financial penalties rather than custodial sentences.

In the Scottish case, this finding may be accounted for in part by reforms elsewhere in the justice system. Since more and more 'low-level' offences and offenders have been diverted from court processes altogether (often through warnings, fixed penalties and other direct measures applied by prosecutors), the profile of the population coming to court for sentencing today is different from that in the 1970s.

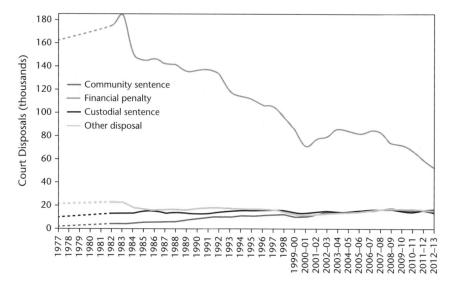

FIGURE 10.2   Court disposals in Scotland, 1977–2013

If that population now includes a higher proportion of more serious offences and offenders, then that might account for the decline of the fine *as court-imposed sanction*.

However, since the total number of convictions has also fallen significantly in Scotland over the same period, the rise in the prison population and the apparent failure of community sanctions to do much to arrest that rise remains a matter of concern. Indeed, administrative data about the criminal histories of people receiving community and custodial sentences in Scotland does not provide strong evidence that community sentences are successfully diverting higher-tariff offenders.[10]

With respect to the questions of comparative criminal justice that concern us in this book, we can draw some lessons from the Scottish case. Certainly it seems that changes in the constitutional dynamics of the state are likely to have profound effects on the adaptation and legitimation of community punishment. We know that economic, political, cultural and social forces all play a part in shaping penality; but we need to recognise that, within the broad term 'political', we need to think not just (and perhaps not so much) about the hurly-burly of penal politics (worrisome though that often is) and more about the changing constitutional and institutional dynamics of political fields and penal–political subfields. As Garland (2013) has recently advised, we need to much more carefully map the shifting contours of the penal state if we are to understand the forms of penality it nurtures and neglects.

We can also see that in Scotland the core reductionist narrative for community sanctions has perhaps changed relatively little in the last century – although, crucially, *reductionism* has progressively come to be displaced as the main aim by another objective that was once its subordinate – *rehabilitation*. In recent decades, the central focus of policy and practice debate and development has been on which objectives, methods and practices (and which organisational arrangements and which practitioners) might allow community sentences to secure credibility by achieving positive rehabilitative effects. However, in this context, two particular propositions have proved especially durable in Scotland (at least since the 1930s), even if they have been tested at times: (1) the casework relationship is the prime vehicle for supporting change; and (2) locally connected and delivered services are best placed to support change.

Within the framework of these two propositions, discourses and practices have, however, evolved and adapted significantly. Crudely it is possible to trace discursive shifts from a primary emphasis on robust supervision (from inception to the 1930s) to a focus on delivering professional social work first to treat delinquency and then to provide welfarist social education (from the 1930s to the 1970s); and then to criminal justice social work as a responsibilising endeavour (in the 1980s and 1990s); and then towards risk management and public protection (in the 1990s and 2000s) (McNeill 2005). More recently, a new emphasis on reparation has emerged (discussed above) (McNeill 2010, 2011). The narrative that is missing (for the most part) in the Scottish story has been the punitive one (Robinson *et al.* 2013), but, given the failure of reductionism, this does not mean of course that community sentencing in Scotland has necessarily succeeded in reducing or constraining the extent or severity of punishment.

I call these *discursive* shifts because the extent to which institutions, cultures and practices have changed is less clear, but from the point of view of legitimation the discursive shifts are themselves telling. Each discursive adaptation seems to represent a response to the development of new forms of criminological and social scientific knowledge. Policymakers and practitioners have tried to deploy this knowledge as a form of cultural capital through which they have (generally) sought to sustain or extend their influence in a field that has been almost continually reconfigured by wider cultural, economic and political developments in the twentieth century.

But in an important sense, valiant though these efforts may have been, they may also have been somewhat misguided or at least incomplete. As Clear and Frost (2013) have recently argued, there are really only two ways to reduce the prison population: we can choose to send fewer people to prison or we can send them there for shorter periods. Short of legislative and sentencing reform, all other approaches – like the continual improvement and/or re-branding of community sanctions, whether as punishment, rehabilitation or reparation – cannot achieve that central reductionist objective, and too often such developments risk a mere expansion of the net of social control, rather than an effort to rein it in (see also McNeill and Beyens 2013; Phelps 2013a, 2013b).

Notes

1 For the most part, direct measures are warnings or financial penalties, but the possibility of diversion, for example, for reparation or mediation, or for help with mental health

problems does exist. However, these latter measures are used relatively rarely overall and to quite different extents in different localities (see Bradford and McQueen 2011), although numbers have grown significant in the last 2 or 3 years. Almost 1,700 cases of diversion to such (supervised) measures were commenced in 2012–2013: see Table 1 at www.scotland.gov.uk/Resource/0045/00451608.pdf.

2 These figures come from Table 7 in 'Criminal proceedings in Scottish Courts, 2012–2013'; see: www.scotland.gov.uk/Resource/0043/00438958.pdf.

3 These figures come from Tables 30 and 31, 'Criminal Justice Social Work Statistics, 2012–2013'; see www.scotland.gov.uk/Resource/0045/00451608.pdf.

4 By way of comparison, the Scottish prison population on 21 November 2014 stood at 8,009, with 1,219 of these people being in pre-trial detention, and 361 of them being on Home Detention Curfew (an electronically monitored form of executive early release) (Scottish Prison Service website: www.sps.gov.uk/Publications/ScottishPrisonPopulation.aspx, accessed 28 November 2014).

5 For example, the Glasgow Discharged Prisoners Aid Society was founded in 1856; see www.theglasgowstory.com/image.php?inum=TGSG00019, accessed 28 November 2014.

6 As the editors note in the Introduction, although community service might have been legitimated from the outset as a reparative sanction, in fact the discourses and practices surrounding it were much more complex (see McIvor 2010). In any case, the McLeish report and the CPO suggested reparation as a central legitimating narrative for all forms of community punishment, not just unpaid work.

7 See: www.scotland.gov.uk/resource/doc/925/0103556.pdf, accessed 28 November 2014.

8 See: www.scotland.gov.uk/Topics/Justice/policies/reducing-reoffending, accessed 29 November 2014.

9 The Scottish data, charts and tables discussed in this section were supplied directly by Justice Analytical Services in the Scottish Government.

10 Personal communications with Peter Conlong, Justice Analytical Services, Scottish Government.

References

Allen, F. (1981) *The Decline of the Rehabilitative Ideal: Penal Policy and Social Purpose*. New Haven: Yale University Press.

Bradford, B. and McQueen, S. (2011) 'Diversion from prosecution to social work in Scotland'. Scottish Centre for Crime and Justice Research Report No. 1/2011. Glasgow: Scottish Centre for Crime and Justice Research. Available at: www.sccjr.ac.uk/wp-content/uploads/2012/10/Diversion%20from%20prosecution.pdf (accessed 19 January 2015).

City of Glasgow (1955) *Probation. A Brief Survey of Fifty Years of the Probation Service of the City of Glasgow 1905–1955*. Glasgow: City of Glasgow Probation Area Committee.

Clear, T. and Frost, N. (2013) *The Punishment Imperative: The Rise and Failure of Mass Incarceration in America*. New York: NYU Press.

Duff, A. (2001) *Punishment, Communication and Community*. New York: Oxford University Press.

Duff, A. (2003) 'Probation, punishment and restorative justice: Should altruism be engaged in punishment?', *The Howard Journal*, 42(1): 181–97.

Garland, D. (1996) 'The limits of the sovereign state: Strategies of crime control in contemporary society', *British Journal of Criminology*, 36(4): 445–71.

Garland, D. (2013) 'Penality and the penal state', *Criminology*, 51(3): 475–517.

Johnstone, G. (1996) *Medical Concepts and Penal Policy*. London, UK: Cavendish.

Justice Department (2001) *Criminal Justice Social Work Services: National Priorities for 2001–2002 and Onwards*. Edinburgh: Scottish Executive.

Kilbrandon Report (1964) *Children and Young Persons (Scotland), Report by the Committee Appointed by the Secretary of State for Scotland*, Cmnd 2306. Edinburgh: HMSO.

McAra, L. (1999) 'The politics of penality: An overview of the development of penal policy in Scotland', in Duff, P. and Hutton, N. (eds) *Criminal Justice in Scotland*. Aldershot: Ashgate/Dartmouth, pp. 355–80.

McAra, L. (2008) 'Crime, criminology and criminal justice in Scotland', *European Journal of Criminology*, 5(4): 481–504.

McConnell, J. (2003) *Respect, Responsibility and Rehabilitation in Modern Scotland*, Apex Lecture 1, September. Edinburgh: Scottish Executive.

McGuinness, P. (2014) *Room for Reparation? An Ethnographic Study into the Implementation of the Community Payback Order*. Unpublished University of Glasgow PhD thesis.

McIvor, G. (2010) 'Paying back: 30 years of unpaid work by offenders in Scotland', *European Journal of Probation*, 2(1): 41–61.

McIvor, G. and McNeill, F. (2007) 'Probation in Scotland: Past, present and future' in Gelsthorpe, L. and Morgan, R. (eds) *The Probation Handbook: A Policy, Practice and Research Handbook*. Cullompton, Devon: Willan.

McNeill, F. (2005) 'Remembering probation in Scotland', *Probation Journal*, 52 (1): 23–38.

McNeill, F. (2009) *'Helping, Holding, Hurting: Recalling and Reforming Punishment'*, the 6th annual Apex Lecture, at the Signet Library, Parliament Square, Edinburgh, 8 September 2009. Available at: https://pure.strath.ac.uk/portal/files/521675/strathprints026701.pdf (accessed 8 April 2015).

McNeill, F. (2010) *Community Payback and the new National Standards for Criminal Justice Social Work*, Briefing Paper 02/10, Glasgow: Scottish Centre for Crime and Justice Research. Available at: www.sccjr.ac.uk/documents/Briefing_Paper_2010_02_community_payback.pdf (accessed 8 April 2015).

McNeill, F. (2011) 'Determined to punish? Scotland's choice', in Hassan, G. and Ilett, R. (eds) *Radical Scotland: Arguments for Self-Determination*. Edinburgh: Luath Press.

McNeill, F. and Beyens, K. (eds) (2013) *Offender Supervision in Europe*. Basingstoke: Palgrave.

McNeill, F. and Dawson, M. (2014) 'Social solidarity, penal evolution and probation', *British Journal of Criminology*, 54(5): 892–907.

McNeill, F. and Whyte, B. (2007) *Reducing Re-offending: Social Work and Community Justice in Scotland*. Cullompton, Devon: Willan.

Mahood, L. (2002) ' "Give him a doing": the birching of young offenders in Scotland', *Canadian Journal of History*, 37(3): 439–58.

Marsland, M. (1977) 'The decline of probation in Scotland', *Social Work Today*, 8(23): 17–18.

Martinson, R. (1974) 'What works? Questions and answers about prison reform', *The Public Interest*, 35: 22–54.

Moore, G. (1978) 'Crisis in Scotland', *The Howard Journal*, 17(1): 32–40.

Moore, G. and Whyte, B. (1998) *Moore and Wood's Social Work and Criminal Law in Scotland*, 3rd edn. Edinburgh: Mercat Press.

Munro, M. and McNeill, F. (2010) 'Fines, community sanctions and measures', in Croall, H. and Mooney, G. (eds) *Criminal Justice in Scotland*. Cullompton, Devon: Willan.

Nelson, S. (1977) 'Why Scotland's after-care is lagging', *Community Care*, 14(12): 87.

Phelps, M. (2013a) 'The paradox of probation: Understanding the expansion of an "alternative" to incarceration during the prison boom', PhD thesis, Princeton University. Ann Arbor: ProQuest/UMI.

Phelps, M. (2013b) 'The paradox of probation: Community supervision in the age of mass incarceration', *Law and Policy*, 35(1–2): 55–80.

Robinson, G., McNeill, F. and Maruna, S. (2013) 'Punishment *in* Society: The Improbable Persistence of Community Sanctions', in Simon, J. and Sparks, R. (eds) *The Sage Handbook of Punishment and Society*. London and New York: Sage, pp. 321–40.

Rose, N. (1989) *Governing the Soul: Shaping of the Private Self*. London: Routledge.

Scottish Government (2010) *National Outcomes and Standards for Social Work Services in the Criminal Justice System*. Edinburgh: Scottish Government.

Scottish Labour (2003) Scottish Labour Manifesto 2003: *On Your Side*. Available at: www.scottishlabour.org.uk/manifesto/ (accessed 5 April 2003).

Scottish Office (1947) *The Probation Service in Scotland. Its Objects and Its Organisation*. Edinburgh: HMSO.

Scottish Office (1955) *The Probation Service in Scotland*. Edinburgh: HMSO.

Scottish Office (1961) *The Probation Service in Scotland*. Edinburgh: HMSO.

Scottish Office (1998) *Community Sentencing: The Tough Option: Review of Criminal Justice Social Work Services*. Edinburgh: Scottish Office Home Department.

Scottish Prisons Commission (2008) *Scotland's Choice*. Edinburgh: Scottish Prisons Commission.

Social Work Services Group, SWSG (1991a) *National Objectives and Standards for Social Work Services in the Criminal Justice System*. Edinburgh: Social Work Services Group.

Social Work Services Group, SWSG (1991b) *Social Work Supervision: Towards Effective Policy and Practice – A Supplement to the National Objectives and Standards for Social Work Services in the Criminal Justice System*. Edinburgh: Social Work Services Group.

Ward, T. and Maruna, S. (2007) *Rehabilitation: Beyond the Risk Paradigm*. London: Routledge.

Weaver, B. and McNeill, F. (2010) 'Public protection in Scotland', in Williams, A. and Nash, M. (eds) *The Handbook of Public Protection*. Cullompton, Devon: Willan.

11

COMMUNITY PUNISHMENTS IN SPAIN

A tale of two administrations

Ester Blay and Elena Larrauri[1]

Introduction

'Community punishment' is not a concept used in Spanish policy, legal discourse or academic literature. Instead, 'alternatives to prison' or 'alternative punishments and measures'[2] are the current expressions used to refer to fines, suspended sentences, with and without requirements, and unpaid work. One reason why academics and practitioners keep referring to alternatives to prison is probably that the main rationale for defending community punishments is to avoid a prison sentence; the goal that is emphasized is not so much to achieve something positive (through supervision in the community), but to avoid something negative (imprisonment). A second reason that might explain the lack of attraction of the concept of 'community punishment' is probably that, although judges when sentencing take into consideration the rehabilitation needs of offenders, their main thrust is to provide a proportionate penal response, which can often be more easily achieved through a fine. The final reason is perhaps that there is no 'probation system' (and no 'probation officers' as such) in Spain. Historically, suspended sentences carried no requirements (except not to reoffend, which was supposed to be achieved by the threat of the prison sentence). Although 'supervision' and 'control' have been increasing (see the third and fourth sections below: 'Development', and 'Recent trends'), we may presume that in Spain both elements are still relatively rare; even in Catalonia, where supervision in the community is more developed, the terms 'probation' or 'community punishments' still tend not to appear as such.[3]

For the purposes of this chapter, we understand 'community punishment' as referring to those sentences that do not consist of a deprivation of liberty in a prison or mental health institution or detention centre but do involve some level of supervision by an agent whose mission is to enforce the sentence imposed by a penal judge by controlling and assisting the offender.

It is important from the outset to underline that there are two criminal justice administrations in Spain; whereas the criminal code and the judicial system is common to all Spanish territory, the implementation of sentences (both prison sentences and community punishments) is carried out by two administrations: the Catalan[4] and the Spanish.

It is also important to highlight some features of the Spanish jurisdiction that might have an impact on the way community punishments are imposed and enforced: a) in Spain *sentencing is narrowly determined by law*. This gives judges the impression that their discretion to resort to community punishments is very limited; b) for the vast majority of offences, imposing *a prison sentence is an option* given by the lawmaker (i.e. the parliament via the Criminal Code), which gives an indication that prison is an appropriate response in that case. The custody threshold (that is, when a custodial sentence is considered appropriate) is determined by law and it currently stands at 3 months;[5] c) when the sentence is up to 2 years, judges may still avoid entrance into prison by *suspending sentences*, but only if the person has no previous criminal record;[6] d) there is no *'sentencing hearing'* and no pre-sentence report; this means that the information about the offender available to the sentencing judge is limited and, to a certain extent, this might lead him or her to rely more on the seriousness of the offence and less on the individual information that would justify the use of a community punishment.

Until recently in Spain, community punishments were limited to suspended sentences.[7] The use of suspended sentences might be considered a 'history of success' in light of their widespread use (Cid and Larrauri 2002, 2009) and their impact on decarceration. One could suspect that prison rates in Spain would be even higher if suspended sentences were not available to judges (Cid 2008; Díez Ripollés 2006). However, as in other European jurisdictions (Snacken *et al.* 2014), suspended sentences have not usually been granted on the basis of an individual analysis of the case and have *not involved any supervision*. This might be due to the fact that the law establishes very strict requirements in order for judges to grant suspensions (prison sentences must be two years or less and the defendant must have no criminal record) and perhaps also reflects a form of judicial education and culture that emphasizes desert considerations over rehabilitation (in Beyens and Scheirs' (2010) terms, a 'neoclassic orientation'). Additionally, individual information on the offender is not available, since generally, as we have mentioned, there are no pre-sentence reports available to the courts (Larrauri 2012; Larrauri and Zorrilla 2014).

The major change in this system (based on prison, suspended sentence, and fines[8]) came as a result of the new democratic 1995 Criminal Code (Cid and Larrauri 1997, 2005), which introduced: a) the possibility for the judge to substitute prison sentences imposed on recidivist offenders for fines or home arrest; b) the possibility for the judge to impose requirements (beyond merely not reoffending) to suspended and substituted sentences; and c) community service or unpaid work as a sentence. From this moment on, a new system began to develop: this system included new penalties available to judges; a supervision system, albeit limited, by the 'probation service'; and judicial supervision of the implementation of these penalties (Blay 2011). This new supervision system is more developed in Catalonia than Spain (Martin and Larrauri 2012) and, although it does not carry the name of 'probation',[9] it does involve supervision of unpaid work sentences and the requirements attached to suspended sentences (mainly but not exclusively attendance at educational treatment or drug-abuse programmes) by social workers (employed or subcontracted by the Justice Department).

Today, then, community punishments in Spain basically consist of 'front end' measures such as unpaid work (*trabajo en beneficio de la comunidad*), suspended sentences with some requirements (*suspensión de la pena con reglas de conducta*) and a specific suspended sentence for drug users (*suspensión especial para drogodependientes*); and as 'back end' (or release) measures, the two main possibilities being open prison[10] (*régimen abierto*) and parole (*libertad condicional*).[11]

The landscape of punishment cannot be fully pictured, however, without reference to the growing field of *prohibition orders* available to the sentencing judge when the offender is found guilty. These orders, which may have a victim-protection rationale (e.g. prohibition to approach or communicate with the victim) or an incapacitative one (e.g. prohibition to drive, to undertake specific jobs), are important because they signal a shift, both towards the consideration of victims' needs, and towards placing increasing importance on 'preventive justice' (Ashworth and Zedner 2014) by the courts through specific tailored punishments (imposed in addition to other sentences). These are to some extent 'supervised' by 'probation officers'.

Foundations

The possibility of conditionally suspending prison sentences was introduced in Spain in 1908 following the Franco-Belgian *sursis* model (Navarro 2002); subsequently, the penal landscape was constituted mainly by imprisonment, suspended sentences and fines.

As we mentioned in the Introduction, the major shift for community punishments in Spain came about in 1995 (Cid and Larrauri 1997). The new Criminal Code aimed precisely at increasing the use of alternatives to prison. Thus, in the first place, the Code allowed for prison sentences of up to 2 years to be suspended, instead of prison sentences of up to 1 year as was the case previously. Moreover, new alternatives were introduced: unpaid work, the possibility of substituting prison sentences and of adding requirements to suspended sentences; the possibility of suspending a prison sentence of up to 3 years for recidivist offenders with a drug abuse problem (previously 2 years); and the possibility of substituting prison sentences of up to 2 years by fines or home arrest for recidivist offenders.

Rehabilitation (in the particular wording of 're-education and social reintegration', *reeducación* and *reinserción social*) is spelled out in the 1978 Constitution as an end at which punishments should aim.[12] However, and because the professionals drafting the new Code were heavily influenced by critiques of rehabilitation at that time, the main reason to introduce these new punishments was probably not so much influenced by rehabilitation as by 'decarceration' goals. The idea was not so much to rehabilitate or *re*-socialize with community punishments, but to avoid the *de*-socialization which imprisonment involved (see Muñoz Conde 1979, 1985; Larrauri 2001).

Although there is an argument that these punishments can achieve better rehabilitation and reintegration than imprisonment, it is important to note that another main thrust for applying them is proportionality. According to this logic, alternatives to imprisonment for minor offences are developed not because they are more rehabilitative, but rather because prison is deemed to be too severe a punishment for certain offences and in certain circumstances in the first place (Mir 1984). This emphasis on the proportionality of the sentence (rather than on supervision) and on avoiding prison's desocializing effects (rather than rehabilitating) is probably also part of the explanation of the slow growth of the organization needed to supervise the implementation of these community punishments.

The importance of philosophies such as proportionality might also help explain why judges are credited with imposing these community punishments in an 'automatic' way (i.e. with scant individual information and rarely with individually tailored requirements). The ideas of the severity of the offence and the determination of punishment by the law are the main explanations for imposing any sentence in Spanish judicial culture. Moreover, according to our judicial culture, alternatives to prison are primarily for first-time offenders, who do not need (nor deserve) intervention or control. As a result, for these first-time offenders, fines and suspended sentences (with no requirements but not to reoffend) are the appropriate responses. Once the person has a criminal record, he or she no longer 'deserves' the alternatives to imprisonment and in general will get a prison sentence.

After Franco's dictatorship the so-called Criminal Code of Democracy (the 1995 Criminal Code) imported some elements from the English tradition, such as community service orders and the possibility of adding requirements to a suspended sentence, involving some form of supervision, though not probation as an autonomous punishment (Cid and Larrauri 1997). This led to the development of an incipient probation system, which was more visible in Catalonia. The Catalan administration developed a system for adults from within the juvenile system (Martin and Larrauri 2012). This system rested on the principal elements which characterize probation elsewhere: pre-sentence reports and supervision in the form of interviews and/or in the form of compulsory attendance to an educational programme; programmes mainly focused on gender violence, driving offences and treatment for drug offenders.

Although more requirements were added to supervision orders, the people on whom these community punishments were imposed were mainly the same as before: first-time offenders (Blay 2010). This is mainly due to the requirements for suspending a prison sentence; that is, suspension only applies to prison sentences no longer than 2 years and for those without criminal records.[13] These rules, added to a judicial culture that sees alternatives as something to be granted only 'once' and which sees such sanctions as something less than 'real' punishment, which is still embodied only by the prison, might explain the reason why, despite the Criminal Code of Democracy (1995), the sentencing pattern did not change radically.

Development

More recently, the narratives around community punishments in Spain have entered a new stage – moving beyond proportionality and decarceration. After a first stage of a penal system based almost exclusively on prison, suspended sentences and fines, and the later introduction of alternatives to prison in the 1995 democratic Criminal Code, this (third) stage can be said to begin in 2003, when a major reform of the criminal code took place.

The climate in 2003 was one of soaring imprisonment rates (which had been growing since the 1970s; González Sánchez 2011) and of growing punitivism (i.e., the reform, for example, made the requirements to have access to open prisons more demanding). At the same time, however, these reforms enlarged considerably the scope for community penalties: they introduced unpaid work as a direct punishment for the less serious forms of domestic violence (thus judges had the direct choice between prison and unpaid work);[14] and they established the possibility of unpaid work to substitute for prison sentences for recidivists (while maintaining suspended sentences for first-time offenders).[15] These reforms additionally introduced prohibition orders, such as the prohibition on approaching a certain place or on communicating with the victim (*penas de alejamiento*), which may be and often *have to* be imposed by judges (because the law requires it) together with, or as part of, community punishments.

In this stage the justification for punishments included a strong new emphasis on protecting the victim. The idea was probably to introduce more intensive and therefore *credible* alternatives to prison for recidivists (i.e., more requirements, controlled and supervised). Thus, for example, if prison sentences for intimate-partner violence are suspended or substituted, requirements of attending an educational programme and prohibition orders must *always* be imposed, the law not giving room for judges to decide otherwise.

Although more requirements were added, this probably did not change the main picture: culturally, community punishments are considered only adequate for first-time offenders, as an act of mercy for a first offence. They are not seen as 'real' punishments, partly due to inadequate or nonexistent supervision (in Spain) and many practical enforcement problems which create a perception that these are 'never enforced' (Blay 2007).[16]

More recent evidence, from our data gathered from 2012 onwards, however, indicates that more community punishments are being imposed on repeat offenders, that is, prison sentences are beginning to be substituted, and increasingly unpaid work orders and fines are imposed on offenders with criminal records, so this picture could be changing (see 'Recent trends', below).[17]

Finally, reparation for the victim had only been a visible feature of the juvenile system, and although there were attempts to introduce victim–offender mediation for adults, they really never took hold, and even though they are still functioning they are kept at the stage of 'experimental pilot' and at the margins of the sentencing system.[18] There are some very recent (2013–2014) initiatives to increase the scope for mediation in the area of criminal law. Though these initiatives are getting stronger, they are driven by individual judges and not so much by law-makers (J. A. Rodríguez, personal communication). Beyond specific attempts to introduce reparation schemes, a narrative of reparation has also been used in political, administrative and judicial discourses when justifying the introduction or use of unpaid work as a sentence.

Recent trends

We will now explain the development of community punishments in terms of numbers and the problems they currently face. In this section we will concentrate on *suspended sentences* (with an obligation to attend an educational programme, or drug-treatment programme) and *unpaid work*. Although some suspended sentences do have other requirements (such as an interview with the administration officer), these are harder to quantify and little is known or published about them. Table 11.1 shows the dimension of the penal field in terms of *sentences imposed* by the courts in Spain.

Table 11.1 shows the number of sentences imposed by Spanish courts between 2007 and 2013. This does not reflect how many prison sentences have been suspended or substituted, since this statistic is not published. As far as we know, prison sentences are suspended in 84 per cent of the cases where it is legally possible to suspend, and they are substituted only in 12 per cent of the cases where they may be substituted (Cid and Larrauri 2002). The table reflects the fluctuation in unpaid work sentences and the general increase in the number of prohibition orders imposed.

In order to picture *how much* supervision in the community there is, consider that in Spain in December 2013 there were 56,103 prison inmates (sentenced), and there were approximately 52,203 individuals under supervision in the community.[19]

Figure 11.1 offers some data related to the Catalan Administration; it reflects the offences that community punishments are used for and the absolute number of individuals serving community punishments (mainly unpaid work and suspended sentences with requirements) in Catalonia.

From Table 11.1 and Figure 11.1, and a review of available literature, we can offer the following reflections on the evolution and current application of community punishments following the logic of rehabilitative, punitive, reparative and managerial discourses (Robinson *et al.* 2013).

How community punishments are used

Community punishments are used to punish specific types of offences. The penal reform of 2003 allowed *domestic violence* or *intimate-partner violence* and *driving offences* to be punished by a community sentence. Thus, in the case of unpaid work, for

TABLE 11.1 Evolution of imprisonment and fines and unpaid work (dimension of or in the penal field) for Spain, including Catalonia

	2007	2008	2009	2010	2011	2012	2013
Prison	121,217	129,890	139,663	141,849	135,713	142,444	153,950
Privation of liberty for fine default[a]	11,796	16,734	11,023	7,873	7,202	1,667	41
Prohibition from a specific job	70,813	84,852	89,331	94,312	93,566	103,619	111,335
Prohibition to drive	57,916	79,664	79,699	75,964	79,453	74,145	72,197
Prohibition to bear arms	26,983	29,943	31,175	31,952	28,966	28,223	28,578
Prohibition to approach the victim[b]	27,437	27,413	–	34,881	30,707	30,516	32,378
Prohibition to communicate with the victim	10,895	19,435	4,269	4,959	10,265	10,934	28,155
Unpaid work	13,803	91,045	110,659	102,007	56,426[c]	54,070	56,769
Fine	96,717	145,819	158,250	126,199	104,783	108,373	121,971

[a]The sharp drop between 2012 and 2013 reflects a change to the classification of fine defaulters, who from 2013 are included in one of three other categories of: prison, unpaid work, house arrest.

[b]No data for 2009 was published on the prohibition to approach the victim.

[c]This sharp drop in the number of unpaid work sentences is due to a change in the Criminal code introduced in 2010 that allowed judges to punish driving offences with prison, a fine or unpaid work, instead of prison or a fine and unpaid work, which we refer to when dealing with recent trends.

Source: National Institute of Statistics.

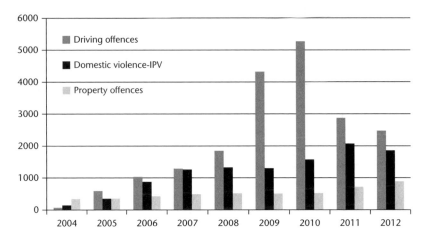

FIGURE 11.1   Evolution of unpaid work and suspension with requirements in Catalonia: type of offence

Source: Data from the Catalan Service of Alternative Measures.

example, it is established as a direct punishment[20] for intimate-partner violence, and the judge may choose between prison and unpaid work. The rationale of the reform was that prison should only be used for the more serious cases, and fines were not appropriate to punish domestic violence (they could affect the victim's right to compensation). Unpaid work was for this offence just punitive enough to be acceptable as an alternative to prison. In the case of driving offences, the rationale was probably to increase the punitive bite of the fine (see the next section) as an alternative to imprisonment.

This leads, in practice, to community sentences being used mainly for intimate-partner violence and driving offences, as reflected in Figure 11.1. Increases and decreases in the use of community sentences directly correlate to reforms in the criminal code in these two categories of offences.

The severity of community sentences

The penal reform of 2003 increased the severity of community sentences. This evolution is reflected in the increase in the maximum number of hours or days of unpaid work, which were initially up to 380 hours and were increased to 180 days of work (amounting to 1,440 hours of work), and in the possibility, and in certain cases the legal obligation, to add obligations to suspended sentences after the 2003 Criminal code reform. These punitive increases were justified in terms of unpaid work needing to reinforce its punitive credentials if it was going to function as an *alternative* to prison. Suspended sentences with the additional requirement of attending an educational programme have certainly witnessed an increase, because from 2003 onwards, when a judge has decided to suspend or substitute a prison sentence for intimate-partner violence, the Code establishes that these requirements *must* be imposed. This reform was justified in terms of providing an alternative response to prison with more requirements, hence more *punitive* and with more content than 'only suspending' the sentence. As far as we know, besides intimate-partner violence and, to a lesser extent, driving safety programmes in cases of suspending or substituting prison sentences for driving offences, judges make little more use of requirements for other types of offences (Varona and Blay forthcoming).

Development of different forms of supervision

Incipiently since 1995, but more importantly since 2003, we have witnessed the development of different forms of supervision. The two administrations responsible for supervising offenders in the community (Spain and Catalonia) have developed a slightly different orientation. Basic regulation on supervision is common to both territories, but its terms are vague enough to allow for considerable variation in how punishments are implemented by supervisors and, probably, experienced by offenders. Although more research is needed on these variations, we suggest that the Catalan administration has more of a 'supervision and *probation*' ideology, reflected both at the level of official discourse of senior civil servants and working practices of individual supervisors (Blay forthcoming), whereas the Spanish Administration has a more 'sentence enforcement' orientation.

The nature and extent of supervision by Spain's equivalent of probation officers has not to our knowledge been researched. It is difficult therefore to ascertain to what extent individual supervision (in the sense of a supervisory relationship between offender and officer) actually exists and what it consists of. However, an indication of this different orientation[21] might be seen in the fact that the supervision of community sentences in most of Spain is located within the Prison Service. In contrast, as we have mentioned above, in Catalonia probation officers (*delegats d'execució de mesures*) came from the juvenile system, and these professionals, mainly social workers and psychologists, play a central role in the implementation of suspensions with requirements and unpaid work in Catalonia.

Risk-assessment practices

Since 2003 we have seen the introduction of risk-assessment practices in the area of community sentences. Several legal reforms affecting mainly driving offences (see 'The relevance of available resources', below, and Note 21) have led to a reduction in the number of community sentences being implemented (Figure 11.1). This has been used as an opportunity by the Catalan administration to revise how supervision of unpaid work orders takes place. A risk-assessment procedure[22] has been introduced, in which offenders are tiered in three levels of risk and granted more or less intense levels of monitoring according to this assessment.[23] As a consequence, besides the enforcement of unpaid work, attendance at follow-up interviews with the supervisor are part of the community punishment for medium- and high-risk cases. As far as we know, this has not taken place in the Spanish context.

Risk-assessment instruments are used in Catalonia by probation officers in cases of suspended sentences with requirements related to intimate partner violence offences[24] in order to determine priority and intensity in the management of cases (i.e., orders for high-risk offenders shall be prioritized and more intensely supervised), and by psychologists, who implement education and treatment programmes. Probation officers assess risk on the basis of the content of the sentence and an interview with the offender, but psychologists of the institution that delivers the programme use a standardized instrument, an adapted version of the Spouse Assault Risk Assessment instrument (SARA) (Andrés-Pueyo and López 2005; Andrés-Pueyo et al. 2008 for an evaluation). Part of the future of community punishments seems to be linked to the use of risk-assessment tools.

Formalization and standardization of judicial decision-making

Specialized courts (*Jueces de Ejecución*) in the implementation of sentences (i.e., post-sentencing decisions, such as suspending or substituting a prison sentence and imposing requirements, as well as supervising their enforcement) were introduced in 2000 in large constituencies, mainly with the aim of facilitating an expedient enforcement of sentences. In spite of this, formalization and standardization due to an enormous workload seem to be continuing trends by the new specialized courts, both at the level of judicial imposition of community punishments and at the level of their supervision.

Community punishments are very standardized: although judges can choose among many requirements when suspending or substituting a prison sentence, judges tend not to make use of this discretion, even though the Criminal Code would allow them to do so. As noted above, this may be explained in part by the scarce use of pre-sentence reports by judges and thus the lack of personal and social information on the offender needed to individualize the punishment (Larrauri 2012; Larrauri and Zorrilla 2014 on pre-sentence reports). Additional explanations of this lack of creativity in imposing community punishments might be the absence of an infrastructure in Spain to implement them, and high workloads in the Courts.

Regarding judicial supervision, this trend towards formalization is also explained, in part, by high workloads in the courts (mainly as a result of the increase in intimate-partner violence and driving offences, formerly misdemeanors or administrative infractions). In the context of a neoclassical culture (Beyens and Scheirs 2010), judges have adapted to an increase in the amount of work they have to deal with (not accompanied by an increase in resources) by supervising the enforcement of orders in a very formal manner (e.g. by limiting their control to hours worked or hours spent in a treatment programme) (Blay 2011). Moreover, judges do not tend to perceive that individual rights might be involved and/or infringed in the enforcement of community orders, so they tend to regard their supervisory task in this area as unworthy of judicial attention (contrary to what happens with prison sentences, where it is very obvious that individual rights are involved) (Blay 2011). Also in judicial supervision, prison is seen as 'the only real punishment'.

The relevance of available resources

Since 2003 some developments in community punishments have indicated a marked managerial trend (Robinson *et al.* 2013). Community punishments have been defended as *cheaper* responses to crime than prison. For example, up to 2012, Catalan official statistics regularly featured the cost of 1 day in prison compared with 1 day of community supervision. This idea of cheaper responses, together with the continental tradition of alternatives to prison not involving supervision (being suspended sentences and/or fines and thus needing few resources), has led to little public funding being allocated to the development of the appropriate personnel and infrastructure to implement them. This explains in part the limited development of a probation service as such in Spain.

The lack of sufficient resources has sometimes led to dramatic situations where orders could not be enforced and the statute of limitations has prevailed; in some areas of Spain when such problems were at their worst, up to 90 per cent of unpaid work orders expired (Blay 2010). The response to this situation (from 2007 to 2010) was not an increase in resources but, rather, changes in regulation. On the one hand, the Criminal Code was reformed, allowing judges to punish driving offences with prison, fines *or* unpaid work (instead of prison or fines *and* unpaid work). In practice, this led to an important reduction of the use of unpaid work for these offences (see Table 11.1). On the other hand, in order to facilitate the implementation of large numbers of orders, the Code allowed these sentences to be served in the form of group educational programmes, which were easier (cheaper) to organize than individual job placements for large numbers of offenders. The logic behind these reforms was to make the system sustainable, and thus it was a managerial adaptation (adapting community sentences to resources, rather than the other way around).

A further development, privatization of the supervision of offenders, has also been resorted to in Catalonia (but not, as far as we know, in the rest of Spain), where supervision of community punishments is regularly contracted out to non-profit organizations because it is deemed more appropriate from a managerial point of view (Larrauri 2010; Blay 2010; Martin and Larrauri 2012).

How legitimate are community punishments?

The legitimacy of community sentences was arguably at its highest when they were only an aspiration to be introduced in Spain. In the second stage, when they were introduced in the new criminal code in 1995, legitimacy was not drastically damaged, because their scarce presence in the punishment system was attributed to a lack of use by judges (Cid and Larrauri 2002).[25] From 2003 their legitimacy has been damaged mainly by law reforms that have made it mandatory to implement them and that have led to a great increase in the number of sentences being passed (mainly unpaid work for driving offences and educational programmes for intimate-partner violence). Since the law-maker provided no additional means to ensure this greater number of sentences could be appropriately implemented, this led, as we have seen, to non-compliance with or non-execution of a vast majority of sentences.

Since legitimacy has different audiences, maybe it is helpful to distinguish among judges, offenders and the justice administration. Our contention would be that community punishments are struggling for legitimacy in the sense that they remain somehow an alien concept and are not yet an embedded part of the penal landscape, for the reasons previously explained (see Introduction).

On the other hand, how do we measure the legitimacy of community punishments? Being used by *judges* might give some idea of their legitimacy (especially when they may impose other punishments), and in this sense, as the statistics above have shown, they would seem to hold a certain legitimacy for them. However, according to our own qualitative research on the views of the majority of judges (Blay and Larrauri 2011; Blay 2011), sometimes a community sentence is used because judges do not want to resort to prison for a given offence in terms of proportionality, and a fine is not available, not because they think a community sentence is the most appropriate response.

An example of their limited legitimacy for the law-maker might be the process followed since 2003: introducing unpaid work and educational programmes for only two types of offence, making them mandatory, not providing any additional means to ensure they could be effectively implemented and, finally, changing again the law to try to limit their scope when it was clear that the system could not cope with the vast number of orders.[26] We would expect that a parliament that believes in community sentences would at least promote the possibility of their implementation for other offences (particularly property crime), and create and appropriately fund a system of probation officers that would allow for their supervision, and which could finally convince judges that the option is not merely one between prison and impunity.

Regarding the *Administration* (which has to supervise and control offenders sentenced to educational programmes and unpaid work), we can observe a 'tale of two cities'. The Catalan *administration* has made an effort to develop front-end measures, because both at a senior and at a practitioner level, officers identify themselves as *doing probation*. This may be linked to the fact that the adults' system stems from the earlier development of the juvenile system, based on pre-sentence reports and supervision in the community; it could also be linked to the religious tradition of the political party that has had the responsibility for the Justice Department for most of the time and, finally, it may reflect a European influence.[27] This identity is reflected in the fact that the Catalan administration: a) does pre-sentence reports; b) has a structure of probation officers; c) has developed an accreditation process for non-profit organizations delivering supervision; d) has developed risk-assessment procedures and instruments for offenders; e) makes an effort to ensure the coordination between the Administration and the courts specialized in the implementation of sentences (*Jueces de Ejecución*); f) has provisions for implementing community sentences not only for primary offenders, but also for higher risk and repeat offenders (Blay 2011, forthcoming).

No research has been published on the developments in Spain at an administrative level, so our knowledge stems from partial and anecdotal evidence. As far as we have been able to establish, we can point to the following traits of the Spanish administration of community sentences: a) there is no mention of pre-sentence reports in regulations and there is no administrative body charged with preparing them; b) the supervision of offenders in the community is carried out by correctional social services (called 'open centres', but physically in prisons); c) the delivery of the treatment and educational programmes is carried out by (public but) ad hoc institutions that do not have as sole purpose the supervision of offenders; d) no generalized use of specific risk-assessment practices in the supervision and control of educational programmes and unpaid work; e) no comprehensive effort to establish a coordination between judges and the Administration on the implementation of community punishments. Moreover, the participation in European forums tends to be minimal, albeit written reports for the European Organization for Probation (CEP), for example, have been produced.[28]

Reflections

'Punishment in the community' *as a concept* does not really make sense in Spain: the expression is not used in political, social or legal discourse; and in academic discourse it is a translation of the English expression and not a natural term. So, in this sense, community punishment is an alien concept and 'alternatives to prison' is the preferred term.

The alternatives-to-prison model in Spain is still largely based on suspended sentences and fines, more with an emphasis on a reductionist aim than on supervision (understood as intervention, help and control by the administration). Unpaid work and educational programmes have been introduced and used extensively, especially since 2003, and this certainly may reflect the limitations of an alternative system based on fines with no supervision. However, no probation (or an alternative supervision system) has been developed, reinforcing therefore the lack of traction of 'community sentences'. The concept faces the same problems in Catalonia, but the supervision system is more developed for the reasons explained (see 'How legitimate are community punishments?', above) and probably due to the previous existence of the juvenile justice system, which has a long tradition of providing supervision as a way of helping juveniles *and* reducing confinement.

Punishments in the community may be seen to challenge the punitive penal climate in the sense that they offer judges the possibility of avoiding prison sentences for certain offences either directly or suspending or substituting prison sentences. However, at the same time, *they confirm a punitive penal climate*. They reflect increased severity in the sense that community punishments have evolved towards being more punitive than they were (e.g. longer unpaid work hours), and they often have a component of prohibition or control (prohibition from approaching certain places or the victim as a standard requirement). In part because there is no tradition, and probably not enough resources for supportive supervision in the community, punishment in the community is in practice primarily about control. Prohibition orders and/or requirements, such as those prohibiting certain professions or activities, for example driving, or prohibiting the offender from approaching or communicating with the victim, proliferate and are very often imposed on the very same individuals with community punishments involving supervision (and, as we mentioned, in Catalonia these requirements are to a certain extent being controlled by the probation officers – *Delegats d'execucio de mesures*). Moreover, the reaction to continuous breach in the case of a suspended or a substituted prison sentence is still a prison sentence, therefore we do not exclude the possibility that some people enter prison for breaching the education programme or the unpaid work and exhibiting a reluctant attitude, rather than for the seriousness of the original offence.

However, community punishment is not a static field and it obviously reflects wider social changes. After their introduction and limited use for some years, we witnessed a sharp proliferation of community punishments due to legal reforms enacted in 2003 and 2007, and further law reforms to restrict their scope (2010). It should not be ruled out that developments such as the introduction of risk assessment, better programmes, the European influence, economic reasons, the limitations of fines and unsupervised punishments and technological developments (electronic monitoring) all produce further moves from our traditional alternatives-to-prison system.

In sum: community punishments are applied for a number of restricted offences in part because the main handicap they face is the strong cultural idea that they are not 'real' punishments. This is why they are only applied mainly to two types of offence and to a large extent to first-time offenders. This is probably also why, beyond legal reforms in the Criminal Code, no actual structure to implement community punishments has been created (introduction of pre-sentence reports and probation officers). When they are implemented, they are regarded as a 'one time' opportunity, and therefore not often imposed on people who have a criminal record. Although some community punishments involve 'supervision', this supervision has faced the problems of having to handle a very big increase in numbers over a short period of time. This has meant that supervision has developed in a formalized way and, on occasions, been privatized.

However, supervision has become more sophisticated in recent years due to the decreasing numbers and probably due also to the influence of European scholarship (Morgenstern and Larrauri 2014). This means that risk assessments are being introduced and that, besides offender behaviour programmes, supervision is being carried out through interviews by 'probation' workers, and that repeat offenders are increasingly kept outside prison (Blay forthcoming). This development is, however, different and more advanced in Catalonia than in Spain, thus leading to the aforementioned tale of two cities.

In addition to these traditional community punishments (educational programmes and unpaid work), we witness that an array of 'prohibition orders' is being imposed by the courts on the same individuals. This is an indicator of the concerns to protect victims and maybe also a wish to enhance the punitive bite of community punishments. This implies that community punishments have a control dimension that might lead to an increased rate of breach. Unfortunately in some cases when the breach is persistent or the attitude is defiant, some of these offenders might end up in prison for these reasons rather than by virtue of the seriousness of the original offence.

Notes

1   This research has been carried out under Research Projects DER2012-32150 '*Super-visión en la comunidad: intervención en la fase de ejecución de las sentencias. Especial énfasis en la violencia de género*', funded by the Ministerio de Economía y Competitividad (MINECO) and '*Penologia europea: La seva influència en el sistema de penes espanyol*', Generalitat de Catalunya, Agaur, SGR 2014-2016. We are grateful to Marta Martí for her help with the references and to Consuelo Murillo for her thoughts on the breach of community punishments.
2   For example, the Royal Decree that regulates them provides a list but no generic name; the Spanish Interior Minister speaks of 'Alternative Measures' and the Catalan Justice Department of 'Alternative Penal Measures'.
3   There might be other reasons. The word 'community' is not frequently used in common language.
4   Catalonia is one of 17 Spanish autonomous regions, but the only one with powers to implement sentences.
5   Only when a prison sentence of less than 3 months is imposed is it automatically suspended or transformed into a fine or an unpaid work order.
6   For a comprehensive review of research on suspended sentences, see Cid (2009).
7   There are of course fines; however, these carry no supervision. Therefore we focus on the suspended sentence, which at least carries some requirements (i.e. not to reoffend) and therefore implies a 'control' element.
8   There are of course other types of punishment available to judges, such as disqualification orders; however, these tend to be used in addition to prison, fines or suspended sentences.
9   We tend to write 'probation' in quotation marks because the origins, characteristic elements and evolution of probation have not happened in Spain in similar ways as in the UK and there is no Probation Service as such. Sentences tend to be more determinate, there is no sentencing hearing, there is no general use of pre-sentence reports and supervision tends to involve only attending specific programmes. All these elements that characterize probation can only be found in a very limited way, in Spain, and perhaps in a less limited way in the Catalan system.
10   Open prison usually involves individuals spending the day out of prison, either working or studying, and going back to prison for the night.
11   Although open prisons and parole have been analysed by Spanish scholars, the focus has been on the problems involved in gaining access to them, not on the supervision or experience of them.
12   The exact wording of the Constitutional precept is that *deprivations of liberty* 'shall be oriented towards reeducation and social reintegration' (art. 25 of the 1978 Constitution);

a wide reading of the precept, common in literature, extends this orientation to punishments other than imprisonment.

13 And substitution of prison sentences, which was possible for repeat offenders, was scarcely used (Cid and Larrauri 2002).

14 In the 1995 criminal code, unpaid work could only be used as a substitute for home arrest and in cases of fine default, hence the initial rare use of this sentence.

15 Substitution of prison sentences for recidivists has been possible since 1995, but only by a fine. It was thought that allowing judges to substitute prison sentences also with unpaid work would increase its use by judges.

16 We do not have general reliable data on judicial decision-making since the 1998 sample used by Cid and Larrauri 2002, although this conclusion may be inferred from other related studies (Antón and Larrauri 2009; Blay 2011).

17 Preliminary statistical analysis of the results of a pilot study undertaken in Barcelona, involving 200 judicial rulings, show that 35 per cent of offenders receiving sentences of unpaid work have criminal records, as do 23 per cent of those who are fined (Varona and Blay forthcoming).

18 In 2011 there were 1,234 cases diverted to mediation, and 1,037 in the next year.

19 This is approximate, because it is the number of sentences, not of offenders, under supervision. The number of offenders does not regularly appear in the Spanish statistic.

20 This means judges do not have to resort to a suspended sentence or substitute a prison sentence, which involve longer procedures, but may directly grant a community sentence.

21 See also some more differences in Risk-assessment practices, below.

22 No instrument is used to assess risk in unpaid work cases, but supervisors use a previously established list of items thought to be relevant for this assessment.

23 There is further need to study the type of supervision undertaken: the weight, length, depth and quality of the supervision, beyond legal regulation (Blay forthcoming).

24 Risk-assessment tools are also used in the prison context in Spain to adopt some decisions (Martínez Garay 2014) and in the Catalan system (RISCANVI; Nguyen et al. 2011). Additionally they might also be used by the police, who are responsible for implementing victim protection and prohibition orders (Instrucción 5/2008 General Secretary of State for Security).

25 From 1995 to 2003 it was not uncommon to hear that the Administration was providing more places for serving unpaid work than sentences imposed by judges (Blay 2007).

26 An additional indication is the abolition of the possibility of asking for a pre-sentence report, which is now not even mentioned in the new Royal Decree (Larrauri and Zorrilla 2014).

27 For example Marc Cerón, Director of the Reparation and Penal Execution in the Community of the Catalan Administration, has been the President of the European Organization of Probation, CEP, since May 2010.

28 See the online report on Spain in the CEP knowledgebase, for example (http://www.cep-probation.org/uploaded_files/Summary%20information%20on%20Spain.pdf).

References

Andrés-Pueyo, A. and López, S. (2005) *SARA: Manual para La valoración del riesgo de violencia contra La pareja*. Barcelona: Publicacions i Edicions de La Universitat de Barcelona.

Andrés-Pueyo, A., López, S. and Álvarez, E. (2008) 'Valoración del riesgo de violencia contra La pareja por medio de La SARA', *Papeles del Psicólogo* 29(1): 107–22.

Antón, L. and Larrauri, E. (2009) 'Violencia de género ocasional: un análisis de las penas ejecutadas', *Revista Espa nola de Investigación Criminológica* 7: 1–26. Available at: www.criminologia.net/pdf/reic/ano7-2009/a72009art2.pdf (accessed 26 November 2014).

Ashworth, A. and Zedner, L. (2014) *Preventive Justice*. Oxford: Oxford University Press.

Beyens, K. and Scheirs, V. (2010) 'Encounters of a different kind: Social enquiry and sentencing in Belgium', *Punishment & Society* 12(3): 309–28.

Blay, E. (2007) 'Nueve tópicos acerca del trabajo en beneficio de La comunidad: La necesidad de una discusión basada en conocimientos empíricos', *Indret: Revista para el Análisis del Derecho* (4): 1–18. Available at: www.indret.com/pdf/474_es.pdf (accessed 26 November 2014).

Blay, E. (2010) '"It could be us": Recent transformations in the use of community service as a punishment in Spain', *European Journal of Probation* March 2: 62–81.

Blay, E. (2011) 'El papel de los jueces en La ejecución de las penas comunitarias: una investigación empírica y algunas propuestas para La reflexión', in Larrauri, E. and Blay, E. (eds) *Penas comunitarias en Europa*. Madrid: Trotta, pp. 60–82.

Blay, E. (forthcoming) *Individual Supervision Practices by Catalan Probation Officers*.

Blay, E. and Larrauri, E. (2011) 'La supervisión de los delincuentes en libertad', in Larrauri, E. and Blay, E. (eds) *Penas Comunitarias en Europa*. Madrid: Trotta, pp. 9–19.

Cid, J. (2008) 'El incremento de La población reclusa en España entre 1996–2006: diagnóstico y remedios', *Revista Española de Investigación Criminológica* (6): 1–31. Available at: www.criminologia.net/pdf/reic/ano6-2008/a62008art2.pdf (accessed 26 November 2014).

Cid, J. (2009) *La Elección Del Castigo: Suspensión de La Pena o 'Probation' Versus Prisión*. Barcelona: Bosch.

Cid, J. and Larrauri, E. (eds). (1997) *Penas Alternativas a La Prisión*. Barcelona: Bosch.

Cid, J. and Larrauri, E. (eds). (2002) *Jueces Penales y Penas en España: Aplicación de las Penas Alternativas a La Privación de Libertad en los Juzgados de lo Penal*. Valencia: Tirant lo Blanch.

Cid, J. and Larrauri, E. (eds). (2005) *Delincuencia Violenta: ¿Prevenir, Castigar o Rehabilitar?*. Valencia: Tirant lo Blanch.

Cid, J. and Larrauri, E. (2009) 'Development of crime, social change, mass media, crime policy, sanctioning practice and their impact on prison population rates. National Report: Spain', in Dünkel, F., Lappi-Sepälä, T., Morgenstern, C. and Van Zyl Smit, D. (eds) *Kriminalität, Kriminalpolitik, Strafrechtliche Sanktionspraxis und Gefangenenraten im Europäischen Vergleich: Band II*. Germany: Forum, pp. 805–39.

Díez Ripollés, J. L. (2006) 'La evolución del sistema de penas en España: 1975–2003', *Revista Electrónica de Ciencia Penal y Criminología* 8(7): 1–25. Available at: http://criminet.ugr.es/recpc/08/recpc08-07.pdf (accessed 26 November 2014).

González Sánchez, I. (2011) 'Aumento de presos y Código Penal. una explicación insuficiente', *Revista Electrónica de Ciencia Penal y Criminología* 13-04: 1–22. Available at: http://criminet.ugr.es/recpc/13/recpc13-04.pdf (accessed 26 November 2014).

Larrauri, E. (2001) 'Aportación de las ciencias sociales a La elaboración de reformas en La legislación penal', in Díez Ripollés, J. L. and Cerezo Domínguez, A. (eds) *Los Problemas de La Investigación Empírica en Criminología: La Situación Española*. Valencia: Tirant lo Blanch, pp. 93–107.

Larrauri, E. (2010) 'Los programas formativos como medida penal alternativa en los casos de violencia de género ocasional', *Revista Española de Investigación Criminológica* (8): 1–26. Available at: www.criminologia.net/pdf/reic/ano8-2010/a82010art1.pdf (accessed 26 November 2014).

Larrauri, E. (2012) '¿Es necesario un informe social para decidir acerca de La pena?' *Jueces para La Democracia* 72: 105–9.

Larrauri, E. and Zorrilla, N. (2014) 'Informe social y supervisión efectiva en La comunidad: especial referencia a delitos de violencia de género ocasional', *Indret: Revista para el Análisis del Derecho* 3: 1–29. Available at: www.indret.com/pdf/1058_es.pdf (accessed 26 November 2014).

Martin, J. and Larrauri, E. (2012) 'Probation in Europe: Catalonia', in van Kalmthout, A. and Durnescu, I. (eds) *Probation in Europe. 2013–2014 Edition*. Utrecht: CEP, Conférence Permanente Européene de La Probation, pp. 1–46. Available at: www.cepprobation.org/uploaded_files/Probation-in-Europe-2013-Chapter-Catalonia.pdf (accessed 26 November 2014).

Martínez Garay, L. (2014) 'La incertidumbre de los pronósticos de peligrosidad: consecuencias para La dogmática de las medidas de seguridad', *Indret: Revista para el Análisis del Derecho* 2: 1–77. Available at: www.indret.com/pdf/1043...pdf (accessed 26 November 2014).

Mir Puig, S. (1984) *Derecho Penal: Parte General*, 1st edn. Barcelona: Reppertor.

Morgenstern, C. and Larrauri, E. (2014) 'European norms, policy and practice', in McNeill, F. and Beyens, K. (eds) *Offender Supervision in Europe*. Croydon: Palgrave Macmillan, pp. 125–54.

Muñoz Conde, F. J. (1979) 'La resocialización del delincuente: análisis y crítica de un mito', *Sistema: Revista de ciencias sociales* 31: 73–84.

Muñoz Conde, F. J. (1985) *Derecho Penal y Control Social*. Jerez de La Frontera: Fundación Universitaria de Jerez, D.L.

Navarro, C. (2002) *Suspensión y Modificación de La Condena Penal*. Barcelona: Bosch.

Nguyen, T., Arbach-Lucioni, K. and Andrés-Pueyo, A. (2011) 'Factores de riesgo de La reincidencia violenta en La población penitenciaria', *Revista de Derecho Penal y Criminología*, 3(6): 293–4.

Robinson, G., McNeill, F. and Maruna, S. (2013) 'Punishment in society: The improbable persistence of probation and other community sanctions and measures', in Simon, J. and Sparks, R. (eds) *The SAGE Handbook of Punishment and Society*. London: Sage.

Snacken, S., Van Zyl Smit, D. and Beyens, K. (2014) 'European sentencing practices', in Body-Gendrot, S., Hough, M., Kerezsi, K., Lévy, R. and Snacken, S. (eds) *The Routledge Handbook of European Criminology*. London: Routledge.

Varona, D. and Blay, E. (forthcoming) 'Aplicación judicial del sistema de penas del Código Penal', Resultados de un estudio piloto en los Juzgados de Ejecución de Barcelona.

12

PHILANTHROPY, WELFARE STATE AND MANAGERIAL TREATMENT

Three phases of community punishment in Sweden

Kerstin Svensson

Introduction

Sweden is well known for its welfare state, a welfare state that was at its strongest in the 1970s. As this chapter will take us both further back into history and forward to the present, it is important to add that citizens' reliance on the central state is part of a deep and durable tradition in Sweden. Since the establishment of the state of Sweden 500 years ago, the patriarchal state has taken different forms and shapes, amongst which the late twentieth-century welfare state is the most well known in the international context.

In analysing the development of punishment in the community in Sweden, it is important to bear such relations between the state and the population in mind. In a patriarchal state, the government takes care of the population. In Sweden this is shown through the close connection between public poor-relief and punishment. The discussion about penal measures has throughout history been tied with the question about how to deal with poverty.

Sweden is not only an example of a state with a strong patriarchal tradition, but also of state that has been unharmed (by external aggression) for more than 200 years. The changes in the penal system have been both slow and durable, perhaps because the foundations of the system have seldom been exposed to external threats.

In this chapter, I will give a brief history of the evolution of punishment in the community in Sweden. Development in Scandinavian countries has many similarities. Sweden, Denmark and Norway have throughout history made similar changes in more or less the same period, but still, there are too many differences between the countries to tell a single story of Scandinavian development. Recently, Pratt and Eriksson (2012) have detected a Scandinavian culture of control based on imported ideas from the USA. While a development towards a more punitive penal culture is seen in all the Scandinavian countries, there remains a significant difference in the degree and nature of public interest in crime and punishment between Scandinavia and the Anglophone world. And, evidently, there is a huge difference in prison rates between Scandinavia and the Anglophone world. Nevertheless, within Scandinavia there are different countries, different jurisdictions and different values. Bonde-son (2005) draws this very conclusion from her study of opinions on legal and moral issues: 'despite all historical, religious, economic and political homogeneity, it appears that value orientations are rather heterogeneous. . . There is no uniform pattern of values in the Scandinavian countries' (p. 441).

This chapter starts in the early nineteenth century and continues chronologically to the present day. Covering such a long period in a short text demands a choice of what is most important. Accordingly, I have chosen to focus on turning points in this penal evolution as well as on central aspects of contemporary punishment in the community. That means that there are several parts of the history that are left out or glossed over. In order to make the turning points in the penal system understandable, I will also give some glimpses of the nature of Swedish society when these turns were taken.

As this story focuses on the evolution of current forms of punishment in the community, a short explanation of the current legal system and punishment is nec-essary. In the Swedish Penal Code there are two punishments: prison and fines. All other sanctions are alternatives to prison and can be used in sentencing only where prison is the stated penalty in the Penal Code. There is one state agency for implementing penal sanctions: The Prison and Probation Service. 'Probation' is the term used for the alternative sanctions, but also for the agency responsible for supervision of offenders sentenced to imprisonment and supervised after release on parole, or serving their sentence with electronic monitoring. In a literal trans-lation, the Swedish term for the probation service, '*frivård*', would be 'free care', or 'care in the community'; but in general the English translation is 'probation service'.

Alternatives to prison, according to the Penal Law, are sorted into two main cat-egories: the conditional sentence and probation. A conditional sentence is a term of imprisonment which, in practice, is not served, and its length is not stated at sentencing. To get a conditional sentence means to have it recorded in the crim-inal record (as a criminal sentence) and that the suspension may be revoked if a new crime is committed within 2 years. Probation is given as a sentence in its own right; in Swedish it is called '*skyddstillsyn*', which literally translated to English means 'protective care'. A sentence of probation is served through 1 year of super-vision and it can be combined with different conditions: drug treatment, attending programmes within the probation service; psychiatric treatment, etc. 'Community service', a concept that also is a literal translation from Swedish to English, can be added both to a conditional sentence and to probation, which means that a person sentenced to a conditional sentence with community service is in contact with the probation service for the purposes of doing the community service, but for nothing else. For a person sentenced to probation with community service, the community service is just one part of the contact with the probation service and thus integrated with the supervision; and it may also be combined with other conditions.

Apart from these alternatives to prison sentences, there are also alternatives that involve other agencies, mainly social or psychiatric services. I will not go into detail about these, as they are used for a marginal number of offenders. Neither will I describe youth justice, as it is a complicated mix of the penal system and social services and has a distinctive history of its own. Therefore, in this chapter the focus is on adult offenders and the sanctions used for punishment in the community. Finally, I will not talk about fines, even if fines remain by far the most common sanction in Sweden, a situation that has endured since medieval times (Österberg 1996). From the mid-nineteenth century until the mid-twentieth century, 95 per cent of all sanctions were fines. Since 1945, the use of other sanctions has increased, and fines now represent 86 per cent of sanctions (von Hofer 2011). Von Hofer states, in his statistical analyses of crime and punishment in Sweden between 1750 and 2010, that penologists argue that punishments are given to protect major social values. Yet the image given by studies of Swedish penal law and its implementation is that minor crime against social values is, in practice, more often punished, which is revealed by the dominance of fines among sanctions. Further, the fine is a sanction that also can be combined with both conditional sentences and probation.

My focus is on the development of probation as a sentence 'instead of prison'. However, as mentioned above, the probation service also takes care of the supervision of parolees. Parole is mandatory in Sweden after serving two-thirds of the prison sentence, and supervision of parolees normally takes place for one year, whatever the length of the sentence. The rules for probation and parole differ somewhat, but in practice the year of supervision is the same and is implemented by the same agency.

The probation service implements one further kind of punishment in the community: electronic monitoring, which is in Sweden a way of serving a prison sentence. The court has to first decide to impose a prison sentence. The Prison and Probation Service can, after investigation, under certain circumstances and with the consent of the offender, decide that a short prison sentence can be served through electronic monitoring. As probation and parole have many similarities and electronic monitoring is also carried out by the probation service, there will be some references also to those two ways of serving a prison sentence, or part of it, in the community. However, my main focus remains on the main sentence to punishment in the community: probation.

The main material for this chapter was collected for a publication in Swedish, which also is the source for much of the text in this chapter (Svensson 2001). The sources are secondary literature, governmental reports and propositions for legal changes. The more contemporary information, as well as some additional material, has been gathered directly for this chapter through literature, national statistics and information published by the Prison and Probation Service.

Initiatives and inception

Philanthropy in a poor country

Modern ideas of punishment in the community came to Sweden from Western influences during the nineteenth century. They were discussed as ways to deal with the critique of prisons, but, before they could become accepted, such ideas had to find a wider group of advocates and agents. Already, in 1809, when the nation state we know today as Sweden was formed, ideas about reforms of the penal system were being discussed in government. The ideas came from North America, mainly the USA, and pointed at the possibility of making punishment reintegrative. The idea of reintegration had a high moral value, as it was a question of educating the population, especially 'social education' of the poor. A committee was put to work and in their report they referenced positive experiences of prison regimes in the USA. Parallel to the discussion on how to organize prisons, there was a discussion in the government, from the early nineteenth century, about how to organize poor relief in the community (Wieselgren 1895). In 1825 a central, national administration was organised for the prisons. In 1830 the first proposal was made about organising some kind of philanthropic associations for poor relief. The idea was that the highest regional representatives for the state should chair the associations, and members of the bourgeoisie should be involved to support poor families as well as former prisoners.

In the mid-nineteenth century Sweden was still a poor country with an agrarian economy. Industrialisation had begun on a small scale, but the vast majority of the population still lived in rural areas under poor conditions. From the mid-nineteenth century to the early twentieth century, a quarter of the population (1 million people) emigrated from Sweden, most often to the USA. But there was also, in parallel, strong growth in the birth rate, so that in the early twentieth century the population was more or less as big as in the mid-nineteenth century, despite large-scale emigration. The large poor population was seen as a threat to the emerging bourgeoisie; in the 1840s the incarceration rate was at its height in Sweden, with vagrancy being one of the main reasons for imprisonment (Snare 1992). In this period we see the first social reforms in Sweden, as laws on poor relief and public elementary schools were passed. As others have pointed out, social and penal reforms were combined as a way of governing the population and making the working classes amenable to the needs of an industrial economy (see Rusche and Kirschheimer 1939; Melossi and Pavarini 1981; Foucault 1979).

In this social context, associations for poor relief and for support for ex-prisoners came to be established in parallel with an extensive prisons building programme based on ideas combining elements of the Philadelphia and Auburn systems in the USA. The prisons were built as for the Philadelphia system, with its larger prison cells, where the prisoners were supposed to spend their time in solitude. But the daily work carried a stronger influence from the Auburn system, as the prisoners spent much time outside their cells, working together in the prisons' workshops and just spending the nights in solitude. An ideology of treatment as a tool for reintegration and for making good workers out of offenders started to grow. The Penal Law was reformed in 1864 so that corporal punishments were more or less replaced by prison, and the idea of reformation through the prison sentence was established. As a consequence of this ideology, the idea of 'caring power' grew. By supporting offenders, they were also to be controlled in the community, not only in prison. In these early days of the process, this was more an idea than a practice and there were no legal tools to support the task (Svensson 2001).

Legislation and definition of the supervisors

In 1890 there was a meeting for Scandinavian legal professions in Copenhagen, where the main theme was that short prison sentences were seen as being destructive and where it was argued that they should be replaced by conditional sentences. However, the discussion came to be more about whether the court could assess the criminal as a person, and the idea of introducing a conditional sentence was dropped (Eriksson 1995). The same year, and again in 1893, proposals on implementing conditional sentences in the legal system were put to the Swedish parliament based on experiences from the USA, but these proposals were rejected with reference to the meeting in Copenhagen. When the question was raised again in 1894, two members of the parliament supported it, which made the debate continue. In 1900 a committee was put to work on a proposal on how conditional sentences could be implemented (Rydin 1901).

At the turn of the century, around 1900, industrialisation developed quickly in Sweden after several technical innovations. As a complement to the bourgeois philanthropic associations from the nineteenth century, the labour movement started to grow strong. As families moved into the cities for work in the new factories, new social problems emerged. A major issue was that the children were left alone when their parents went to work in the factories. In 1902 a Child Protection Act was enacted. In this, the treatment of children was separated from that of adults, thereby removing them from prisons. The age of criminal responsibility was set at 15 years, because at that age the children of the poor typically finished their education. This separation of children and adults was the first step in a differentiation of categories of offenders, linked to attempts to keep some groups out of prison.

These first steps in the evolution of punishment in the community bear a lot of resemblance to what Jonathan Simon (1993) calls the 'disciplinary period' in his study of parole in California. The fundamental idea was to make offenders work, or even to make poor people work, as vagrancy was still a crime. A lot of social reforms came in the early twentieth century, parallel to the needs of the workforce in the factories and to the growing labour movement. The 'social issue', as the debate on poverty, poor relief and social reforms has been named, became an important issue that gathered a lot of people in associations of different kinds. These associations, the 'Poor Relief People' (Lundkvist 1997), had strong political influence. In associations of the legal professions, discussions were held about the most suitable ways to punish. Three main assumptions shaped these ideas: (1) there is a connection between the crime and the criminal's mind; (2) there is a connection between the criminal's action and his future actions; and (3) crime influences the mind of the criminal (Stjernberg 1905).

In 1906 laws on conditional sentences and parole were enacted. In order to receive a conditional sentence, first there had to be an assessment of the offender. Based on influences from the USA, the poor-relief people demanded that a pre-sentence report should be part of the legal process to facilitate this assessment. In 1910 legislation about pre-sentence reports was passed. However, conditional sentences did not entail supervision. Support could be given through civil society associations, but it was just support; no control was built into the sanction. After debates in the parliament, the law was altered in 1918 and the next step in differentiation and categorisation was taken. From now on, there were two types of alternatives to prison: conditional sentences with and without supervision. The law on pre-sentence reports was altered to fit the new legislation, and the court had to decide between the two based on an assessment of the offender; and supervision had to be given to those who were assessed as having some kind of social problems, as they were seen as being in 'need of guidance to improve' (Sakkunniga 1917). With the legal reform in 1918 the possibility to sentence an offender to the loss of civil rights[1] was abandoned, as were the last forms of corporal punishment.

Supervision as a way to support and control was inspired by work with offenders in the USA, but also from child protection and poor relief in Sweden. The concept used in Swedish, '*övervakning*', would more typically be translated as 'surveillance'; but, as both control and support had influence on the idea, the concept of 'supervision' is closer. The ideas of controlling and supporting offenders in the community were closely connected to ideas of methods for working with other categories of people, not least children and alcohol abusers. The concept of 'social work' came into use in the first years of the twentieth century, and a debate grew about who was best suited to provide supervision: educated and employed civil servants or volunteers (CSA 1906). This was a big issue for several years; the debate ended in a compromise. In the supervision of offenders, as well as in the social services' work with children, youth and poor families, a combination of civil servants and laymen was to be used. Each of them should do what they were best suited for. Civil servants should take care of the formalities and control the implementation of the sanction, and laymen supervisors should have the closer, personal contact with the supervisee.

In this manner, punishment in the community was formed in the early twentieth century and the legal framework was set. This was achieved mainly through governmental initiatives, even if the ideas also came from other countries and developed in professional groups, such as the legal professions. The fundamental features of the evolving approach were that there should be a social investigation, a pre-sentence report, for assessing whether an alternative to prison was to be imposed. Further, there should be a differentiation between offenders that were to be supervised or not supervised, so that offenders with social problems should be supervised, and those more established in society were supposed to manage by themselves while they underwent the implementation of the sanction. The supervising work should be shared between employed civil servants and laymen supervisors.

The welfare state era

During the first decades of the twentieth century, growth in the economy founded on strong industrial development also led to strengthening of the labour movement in Sweden. In 1932 the social democrats came to form a government and an era of long political stability started. The social democrats governed Sweden for 44 years, until the election of 1976. During these years the world-famous welfare state was built through social reforms in a strong and stable economy. At the same time the patriarchal state came to be more and more about the government and the power of the king was successively reduced. One of the reasons behind the stable economic growth was that Sweden was not directly involved in the world wars. Social issues dominated politics, and criminal policy was regarded as a part of social policy, as crime was seen as one of the social problems that could be solved through reforms. The reforms were often based on research, mainly from political economy, but also from social medicine, psychiatry and a growing field of social sciences.

Rehabilitation

If the idea of rehabilitating and reintegrating offenders had been implemented in the penal law by the turn of the twentieth century, it became more and more refined. In the 1930s ideas were developed through the evolution of the welfare state. It was said in preparatory work for a law on changes in the organisation of implementation of sentences in 1933 that 'no punishment, if it would have any aim, should lack supportive work with offenders, and no supportive work should be given to offenders, without being part of the criminal justice system' (*Betänkande* 1933, p. 30).

Social democratic ideas about the importance of state-run agencies for social reforms and of the importance of education and skilled workers led to reformation of punishment in the community. A state-run probation service was introduced in 1942, on the basis of the aforementioned proposal from 1933. This was called '*skyddskonsulenter*'; in a literal translation to English, they would be named 'protection consultants', but the term is usually translated as 'probation managers'. The professional requirements for this occupation included social work qualifications; but, from the start, the task of these social workers was to support and control the work organised by the associations for supervision of offenders, not to work with the offenders directly.

However, the ideas of punishment in the community were not fully accepted by society. When, in July 1944, a young man received a conditional sentence with supervision for assault, several newspapers wrote about it. The sentence was 3 years of supervision, to pay a sum to the victim and a strict instruction to be sober.

This last element of the sanction was to be implemented through membership and participation in the activities of a temperance association. This caught public attention and the discussion came to be about whether it was a punishment to be sober. The judge, who had also been part of the government and later would become Minister of Justice, argued that the educative aspect of the sentence was of great importance for the community. He also said that the punitive element of the sentence was reflected in a high payment to the victim. The fact that he did not state how long the suspended period of imprisonment might be, he argued, only enhanced the deterrent effects of the sentence (*Skånska Dagbladet* 1944).

The laws on conditional sentences and conditional release had had the same constitution since 1918 (Strahl 1944). In 1945 new laws on conditional sentence and early release were enacted. What was formerly conditional release became mandatory early release after five-sixths of the prison time was served. After that, the offender would be supervised in the community. These reforms were based on the idea that there should be treatment in prison that should be followed up through treatment in the community. Mandatory early release was constructed so that it would also reach those who had bad prognoses for being integrated in the community, as they were the ones most likely to be in need of supervision and treatment (Strahl 1944). In the discussions of the late 1930s and early 1940s, a concept of punishment in the community became more and more used: '*kriminalvård* i frihet'. In a literal translation it would be close to 'punishment and treatment in freedom', in which the concept of 'freedom' was important. In a proposal for changes in the organisation for the implementation of sanctions in 1949, it was said that 'it is of highest social interest that those punishments in the community that replace incarceration have an organisation that is rational and effective' (Fångvårdsstyrelsen 1949). It was also stated that staff in the organisation for implementation of sanctions should be prepared for their work through experiences from both prisons and punishment in the community. A manager in the national organisation for implementing sentences at that time said that it was a sign of a criminal policy that strove to 'preserve the most precious thing man owns, second to life, namely freedom' (Schillander-Lundgren *et al.* 1991, p. 21). The arguments for this form of punishment were, on the one hand, the possibility of punishing outside of prison because of new methods of individual supervision. On the other hand, support and treatment was a superordinate aspect in the debate. 'Punishment' was only used in relation to the Penal Code and the practice in courts, while support and treatment was in focus in the implementation of the sentence.

Ever since 1910, there had been committees working on a new Penal Code. After decades of investigations and debates, this was enacted in 1965. This code followed from a lineage of ideas about rehabilitation and reintegration that had developed during more than 100 years. Punishment was now said to be implemented primarily in the community, as all forms of punishment had a reintegrative aim and reintegration should be completed in the community. Alternatives to prison should be used wherever possible, and prison sentences should be served in contact with the community. That laid the ground for extensive possibilities of furlough during prison time and for visits in prison from family members, as well as for extensive possibilities of work outside prison or of residence at a treatment centre while serving a prison sentence. It also made way for professionals from employment agencies, the social services, treatment centres and other organisations visiting prisons regularly, and even for the prison staff, to bring prisoners to leisure activities in the community, especially from the open prisons.

The conditional sentence had since 1918 existed in two forms: with or without supervision. Now a new sanction was introduced, *skyddstillsyn*, usually translated as 'probation'. It became a sanction of its own in 1965, but with its main characteristics from the conditional sentences with supervision. The law allowed that the court could sentence to probation instead of prison sentences of up to one year, or two years in the case of young adults. The difference between conditional sentences and probation was that if the offender had any need for assistance in his rehabilitation, that is, if she or he had some kind of social or psychological problems, then probation should be used.

A reformation of the national administration for implementation of sanctions followed the changed Penal Code. This has been called 'the probation reform'. The central administration now got the name of 'Prison and Probation Service'. Bondeson (1977) suggests that, after 10 years, the number of sentences to probation had only increased modestly, while the use of conditional sentences (without supervision) had more than doubled in frequency. Nevertheless, the state organisation for probation grew hugely during the 1970s. The probation officers became managers for their local organisations, and the new category of workers were named 'treatment assistants', as they would assist the probation officer as well as the offender in the implementation of the sentence and in the treatment that was included. In parallel there were still to be volunteers working in the direct supervision of offenders in cooperation with and as a supplement to the treatment assistants. At that time, the number of educated social workers in Sweden was not sufficient to meet demand. The social services were also growing, and the new training courses that had started in the late 1960s and early 1970s could not supply enough new recruits. Therefore, in recruiting staff to the probation service, the terminology 'social workers or similar' was used. This concept is still in use, but, as we will see, other ways of understanding the phrase developed later.

In the 1970s, then, we see the peak of the treatment ideology as well as of the welfare state. This period is comparable to what Jonathan Simon (1993) has called the 'clinical period' in US parole: a period when the treatment ideology has been strong and supervision focussed on case work and individual meetings with clients.

Legitimacy crisis

In the mid-1970s, the welfare state came to be questioned more and more. In 1976, the social democrats lost the election, and a liberal–conservative coalition government took power. A parallel critique arose of the penal system's alleged ineffectiveness. Crime and punishment came onto the political agenda.

In the 1970s, the development of community punishment also came to be questioned. Martinson's (1974) article and the related discussion about 'nothing works' had an impact, but studies were also undertaken in Sweden. Three comprehensive studies came to influence the discussion: a follow-up of the probation reform, an experimental study and a proposal for a new penal system. In the first of these, the criminologist Ulla Bondeson (1977) presented a systematic analysis of the practice of implementing community punishments following up the probation reform. Bondeson's study showed in all aspects that the legislator's intentions were not implemented in practice. Her principal conclusion was that probation and parole had not fulfilled their aims in giving treatment. On the contrary, they had moved prison to the neighbourhood of the offenders. She revealed vague and varied practice. Further, she showed that judges had a varied practice in sentencing, because the legal framework was vague.

In the same year, 1977, The Swedish National Council for Crime Prevention presented a suggestion for a new penal system (BRÅ 1977). Here they criticised the penal system for not being as humane and not as focussed on treatment as was suggested in the penal policy behind the legislation. The critics focussed on insufficient predictability, low proportionality between crime and punishment and false ideas about the causes of criminality, as well as on the fact that the results were not as expected. All these criticisms were applied to community punishment.

In addition, an experimental study was conducted as a comparison between probation services with similar groups of offenders (Kühlhorn 1972; Kühlhorn et al. 1979). This experiment started as a test of whether allocating more resources to the probation service would produce lower rates of reconviction. In the experimental group the offenders were categorized according to level of risk of reoffending. The higher the risk, the more contact they should have with the supervisor. Extra resources were given to the experimental service, while a normal distribution of resources was given to the control service. The results of this study showed that the reconviction rates were *higher* for the group that were supervised in the probation service, with more resources than for the control group. The resources were shown to stay within the services; they did not lead to more resources for the clients, but for more differentiated office work. The conclusion drawn from this was that the probation service was in a crisis; it lacked both content and identity (*Kriminalvården* no 1/1978).

In 1980 a new Social Service Act was enacted. It was an Act that gathered together all social services. It had been prepared over a long time and carried in it all the ideologies of the welfare state. Discussions about including the probation service alongside other social services were held during the late 1970s and early 1980s. In the end the idea was rejected, as it was said that the social services were not suited for implementing punishment in the community, because they were even less structured and controlling than the probation service (SOU 1981: 90). This marks a point where the development of the treatment ideology in the welfare state's legal system came to an end and the distinction between the social services and the probation service was clarified.

The criminologist Nils Christie (1982) has explained the defeat of the treatment ideology by pointing to the fact that it became explicit that community punishment was more punishment than treatment, despite the discourse of rehabilitation. The treatments used did not work, so the reconviction rates did not decrease. Another part of the explanation was that the labour movement reacted to the under-provision of treatment to the poor, as it was their constituency that was adversely affected. The dominant ideology became more directly punitive, but still it was held that punishment should give room for treatment. There was a subtle change in nuances, with the combination of support and control remaining.

The punitive turn

In the early 1980s the prisons were full, but still there were public and political demands for more severe punishments. The number of reported crimes had risen since the mid-1940s and the treatment ideology did not show the expected results. The neoclassical penology returned and a more simplified, predictable punitive system was demanded by the government (SOU 1981: 90). Until 1983, all parolees had been put under supervision. When a decision was taken to introduce early release after serving half of the prison sentence, it brought with it the need for a discretionary decision by the probation service. They should decide whether the parolee should be supervised, on the basis of need of support for reintegration. The ideas behind the reform were to decrease the prison population, but also to enhance the probation service. Through a more effective probation service, short prison sentences could be avoided and community punishment could regain credibility in the public eye and be a 'real' alternative to imprisonment, that is, a more explicit punishment in the community.

In 1977 rules and guidelines for the probation service had been implemented (Frivårdsförordningen 1977), despite protests from the probation workers. They integrated work with probationers and parolees and were built on known practice. Some structured measures were added, such as that the probation officer should visit the offenders' homes within the first month of supervision and that a plan for the treatment should be made and documented. This was argued to be a question of efficiency in the penal system, not as a measure for the offender's rehabilitation. After that, education of probation officers in management, methods and law grew within the Prison and Probation Service. The idea was to make the distinction between the social services and punishment in the community more explicit, also in practice (*Kriminalvården* no 5/1985). One aspect in this distinction was the focus on 'the dangerous offender'; a discussion in society that affected practice in the probation services and led to more closed and secured offices as well as to a more distant relationship between supervisor and supervisee.

In the late 1980s, several new sanctions were implemented, but still mainly as different versions of probation. The first to come was 'contract treatment' from 1988. This was formally a sentence to probation combined with a strict instruction in the form of a contract, where the offender should undergo treatment in a form that was specified before the sentence was given. The treatment should correlate to the causes of the crime committed, which in practice mainly meant treatment for substance abuse for offenders who committed a drug- or alcohol-related crime. The innovation with this sanction was that it was not only specified, it also included an explicit definition of the prison sentence it was replacing. For the first time, a community punishment was to be combined with the court's decision of a fixed prison sentence. In the sentences it was written thus: 'If prison had been chosen, a prison term of X months would have been the sentence'.

This new sanction came at a time of major changes in the penal system. In 1989 the fundamental idea in the Criminal Code was altered. Before, sanctions had been based on the two aspects of general prevention (deterrence) and individual prevention (treatment). From now on, the sanctions were to be built on the basis of the severity of the crime. Focus shifted from the offender to the crime. One immediate consequence was that the use of narcotics became criminalised. Using drugs had been regarded as a symptom of social problems; now it was to be seen as an individual failure and a crime.

In a few years at the end of the 1980s, 25 per cent of probation officers left their jobs. Most of them argued that it was a question of low salary, but more than half of them argued that the room for discretionary social work had diminished (Svensson 2001). As a reaction to the flight of staff, the Prison and Probation Service argued for a more explicit probation service and a reorganisation. With the new organisation came new titles. The probation officers that used to be 'protective consultants' and 'treatment assistants' came in 1991 to be 'probation managers' and 'probation inspectors'. The change in title manifested the shifting focus from protection, treatment and support to a more managerial probation service with control and structure in focus. As Foucault (1982) has put it, this is a discontinuity that forms a new field. It is something new, but it is built on the legacy from its predecessor, and thereby the patterns are reproduced also in the new field.

A new probation service and new sanctions and measures

Crime and punishment were high on the agenda in the election for the Swedish government in 1991. It was one of the main issues that the conservative party campaigned on. Their posters were dominated by phrases such as 'They should be locked up, so you can be outside'. After winning the election, the conservative government took several initiatives in the field of criminal policy. The focus on offenders' rehabilitation was more or less replaced by caring for victims in the public debate.

In 1994, the Swedish Crime Victim Compensation and Support Authority was formed. The construction of funding for this organisation was an innovation, as it also holds a Crime Victim Fund. This fund is mainly built up through fees paid by convicted offenders and used for funding organisations and activities for victim protection and support, as well as for research in this area. Every offender convicted for a crime that could result in a prison sentence has to pay 800 SEK (equivalent to approximately 80 euros), which generates around 50 million SEK to the fund every year. This fee is not damages and not a fine, but it is an additional part of the sentence.

The next new sanction to be ratified was community service. It started as a trial in four cities in 1990, was extended to a national trial in 1994 and implemented permanently in the legislation in 1999 (Regeringens proposition 1997/98). Community service was constituted in the same way as contract treatment; that is, it is a sentence to probation with a strict instruction, herein the form of a certain amount of hours for community service. This was to be combined with the court's decision of a fixed prison sentence. The offender did not have to sign a contract, but had to consent to be sentenced to community service.

Community service means to be sentenced to work. During the strong welfare state, work had been regarded as a *right*, and therefore work could not be imposed as a punishment. Through community service, however, work returned as a punishment. Community service has, ever since its first implementation, been regarded positively in Sweden. The idea of working serves both the ideas of reintegration through work and of payback to society through work.

The third innovation in the development of community punishment was electronic monitoring, which became possible in 1994 as a trial in some regions, from 1996 as a nationwide trial and was made permanent from 1999 (Regeringens proposition 1997/98). Whilst the first two, contract treatment and community service, had been specified as alternatives to imprisonment in sentencing, electronic monitoring was constructed as a way of serving a prison sentence. Thereby, the court had to assess the severity of the crime and consider the offender's history and present situation, and after that decide whether any alternative to imprisonment could be used. If not, the sentence should be prison and, before referral to a specific prison, the probation service should investigate whether the prison sentence could be served at home under electronic monitoring. This way, electronic monitoring became a discretionary decision by the probation service, not a sentence by the court. The probation service also had to fulfil the implementation of electronic monitoring, which made it the central agency for electronic monitoring even if it was a way of serving a prison sentence. Later, electronic monitoring was expanded to replace a sentence of up to one year of prison, and a 'back door' system also developed, with electronic monitoring as a part of early release from prison.

These three novelties in the penal system conspired to alter the status of community punishment, as they emphasized the punitive and controlling aspects over the supportive aspects that for a long time had dominated the discourse. Community service and electronic monitoring were introduced as common sanctions at the same time that early release from prison was changed (from being given after half of the sentence served to two-thirds) (Regeringens proposition 1997/98). However, the main activity and the core ingredient in community punishment remained supervision, which was still a vague practice as there were very few rules or guidelines.

In the mid-1990s the ideas of programmes and evidence-based practice reached Sweden. Now, as at the inception of probation, the new ideas came from the west. In 1995 a group within the Prison and Probation Service central administration started to work towards implementation of ideas from 'What Works' research. In 1996 a national event was held for presenting structured programmes in prison and probation. At this time, it was a really wide variety of activities that was presented in the name of 'programmes'. In some cases they were imported programmes, mainly from Canada (with cognitive skills programmes the most dominant). In other cases, the reference was to more traditional activities, mainly in prisons, which were named 'programmes', but without scientific support. In 1999 a national group for coordinating programmes was put to work and in 2002 a committee for accreditation of programmes was established (Lardén 2014). From this point the idea of programmes that were, or could be, evaluated and evidence based has been a central aspect of practice in both prisons and in the community. While incarceration is the most obvious part of a prison sentence, programmes and their specific strict instructions also restructured community punishments.

Through these measures, community punishment was reformed into a model similar to what Jonathan Simon (1993) called the 'managerial' model of parole in California: that is, a way of working where administration of sanctions and of offenders dominates over working with the offenders. The managerial aspects came into the Swedish probation service through an emphasis on documentation, structure and results. Furthermore, in the early 2000s the concept of risk came to dominate the discourse and practice of offender assessments. Nevertheless, the introduction of ideas of structure, results and even of documentation has been assessed by some as a new form of treatment ideology (Kyvsgaard 2006). However, in contrast to the former treatment ideology with its roots in humanism and philanthropy, contemporary treatment ideology has scientific and managerial overtones. In practice, the tradition from the 'old' treatment ideology is still strong among probation officers, but in all central guidelines for the practice the main issues are risk and risk assessment. There is thereby a gap between what the probation service is supposed to do and what it is actually doing (see Persson and Svensson 2012).

Continuity and change

In the twenty-first century we have not yet seen any significant changes in the development of community punishment in Sweden. As always, there are ongoing changes in the organisation of the Prison and Probation Service. The managerialisation of the work through changes in assessments, documentation and bureaucracy, as well as structured methods of practice, are continuously developing. There are also different ways in which scientific advisors influence practices (for example, via accreditation processes). These scientific advisors, with their everyday practice in universities and only loose connections to the Prison and Probation Service, are also involved in the process of implementing and evaluating the practice. However, there have not been any significant legal changes in the sanctions themselves.

There is almost no debate about criminal policy in the twenty-first century: when crime is discussed it is almost exclusively about the security of abused women and children rather than about reactions to offending. The cases that have caused discussion about punishments have been directly related to dramatic incidents related to security issues in prisons. No debate has been held about community punishment and almost none about the penal system.

In 2012 a committee presented a proposal for changes in the Penal Code (SOU 2012: 34). The proposal took as its starting point a critique of the existing system. They pointed at problems with a complex variety of alternatives to imprisonment. Although the Penal Code until now has only had two punishments (fines and imprisonment), the most commonly used sanctions (after fines, community punishments) are not specified in the Penal Code, but rather are left at the courts' and judges' discretion. Court practice is thereby not predictable, the committee said. The alternatives to imprisonment do not, in most cases, express the severity of the crime through a pronounced term of imprisonment. Expressing the custodial sentence that is being suspended conditionally is only valid for contract treatment and community service. The committee therefore argued for a reform where the community punishments were imposed as independent sanctions, not as alternatives to imprisonment, and in which the severity of the crime should be more explicitly reflected in the sanction. The committee argued that probation should be removed and replaced by a 'conditional prison sentence' that could be combined with a variety of measures graded in a scale in relation to the severity of the crime and conviction. Thereby, the different sanctions would be standalone sanctions and not explicit 'alternatives'. They also argued that more resources should be given to the probation service for enhancing the content of conditional prison sentences.

On the one hand, these proposals reflect the trend towards focusing more on crime and punishment than on the offender and causes of crime. On the other hand, if the proposals were to be accepted, the distance travelled away from the ideologies of the welfare state would be made even more explicit. But 2 years have passed since these proposals were made and no initiative has been taken for implementation.

More generally, a managerial trend influenced by new public management dominates the public sector in Sweden. Privatisation has been a strong influence on many human public service organisations. Schools, medical care, child care, care of the elderly and employment agencies, all important parts of the welfare state, have been privatised in the twenty-first century. For criminal justice, until now, there have been only a few small areas where private agencies have operated. There are some private security companies taking care of checking offenders on electronic monitoring or community service, but, so far, implementing punishment has remained a task for state agencies.

Since the early 1990s there has been a slight decrease in reported crimes. During the last 10 years (up to 2014), the number of prisoners has decreased by 15 per cent, the number of offenders on electronic monitoring has decreased by a third and the number of parolees under supervision has fallen by 23 per cent. At the same time, the number of offenders under probation has increased slightly. Between 2004 and 2009, they increased by 15 per cent but, since then, numbers have decreased, so that the number of probationers in 2013 was just 2 per cent higher than in 2004. In total there have been, during the last 10 years, around 12,000 persons under supervision every year in Sweden, of which 12 per cent are women. If we add offenders being monitored electronically, the number is 14,000 persons serving community punishments, a rate of 145 per 100,000. That is double, or slightly more than double, the prison rate for Sweden (Kriminalvården 2014).

A survey of judges in 2009 showed that they demanded *both* more rehabilitation and more control in the probation service. They asked for more explicit content/requirements (including programmes) in community punishments, but were also positive about longer periods of supervision in cases where offenders needed more support (BRÅ 2010). We can see therefore that there are still remains of the treatment ideology in the minds of Swedish judges, even if their demand for more explicit measures reflects contemporary managerialisation.

Conclusion

In the long history of community punishment in Sweden, we can see both continuity and change. For a long time there was a close connection between agencies for the social services and community sanctions. In the punitive turn in the 1990s, criminal justice agencies separated themselves from the social services, but, later on, social services were themselves inspired by methods and ideas from the Prison and Probation Service. The idea of working with structured programmes came to the Prison and Probation Service in the mid-1990s. Some years thereafter the same ideas were implemented in the social services. Legislation governing social services introduced more strict regulation in 2001, and today the same tools and models are being used by both agencies. It is not only the probation service that has developed towards more structure and more punitivity; we can see the same trend in all kinds of human service organisations. The welfare state understanding of the idea of a caring power relationship between the professional and the client is in many ways replaced by a managerial understanding of the relationship where the client is more of an object for interventions than a subject in a partnership for change.

Sweden has a history of a strong welfare state, which was built from a poor rural country with huge emigration into a strong industrial society. Now, in the post-industrial, global era, there are still some ideological remains of the welfare state; but in most aspects, Sweden is a part of a global trend and lacks a stable state. Throughout its history in Sweden, community punishment has been regarded as punishment, but as a punishment with an aim to integrate. Nowadays, it is still regarded as punishment, but it is not so evident that the aim is still to integrate. Punishment in the community is on the one hand a central part of the criminal justice system in Sweden, on the other hand an unknown and undebated part. The main elements, supervision of offenders by professionals and volunteers, have remained; but the characteristics of the implementation of the sentence have changed as the focus in criminal policy has changed from the offender towards the offence. There are still explicit ideas about treatment, but now treatment is to be arranged in more structured programmes and managed in a more transparent way. In the early days, when the ideas of punishment in the community started to be developed in Sweden, it was related to poor relief and educating the poor. Today, poor relief, or the social services, are witnessing the same development as the criminal justice system. The individual is held responsible for his or her actions, and the help provided is pre-packed in fixed programmes where the individuals have to adjust to the given schemes rather than the other way around. Even if there has been change, the legitimacy of punishment in the community has rarely been questioned, although it is also true that it is rarely explicitly endorsed; rather, it is taken for granted as part of the criminal justice landscape in Sweden.

Note

1. Those who had been sentenced to loss of civil rights were not allowed to vote, to give witness or to be employed in public service during a period set in the sentence.

References

Betänkande med förslag till organisation av det frivilliga skydds- och hjälparbetet beträffande frigivna fångar. (1933) [*Report with a proposal for the organization of the voluntary protection and assistance work on released prisoners.*] Stockholm: Nord. bokh. i distr.

Bondeson, Ulla (1977) *Kriminalvård i frihet. Intentioner och verklighet* [*Alternatives to Imprisonment. Intentions and Reality*]. Stockholm: Liber.

Bondeson, Ulla (2005) 'Perceptions of Criminal Justice Policy in Scandinavia', in Bondeson, U. (ed.) *Crime and Justice in Scandinavia.* Copenhagen: Forlaget Thomson, pp. 427–44.

BRÅ (1977) *Nytt straffsystem: idéer och förslag.* [*A new penal system: ideas and suggestions*]. Brottsförebyggande rådet. Arbetsgruppen rörande kriminalpolitik. Stockholm: LiberFörlag/Allmänna förlaget.

BRÅ (2010) *Frivården i Sverige. En kartläggning* [*Probation Service in Sweden. A mapping.*] Stockholm: Brottsförebyggande rådet.

Christie, Nils (1982) *Limits to Pain.* Oxford: Robertson.

CSA (1906) 'Tjänstemannasystem och vårdaresystem i svenska städers fattigvård'. [Public administration and carers in poor relief in Swedish cities] in Centralförbundets för socialt arbete, Fattigvårdskommittén, *Fattigvård och folkförsäkring*, no. 5. Stockholm: Ekmans.

Eriksson, Torsten (1995) *Kriminalvård. Idéer och experiment. Kriminologisk handbok.* [*Criminal Justice. Ideas and Experiments. Criminological handbook.*] Norrköping: KVS Förlag.

Fångvårdsstyrelsen (1949) *Kriminalvård i frihet: Fångvårdsstyrelsens utredning angående skyddsarbetets organisation m. m.* (1949) [Punishment in the community. The prison authority's investigation of the organization of probation work] Stockholm.

Foucault, Michel (1979) *Discipline and Punish: The birth of the prison.* Harmondsworth: Penguin.

Foucault, Michel (1982) *The Archaeology of Knowledge and the Discourse on Language.* 1. Pantheon paperback edn. New York: Pantheon.

Frivårdsförordningen [Probation regulations] SFS 1977:329.

Kriminalvården no 1 1978 [An internal publication for prison and probation staff].

Kriminalvården no 5 1985 [An internal publication for prison and probation staff].

Kriminalvården (2014) 'Statistik och fakta' ['Statistics and facts for the Prison and Probation Services']. Available: www.kriminalvarden.se/forskning-och-statistik/statistik-och-fakta.

Kühlhorn, Eckart (1972) *Frivårdsförsöket i Sundsvall.* [*The probation experiment in Sundsvall*]. Rapport från projektet Frivårdsförstärkning. Stockholm.

Kühlhorn, Eckart, Johansson, Leif and Lundberg, Inga-Lill (1979) *Frivård och rehabilitering* [*Probation and Rehabilitation*]. BRÅ-rapport n1979:3. Stockholm: Liber.

Kyvsgaard, Britta (ed.) (2006) *Hvad virker – hvad virker ikke? kundskabsbaseret kriminalpolitik og praksis. [What Works – What Doesn't? Knowledge-based criminal policy and practice.]* Kbh.: Jurist – og Økonomforbundets Forlag.

Lardén, Martin (2014) *Utvärdering av Kriminalvårdens Behandlingsprogram.* Norrköping: Kriminalvården.

Lundkvist, Lennart (1997) *Fattigvårdsfolket. Ett nätverk i den sociala frågan 1900–1920.* [*The Poor Relief People. A Network in Social Issues 1900–1920*] Lund: Studentlitteratur.

Martinson, Robert (1974) 'What works? Questions and answers about prison reform', *The Public Interest*, Spring, pp. 22–54.

Melossi, Dario and Pavarini, Massimo (1981) *The Prison and the Factory.* Totowa: Barnes & Noble.

Österberg, Eva (1996) 'Våld och ära, böter och skam [*Violence and Honour, Fine and Shame*]. Kriminalitet och straff i Sverige från medeltid till nutid', in Åkerström, M. (ed.), *Kriminalitet, Kultur, Kontroll.* Stockholm: Carlssons.

Persson, Anders and Svensson, Kerstin (2012) 'Shades of professionalism: Risk assessment in pre-sentence reports in Sweden', *European Journal of Criminology*, March, 9: 176–90.

Pratt, John and Eriksson, Anna (2012) 'In defence of Scandinavian exceptionalism', in Ugelvik, T. and Dullum, J. (eds) *Penal Exceptionalism? Nordic Prison Policy and Practice.* London and New York: Routledge, pp. 235–60.

Regeringens proposition 1997/98:96: vissa reformer av påföljdssystemet. [*Governmental proposition 1997/98:96: some reforms of the criminal sanctions.*] (1998) Stockholm.

Rusche, Georg and Kirschheimer, Otto (1939) *Punishment and Social Structure.* New York: Russell and Russell.

Rydin, Artur (1901) *Om villkorlig dom.* [*On Conditional Sentence.*] Verdandis småskrifter 102. Stockholm: Albert Bonnier förlag.

Sakkunniga (1917) *Förslag till lag angående villkorlig straffdom och lag om ändrad lydelse av 1, 6, 7 och 8 §§ i lagen den 22 juni 1906 angående villkorlig frigivning m.m. [Proposal for legislation on conditional sentence and changes in paragraphs 1, 6, 7 and 8 in law June 22 1906 on conditional release*]. Sakkunniga av vissa till strafflagstiftningen hörande frågor.

Schillander-Lundgren *et al.* (1991) *50 år med frivården* [*50 years with the Probation Service*]. Norrköping: KVS Förlag.

Simon, Jonathan (1993) *Poor Discipline. Parole and the Social Control of the Underclass, 1890–1990.* Chicago and London: University of Chicago Press.

Skånska Dagbladet 28 July 1944 [Local newspaper].

Snare, Annika (1992) *Work, War, Prison and Welfare. Control of the laboring poor in Sweden.* Kriminalistisk Instituts skriftserie no 4. Copenhagen: Department of Criminology.

SOU 1981:90 *Frivårdspåföljder* [*Alternatives to Imprisonment*]. Statens Offentliga Utredningar.

SOU 2012:34 *Påföljdsutredningen.* [*Criminal Sanctions Inquiry*]. Statens Offentliga Utredningar. Available summary in English: www.regeringen.se/content/1/c6/19/40/93/929ae311.pdf.

Strahl, Ivar (1944) *Villkorlig dom och villkorlig frigivning samt det därtill knutna skyddsarbetet.* [*Conditional Sentence and Conditional Release and the Connected Care Work*]. Stockholm: P. A. Norstedt & Söner.

Stjernberg, Nils (1905) *Den nya svenska strafflagstiftningen angående minderåriga förbrytare, tillika ett bidrag till spörsmålen angående villkorlig straffskyldighet.* [*The New Swedish Penal Code for Youth Offenders, and a Contribution to the Questions on Conditional Punishments*]. Stockholm: Almqvist & Wiksell.

Svensson, K. (2001) '*I stället för fängelse?: en studie av vårdande makt, straff och socialt arbete i frivård*' [Alternatives to imprisonment? A study of caring power, punishment and social work in supervision of offenders], Dissertation. Lund: Lund University. Available, with summary in English, at: http://lup.lub.lu.se/luur/download?func=downloadFile& recordOId=20358&fileOId=791410.

von Hofer, Hanns (2011) *Brott och straff i Sverige. Historisk kriminalstatistik 1750–2010.* [*Crime and Punishment in Sweden. Historic criminal statistics 1750–2010*]. Diagram, tabeller och kommentarer. Stockholm: Stockholm University, Department of Criminology.

Wieselgren, Sigfrid (1895) *Sveriges fängelser och fångvård från äldre tider till våra dagar. Ett bidrag till svensk kulturhistoria.* [*Sweden's Prisons and Prison Care from Older Days to Our Days. A contribution to Swedish cultural history.*] Stockholm: Norstedts.

13

CONCLUSION

Community punishment and the penal state

Fergus McNeill and Gwen Robinson

Introduction

As we noted in the Introduction, this book is the second to be produced by members of the COST Action on *Offender Supervision in Europe* (see: www.offendersupervision.eu). Our first collection (McNeill and Beyens 2013) made the case for studying 'mass supervision' (see also McNeill 2013; Phelps 2013) and for studying it comparatively (Beyens and McNeill 2013). It also provided an overview of existing European research on how supervision is experienced, practised and governed, and on associated decision-making processes.

The concluding chapter of that first volume (Beyens and McNeill 2013) was one of two embarkation points for the European tour that this collection presents. The second was a book chapter by Robinson *et al.* (2013) that explored the various adaptations through which community punishment (or more specifically probation as a penal institution) has survived the harsh penal climate of late modernity; that chapter's analysis was based mainly on developments in the UK and the USA. These two chapters provided the conceptual and methodological foundations for this volume.

Beyens and McNeill's (2013) examination of why, how and through (or with) whom we might best study supervision comparatively informed our central approach, which was to collaborate with a number of scholars that we knew we could trust as guides to their jurisdictions. As Beyens and McNeill (2013) noted in their chapter – and as we noted in our Introduction – there is no such thing as an impartial guide; the picture that one gets of the place (or topic) is bound to be coloured by the guide's interests and perspectives, but this is hardly a problem that is confined to comparative research on supervision, indeed, it is one of the central challenges of all social research.

Partly to address that challenge – and partly to give our collaboration and our comparative analysis some structure and focus – we looked to the chapter by

Robinson *et al.* (2013) to set out our conceptual framework. As well as inviting our contributors to read that chapter, we set them a number of questions derived from it: questions about the development of, adaptation of and prospects for community punishment (see Appendix 1). Centrally, we sought to understand and to compare how institutions of community punishment (through which offender supervision is delivered) in different European jurisdictions have been legitimated throughout the process of their evolution in each place. More specifically, we asked whether the four legitimising narratives that Robinson *et al.* (2013) identified as being key to probation's adaptation in Anglophone jurisdictions – punitive, managerial, rehabilitative and reparative – recurred in the European jurisdictions in question.

This book therefore tackles one of the core challenges facing the COST Action on *Offender Supervision in Europe*, one that was somewhat lost in the first volume's focus on specific aspects of supervision. That challenge was and remains to examine how supervision is shaped by its social, economic, political, cultural, legal and organisational contexts. As Beyens and McNeill (2013) make clear, this is important not just to make sense of these institutions as they exist today for the purposes of critique; it is also important to the project of reimagining them for the purposes of reform.

In this concluding chapter, we summarise what we have learned from our erstwhile guides, beginning by examining *how* our contributors took on the challenges we set, before returning to the controversy around the book's title, *Community Punishment: European Perspectives*. We go on to examine the extent to which the four narratives recurred and made sense in the jurisdictions in question, before concluding with a discussion of community punishment both as a barometer of the penal climate and as an institution of 'the penal state' (Garland 2013).

Approaching community punishment

We have already noted above (and in our Introduction) the question of the partiality of our guides (see Portelli 2006); necessarily, they can only paint their pictures from the positions they occupy – and their perspectives will affect the pictures they present. However, readers may have noted that they have also painted with somewhat different materials and in different styles. There are two main reasons for this; one of them more pragmatic and one perhaps more principled. We were struck that some guides had very little existing material to work with (e.g. Durnescu), either in the way of reliable official data about supervision or in the way of previous empirical research and scholarship. Indeed, some authors undertook new research or drew on ongoing projects to support the development of their arguments (e.g. Blay and Larrauri, Carr). Others suffered an embarrassment of riches (e.g. Robinson). In the former case, it was a much more challenging task to offer the sort of analysis that we sought, since it fell to the contributor to sketch that analysis more or less from scratch; in the latter case, the contributor had the luxury (and the challenge) of synthesising a number of existing studies and sources, examined anew in light of the questions we set.

The second, perhaps more principled, reason for these different choices of material reflects the disciplinary positions of the contributors. Some have been trained principally to analyse and make use of legal materials and so provide considerable detail on the evolution of the law as it pertains to community punishment (e.g. Blay and Larrauri, Herzog-Evans, Morgenstern). For lawyers and socio-legal scholars, the law is perhaps seen as a primary source and product of processes of legitimation, and as the framework around which institutions and practices are constructed.[1] Others lay particular emphasis on and devote considerable attention to the historical background of community punishment and thus to the enduring legacy of its conditions of emergence (e.g. Healy, Svensson); analysis and reanalysis of the past, after all, often provides the discursive resources to construct and reconstruct the present. Yet others lay stress on the contestation of legitimacy most clearly evidenced (at least in democratic states) in policy, practice and media discourses (e.g. Boone, Beyens, Robinson). In some chapters, this contestation is seen in the context of wider and more fundamental or political–constitutional struggles over the characters of states in transition (e.g. Carr, Healy, McNeill); sometimes these transitions and their penal effects can only be understood in transnational context (e.g. Durnescu).

As editors, we are not in the least troubled by this diversity. Indeed, we think that the overall effect is extremely illuminating. Each of the chapters has its own strong character; certainly they all paint fascinating pictures with the materials they found or selected. The fact that they also reveal a little about their authors is no bad thing if it permits the reader to take some account of the issues of partiality and perspective we have discussed above. Moreover, the similarities and differences in approach between our contributors may have as much to teach us as the similarities and differences in their conclusions. In this respect, each author's approach poses intriguing questions for their colleagues. To pick on our own contributions, for example: what might Robinson's chapter have looked like if it had followed Herzog-Evans's or Morgenstern's example and placed more emphasis on the evolution of the law of community punishment as opposed to its policy and practice discourses? And what might McNeill's chapter have looked like if it had started, like Svensson's, with a clearer account of the historical relationships between punishment and welfare in Scotland, or if, like Durnescu's, it paid more attention to transnational influences on states in transition?

As a collection therefore, this book's chapters illustrate the range of possibilities for further developing our individual analyses of community punishment in our own jurisdictions. For any one of us to offer a *comprehensive* analysis of how supervision has been shaped by its social, economic, political, cultural, legal and organisational contexts would have required a book rather than a chapter. In any case, comprehensiveness was not the challenge that we set as editors. But nonetheless, the book as a whole succeeds in illustrating the many different aspects that such an analysis might be required to address, and the range of materials that it might need to employ.

Questioning 'community punishment'

> [W]e face not only the inter-language challenges of European comparative work but also the intriguing task of finding out how seemingly similar ideas and practices are named, formed and framed in different contexts. To make it even more complex, these ideas and concepts are not necessarily fixed or stable; they change within each jurisdiction over time.
>
> *(Beyens and McNeill 2013: 164)*

In our field, as in many others, language is both powerful and problematic – and not just because of the challenges of translation (see Herzog-Evans 2011). Both editors and contributors faced the challenges posed by the lack of a common language to describe the neglected penal sub-field that we put at the heart of our analyses (see Robinson in press). We noted at the outset that using the term 'community punishment' in the title of this book was contentious – and even a little provocative. Indeed, we asked all of our contributors to reflect upon it in their chapters and, as we hoped, these reflections proved to be interesting.

Although some of our contributors were relatively content with using this term (Beyens, Morgenstern), others suggested that 'punishment' is a word rarely used by those who practise offender supervision in the community. It seems especially problematic for those in jurisdictions where supervision is or has been strongly associated with social work (e.g. Scotland, Republic of Ireland), even if the term has latterly come to be accepted in some of those places (e.g. Sweden). But the term 'punishment' is also problematic – and technically inaccurate – in jurisdictions where supervision is part of a conditional *suspension* of punishment (such as the original probation order in England and Wales) and/or where it is defined as a modality of the *implementation or execution* of punishment rather than being a punishment *per se*. In the case of suspended punishment, supervision aims to avoid the harms that punishment creates; in the case of supervision as a modality of the implementation of punishment, supervision aims to minimise these harms and to support reintegration after punishment (see Morgenstern).

Of course, as some contributors point out in their chapters (Beyens, McNeill), whatever practitioners think about what they are doing, and whatever the legal status of it, in one sense the final arbiters of the appropriateness of the term 'punishment' might be people under supervision themselves; and there are relatively few studies of their views (see Durnescu *et al.* 2013).

We were perhaps a little more surprised to find that the term 'community' was also controversial, particularly for Herzog-Evans, who explains that in France the term 'community' typically connotes that which divides or separates citizens of the French state; as such, its use violates the very principles of fraternity and unity which are often implied in its English usage. But even in its English usage, the term 'community' posed challenges for Carr, writing about and from a jurisdiction where relationships between the (British) state and the (Northern Irish) communities to which it relates have a fraught, complex and dangerous past and present – and where these conflicted relationships have required unique and intriguing responses from probation practitioners.

The more neutral German term translated as 'ambulant' is an interesting and much less ideologically loaded alternative (see Morgenstern). Rather than speaking of the locus of the sanction or measure, it speaks to its characteristic mobility (in implicit contrast to the fixity of the prison). And indeed, albeit in a disquieting way, 'ambulant' might turn out to be a strangely fitting term in those jurisdictions where electronic monitoring (EM) is emerging in forms that stress penal supervision divorced from rehabilitative support (see Beyens). The somewhat dystopian notion of 'ambulant punishment' or even the 'ambulant prison' (moving with and adapted to the 'free' prisoner) seems not so remote in this context; certainly there is little about such forms of EM that would define then as *community* punishments (using the term 'community' in its positive sense).

But perhaps Herzog-Evans' rebuke for her monolingual and Anglophone editors has wider import. It demands that anyone who wishes to use the term 'community' in the context of institutions and practices of offender supervision should specify more clearly what they mean to imply about the role of community as a locus for supervision and/or as an actor in supervision (Bottoms 2008; Worrall and Hoy 2005). Ultimately, perhaps the simple conclusion we can draw is that 'community punishment' is certainly not a term that 'works' unproblematically across time and space.

Legitimisation and adaptation: The four narratives

We asked our contributors to analyse the development of, adaptation of and prospects for community punishment in their jurisdictions. Having read and re-read all of the chapters in this collection, an obvious question we might ask is whether the jurisdictions in question share much in common. Although our initial response might be negative, on closer examination it seems that we need to break down that question more carefully into its constituent parts.

Certainly, it seems possible to conclude that community punishment in most of these jurisdictions may have had somewhat more in common at its points of origin than subsequently. Or perhaps we can more accurately say that the original impulses to create institutions of community punishment seem similar in many places. Though perhaps to varying degrees, almost all jurisdictions tells a similar story about *fin de siècle* unease concerning the human and social costs of imprisonment (see McNeill and Dawson 2014). But almost as soon as the institutions of community punishment began to develop, their evolution took different forms. Indeed, the metaphor of evolution is apposite here, since it seems that the species of community punishment that emerge are necessarily specifically adapted to their peculiar conditions.

Thus, for example, the legal architecture used to provide and promote community punishments clearly varied in important ways between jurisdictions with common law and codified legal traditions. The legal status of community punishment tends to be broadly similar within each of these traditions, though somewhat different between them. In common law systems, probation initially emerges as a court order imposed *instead of a sentence*, while in codified legal systems it emerges within the framework of *conditionally suspended sentences* of imprisonment. That said, supervision emerges in different forms and at different times in different places, especially *within* the codified legal tradition; it also changes over time *within* jurisdictions in both traditions. Indeed, supervision in the context of suspended sentences of imprisonment (as opposed to unsupervised suspended sentences) is still relatively new in some continental countries (see also Van Zyl Smit *et al.* 2015). Moreover, in both types of jurisdictions, different forms of community punishments have emerged as 'autonomous' sanctions or penalties imposed neither 'instead of' a prison sentence nor linked in any way to a suspension of sentence (see Beyens and Robinson for two quite different examples). There is then some evidence of convergence around the development of *autonomous* supervised sanctions. More generally, changes in the legal architecture of supervision often seem to emerge, even in quite different systems, as a way of 'toughening up' supervision. These legal reforms are often associated with rebranding supervision in an effort to boost judicial and public confidence. As such, this legal trend (if it amounts to a trend) can be linked to the '*punitive*' adaptation referred to by Robinson *et al.* (2013), even if it is linked to reductionist aspirations in some jurisdictions (see, for example, McNeill).

But redesigning the legal architecture of supervision might also be interpreted as a '*managerialist*' adaptation, since it is often a technical or a systemic fix to the political problems associated with growing prison populations and their fiscal and social costs. In part these changes seem to be about inventing and pulling new levers to channel 'flows' from one penal tributary to another. For civil servants charged with finding ways to reduce the financial costs of imprisonment without suffering the political costs of appearing 'soft on crime', these kinds of systemic fixes have an obvious appeal. We might conclude that, although the extent and nature of the cultural and political pressures associated with 'populist punitiveness' (Bottoms 1995) may differ in the jurisdictions in question, the search for systemic fixes to prison growth is common to most if not all of them.

For that reason, it is perhaps not surprising that, since the inception of community punishment, policy transfer has played an important role in diffusing innovation, thus creating some commonalities between jurisdictions. In this respect, as scholars we might have expected to receive numerous accounts of the importance of a compelling 'scientific' basis for penal innovation. But, in fact, the familiar stories of 'Nothing Works' and of 'What Works?' (see Raynor and Robinson 2009) are minor sub-plots of this book, largely confined to the UK jurisdictions, the Netherlands and Sweden; and even there their impact is variable and their importance is questionable. Our comparative method perhaps helps us to explain this. Research evidence about the effectiveness of rehabilitative interventions only finds an interested *political* and policy audience in jurisdictions where rehabilitation is understood in a particular way; that is, more as a process and outcome of intervention than as a legal right of the punished (see Morgenstern on 'resocialisation'). And even in such jurisdictions, it only finds influence where rehabilitation remains an important justifying aim of punishment. Hence, in most of the codified legal jurisdictions, the evidence base about *rehabilitation as correction* is often braided with (and even subordinate to) legal principles and arguments about *rehabilitation as a right*. That said, there are some signs that the more correctional form of rehabilitation is becoming more significant in some continental jurisdictions (see Blay and Larrauri).

Overall, it seems that although the most significant and best-travelled penal innovations may have boasted associated scientific support, their successes have perhaps owed more to their political appeal, to their cultural and systemic 'fit', and to their potential systems' effects (in reducing imprisonment) rather than to scientific evidence about 'what works?' (to reduce reoffending). The development of community service is perhaps the most obvious and important example, although the more recent emergence and expansion of EM may turn out to be more important and more consequential (Nellis *et al.* 2013).

These two innovations are interesting in different ways. Again recalling the four narratives of Robinson *et al.* (2013), we might conclude that, despite the success of community service (at least in terms of its spread and uptake, leaving aside the question of its effects), this collection provides precious little evidence that the '*reparative*' narrative has been important in the legitimation of community punishment, except perhaps in the Republic of Ireland and in Scotland – and even there only in the last few years (see McNeill).

The more recent increases in the use of EM across *and* within many of the jurisdictions discussed in this volume might represent another sort of *managerial* adaptation, but at least in some places EM also seems to be associated both with the *punitive* adaptation and with the narrative of *incapacitation* that Robinson *et al.* (2013) mention but fail to elaborate in their chapter. Arguably part of the success of both community service and EM rests in their simultaneous appeal to multiple narratives – punitive, rehabilitative, reparative, managerial and incapacitating.

In asking our contributors to consider how well these legitimising narratives travel, we imposed (perhaps implicitly) a *vertical* comparison on our guides, asking them to compare developments in their jurisdictions with this pre-existing model; and we left ourselves with the challenge of making *horizontal* comparisons between the jurisdictions of the sorts that we have begun to sketch above (on vertical and horizontal comparison, see Morgenstern and Larrauri 2013). However, we have to recognise that, with hindsight, this approach might itself be criticised for being Anglocentric. Drawing our analytical framework from the chapter by Robinson *et al.* (2013) ran the risk of treating the USA and the UK as the default cases (against which to compare), when in fact they may be outliers.

For this reason, we have not sought to hold our contributors too closely to the framework we suggested and, as readers will already have noted, in many cases they have been compelled to range some way beyond their terms of reference to make sense of the evolution of community punishment in their jurisdictions. Indeed, it turns out that it is not just that our four legitimising narratives proved inadequate to the task of explaining diverse forms of penal evolution; even the assumption that community punishment has faced significant problems of legitimacy turns out to be faulty in some cases. Romania is a fascinating example in this respect. As Durnescu makes clear, in the absence of democratic accountability, processes of legitimation take quite different (and less public) forms. And even when democracy comes, the challenges of *proving* the State is democratic and, crucially, that it is 'European' require a different legitimising project; one that has as its audience not politicians, judges or members of the public in Romania, but rather politicians and bureaucrats in Brussels.

In understanding the evolution of community punishment in Central and Eastern European states then, 'Europeanisation' may be a critically important legit-imising narrative. But, in fact, several of our contributors illustrate a range of relationships between community punishment and projects of *state-building* even in the established liberal democracies of Western Europe (Carr, McNeill). More gen-erally, if we think not of state or nation-building but of projects of *state-sustaining*, then all of our contributors have had much to say, directly or indirectly, about the relationships between community punishment, the 'penal state' and the state itself. It is to these relationships that we turn in conclusion.

Conclusion: Penal fields, penal states and penal climates

In both of the published pieces that we mentioned at the outset of this chapter as our 'points of embarkation', reference is made to Joshua Page's recent work on 'the penal field' (Page 2011, 2013). Page argues that accounts of penal change require careful analyses not just of the social forces that operate on the field (i.e. those forces that come from wider social changes), but also of the relations and dynamics 'inside' the penal field itself, in its various subfields and in its interactions with other fields of social action. Drawing on the work of Pierre Bourdieu, Page points to the importance of explaining the relationships between the 'habitus' or dispositions of penal actors and their ownership of and struggles over various forms of capital within and across penality and its intersecting fields. Although we did not refer to Page's work in setting the agenda for this book, some of the chapters in this collection offer accounts of how community punishment's senior managers, practitioners and advocates have sought to secure such capital in their differently configured penal fields. A common thread across the jurisdictions is the perennial marginality and insecurity of these actors despite the proliferation of the volume and range of 'services' they offer.

However, the analysis intended in this collection requires us to look beyond rela-tions *within* the field to make sense of developments. In a sense, the sorts of field analysis that Page recommends help us with the question of *how and with what conse-quences* adaptation has been accomplished; but the wider questions of *why* adaptation has been necessary and *which* adaptations have prevailed perhaps requires a differ-ent sort of analysis. Nonetheless, to 'level up' too far – to the structural, social and cultural changes associated with late modernity and with globalisation – risks leaving us ill equipped to account for the persistence of so much difference between the jurisdictions.

This is the same conundrum that David Garland has recently begun to address. In his plenary address at the European Society of Criminology conference in Budapest in 2013 on 'Cultures of Control and Penal States', and in subsequent publications (Garland 2013), his central argument has been that, in seeking to understand and explain historical and contemporary changes in penal systems, policies and practices, a shift in focus is required. He urges more attention to the ways in which political mechanisms and institutions (penal states) translate social and cultural forces into particular penal outcomes. Though Garland has done as much as anyone (particularly in his 2001 book *The Culture of Control*) to elaborate these broader social and cultural currents, he suggested we need to escape our 'sociological bias' – looking for deep background causes – and to study proximate causes too.

For Garland, the term 'the penal state' is not critical or evaluative, it is descriptive. It refers to the governmental authorities that make penal rules (as Joshua Page might put it, these authorities influence the way the field is legally and politically structured), exercising penal governance and leadership, rather than to the penal apparatus itself. As such it involves elements of the Executive, the Parliament and the Judiciary, as well as the leadership of criminal justice agencies. Garland explains five key dimensions by which penal states might vary, and our chapters provide some interesting accounts of difference in each dimension:

1. *State autonomy* refers to the extent to which the state is independent of social forces refracted through the institutions of civil society or, conversely, to what extent social forces dictate state conduct. Romania, in the Communist era, perhaps provides an example of a state that was relatively strong *vis-à-vis* a weaker civil society (see Durnescu). Belgium perhaps provides an example of a weaker state forced to respond to public and media reaction to the Dutroux case (see Beyens).

2. *Internal autonomy* refers to the relative independence of the penal state within the state itself and thus to its degree of independence from other state institutions. In other words, it concerns the extent to which penal officials themselves have the power to shape penal outcomes. Scotland, before devolution, is an interesting example in this respect, in that a weak arm of the UK Executive (the Scottish Office) with limited political legitimacy lacked the resources to impose changes in the nature of community punishment (see McNeill).

3. *Control* refers to the ways that different nations allocate the power to punish differently – at the national, regional or local level – and sometimes share this power in significant ways with others through transnational institutions. In our case, looking outwards, we might consider the role of the EU and the Council of Europe, as well as the European Court of Human

Rights. The European influence can pull in two different directions – one concerned with human rights and one concerned with cross-border cooperation in pursuit of managerial efficiency. Looking inwards, we might consider the relative autonomy of regional or local governments (and of local as opposed to national forms of penal state). Once again, the importance of 'Europeanisation' in Durnescu's chapter illustrates the salience of externally allocated (or appropriated) power, though Morgenstern's chapter also shows in a different way how European institutions can influence a 'strong' and well-established state.

Control is also distributed differently across the penal process: different actors compete for control (prosecutors, judges, prison officials, probation services, public or private partnerships). These distributions of power change over time, much as Page's (2013) field analysis suggests. Herzog-Evans' chapter illustrates these issues well in relation to the power of the prisons administration over French probation and the progressively weakened position of the Juges de l'Application des Peines. Robinson's chapter points to the implications of the current part-privatisation of probation services in England and Wales.

4.   *Modes of power* refers to quantitative and qualitative aspects of penal power; to how much power is exercised, but also to the ways in which it is exercised. Inevitably this also involves modes of knowledge expressed in how penal actors think about penal objectives, techniques and practices. These modes of power have both negative and positive dimensions; they involve both incapacitating and capacity-building forms of penal power. Both Svensson's and Robinson's chapters illustrate very effectively how and why once-preferred (capacity-building or welfarist) forms of penal power came to be adjusted or displaced by more punitive and incapacitating forms, even in very different states.

5.   *Power resources* refers to the extent to which a penal state has capacity. This is not just about the scale of the available infrastructure (i.e. numbers of prison places or probation officers) but all sorts of systems capacity – institutional, professional and academic. It speaks not just to economic or physical capital, but also to the cultural capital represented in knowledge, research and evidence. In this respect, Garland noted that negative, incapacitating penal power is easier to operationalise, not least because it can operate in relative isolation; by contrast, positive (capacity-building) power requires coordination with social services and with economic forces outside penality.

We have already discussed above how systemic 'fixes' and adjustments and new methods (both legal and 'scientific') both affect and reflect penal and social resources. In broad terms and in most jurisdictions, we can perhaps identify a trend towards divestment from welfare in favour of control (see Wacquant 2009), at least insofar as this is reflected in the redesign of 'tougher' community punishments.

Garland's analysis of the 'penal state', then, offers useful resources for the sorts of horizontal comparisons we are interested in. However, the COST Action has also benefitted from exposure to cutting-edge doctoral research on comparative criminal justice which, while largely consistent with Garland's framework, highlights other dimensions that he neglects or downplays. Brangan (2013), in an address to a meeting of the Action, stressed the need to complement an analysis of the institutional dynamics of penal states and systems with an appreciation of the influences of culture and of human agency. She argued that, once we have mapped out the institutions which inform penal practice, 'the next comparative step we need to take is to fill these institutions with the dynamism of agency, examining the cultural currents that exist *inside* these criminal justice occupational sites' (Brangan 2013[2], emphasis added).

By attending to culture and agency, Brangan argued, we can assess 'the embedded mores, values, beliefs, penal sensibilities and fears of penal actors', which all contribute to an 'institutional ethos' or shared view of the world. Crucially, she also suggested the importance of an explanatory factor that we sometimes neglect: 'happenstance'. Both chance events and human agency may be vital sources of and resources for change in penality. To the extent that our chapters reveal both the importance of key actors in the evolution of community punishment and the vulnerability of its institutions to 'events' (and, in particular, to tragic high-profile cases; see, for example, the chapters by Beyens and Boone), they endorse Brangan's important caution about happenstance.

Brangan (2013) also adds to Garland's framework the importance of historical legacy and path dependency, suggesting that, if we are to understand persistent differences between jurisdictions, we need to reflect upon their distinct histories. Even if, as we have stressed above, the conditions of emergence of community punishment are similar in many jurisdictions, this only serves to underscore the importance of understanding historically their paths towards divergence. In this respect, the stress that several of our authors place on history is both telling and well justified, although we would tend to see this as invoking a Foucauldian 'history of the present', one that pays particular attention to the conditions of possibility that generate or permit shifts in governmental strategies through which different discourses emerge (see also Garland 2014).

Perhaps in this last section we have begun to hint at and answer the important question of why we undertake comparative analyses of community punishment. There are two obvious reasons. One is to understand community punishment better; but we also aim to better understand punishment itself and, through it, the states we live in. Drake (2012) has recently argued that the prison is 'a useful barometer for tracing the methods and parameters of state power' (p. 14). We have no problem with that idea or with the merits of such work. Drake focuses in particular on the shared quest for security that she found in the high-security estate and in the wider social realm post-9/11. But the most severe end of the penal system is neither the only nor necessarily the best barometer (at least on its own) of state power, even if it is its most severe (domestic) form. Indeed, Drake (2012) bases her observations on Christie's analysis from a decade ago (in *A Suitable Amount of Crime*):

> Penal systems carry deep meanings. They convey information on central features of the states they represent. Nothing told more about Nazi Germany, about the USSR or about Maoist China than their penal apparatus – from their police practice, via courts to prisons, camps and Gulags. In concrete cases, we can evaluate states according to their penal systems.
>
> *(Christie 2004: 101)*

Christie thus recognises the need to look at *the full range of penal practices* in order to assess the penal climate (and with it the character of the penal state). Drake (2012) herself acknowledges that 'the question of whether imprisonment rates are the best indicator of punitiveness or penal severity remains unanswered' (p. 18).

The challenge this leaves for scholars of community punishment is to examine and assess exactly what the institutions and practices that concern us can contribute to developing more finely tuned barometers of penal change in particular and of state power more generally. Whereas our first collection (McNeill and Beyens 2013) made this case by drawing attention to the growth of offender supervision within and across jurisdictions, and to its intensifying forms, this collection goes significantly further in connecting developments in community punishment with their social contexts. We have been confronted with a dizzying array of contextual factors that at different times and in different places have proved crucial to the evolution of community punishment. To move towards unifying these insights into a single model of that evolution is a tempting prospect, since it might substantiate or improve accounts of penal change and, more generally, of the changing character of the late-modern state itself. But it may also be a 'fool's errand' inasmuch as a model that can fit everywhere might not tell us too much about anywhere.

Setting aside that dilemma for the moment, perhaps we can end our European tour confident at least that, thanks to our guides, we have developed a better understanding of a range of jurisdictions and, through them, a better understanding of what influences the development of and prospects for community punishment. As individual scholars, we now have the resource that this book provides; a set of case studies of the evolution of community punishment under different social conditions and in different social contexts. As we have suggested above in relation to our own chapters, those case studies have already succeeded in posing new questions and opening up new analytical possibilities that had not occurred to us before.

Such are the pleasures of travelling to interesting places and in good company. We may be left with more questions than answers, but perhaps we have become a little wiser along the way.

Notes

1   As one of our contributors (Martine Herzog-Evans) has suggested, this legal focus may also be a result of how different states seek to engineer penal development in particular

jurisdictions. Some states may rely more on law, others may rely, for example, on attempts to influence practice through training or research.

2   See www.offendersupervision.eu/blog-post/a-framework-for-comparative-research-on-supervision, accessed 30 December 2014.

References

Beyens, K. and McNeill, F. (2013) 'Conclusion: studying mass supervision comparatively', in F. McNeill and K. Beyens (eds) *Offender Supervision in Europe*. Basingstoke: Palgrave Macmillan, pp. 155–70.

Bottoms, A. E. (1995) 'The philosophy and politics of punishment and sentencing', in C. Clarkson and R. Morgan (eds) *The Politics of Sentencing Reform*. Oxford: Clarendon Press, pp. 17–50.

Bottoms, A. E. (2008) 'The community dimension of community penalties', *Howard Journal of Community Justice* 47(2): 146–169.

Brangan, L. (2013) 'A framework for comparative research on supervision?', *Offender Supervision in Europe* blog-site (www.offendersupervision.eu/blog-post/a-framework-for-comparative-research-on-supervision, accessed 26 January 2015).

Christie, N. (2004) *A Suitable Amount of Crime*. London: Routledge.

Drake, D. (2012) *Prisons, Punishment and the Pursuit of Security*. Basingstoke: Palgrave Macmillan.

Durnescu, I., Enengl, C. and Grafl, G. (2013) 'Experiencing supervision', in McNeill, F. and Beyens, K. (eds) *Offender Supervision in Europe*. Basingstoke: Palgrave, pp. 19–50.

Garland, D. (2001) *The Culture of Control*. Oxford: Oxford University Press.

Garland, D. (2013) 'Penality and the penal state', *Criminology* 51(3): 475–517.

Garland, D. (2014) 'What is a "history of the present"? On Foucault's genealogies and their critical preconditions', *Punishment and Society* 16(4): 365–84.

Herzog-Evans, M. (2011) 'What's in a name: penological and institutional connotations of probation officers' labelling in Europe', *Eurovista* 2(3): 121–33.

McNeill, F. (2013) 'Community sanctions and European penology', in Daems, T., Snacken, S and Van Zyl Smit, D. (eds) *European Penology*. Oxford: Hart Publishing, pp. 171–91.

McNeill, F. and Beyens, K. (eds) (2013) *Offender Supervision in Europe*. Basingstoke: Palgrave Macmillan.

McNeill, F. and Dawson, M. (2014) 'Social solidarity, penal evolution and probation', *British Journal of Criminology* 54(5): 892–907.

Morgenstern, C. and Larrauri, E. (2013) 'European norms, policy and practice', in McNeill, F. and Beyens, K. (eds) *Offender Supervision in Europe*. Basingstoke: Palgrave, pp. 125–54.

Nellis, M., Beyens, K. and Kaminski, D. (2013) *Electronically Monitored Punishment: International and Critical Perspectives*. London: Routledge.

Page, J. (2011) *The Toughest Beat: Politics, Punishment, and the Prison Officers' Union in California*. New York: Oxford University Press.

Page, J. (2013) 'Punishment and the penal field', in J. Simon and R. Sparks (eds) *The SAGE Handbook of Punishment and Society*. London: Sage, pp. 152–66.

Phelps, M. (2013) 'The paradox of probation: Community supervision in the age of mass incarceration', *Law & Policy* 35(1–2): 51–80.

Portelli, A. (2006) 'What makes oral history different?' in Perks, R. and Thomson, A. (eds) *The Oral History Reader*, 2nd edn. London: Routledge, pp. 32–41.

Raynor, P. and Robinson, G. (2009) *Rehabilitation, Crime and Justice*. Basingstoke: Palgrave Macmillan.

Robinson, G. (in press) 'The Cinderella complex: punishment, society and community sanctions', *Punishment & Society*, in press.

Robinson, G., McNeill, F. and Maruna, S. (2013) 'Punishment in society: The improbable persistence of probation and other community sanctions and measures', in J. Simon and R. Sparks (eds) *SAGE Handbook of Punishment and Society*. London: Sage, pp. 321–40.

Van Zyl Smit, D., Snacken, S. and Hayes, D. (2015) '"One cannot legislate kindness": Ambiguities in European legal instruments on non-custodial sanctions', *Punishment & Society* 17(1): 3–26.

Wacquant, L. (2009) *Punishing the Poor: The Neoliberal Government of Insecurity*. Durham, NC: Duke University Press.

Worrall, A. and Hoy, C. (2005) *Punishment in the Community: Managing Offenders, Making Choices*'. Cullompton, Devon: Willan.

APPENDIX

Questions for contributors

Below is a list of questions contributors to this volume were asked to address:

Foundations

- What were the 'conditions of emergence' of early forms of community punishment in (the jurisdiction)?
- How were they initially justified?
- How and with whom were they intended to be used?

Development

- How have forms of community punishment evolved since their inception?
- What (global/local) conditions or changes (social, economic, political, cultural etc.) have influenced their development?
- Have there been moments of crisis in respect of the legitimacy of community punishment? What happened?
- What is the current size and shape of community punishment? Is it an expanding or contracting part of the penal field?
- What narratives or rationales currently underpin community punishment? Are these contested?
- What does the future hold for community punishment in (the jurisdiction)?

Reflections

- Does 'community punishment' make sense conceptually in (the jurisdiction)?
- Why/why not? What (alternative) terms are actually used to describe the part of the penal field which is the subject of this book?

- What does an understanding of community punishment contribute to an understanding of the 'penal climate' in (the jurisdiction) (e.g. in terms of stability vs turbulence; penal moderation vs punitiveness)? Does it tend to confirm or challenge existing accounts?
- What are the most important questions which your analysis raises (about community punishment; about national penal policies; for comparative research, etc.)?

INDEX